A CENTURY OF DEBT CRISES

IN LATIN AMERICA

A CENTURY

OF DEBT CRISES

IN LATIN

AMERICA

From Independence
to the Great Depression,
1820–1930

Carlos Marichal

PRINCETON UNIVERSITY PRESS

PRINCETON, NEW JERSEY

Copyright © 1989 by Princeton University Press
Published by Princeton University Press, 41 William Street,
Princeton, New Jersey 08540
In the United Kingdom: Princeton University Press, Guildford, Surrey

Library of Congress Cataloging-in-Publication Data
Marichal, Carlos.
A century of debt crises in Latin America : from independence to the
Great Depression, 1820–1930 / Carlos Marichal
p.   cm.
Bibliography: p.
Includes index
ISBN 0-691-07792-4 (alk. paper) ISBN 0-691-02299-2 (pbk.)
1. Debts, External—Latin America—History. I. Title.
HJ8514.5.M357 1989
336.3'435'098—dc19   88-17843

Publication of this book has been aided by the Whitney Darrow Fund of Princeton
University Press

This book has been composed in Linotron Times Roman

Clothbound editions of Princeton University Press books are printed
on acid-free paper, and binding materials are chosen for strength and durability.
Paperbacks, although satisfactory for personal collections, are not usually
suitable for library rebinding

Printed in the United States of America by Princeton University Press,
Princeton, New Jersey

To Juan and Solita

CONTENTS

List of Figures   ix
List of Tables   xi
Acknowledgments   xiii

INTRODUCTION   3

CHAPTER 1
Independence: Silver and Loans   12

CHAPTER 2
The Crash of 1825   43

CHAPTER 3
The Rediscovery of Latin America, 1850–1873   68

CHAPTER 4
The First World Debt Crisis   98

CHAPTER 5
Loan Frenzy in the Río de la Plata, 1880–1890   126

CHAPTER 6
The Baring Panic of 1890   149

CHAPTER 7
Dollar Diplomacy and the Loan Boom of the 1920s   171

CHAPTER 8
The Great Depression and Latin American Defaults   201

EPILOGUE   229

Appendix A   Foreign Loans to Latin American Governments, 1850–1873   243

Appendix B   Foreign Loans to Latin American Governments, 1880–1890   247

Appendix C   Foreign Loans to Latin American Governments, 1920–1930   251

Appendix D   A Guide to the Principal Foreign Banking Houses Engaged in the Issue of Latin American Loans during the Nineteenth and Early Twentieth Centuries   257

Bibliographical Note   269

Index   275

LIST OF FIGURES

FIGURE 1
Mercantile and Financial Relations between Great Britain and
Latin America in the Early 1820s   21

FIGURE 2
British Exports to Latin America, 1820–1830   48

FIGURE 3
Price Trends of Argentine 1824 External Bonds on the London
Stock Exchange, 1825–1860   58

FIGURE 4
Latin American Exports to Great Britain, 1855–1880   75

FIGURE 5
British Exports of Capital and Merchandise to Latin America,
1855–1880   76

FIGURE 6
Market Prices of Peruvian, Argentine, and Brazilian External
Bonds on the London Stock Exchange, 1870–1880   109

FIGURE 7
Market Prices of Costa Rica, Honduras, Santo Domingo, and
Paraguay Bonds on the London Stock Exchange, 1868–1874   111

FIGURE 8
British Exports and Capital Issues for Argentina, 1882–1902   138

FIGURE 9
Latin American Exports to All Nations, 1910–1929   176

FIGURE 10
United States Exports and Loans to Latin America, 1915–1931   183

LIST OF FIGURES

FIGURE 11

Market Prices of Latin American Gold Bonds on the New York
Stock Exchange, 1930–1936   205

FIGURE 12

Latin American Total Exports, 1928–1938   209

LIST OF TABLES

TABLE 1
Latin American Government Issues Floated in England,
1822–1825   28

TABLE 2
Defaults and Renegotiations of Latin American Loans of the
1820s   59

TABLE 3
Foreign Loans to Latin American Governments, 1850–1875   80

TABLE 4
Defaults and Settlements of Latin American Loans Following
the Crisis of 1873   120

TABLE 5
Foreign Loans of Five Latin American States, 1880–1890   128

TABLE 6
Argentine Foreign Debt Renegotiations, 1890–1906   165

TABLE 7
Foreign Loans to Latin American Governments, 1920–1930   185

TABLE 8
Status of Latin American Debts and Defaults, 1931–1950   212

ACKNOWLEDGMENTS

THE PRESENT work had a long gestation period, during which I accumulated a large number of personal debts that I want to acknowledge. On the other hand, I received no grants or financial assistance in the course of my research and writing, even though at times they were sorely needed. It is just as well that a critical analysis of foreign indebtedness be free of any monetary debts.

My interest in the history of Latin American foreign debts grew out of research on the economic history of Argentina carried out a decade ago. The individual who contributed most to deepen my understanding of this subject was Luis Victor Sommi—historian, political activist, and humanist, now unfortunately deceased. Also of critical importance was my contact with researchers of NACLA, the North American Congress on Latin America, of New York, especially with Michael Locker and Carlos Díaz Ritter, who stressed the value of studying the history of financial groups.

Subsequently in Mexico, where I have lived and taught since 1979, many individuals provided encouragement, stimulus, and fruitful critiques. In 1980 Samuel Lichtenztejn and José Quijano urged me to prepare for a conference a paper that helped me formulate ideas on the comparative history of Latin American finances. At seminars held at the Universidad Autónoma Metropolitana in Mexico City, the following colleagues listened with patience and commented intelligently on the hypotheses I presented: Carlos Sempat Assadourian, Daniel Cataife, José Carlos Chiaramonte, Juan Carlos Garavaglia, Hira de Gortari, Leonor Ludlow, and Jan Patula. My colleague from Haiti, Guy Pierre, greatly assisted me in the study of economic cycles. Once the preliminary drafts had been transformed into a manuscript, the following people were so good as to read and comment on some or all of the chapters: Nicolás Sánchez Albornoz, Paul Bushkovitch, William Callahan, Barbara Tenenbaum, and John Womack. Their observations and criticisms were invaluable.

My good friends Adela Harispuru and Margot Andersen Imbert provided me with difficult-to-obtain bibliographical materials and information. The librarians of the following institutions were particularly helpful: Widener Library (Harvard University), the Hispanic Division of the Library of Congress, the library of the Ministerio de Economía in Buenos Aires, and the library of the Secretaría de Relaciones Exteriores in Mexico City. Magdalena Fernández, Tehila Liberman, and Irma Escobar Reyes helped me with secretarial chores. Enrique Vega did work on the graphic material, and Jorge Orozco Zuart assisted with the appendixes. I would also like to thank the two anonymous readers who reviewed the manuscript on behalf of Princeton University Press for their many useful observations, Peggy Hoover for her meticulous and intelligent work as copyeditor of the manuscript, and Sanford G. Thatcher, editor-in-chief of the Press, for his punctual letters and his support.

My greatest debt I mention last. This study would not have been possible without the assistance in many things, great and small, of my wife and companion, Soledad González, of my parents, and of my parents-in-law through a now-long stretch of years during which my explorations of the Latin American past often seemed a difficult though never fruitless task. I can only hope that the present study reflects in some measure the affection they have so liberally bestowed on me.

A CENTURY OF DEBT CRISES

IN LATIN AMERICA

THE WORLD debt crisis began in the early 1980s, but its end is still not in sight. The enormous financial burden on the less-developed nations of the world has already had such a devastating impact that we should not expect a sustained economic recovery in the near future. The dramatic rise in unemployment levels in most Asian, African, and Latin American countries in recent years has been accompanied by an equally striking drop in the per capita income of the majority of the population, causing hardship and provoking discontent. The financial debacle has therefore sown the seeds of increasingly widespread social and political protests.

The impact of the debt crisis has been felt most harshly in Latin America, which is struggling to free itself of an oppressive load of $350,000,000,000 in foreign debts. Much attention has been directed to the plight of the big debtors—Brazil, Mexico, Argentina, and Venezuela—but the smaller countries are beset with similar problems. The external debts of Bolivia, Ecuador, Peru, and the Central American and Caribbean nations have disrupted their economies and immeasurably intensified the suffering of the poorest peoples of the Western Hemisphere.

The debt crisis caught bankers, politicians, and economists, as well as almost everyone else, off guard—partly because the swings in the international economy have become increasingly acute during the last decade. None of the participants in the great loan boom of the late 1970s expected that the boom would end in the debt crisis of the 1980s. The euphoria of prosperity mesmerized everyone engaged in these financial negotiations and obscured the signs of increasing instability in the world capitalist economy. But it is also possible that the lack of a historical perspective made it difficult to comprehend the cyclical nature of the loan flows and the inevitability of a financial upheaval.

The present debt crisis is not an unprecedented event, but part of a chain of recurrent crises throughout the history of Latin America. During more than a century and a half the Latin American nations have repeatedly experienced international financial storms that greatly damaged their economies and strapped them into an apparently irrevocable succession of boom and bust cycles that reinforce underdevelopment. The debt cataclysm of the 1980s is greater than those of the past because of the huge volume of financial resources now at stake and because of the increasingly complex structure of the economies of modern Latin America. However, the dimensions of the current dilemma do not imply that nothing can be learned from similar past experience. The evolution of the diverse societies of Latin America has been molded by a complex set of historical factors that are not merely a legacy but also a continuing reality.

Since the early nineteenth century, Latin American elites have looked abroad for loan capital to build and modernize their states and economies. The inflow of funds stimulated growth for relatively short time periods, but international commercial and financial crises invariably cut short the flow of funds from abroad and drove the debtor nations to bankruptcy. The outcome was a series of debt crises that accentuated the economic contradictions and political conflicts with the powerful creditor nations of Western Europe and later with the United States.

It was in the 1820s, when the Latin American peoples were fighting for independence, that foreign loans began to play an important role in the history of the region. All the most distinguished patriot leaders—Bolívar, San Martín, O'Higgins, Rivadavia—sought loans from Europe to consolidate independence and to promote trade. The illusions of prosperity were shattered by the European financial crisis of 1825–26, which was followed shortly by the defaults of most Latin American governments. This was the first Latin American debt crisis. Subsequently, there came a succession of new loan booms, followed by debt crises in 1873, 1890, and 1931.

The present study is a survey of the most important Latin American debt crises from independence to the depression of the 1930s. In order to understand the dynamics of each crisis it is necessary to explore both the causes and consequences of each. For this reason the focus here will be on the broader concept of the "loan cycle," which includes two stages: that of the loan boom and that of the debt crisis. Each loan cycle is characterized by an upswing, a period of prosperity during which Latin American states contracted a large number of loans abroad, and a downswing, which was usually the result of an international financial crisis that caused economic distress in Latin America and frequently led to a string of defaults.

The chapters of this book make up a sequence of pairs that follow this two-stage outline. Chapters 1 and 2 deal with the first Latin American loan boom of 1822–25 and with the first regional debt crisis that followed. Chapters 3 and 4 focus on the loan expansion of the 1860s and early 1870s, which was cut short by the world depression of 1873. Chapters 5 and 6 concentrate on the loan frenzy of the 1880s, when Argentina became the largest Latin American debtor, and on the Anglo-Argentine financial panic of 1890. Chapters 7 and 8 analyze the loan boom of the 1920s and the effects of the Great Depression of the 1930s on Latin American finances.

4

Such a broad historical canvas requires a comparative approach that goes beyond the boundaries of "national" financial histories. Moreover, a central tenet of the present study is that the Latin American debt crises of the past cannot be understood solely in the light of the experience of an individual country, but must be viewed as the expression of trends common to many nations of the subcontinent.

In order to identify these trends, it is essential first to collect and compare the facts. In which decades were the largest number of loans issued by the Latin American states? What was their value and purpose? Which were the principal banking houses involved in placing the bonds in foreign capital markets? How did the loans fit into the economic strategies of the governments contracting the loans? The present study addresses itself to these questions by reviewing a large body of information found in the secondary literature and by complementing it with data from primary sources, financial journals, government documents and bondholder reports. Because the amount of information is so great, it is impossible to deal in detail with all the foreign financial transactions of the diverse Latin American nations in each chapter. Therefore preference is given to the states that were the largest debtors in the different periods under review. A complete synopsis of relevant Latin American debt statistics can be found in the tables throughout the text and in Appendixes A, B, and C.

One can also argue that a comparative study of the major Latin American loan cycles during the nineteenth and early twentieth centuries offers an opportunity to explore a series of important theoretical questions and propositions. Because these questions and hypotheses thread their way through each chapter of this book, we shall comment briefly on them in order to introduce the general thrust of the arguments to be presented.

That loan booms and subsequent debt crises have been a permanent feature of Latin American history since independence suggests that there are deep-rooted structural causes which explain their dynamics. A fundamental hypothesis of this study is that the pattern of the loan cycles was not circumstantial, but rather the result of the interaction between the economic cycles of the more-advanced capitalist nations and the processes of economic change in Latin America. To be more specific, the loan booms gained strength as a result of phases of expansion of the world economy, which tended to stimulate the accumulation and export of excess capital from international money markets to Latin America. Conversely, the debt crises coincided with widespread downswings of the economies of industrialized nations, which provoked a sharp reduction of the outward flow of financial resources. These fluctuations submitted the economies of the Latin American nations to the dominant trends of world capitalism, but it is my specific

5

purpose to emphasize the degree to which such swings decisively influenced the course of the financial policies of the governments of the region.

The nature and duration of the long, medium, and short "waves" of
capitalist economies are much-debated in the literature on business cycles
in the history of the United States and Europe, but among economic historians of Latin America discussion of these questions has been more limited,
focusing principally on trade cycles, particularly the cycles of specific export commodities. This study broadens this perspective by combining the
available information on the trends of Latin American foreign trade with
data on the flow of international loans. The resulting analysis provides a
new, if tentative, outline of the impact of the major waves of economic
expansion and depression, as well as of the key financial crises, in the different Latin American nations, which can help improve on the rather im-
precise economic periodization offered by, for example, the exponents of
the so-called "dependency school," such as Fernando Henrique Cardoso
and Enzo Faletto. The latter emphasized the importance of the crisis of
1929 as a major turning-point in the history of Latin America, but they paid
less attention to the effects of international economic cycles and crises upon
the economies of the region in previous decades.

A global analysis of the historical pattern of foreign trade and loans con-
firms that to the extent that capitalism did advance in Latin America it was
subject in great measure to the dynamics of the economies of the industrial
nations of the North Atlantic. The successive foreign loan booms of the
nineteenth and early twentieth centuries were closely linked to the international cycles of capital exports. The explanation of the forces that impelled
capital exports has been the subject of a long-standing debate among economists and historians. The discussion was initiated at the turn of the century
by Marxist theoreticians who focused on the analysis of imperialism, and
their views continue to be highly influential as well as polemical. Lenin,
for example, emphasized the accumulation of surplus capital in the imperial
nations which required profitable outlets for investment. Rosa Luxemburg,
on the other hand, argued that it was the need to finance the export of surplus production which led the industrial nations to extend credit to the less-
developed countries. Subsequently, non-Marxist writers such as Herbert
Feis, Leland Jenks, Alec Cairncross, and, more recently, Charles Kindleberger have deepened our knowledge of the historical pattern of capital
exports and the ways in which they both stimulated trade and increased the
resources available for economic growth on a worldwide scale.

The loans injected capital into Latin America, but they also led to a reverse flow of funds in the shape of interest and amortization payments. This
outward flow weighed more heavily on some nations than others, depending on the size of their external debt as well as on their resources. In the

6

long run, all the debtor nations were committed to pay back a sum much larger than what they had originally received. Such circumstances made the debtors easy prey for an ever-growing circle of foreign financiers who urged them to take more loans with which to pay off previous debts. At the apogee of this loan frenzy, dozens of rival banking firms stirred up speculation so much that an explosion became inevitable.

The debt crises that followed the boom were usually triggered by a stock market crash in London or at some other financial center, by the collapse of one or more leading international banks, and/or by the news of the imminent default of a given Latin American government. Regardless of the specific origin, the financial panic intensified both the international economic crisis and the local crisis.

For contemporary observers in the creditor nations, however, the causes of the debt crises were ascribed not to the turmoil in the money markets of the nations of the center, but rather to the wayward actions of the debtor nations of the periphery. As early as the 1830s the respected British economist Thomas Tooke argued that the Latin American loans of 1822–25 had been responsible for the outbreak of the crash of 1825 in London. Likewise, in the 1870s the British Parliament carried out a major inquiry on foreign loans, the object of which was to demonstrate that the Latin American debts were a major factor in unleashing the great crisis of 1873. And sixty years later, in 1931, in the midst of the worst banking crisis in the history of North America, the United States Senate launched an official investigation into the Latin American loans issued during the 1920s, apparently trying to show that these transactions were a chief cause of the financial pandemonium of the early 1930s.

The following chapters argue that the debt crises were the consequence of international economic crises, not the cause. After the breakdown of the financial and industrial machinery in the creditor nations, the flow of loans to Latin America would be abruptly frozen. Frequently there would be numerous defaults, although in most instances a few states were able to continue paying interest and amortization payments. Then there came a complex phase of debt crisis resolution. Negotiations among bankers and politicians became enmeshed in a web of contradictions that seldom permitted short-term solutions. Thus the effects of the crisis continued to weigh heavily on the debt-ridden Latin American societies, often for decades.

Most foreign loan booms ended in debt crises, but not all. One important exception does not fit into the pattern previously described. Throughout Latin America between 1900 and 1914, there was a great loan frenzy that concluded as a direct consequence of the outbreak of World War I, not as a result of an international economic depression. The effects of the war on

Latin America were quite different from the effects of the major economic crises of the past. In the first place, although capital flows from abroad were frozen after 1914, only one state—Mexico—actually defaulted. The other Latin American nations continued to make regular payments to the foreign bondholders. The wartime export boom, which allowed most of the Latin American economies to accumulate large monetary reserves, was probably the reason for that. The result was unexpected. In the midst of a period of tremendous commercial expansion (1915–20), the Latin American governments did not take any new (long-term) foreign loans, but rather proceeded to liquidate a substantial part of their debts.

During the war years, therefore, Latin America became a net capital exporter rather than a capital importer as it had been before 1914. The reasons for this bring up a number of difficult questions. Some of these questions are touched on in Chapter 7, but additional research is needed to clarify the singular nature of the impact of the war on the Latin American economies. The situation during the 1920s was quite different. In that decade, despite a substantial drop in regional exports, most of the Latin American states sharply increased their foreign loan activity. Here again, one must recognize the particular characteristics of each economic cycle and the cycle's influence on the degree of loan activity.

The negotiation of foreign loans was not affected solely by international conditions. Local political, economic, and social circumstances played an equally decisive role. In this respect it should be noted that all the loans dealt with in the present work were government bond issues and that the fundamental objective here is to analyze the historical evolution of public rather than private debts. In short, the technicalities of the foreign credit transactions should not obscure the fact that the loans were *political instruments* intended to accomplish a varied set of economic, military, and/or social goals.

Such a viewpoint leads one to ask whether traditional theories—in particular the classic Marxist analyses of imperialism—provide us with all the necessary instruments to explain the nature of the relationship between international economic forces and local power structures in the dependent nations. It is no secret that the early theoretical studies of imperialism, such as those of Lenin, Luxemburg, and Bukharin, were concerned fundamentally with the political and economic dynamics of the industrialized nations instead of with those of the countries of the periphery. Their interpretation of capital exports brilliantly explained the fundamental forces that lay behind the great rise in foreign investments in the last quarter of the nineteenth century. But they paid relatively little attention to the specific characteristics of government loans as one important form of capital exports, and they had even less to say about the way the loan proceeds were invested by the ruling elites of the less-developed nations, whether colonial territories or independent states. These early theoreticians were looking at the phenomenon of imperialism from the center outward, and not vice versa.

More recent theoretical works—for example, those of Paul Baran and Samir Amin—and historico-economic studies, such as those of Celso Furtado and André Gunder Frank, have opened new perspectives by exploring the different dynamics of capitalism in the center and in the periphery. This new focus suggests that certain key problems, such as the role of state finances in the evolution of capitalism in the dependent countries, must be studied in greater depth.

A historical analysis of the Latin American experience demonstrates that in all cases the loans were tools of government policy and as such cannot be separated from the study of the public finances of the different republics. Foreign credit was only one means, albeit an important one, of obtaining resources for the national treasuries. The issue of bonds abroad depended not only on the availability of funds in the foreign money markets, but also on the decisions made by the Latin American elites to seek capital to implement their political and economic programs. Study of the foreign loans therefore needs to include analysis of the changing context of financial policies with respect to taxation, money supply, and sources of both local and external credit.

How Latin American governments raised money is a central question that must be examined in order to explain the nature and scope of their financial strategies. But it is equally important to ask how they spent their resources. How were the loan monies actually invested? Did the loans accelerate a local process of capitalist development, or was the foreign gold used for nonproductive purposes? The questions outnumber the answers. Appendixes A, B, and C, and the tables throughout this study, give the official objectives of each loan, although in many cases governments actually used the proceeds for other purposes. Ascertaining the precise destiny of each loan, however, requires much future research and is beyond the scope of the present study. Nonetheless, the statistical data I collected from a broad range of sources can provide general guidance. The following pages show that the Latin American experience with foreign loans was varied. In the 1820s the bulk of the money came in the form of war loans. During the 1860s and early 1870s, much loan capital was invested in railway construction. In the 1880s, railway and port loans were also important. Later, in the 1920s, most foreign funds were destined for urban modernization projects. Yet throughout there were many instances of other types of loans, some of them for refinancing of old debts, others of a highly speculative nature.

To understand the loan strategies of the different states, one must examine the ideologies and programs of the Latin American elites engaged in issuing bonds abroad, as well as the designs of the bankers who provided the money. Economic and social historians of Latin America have dealt with such questions by analyzing the alliances forged between foreign capitalists and national elites, between bankers and politicians. The importance of these alliances is emphasized in each chapter that follows. Politicians, financiers, merchants, landowners, and miners all favored foreign loans in periods of prosperity because they believed that the inflow of foreign gold would stimulate the economy and benefit their own particular business enterprises. They used state loans as a means of directly or indirectly promoting private accumulation. For example, a foreign loan for construction of a state-owned railway benefited a broad array of native and foreign capitalists. The bankers profited by charging fees for the sale of the bonds. The railway contractors earned large sums from the construction business. Native merchants made money by charging commissions on the importation of equipment required for the railway. Landowners benefited by the rise in prices of real-estate properties near the new lines. And local politicians took their portions off the top of both the loan contracts and the construction contracts.

The Latin American propertied classes and the foreign bankers were the principal protagonists and the main beneficiaries of the international loan business. They used state finances as a vehicle for promotion of private interests, for personal enrichment, and for consolidation of power. But who was expected to pay for the foreign debts? Politicians preferred to avoid giving an explicit answer to this question because it was known that in the final analysis the entire population would have to carry the burden of repaying loans that had benefited only a minority. Such deception was built into the political system.

The loans were usually proposed by the executive branch of government and ratified by the national or provincial legislatures. Nevertheless, there was rarely any broad popular discussion of these important financial issues. This is a significant point, because it meant that the loan negotiations rarely became public and could therefore be treated as private business transactions between local politicians and foreign financiers. Neither government officials nor bankers wanted public scrutiny of this high-level wheeling and dealing. They believed—with some reason—that the divulging of information might jeopardize the "delicate" negotiations between the power brokers taking the loans and the money brokers who provided the funds.

Indeed, no government of the nineteenth or even the twentieth century has been eager to provide its citizens with a straightforward and clear account of the international credit operations it has undertaken. Secrecy is one of the prerogatives of power, and control over information related to public credit is enormously useful to those in power.

The Latin American experience demonstrates that such secretive tactics had pernicious consequences. During the loan booms, the public was led to believe that the inflow of foreign gold would continue indefinitely. Circumstances changed dramatically after the onset of major economic recessions, when it became clear that a huge financial mortgage had been placed upon the shoulders of the entire population and that the inevitable result would be increased taxation. Not infrequently, popular protests broke out against the administrations that had overborrowed. For example, during the initial stages of the Great Depression (1929–33) more than one Latin American government fell as a consequence of the mass demonstrations and strikes directed against the politicians who had contracted huge foreign debts and against the corruption those debts had engendered. In numerous instances such protests led to outright default.

The financial crises intensified the internal social and political conflicts in the various Latin American republics and accentuated the contradictions between the wealthy creditor nations and the less-developed debtor countries. But were the loan booms and debt crises inevitable? Were there alternatives to an export model of growth predicated on receiving a large number of loans from abroad? What underlying forces impelled politicians and bankers to adopt strategies of economic development that led to ever-greater financial dependency, and to ever more catastrophic economic crises? These are hotly debated questions today. The present work contributes to the discussion by placing them in historical perspective.

A final word: The style I adopted for this study is narrative because I want to offer the reader some sense of the distinctive character of the periods under review, as well as an idea of the social and political context within which financial policies were formulated and implemented. But because this is essentially an economic history, I made an effort to accompany the narrative account with sufficient empirical evidence to document the successive loan booms and crises, all of which left an indelible imprint on the economies and socieites of the Latin American nations.

CHAPTER 1

Independence: Silver and Loans

Every loan
is not merely a speculative hit
But sets a nation or upsets a Throne.
— Byron, *Don Juan* (12.5.6)

Great resources are required to maintain the Navy and Army; it is, therefore, of
the utmost importance to obtain the loan under negotiation in London.

— Simón Bolívar (October 1823)

As THE sun rose over the towering Andes of central Peru on December
9, 1824, two armies prepared for a battle to decide the destiny of
Spain's colonies in South America. The military action lasted scarcely an
hour. At its conclusion, the patriot troops led by General Antonio Sucre
had decisively routed the royalist army led by the Spanish viceroy, La
Serna. The battle of Ayacucho marked the culmination of the struggle for
Latin American independence.[1] Fifteen years of war and revolution had
brought to an end three centuries of imperial rule over a vast territory
stretching from Colorado and California to Tierra del Fuego. The great
empires of Spain and Portugal were dismantled, and in their places there
arose a geographically complex mosaic of nations with varied political
forms, including two confederations, five republics, two federal republics,
and one native empire.[2]

The winning of political independence, however, did not mean that economic autonomy had been achieved. Latin America broke its ancient ties
with the Iberian monarchies, but it did not cut off links to the outside world.
On the contrary, this vast, rich, and sparsely populated subcontinent became the object of intense attention on the part of bankers, merchants, and
shippers from Europe and the United States. Within a remarkably short

1. The best description of the battle of Ayacucho is in John Miller, *Memoirs of General
Miller in the Service of the Republic of Peru* (London, 1829), 2:192–208. For an excellent
survey of the Latin American wars of independence, see John Lynch, *The Spanish-American
Revolutions, 1808–1826* (New York, 1973).
2. The two confederations were Argentina and Gran Colombia (including Colombia, Venezuela and Ecuador); the five republics were, Chile, Peru, Bolivia, Paraguay, and Haiti; the
two federal republics were Mexico and the states of Central America; and the native empire
was Brazil.

span of time, the new states of Central and South America became enmeshed in a complex web of commercial and financial relationships that progressively tied them to an expanding world economy and its consecutive cycles of expansion and recession, of prosperity and crisis.

The news of Ayacucho arrived at London in February 1825, a propitious moment, for it was precisely then that a great speculative boom had gripped the Stock Exchange. Dozens of new companies came onto the market month by month as stock quotations soared. The financial fever intensified with the announcement that silver-mining enterprises would be formed to exploit the legendary riches of Mexico, Peru, Colombia, and Brazil. The bull market that had commenced in mid-1824 flourished for almost a year, allowing bold speculators as well as conservative bankers undreamed-of opportunities to make a great deal of money.

The speculative mania coincided with a cyclical phase of prosperity for the British economy impelled by expansion of the cotton textile industry, the backbone of the early industrial revolution.[3] Hopes for growth were also stimulated by the introduction of new technology in other fields: The 1820s were the era of the first passenger railways, steam navigation companies, and gas-lighting enterprises that the world had seen. Such innovations attracted the interest of small and large investors throughout England who poured their savings into new ventures, some of them solid, others clearly frauds.[4] The great frenzy prompted the banker Alexander Baring to exclaim, "It seemed as if all Bedlam had broken loose on the Royal Exchange."[5]

The impact of speculation in Latin American securities on the British financial frenzy of 1824–25 should not be underestimated. The number of companies launched on the London market to exploit the natural resources of the newly independent lands did not surpass 46, a fraction of the total 624 companies established during the boom, yet their nominal capital value

3. Statistical data on the economic boom of 1820–25 in Great Britain is in A. Gayer, W. Rostow, and A. Schwartz, *The Growth and Fluctuation of the British Economy, 1790–1850* (Oxford, 1953), 1:171–210.

4. Such companies as the Stockton & Darlington Railway, one of the first railway firms in England, were destined to last. Others, such as the Equitable Loan Co., the aim of which was "to carry on the business of pawnbroking on a large scale," were dupes for the ingenuous. Among the most extravagant ventures was an enterprise presided over by Lords Landsdowne and Liverpool, established with a capital of £1,000,000 in order to cultivate mulberry trees and propagate silkworms in Great Britain and Ireland. For details on the stock exchange frenzy of 1823–25, see William Smart, *Economic Annals of the 19th Century* (London, 1917), chap. 18; John Francis, *Chronicles and Characters of the Stock Exchange* (Boston, 1850), pp. 96–108; and Leland Jenks, *The Migration of British Capital to 1875* (New York, 1927), chap. 2.

5. Smart, *Economic Annals*, p. 296.

was equal to almost 50 percent of all the rest.[6] More important, Latin American loans absorbed £17,000,000 of a total £25,000,000 in foreign government securities sold during these years. In short, the allure of Latin American riches, real or imaginary, was a major factor in one of the earliest stock and bond crazes of modern capitalism.

In 1822 the government of Gran Colombia became the first in Latin America to sign a foreign loan contract with London bankers. It was soon followed by Chile and Peru, and by the year 1825 most of the other newly independent states had accumulated substantial foreign debts. The bonds of the governments of Argentina, Brazil, the Federation of Central America, Chile, Gran Colombia, Mexico, and Peru were bought and sold at high prices on the Royal Exchange, and the rage for these exotic but lucrative securities continued to run strong until the financial crash of December 1825.

The first of Latin American loan booms was thus clearly tied to an expanding cycle of the international economy, a feature that would be repeated in all subsequent loan booms. But the lending and borrowing activity of the 1820s cannot be understood solely in terms of economic cycles. A broader political dimension was also implicit in these transatlantic financial transactions. For Great Britain as well as for the fledgling states of Latin America, the loans were means for attaining a series of strategic goals.

British bankers, merchants, and politicians believed that the loans could help to open doors in Latin America, to increase trade, to gain control of valuable gold and silver mines and to assure British naval predominance in both the Atlantic and the Pacific. For their part, Latin American politicians negotiated loans to finance their armies—engaged in the last stages of the struggle for independence—and to consolidate the new nation-states that had begun to emerge from the ruins of the Spanish and Portuguese empires.

LATIN AMERICA AND THE GREAT POWERS

Although the Latin American elites of the early 1820s sought the diplomatic and financial support of Great Britain, they were not unaware of the dangers of forging close ties with a major European power. Three centuries of colonial rule had left a lasting imprint that would not be soon forgotten. But the leaders of the patriot armies who had fought and were still fighting against Spanish troops knew that their victories were fragile. If the Spanish Crown could obtain the backing of France and the coalition of European

---

6. Based on data in Gayer et al., *Growth and Fluctuation*, pp. 187–189; and J. Fred Rippy, *British Investments in Latin America, 1822–1949* (Minneapolis, 1959), pp. 23–24.

absolute monarchies known as the Holy Alliance, it was possibile that a
new and more powerful military force could be sent across the Atlantic to
reconquer the new republics.[7] The only great power that could counter such
a threat was Great Britain. But British collaboration was not disinterested.
As Simón Bolívar, liberator of Gran Colombia and Peru, observed in a
letter written in May 1823 the British were willing to provide the Latin
American nations with military supplies and war loans for strategic reasons:

> England is the first to be interested in this transaction [a loan for Peru] because she
> desires to form a league with all the free nations of America and Europe against
> the Holy Alliance, in order to put herself at the head of all of these peoples and
> rule the world. . . . It is not in England's interest that . . . Spain maintain a pos-
> session like Peru in America, and therefore prefers that she [Peru] be independent,
> albeit weak and with a fragile government.[8]

This did not mean, however, that the British government had always
favored Latin American independence.[9] During the French occupation of
Spain (1808–14), Great Britain did not openly oppose the Latin American
rebel forces, but authorities at London remained lukewarm toward proposals designed to provoke the permanent separation of the colonies from the
motherland. During the years 1815–20, immediately following the downfall of Napoleon, the conservative foreign secretary, Castlereagh, attempted to reconcile both France and Spain in order to strengthen England's position in the complex postwar constellation of European alliances.
As a result, the rebel movements led by Bolívar and José de San Martín
temporarily lost favor in British ruling circles. Nonetheless, liberal politicians, such as Lord Holland, were able to push through Parliament legislation authorizing the formation of a volunteer corps of British soldiers and
officers to fight for the liberty of the Spanish colonies.[10] At the same time,
dozens of British merchants supplied the insurgents with arms, while London bankers provided the patriot armies with short-term credits to pay for
muskets, cannons and warships.

This ambivalent policy was ended by developments in the critical year

7. A vivid idea of the degree to which such fears impressed themselves on the minds of the
liberators can be found in the correspondence between Bolívar and Sucre in January 1824,
shortly after they had received news of the reestablishment of absolutism in Spain. See Simón
Bolívar, *Cartas, 1823–1825*, ed. R. Blanco-Fombona (Madrid, 1921), pp. 142–146.

8. Bolívar to Sucre, May 26, 1823, in ibid., p. 18.

9. For a classic analysis, see Charles Webster, *Britain and the Independence of Latin America, 1812–1830*, 2 vols. (Oxford, 1938).

10. For an interesting analysis of the British military contribution to Latin American independence, see Eric Lambert, "Los legionarios británicos," in Alberich et al., *Bello y Londres*
(Caracas, 1980), 1:355–376.

of 1823. The decisive turning-point came with the invasion of Spain by more than 100,000 French troops, who proceeded to dismantle the Liberal government in Madrid and reestablish the absolute authority of Ferdinand VII. Liberal opinion in England interpreted the French intervention as a blatant example of the growing power of the Holy Alliance on the European continent. But the invasion was also seen as an exceptional opportunity to consolidate British influence in the Americas. The *Annual Register* noted: "The inglorious triumph of the French beyond the Pyrenees, though productive of present mischief and pregnant with the seeds of much future disorder, has not . . . been entirely without its benefits to the world. It has made the separation between Spain and her late colonies still more complete."[11]

Shortly thereafter the new British foreign secretary, George Canning, a politician of liberal temperament, began to draft proposals for formal recognition of the South American states. The urgency to act was accentuated by fears that rival powers might outpace the British. Already in mid-1822 the United States government had recognized Colombian independence and soon sent diplomatic representatives to Colombia and subsequently to Mexico and Argentina. Canning moved swiftly, and in October 1823 he named British consuls for Buenos Aires, Montevideo, Chile, and Peru, instructing them to initiate negotiations aimed at ratifying commercial treaties with the infant republics. These measures raised the hopes of British merchants and bankers already engaged in promoting trade and loans throughout the vast subcontinent.[12]

BRITISH MERCHANTS AND LATIN AMERICAN TRADE

By sending consuls to the Latin American ports, the British government was de facto extending diplomatic recognition to the new states. In exchange, Canning pressured the leaders of the various nations of the region to ratify accords that would stimulate greater mercantile exchange with Great Britain. The Latin American political elites proved willing to reciprocate for a variety of reasons.

Virtually all the new Latin American leaders—Bernardino Rivadavia in

11. *Annual Register for the Year 1823* (London, 1823), p. iv.

12. The *Times* underlined the economic significance of the new policy, stating: "The announcement of the new relations to spring up between Great Britain and Spanish America has been hailed by the manufacturing and commercial interest of this country with such a burst of satisfaction that Mr. Canning will have to exert himself to follow up a similar national policy whenever occasion may offer" (cited in the *American Monitor* [London, 1824], 1:513). For details, see the classic volume by Robin A. Humphreys, *British Consular Reports on the Trade and Politics of Latin America, 1824–1826* (London, 1940).

Argentina, Bernardo O'Higgins in Chile, Bolívar in Colombia, Agustín Iturbide in Mexico—adopted free-trade policies because they believed more trade would produce greater revenues. In this they were not mistaken, for after independence there was a phenomenal increase in foreign commerce. As a result, the majority of Latin American governments came to rely on import-export taxes as the main source of revenue. In most nations the colonial tax structures were radically restructured. The old taxes on mining production, and the traditional tributes paid by the Indian communities, were abolished. There were exceptions. In Peru and Bolivia the Indian tax continued to be important for several more decades. But generally speaking, Latin American administrations had no alternative but to develop new revenue sources, the most feasible of which proved to be customs duties, not only because they were easily collected but also because they were the least likely to provoke popular protest. In the case of Mexico, customs revenues brought approximately 50 percent of total government income during the 1820s. In Argentina their contribution was even more remarkable, reaching almost 80 percent of total public income during the same decade.[13]

A second important factor that contributed to the establishment of free-trade policies was military in character. The armies and navies of the new states required a large volume of supplies in the way of arms, munitions, and warships, most of which came from abroad. This demand naturally meant lucrative contracts for the foreign suppliers who won the bids on such business.[14]

Finally, there was a financial objective to be reached by means of the commercial treaties. Recognition of the independent status of the Latin American nations would allow them to participate freely and with confidence in transactions on the London money market, because bankers and investors would be assured of the legal and valid status of the external bonds that might be sold by the governments of Chile, Peru, Mexico, or any of the other states of the region.

Adoption of free-trade policies by the Latin American states provided

13. On tax reforms, and esp. the abolition of Indian tribute in this period, see Nicolás Sánchez Albornoz, "Tributo abolido, tributo repuesto. Invariantes socioeconómicos en la época republicana," in the book by the same author entitled *Indios y tributos en el Alto Perú* (Lima, 1978), pp. 187–194. For data on Mexican government revenue, see Barbara Tenenbaum, *The Politics of Penury: Debts and Taxes in Mexico, 1821–1856* (Albuquerque, N.M., 1986), chap. 1, tables 3–5, pp. 24–27. For information on the income of the government of Buenos Aires in the 1820s, see Tulio Halperín Donghi, *Guerra y finanzas en los orígenes del estado argentino, 1791–1850* (Buenos Aires, 1983), pp. 185–213.

14. During 1818–24 Birmingham became the principal military supplier to Latin America. According to Lambert ("Los legionarios," p. 364), "Birmingham had a field day disposing of surplus arms and uniforms from the Napoleonic Wars."

golden opportunities for hundreds of British merchant firms.[15] These firms not only came to dominate an important part of the import-export business of the new republics, but also soon played a critical role in stimulating investments in local gold and silver mines and in the negotiation of government loans. Nonetheless, the enthusiasm of many traders was accompanied by imprudence, as well as ignorance of the clients and markets they were serving. Many merchants had only the vaguest notion of what products would sell in the Latin American market:

The shops and warehouses of Fleet Street and Cheapside had been ransacked for exports, the consideration being not what should be sent but how soon it could arrive. The wool blankets, warming pans and skates which reached tropical Brazil ultimately found employment, the blankets as screens for gold washings, the warming pans (with their lids knocked off) as skimmers for the boiling sugar in the sugar "engenhos," the skates as a source of well-tempered steel for knives and as latches for doors in the Brazilian interior.[16]

Furthermore, by overstocking local warehouses with imported commodities, competing merchants created sudden gluts that caused abrupt declines in prices. The effects of this unbridled mercantile rivalry would later be felt during the crisis of 1825–26.

More-reliable profits were gained from supplying war materiel to the armies of the patriot forces. In the case of Chile, for example, foreign traders developed a flourishing business by selling warships to the newly established national navy. General William Miller, one of the most distinguished officers of both San Martín and Bolívar, noted in his memoirs that the Chilean government and people spared no effort to acquire ten warships, two schooners, and seven gunboats from both the United States and Great Britain. However, the military equipment supplied was often of low quality, and the profits secured by unscrupulous foreign traders were exorbitant.

The same ruinous charges were made for arms and stores. Muskets were sometimes bought at twenty dollars each, and seldom or never at less than ten. A corresponding price was given for military accoutrements, many of which had already been condemned as unserviceable at the Tower of London, and bought up at a low price, for the supply of the patriots or the royalists, whichever the consignees might consider the most eligible customers.[17]

15. British exports to Latin America increased from an annual average of £3,900,000 in 1814–20 to £5,500,000 in 1821–25. See D. Porter, *The Progress of the Nation*, rev. ed. (London, 1912), p. 479.
16. D.C.M. Platt, *Latin America and British Trade, 1806–1914* (London, 1972), p. 23.
17. Miller, *Memoirs*, p. 258.

Not all traders benefited equally from the war and postwar boom, yet the number of mercantile firms opening offices and warehouses in the key points of entry during the early 1820s was extraordinary. In Brazil, sixty British commercial houses operated out of Rio de Janeiro, twenty more in Bahia, and sixteen in Pernambuco. Another forty firms were in business at Buenos Aires, ten at Montevideo, twenty at Lima, and fourteen at Mexico City and Veracruz.[18]

Generally speaking, the most successful houses were those that were able to build up a broad network of commercial and political alliances, both locally and abroad. The example of the Parish Robertson brothers, who had begun a remarkable trading career at Buenos Aires in 1807 at the time of the British occupation of the port, shows the importance of such networks. For several years they were active in Asunción, Paraguay, and then later at the Argentine river port of Corrientes, trading in hides, yerba maté, and tobacco. By 1817, having accumulated a considerable fortune, these enterprising merchants decided to expand operations; they established a commercial house at Buenos Aires and simultaneously opened an agency in Liverpool, England.[19]

During the 1820s the Parish Robertsons combined trade with more ambitious financial transactions. They participated in the issue of foreign loans for the governments of both Buenos Aires and Peru, they promoted mining companies in western Argentina and in the highlands of Bolivia, and they established ranching and colonization companies in the River Plate (Río de la Plata) region. Such a variety of transactions placed them in a special category among Anglo-Argentine merchants. The scope of their activities reflected the advantages of establishing special relationships with leading mercantile and banking firms in Great Britain and with political leaders in Latin America. Other trading houses operating from Buenos Aires, such as those of Thomas Armstrong, Thomas Gowland, or James Brittain, also shipped large amounts of goods, but the range of their business was more limited and their access to foreign credit was restricted.[20]

Throughout Latin America a similar pattern emerged. A number of wealthy and well-connected merchant companies stood out among the rest and were therefore in the best position to secure war supply contracts as

18. Platt, *Latin America*, p. 42.

19. On the Parish Robertsons, see John and William Parish Robertson, *Letters on South America*, 3 vols. (London, 1843); and R. A. Humphreys, "British Merchants and South American Independence," in the volume of essays by the same author entitled *Tradition and Revolt in Latin America* (London, 1972), pp. 113–117.

20. On the activities of British merchants in Argentina, see Vera Reber, *British Merchant Houses in Buenos Aires, 1810–1880* (Cambridge, Mass., 1979); and H. Ferns, *Britain and Argentina in the Nineteenth Century* (Oxford, 1960), chaps. 3–5.

well as to serve governments as agents for negotiation of foreign loans. In Colombia and Venezuela two houses were preeminent: Hylsop & Company and their chief rival, Herring, Powles & Graham. The Hylsops had established themselves shortly after the turn of the century at Kingston, Jamaica. They worked in tandem with their cousins' firm, W. and A. Maxwell & Company of Liverpool, which exported butter, soap, earthenware, hams, and cheese to the Jamaica agency in exchange for such tropical commodities as cocoa, sugar, pimento, and indigo. After 1815 the Hylsops extended their activities to the South American mainland. Maxwell Hylsop became a friend of Bolívar and shortly thereafter was named agent for the Colombian government and contracted to supply arms. Branches of the company were opened at Cartagena and Maracaibo and carried on a flourishing trade, introducing not only war materiel but also British hardware, textiles, and machinery.[21] Hylsops' chief rival—Herring, Powles & Graham—also played a major role in the arms trade of Gran Colombia and then moved into other economic ventures in northern South America. In the early 1820s this merchant firm secured grants of land for mining companies and colonization schemes, arranged the first foreign loan for the Colombian government, and maintained weekly newspapers at Bogotá and Caracas to support British interests.[22]

The critical importance of maintaining broadly based commercial and political ties is also illustrated by the experience of leading British firms operating in Chile, Peru, and Mexico. For instance, the prestigious house of Antony Gibbs & Sons, which had long been involved in the Anglo-Spanish trade, extended its chain of offices to include two new branches at Lima, Peru and at Valparaíso, Chile, in the 1820s.[23] Subsequently it would become one of the most influential and prosperous foreign firms engaged in the Pacific trade of South America. Somewhat less solid but equally far-ranging were the operations of Robert Staples & Company, with agents at Buenos Aires, Lima, and Mexico City. Robert Staples had begun his career in the River Plate region as spokesman for the British mercantile community and as unofficial representative of the Foreign Office.[24] He later found fertile terrain for his financial talents in Mexico in the early 1820s. Soon he gained notoriety as one of the largest creditors of the Mexican government. By then he had associated himself with the London merchant banker

21. On the Hylsops, see Humphreys, *Tradition and Revolt*, pp. 117–121.

22. On Herring, Powles & Graham, see Jenks, *Migration*, pp. 46–47.

23. "In 1826 the house [of Gibbs] had 86 clients in Spain, 26 elsewhere in Europe and 31 in the Americas" (Robert Greenhill, "Merchants and the Latin American Trades: An Introduction," in *Business Imperialism: An Enquiry Based upon British Experience in Latin America*, ed. D.C.M. Platt [Oxford, 1977], p. 162).

24. On the early career of Staples, see Ferns, *Britain and Argentina*, pp. 88–92.

FIGURE 1.

MERCANTILE AND FINANCIAL RELATIONS BETWEEN GREAT BRITAIN AND LATIN AMERICA IN THE EARLY 1820s.

Pattern of Flows of Specie, Bills, Loans and Merchandise

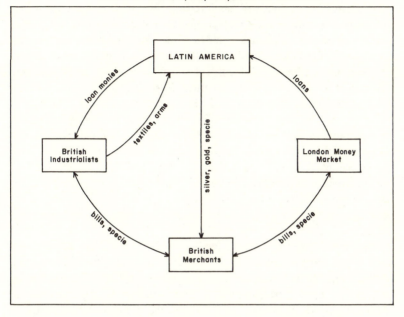

Thomas Kinder, and both were soon active in the promotion of new enterprises, particularly Mexican and Peruvian silver enterprises.

In summary, independence opened up new and dynamic channels of Latin American trade and rapidly tied the region into a web of international mercantile and credit transactions controlled from London, Glasgow, and Liverpool (see Figure 1). But the commercial boom also had a series of negative effects not contemplated by the ideologists of free trade. The massive imports of foreign textiles as well as of military materiel obliged merchants and Latin American government officials to ransack city and countryside in search of metallic currency with which to pay for these supplies. Between 1819 and 1825, for example, Charles Ricketts, British consul at Lima, reported that British men-of-war had carried off 27,000,000 pesos worth of gold and silver from Peru.[25] Precise statistics on bullion exports from other Latin American countries are not available, but the net effect was the same everywhere, leading to a rapid depletion of capital stocks in

25. Humphreys, *British Consular Reports*, p. 195.

21

virtually all regions. Thus, while the surge in trade brought riches to local and foreign merchants, it caused a severe drain of metallic currency as well as of precious metals held by other sectors of the propertied classes, by the church, and by the state treasuries.

The Latin American elites therefore found that trade expansion was not sufficient to revitalize the economies of their new nations. The drain of capital caused by foreign trade could be compensated for only by increasing local production of silver and gold. The regeneration of the silver mines, however, required both political-fiscal reforms and a large amount of new investment. Once again, Latin American politicians were obliged to look to Great Britain for assistance. British capitalists played a critical role in this process, promoting a wave of investment in silver mines throughout the subcontinent: in the Peruvian Andes, in the Brazilian highlands, and in the sierras of central and northern Mexico. The silver-mining boom reinforced the image of Latin American prosperity and, as we shall later see, went hand in hand with the loan boom.

THE LURE OF SILVER

The Latin American silver-mining frenzy of the early 1820s was initiated by a remarkably small group of individuals. They included the partners of a score of merchant houses (several of which we have already mentioned), a handful of London bankers, and a dozen Latin American politicians and diplomats. By virtue of their key position at the crossroads of international politics, trade, and finance, these individuals were to play a dominant role in unleashing forces that shortly culminated in an extraordinary wave of financial speculation on the London Stock Exchange. Paradoxically, the most efficacious instrument at their disposal was not raw power, be it political or economic, but a persuasive psychological tool: the myth of Eldorado.

For centuries the legendary gold and silver mines of Spanish America had captured the imagination of the world and aroused the envy of the European rivals of the Spanish Crown. But now, as the great empire disintegrated, the gates to the mineral treasures of this vast, exotic continent swung open to foreign participation.

Despite the promising prospects—which were described in panegyric terms by the abundant contemporary pamphlet literature—there were serious obstacles. Silver production had declined precipitously with the onset of the wars of independence. In many cases, mine tunnels and shafts had been flooded because of the breakdown of drainage systems. The work force dwindled as large numbers of miners abandoned their homes to march off to war. At the same time, the collapse of the colonial credit system produced severe capital shortages, making it impossible to maintain the mining establishments in proper operating conditions.[26] As the wars came to an end, some improvements were undertaken. Merchants and mine owners initiated drainage operations in a few silver districts, and production there slowly recovered. Yet capital remained scarce. Without additional investment in new machinery, there could be little hope of achieving yields equivalent to those of the late colonial era.

To attract foreign capital to the mines, the political elites of most Latin American states introduced a series of fiscal reforms that eliminated the traditionally heavy taxes on silver and gold production. Furthermore, leading politicians personally took a stake in the early British mining companies. In late 1823 the head of the Argentine government, Bernardino Rivadavia, approved legislation authorizing the formation of companies to exploit the nation's mineral resources. He wrote to his financial agents in London, the firm of Hullett Brothers, urging them to take advantage of the opportunity. He added that he would be interested in investing in such ventures. Similarly, the foreign secretary of the Mexican government, Lucas Alamán, accepted the honorary though influential position as chairman of the board of directors of the United Mexican Mining Association, the first of seven British mining companies established in Mexico in the brief span of one year. Not to be outdone, the diplomatic representatives of Chile, Colombia, and Peru—Mariano Egaña, José María Hurtado, and Antonio de Irisarri, respectively—also assumed posts as heads of new enterprises formed to develop the mineral wealth of their lands.[27]

Latin Americans were not the only politicians involved in this fast-paced mining sweepstakes. The London promoters of these companies spared no efforts to enlist members of the British Parliament as directors. One of the

26. The best description of the mines and the mining crisis is in the monumental work by George Ward, *Mexico in 1827*, 2 vols. (London, 1828), chaps. 4–6; an excellent Spanish translation of this book was published by Fondo de Cultura Económica (Mexico, 1981). For a brief but incisive discussion of the mining collapse in 1810–20, see Tulio Halperín Donghi, *The Aftermath of Revolution in Latin America*, trans. Josephine de Bunsen (New York, 1973), pp. 61–64, 71–75.

27. Hurtado was head of the Colombian Mining Association, Egaña was head of the Chilean Mining Association, and Irisarri was head of the Guatemala Mining Co. and of the Potosí, La Paz, and Peruvian Mining Association. Latin Americans were on the boards of at least ten of the mining companies. For additional details, see Claudio Véliz, "Egaña, Lambert, and the Chilean Mining Association of 1825," *Hispanic American Historical Review* (hereafter *HAHR*) 55 (1975): 637–663; Robert Randall, *Real del Monte: A British Mining Venture in Mexico* (Austin, Tex., 1972); Rippy, *British Investments*, chap. 2; R. A. Humphreys, *Liberation in South America: The Career of James Paroissien* (London, 1952), pp. 122ff. Contemporary sources of information on the mining companies are Henry English, *A Complete View of the Joint-Stock Companies Formed during the Years 1824 and 1825* (London, 1827); and J. Secretan, *Epitome of the Various Foreign Mining Companies* (London, 1824).

largest firms launched in 1824, the New Brazilian Mining Company, placed eight members of Parliament on its twelve-member board of directors.[28] With such tangible political support, investors were unlikely to question the solidity or prospects of the new company at hand. And in order to convince those who were still undecided, eloquent pamphleteers, such as the young Benjamin Disraeli, were hired to prepare detailed and tantalizing reports on the fabulous profits to be earned on the American mining projects.[29]

Contemporaries were struck by the intensity of the monetary passion that broke loose among the English propertied classes as a result of the silver-mining speculation. The *Annual Register* of 1824 described the madness on the stock market:

All the gambling propensities of human nature were constantly solicited into action: and crowds of individuals of every description—the credulous and the suspicious—the crafty and the bold—the raw and the experienced—the intelligent and the ignorant—princes, nobles, placemen, patriots, lawyers, physicians, divines, philosophers, poets, intermingled with women of all ranks and degrees—spinsters, wives and widows—hastened to venture some portion of their property in schemes of which scarcely any thing was known except the name.[30]

By mid-1825, twenty-six different Latin American mining companies had been registered on the Royal Exchange, their shares selling at extraordinary premiums.[31] Seven companies were organized for Mexico, four for Brazil, three each for Peru, Chile, and Colombia, two for Argentina, and one each for Bolivia, the United Provinces of Central America, and Haiti.

The authorized capital of these firms surpassed £24,000,000 but in practice barely £3,000,000 of their stock was paid in by subscribers, so the new associations actually had scarce resources to work with. In most cases the London managers used this small pool of funds to hire mining engineers from England, France, and Germany to do on-site surveys of the gold and silver fields to which the companies intended to lay stake. Such experts as

28. According to Rippy (*British Investments*, p. 24), members of the British Parliament were on the boards of directors of nineteen of the Latin American silver and gold mining companies. For a list of the directors of the New Brazilian Mining Company, see *American Monitor* (1824), 1:512.

29. Apparently Disraeli was himself engaged in speculation in the silver-mine stocks. He was the anonymous author of the 135-page tract entitled ''An Enquiry into the Plans, Progress, and Policy of the American Mining Companies'' (London, 1825). See Véliz, ''Egaña,'' p. 639.

30. *Annual Register, 1824*, p. 3.

31. According to Jenks, *Migration*, p. 54, the Real del Monte stock rose from a price of 70 to 1,200 in a matter of months.

Sir Francis Head, Captain Joseph Andrews, Robert Stephenson, Charles Lambert, General James Paroissien, and James Vetch prepared detailed reports on the mines. In several instances they also published personal accounts, which are still among the most useful and colorful sources of information on the Latin American societies during the postindependence period.[32]

The initial exploration of the mines offered attractive prospects but it later became painfully evident that the success of the numerous silver companies depended less on the support of influential politicians or the technical expertise of engineers and more on the objectives of the wealthy merchants and bankers who were the architects of the mining mania of 1824–25. These money capitalists organized the joint-stock companies and furnished the original funds required to float them. Nevertheless, as financial promoters their objectives were not limited to recovering their investments from mines that would take several years to achieve high levels of production. They were just as anxious to recoup their money quickly by taking advantage of the bull market on the stock exchange and selling off their silver-mining stocks at the highest prices possible.

The speculative and risky character of the early mining boom explains why only a handful of London firms dominated the market for the shares in the new Latin American companies. The principal houses dealing in these securities consisted of a group of aggressive mercantile and financial firms involved in Latin American trade, several of which we have already mentioned. In the case of the Río de la Plata Mining Association, founded in 1824, the chief promoters was Hullett Brothers, a concern engaged in Argentine and Chilean commerce. Similarly, the rival Famatina Silver Mining Company—which had claims to several districts in the province of La Rioja—was established by a group of Anglo-Argentine merchants including the ubiquitous Parish Robertson brothers and the firm of Robert Staples & Company, both working jointly with London financier Thomas Kinder. This group also had interests in the Pasco-Peruvian Mining Company, and at the same time Kinder and Staples served as directors of the Real del Monte Company in Mexico, which was formerly the property of the enormously wealthy counts of Regla.[33]

32. Among the most interesting accounts are Francis B. Head, *Rough Notes of a Trip across the Pampas* (London, 1826); Joseph Andrews, *Journey from Buenos Aires through the Provinces of Cordova, Tucuman and Salta to Potosi*, 2 vols. (London, 1827); and John Miers, *Travels in Chile and La Plata* (London, 1826). On Robert Stephenson, consult J. C. Jeaffreson, *Life of Robert Stephenson*, vol. 1 (London, 1864), chaps. 5–6. On Paroissien, see Humphreys, *Liberation*, pp. 140–141 and passim. On Vetch, see Randall, *Real del Monte*, pp. 51–52 and passim.

33. On the Real del Monte mine in Mexico, see the eyewitness report by Ward, *Mexico in*

In Colombia and Venezuela three mining firms were established in 1824–25 by the previously mentioned merchant houses of Herring, Powles & Graham and Hylsop & Company. The former were more active; they hired the young engineer Robert Stephenson to take charge of its mines, and as early as 1825 Stephenson drew up blueprints for a railway from Caracas to the coast.[34]

Two other London merchant banking firms immersed in the silver business were those of Barclay, Herring, Richardson & Company and B. A. Goldschmidt & Company. The former became the main backers of the Chilean Mining Association and supplied loans to the Chilean, Mexican, and Colombian governments.[35] The Goldschmidts, well known in mercantile and financial circles throughout northern Europe, became progressively involved in Latin American trade and in mining speculation; they promoted two Mexican silver-mining enterprises, at Tlalpujahua and at Real del Catorce, and the larger Colombian Mining Association.[36]

These audacious entrepreneurs, dedicated to peddling silver stocks, combined their interests in the transatlantic trade with financial ventures of increasing magnitude and profitability. Their great opportunity came with the London bull market of 1824–25. And it was neither strange nor surprising that this small circle of traders, bankers, and brokers, who generously plied the Stock Exchange with shares of the silver-mining companies, should also have been dedicated to the much more ambitious and complex business of organizing foreign loans for the governments of the Latin American nations.

1827, chap. 5, sec. 5. On the Argentine mining companies, see Hugo Raúl Galmarini, *Negocios y política en la época de Rivadavia: Braulio Costa y la burguesía comercial porteña, 1820–1830* (Buenos Aires, 1974), chap. 5; and Ferns, *Britain and Argentina*, pp. 134–135.

34. The trading firm of Herring, Powles & Graham (in which T. Richardson, a backer of Overend, Gurney & Co., was a silent partner) became involved in numerous additional projects in the Caribbean region and even projected a canal across Nicaragua. For comments, see Jenks, *Migration*, pp. 55–56.

35. The firm of Barclay, Herring, Richardson & Co. of Winchester House, Broad Street, London, apparently had no links with the more famous Barclay family of Birmingham, which founded and ran the powerful commercial bank now known as Barclay's Bank, but they were linked to the firm of Herring, Powles & Graham through Charles Herring, one of their chief partners. On their role in Chilean mining and short-term loans, see Véliz, "Egaña," p. 649. Their role in Mexican and Colombian loans is detailed in Jaime Rodríguez O., *El nacimiento de Hispanoamérica: Vicente Rocafuerte y el hispanoamericanismo, 1808–1832* (Mexico, 1980), chap. 5.

36. According to Gille, Goldschmidts was one of the important merchant banking firms of London in the early 1820s. It maintained widespread connections with commercial houses in Paris and in northern Germany. See Bertrand Gille, *Histoire de la Maison Rothschild* (Geneva, 1965), 1:159–160. Data on Goldschmidts' investments in Gran Colombia is in David Bushnell, *The Santander Regime in Gran Colombia, 1819–1827* (Newark, Del., 1954), chaps. 7–8.

Latin American Governments and the Loan Boom

While investments in silver mines stimulated economic activity in some regions, they did not solve the grave financial problems of the newborn Latin American states. Because the proceeds from the mines went into the pockets of private capitalists, not to the government, the fundamental dilemma of the finance ministers continued to be fiscal. Rising expenditures rapidly outstripped income and generated large deficits. Moroever, the tax reforms of the 1820s produced contradictory results. The elimination of many old taxes, such as the important *quinto real* levied on the mines, aggravated the fiscal crisis by doing away with major sources of state income. New taxes on imports and exports compensated in part, but they were not sufficient to balance budgets. Inevitably, government officials were obliged to seek credit to cover their deficits, first in the form of forced loans exacted from local merchants, later in the shape of loans contracted with foreign bankers.[37]

It is not surprising that the Latin American governments looked abroad for financial assistance. A decade and more of war and revolution had disrupted and weakened local networks of credit, and loanable capital was scarce and expensive. On the other hand, abundant sources of relatively cheap capital were available outside Latin America, as had been demonstrated by the success of the silver-mining companies in raising capital on the London Stock Exchange.

Latin American finance ministers were quick to learn from this experience and soon sent agents across the Atlantic to solicit long-term credits from European bankers. The success they had selling their bonds is remarkable. Between 1822 and 1825, loans for the Latin American states absorbed the greater part of the foreign government securities sold on the London Stock Exchange (see Table 1). This was no mean feat. Before 1822, almost all foreign loans at London had been destined for and guaranteed by one or another European monarchy or princedom. In contrast, the Mexican, Argentine, Peruvian, and Colombian loans were among the first to be supplied to nations outside Europe. Equally significant, they were among the first to be granted to republics rather than monarchies.[38]

But what were the specific objectives of the Latin American loans, how were they negotiated, and who benefited from them? Politicians, diplo-

37. There are relatively few historical studies of the finances of Latin American governments in the period immediately following independence. The outstanding published works are Miron Burgin, *The Economic Aspects of Argentine Federalism, 1820–1852* (New York, 1946); Halperín, *Guerra y finanzas*; and Bushnell, *Santander Regime*, chaps. 6–8.

38. On the foreign loans issued at London between 1793 and 1821, see "Loans Contracted on Account of Great Britain in Each Year since 1793," in *Parliamentary Papers* (1822), vol. 20, no. 145.

TABLE 1
LATIN AMERICAN GOVERNMENT ISSUES FLOATED IN ENGLAND, 1822–1825

Year and Borrower	Nominal Value (£)	Price to Public[a]	Interest nominal %	Interest "real"[b] %	Sums Realized[c] (£)	Bankers[d]
1822						
Chile	1,000,000	70	6	8.6	700,000	Hulletts
Colombia[e]	2,000,000	84	6	7.1	1,680,000	Herring, Powles & Graham
Peru	450,000	88	6	6.8	396,000	Thomas Kinder; Everett, Walker & Co.
1824						
Brazil	1,200,000	75	5	6.7	900,000	Fletcher, Alexander & Co.; Thomas Wilson & Co.
Buenos Aires	1,000,000	85	6	7.0	850,000	Barings
Colombia	4,750,000	88	6	6.8	4,203,750	Goldschmidts
Mexico	3,200,000	58	5	8.6	1,856,000	Goldschmidts
Peru	750,000	82	6	7.3	615,000	Frys & Chapman
1825						
Brazil	2,000,000	85	5	5.9	1,700,000	Rothschilds
Central America	163,000	73	6	8.2	118,990	Barclay, Herring, Richardson & Co.
Mexico	3,200,000	89	6	6.7	2,872,000	Barclay, Herring, Richardson & Co.
Peru	616,000	78	6	8.2	480,480	Frys & Chapman

SUMMARY BY STATE

State	Total Value of Bonds Issued in London, 1822–25 (£)
Brazil	3,200,000
Buenos Aires	1,000,000
Central America	163,300
Chile	1,000,000
Colombia	6,750,000
Mexico	6,400,000
Peru	1,816,000
TOTAL	20,329,300

[a] Price of bonds sold to investors through the stock exchange.

[b] The calculation of "real" interest is based on the price at which bonds were sold to the public.

[c] "Sums realized" refers to the proceeds presumably received by the bankers and/or loan contractors, but it does not reflect the precise sums transferred to the Latin American governments; the latter sums were invariably much smaller than the former.

[d] Bankers formally in charge of issuing the bonds; other banking firms occasionally participated in distribution.

[e] "Colombia" refers to the government of Gran Colombia (1820–34), which included the future states of Colombia, Venezuela, and Ecuador.

mats, unofficial agents, merchants, bankers, and investors all found themselves engaged in this complex financial drama that had its axis in the Royal Exchange. For each the loans had a different meaning and a different objective. The complex and contradictory web of political and financial forces, personalities, and strategies suggests the importance of distinguishing between the distinct role that each principal actor was destined to play. It is logical to begin with the political elites of the Latin American countries, because they not only provided initial authorization for the loans but also were responsible for spending the funds and supervising repayment.

Traditional historical interpretation suggests that, at best, Latin American political leaders of the 1820s had only vague notions of the objectives for which they contracted foreign loans and, at worst, were simply dupes of the London bankers. Although not wholly erroneous, such a view is misleading on several counts. The contemporary generation of heads of state in the new nations—Bolívar, San Martín, O'Higgins, Rivadavia, Francisco Santander, and Sucre, among others—were not only renowned military strategists and political brokers but also imaginative administrative reformers who drafted constitutions, organized parliamentary bodies, built armies and navies, and transformed the fiscal machinery of their states. As pragmatists, they were acutely aware of the financial basis of political and military power, and they considered foreign loans indispensable for consolidation of both government and army.

The circumstances that led to the authorization and negotiation of the loans varied substantially in each case. We shall select one particularly important case—that of Gran Colombia—to serve as an exemplar of the complexity of contemporary loan politics. First, we look at the historical origins of Gran Colombia, then we turn to the financial situation of the new government in the early 1820s.

TABLE 1 (*cont.*)

SOURCES: Charles Fenn, *A Compendium of the English and Foreign Funds* (London, 1838 and 1878 eds.); J. F. Rippy, *British Investments in Latin America, 1822–1949* (Minneapolis, 1959); Irving Stone, "The Composition and Distribution of British Investments in Latin America, 1865–1913" (Ph.D. diss., Columbia University, 1962); *London Times*, 1822, 1824, 1825; *Annual Register*, 1822, 1824, 1825.

NOTE: In addition to the loans listed, contemporary sources provide scattered information on the following "Latin American" loans: Poyais (nonexistent kingdom in Central America), £200,000 loan, of which £160,000 was issued at London in 1822, price of issue 80, 6% interest rate; Cuba (still a Spanish colony), £450,000 loan, price of issue 91, 6% interest rate, issued in 1824 by Wright & Co.; Guadalajara (a Mexican province), £360,000 of a £600,000 loan, issued at London at the price of 60, the agent being Ellewand & Co. Only one Latin American state loan, that of Haiti, was issued at Paris; this was a 30,000,000 franc loan (£1,200,000) issued in 1825 by a consortium of Paris bankers including Paravey et Cie., Lafitte, Rothschild, Hagerman, and Blanc-Colin.

The formation of the government of Gran Colombia—which included the modern-day nations of Venezuela, Colombia, and Ecuador—was a complex process and central to the entire independence movement in Spanish South America. The first revolutionary outbreaks had taken place in Venezuela in 1811. In later years insurgency spread to Colombia, and by 1819 the Spanish troops in both states had been defeated, although not completely eliminated. It was at this time that Bolívar began to carry out his plan to create a great new state to be called Gran Colombia. To do this it was essential not only to call for elections for a national congress, to ratify a new constitution, and to establish a series of new governmental institutions (ministries of defense, foreign affairs, finance, and interior), but also to reform the colonial tax system, for as in all the Latin American revolutions a principal popular demand was elimination of old and much-hated taxes.

At the Congress of Cúcuta (1821) the representatives of Venezuela and Colombia debated and approved a great many fundamental laws, including several major fiscal reforms. The taxes on internal trade (*alcabalas*), the tribute paid by the Indian communities, and the state alcohol monopoly were abolished. At the same time, several new taxes were introduced—for example, the property tax (*contribución directa*), and others, such as the customs duties (*aduanas*), were expanded. The latter became the most important source of government revenue after 1821, but several important colonial sources of income continued to be operative: the tobacco and salt monopolies, the mints, the tithes, and the stamp tax. As a result, from a strictly fiscal point of view, the new state of Gran Colombia was in a better position than the viceregal government had ever been.[39]

While the income of the government of Gran Colombia appeared to be substantial on paper, several factors made it impossible to avoid deficits. The first was the misappropriation of funds by high- and low-ranking civilian and military officials. In his personal correspondence, Simón Bolívar did not tire of insisting that the strictest measures should be implemented to reduce such practices.[40] But this was easier said than done. When most public employees, as well as the troops and officers of the revolutionary armies, were paid in devalued scrip, it was not likely that local state treasuries would remain untouched. Soldiers on the march had no qualms about ransacking local customs offices, plundering the coffers of the tobacco monopoly, forcing priests to deliver the silver ornaments of their churches, or

---

39. Bushnell, *Santander Regime*, chap. 7.

40. Bolívar wrote to the president of the Peruvian government council on July 22, 1825: "The greater part of the agents of the government are robbing its life-blood [the customs revenues] and this should be proclaimed in all the public papers and everywhere" (Simón Bolívar, *Doctrina del libertador*, ed. Manuel Pérez Vila [Caracas, 1979], p. 204).

expropriating horses, mules, and cattle from large or small ranches.[41] The fiscal situation was also aggravated by the enormous contraband carried on by local and foreign merchants, who assiduously avoided the customs offices. As a result, the finance ministers of Gran Colombia rarely saw more than a fraction of what might be presumed to be the regular income of the state.

Apart from insufficient revenues, certain structural factors made it impossible to balance budgets in the early 1820s. The most important factor was the enormous growth in military expenses. Maintenance of the armed forces required abundant financial resources. Until 1825 the Colombian army consisted of approximately 25,000 troops permanently on duty, a portion of them fighting in Ecuador, Peru, and Bolivia.[42] A large number were cavalry—the famous *lanceros*—and their sustenance was more expensive than that of the regular infantry. In addition, Bolívar and Santander were intent on creating a small but professional navy in order to impede Spanish blockades or full-scale invasions.

Some of the expenses involved in sustaining both army and navy could be covered inexpensively; food and animals could be obtained either by force or by means of war contracts with local merchants, salaries could be defrayed (at least in part) with scrip. But other critical supplies—muskets, munitions, uniforms, swords, cannon, and warships—had to be paid for with hard cash; and most of these had to be imported.

From 1817, Bolívar and the other leaders of Venezuelan and Colombian patriot armies arranged contracts with a considerable number of British merchants to provide military supplies, paid for partly in specie and partly by means of short-term credits. Delays in discharging these credits soon posed serious problems. In 1819 Bolívar's purchasing agent in London, López Méndez, was thrown into debtor's prison as a result of claims by an irate merchant who demanded payment for the arms he had supplied to the insurgent forces.[43] And by 1820 the Colombian government had accumulated debts valued at more than £500,000 with some 200 British manufacturers and merchants who had advanced arms, uniforms, and munitions to the revolutionary army.

41. Bolívar explicitly commanded his fellow officers to collect funds in these diverse ways, as a review of his letters, many of them published by O'Leary, will confirm. An interesting but biased study of the finances of the independence wars could be constructed simply on the basis of the personal correspondence and memoirs of the principal officers of the liberation armies.

42. On Colombian military expenses see Bushnell, *Santander Regime*, esp. chap. 7.

43. On Méndez's activities, see D.A.G. Waddell, "Las relaciones británicas con Venezuela, Nueva Granada y la Gran Colombia, 1810–1829," in Alberich et al., *Bello y Londres*, 1:53–123.

In order to overcome these difficulties, Bolívar resolved to sound out the London merchant banking community on the possibility of raising a long-term loan with which to liquidate the outstanding debts as well as to raise additional funds for his army. So the first major Latin American financial transaction to be negotiated abroad was destined to be a war loan.

In June 1820 the vice-president of Gran Colombia, Francisco Antonio Zea, arrived in London as minister plenipotentiary with powers to settle all existing debts. Although the British foreign secretary, Castlereagh, refused to receive him, Zea soon began negotiating with several financial houses. A year and a half later he signed the first Colombian foreign loan with the merchant-banking firm of Herring, Powles & Graham, representatives of a large body of dissatisfied Anglo-Colombian traders. The contractors took the bonds at 80 percent, a reasonably high price for a government that had not yet obtained diplomatic recognition. These terms were possible because most of the bonds were not sold on the open market, but simply transferred to the legion of individual creditors. Nonetheless, the £2,000,000 operation was subsequently repudiated by the Colombian parliament, and the old disputes were renewed in the London law courts.[44]

Criticism of Zea and the 1822 loan continued in the Colombian press and legislature during early 1823. To avoid having to depend on foreign credit, alternative sources of financing were sought. The most ambitious measure was the ratification of a 500,000-peso internal loan, but the transaction proved to be a failure.[45]

By mid-1823 the Colombian Congress faced a difficult decision: whether to request a new loan and liquidate the accumulated debts abroad, or risk provoking a suspension of trading relationships with Great Britain and an end to all arms shipments precisely at the moment when Bolívar and Sucre were engaged in the most critical campaigns of the war in Peru. There appeared to be no alternative but to negotiate a second financial credit totaling £4,750,000, one of the largest foreign loans issued in London during the 1820s (See Table I).

The bulk of the funds obtained through this second loan were also used for military objectives.[46] A considerable portion (1,000,000 pesos) was re-

44. The obstreperous conduct of Zea, as well as the intense rivalries that developed between the firm of Herring, Powles & Graham and B. A. Goldschmidt for the Colombian loans, provoked a spate of pamphlet literature in the early 1820s, most of it published in London. Three such works are indexed under "Colombian Loan" in the *General Catalogue of Printed Books of the British Museum* (New York, 1967), vol. 5. For additional information, see Anonymous, *Colombia, relación geográfica, topográfica, agrícola, comercial y política* (Bogotá, 1974, a Spanish translation of the English edition published in 1822), pp. lxxxiv–ciii.

45. On the complex negotiations, see Bushnell, *Santander Regime*, chap. 8.

46. Ibid. For additional information on the history of this loan as well as on the loan of 1822, see Vicente Olarte Camacho, *Resumen histórico sobre la deuda externa de Colombia* (Bogotá, 1914), and J. Holguín, *Desde cerca: asuntos colombianos* (Paris, 1908), pp. 1–103.

mitted to Bolívar's army in Peru. An equivalent sum was paid to the Colombian buying agent at London for cancellation of several large short-term debts and for new arms acquisitions. More than 1,000,000 pesos were sent to the United States to pay for the purchase of twelve coastguard gunboats and two modern, well-armed frigates, the *Colombia* and the *Cundinamarca*. At the same time, local Colombian merchants, many of whom had sold provisions on credit to the army, also benefited; they were now able to exchange a huge stock in scrip (*vales*) and promissory notes for £600,000. An additional percentage of the funds went for nonmilitary purposes. A large sum was transferred to the tobbaco monopoly, a state enterprise that had been sacked repeatedly by the army. Another 320,000 pesos were used for agricultural loans, albeit mostly for several important landowners who had close links to the government.

In summary, the two foreign loans of Gran Colombia were not merely speculative operations. The bankers' profits were considerable, as we shall see, but a substantial part of the loan receipts was used for important strategic objectives—namely, the prosecution of the wars of independence.

The Peruvian and Chilean governments soon followed the Colombian example, their needs and aims being almost identical. In 1822, under authorization from Chilean President Bernardo O'Higgins, the London merchant banking firm of Hullett Brothers sold £1,000,000 worth of securities with the ostensible purpose of financing the Chilean navy, the main force defending the Pacific coast of South America against the Spanish fleet.[47]

The first Peruvian external bonds were issued in the same year by the firm of Thomas Kinder and sold in two installments. The money was used to reimburse several dozen British merchants as well as to pay for munitions shipped to Peruvian ports. A second, smaller loan issued in 1825 served to pay arrears of wages to troops, including "generous bonuses for those soldiers who had taken part in the final victorious engagement of the war at Ayacucho."[48] But the proceeds were not sufficient to cover the considerable debts to Gran Colombia incurred for military aid supplied from 1823. In October 1825 Bolívar wrote from the city of Potosí to the Peruvian minister of finance, José de Larrea, urging him to seek a new solution to the debt problem. He wrote:

As always I am thinking of Peru because of her debts, and I would recommend to the government that it should liquidate its national debt by selling all its mines and common lands, which are immense. . . . The State Council should consider this plan, publish it and inform its agents in England. . . . Colombia has already given

47. For the original text of the Chilean loan contract of 1822 and additional information, see *Resumen de la Hacienda Pública de Chile* (Santiago de Chile, 1901).

48. Quotation from W. M. Mathew, "The First Anglo-Peurvian Debt and Its Settlement, 1822–1849," *Journal of Latin American Studies* (hereafter *JLAS*) 2, no. 1 (1970): 83.

as much as she can; and it is this very situation which has made me think of this plan. God save us from the debt and we shall be content.[49]

The news of the success of Gran Colombia, Chile, and Peru in raising loans at London spread rapidly throughout Latin America. In 1822 the Mexican government, headed by the flamboyant general and self-appointed emperor, Agustín Iturbide, also opened negotiations with British bankers, although no Mexican bonds were actually sold until 1824, when the loan and silver-mining craze billowed. The purpose of the Mexican loans was to stabilize state finances and promote economic development, but military requirements were equally important. Overall, a review of the loan disbursements indicates that 20 percent of the £2,500,000 received by the Mexican authorities was used to liquidate claims of British merchants (e.g., Robert Staples, who had provided credits to the government), that approximately 15 percent was used to finance the state tobacco monopoly, and that another 15 percent went to pay for military and naval stores ordered from Great Britain. The remaining funds—nearly 50 percent of the total—went to meet arrears in the salaries and pensions of government employees, the bulk of this sum being used to pay officers and soldiers, for in the mid-1820s the Mexican state was almost synonymous with the army.[50]

The Argentine authorities adopted a markedly different form of loan disbursement. The Buenos Aires government headed by Rivadavia bore a lighter military burden than its sister republics did, and even enjoyed a fiscal surplus. In early 1824 the local parliament authorized a group of wealthy Anglo-Argentine merchants led by Braulio Costa, Felix Castro, and William Parish Robertson to negotiate a £1,000,000 loan in London in order to promote public works, including construction of a modern port at Buenos Aires.[51] The agents signed a contract with the banking house of Baring Brothers, and the bonds soon sold briskly. The proceeds, however, were not spent on the projected public works, but were invested in the first Argentine bank of the nineteenth century, the Banco de Buenos Aires. Additional sums bolstered local credit transactions, because the foreign securities served to amortize outstanding government debts and to facilitate the issue of new internal bonds. In this fashion the Baring loan of 1824 pro-

49. Bolívar, *Doctrina del Libertador*, pp. 207–208.

50. On the early Mexican loans, see Jan Bazant, *Historia de la deuda exterior de México* (Mexico, 1968), pp. 24–40. For complementary details, see Reinhard Liehr, "La deuda exterior de México y los merchant bankers británicos, 1821–1860," *Ibero-Amerikanisches Archiv*, n.f., jg. 9, H.3/4 (1983): 415–439; and Rodríguez O., *El nacimiento*, chap. 6.

51. According to one historian, "The 1824 loan was an attempt to take advantage of a favorable period on the London money market at a time when the Government of Buenos Aires could not raise money locally at less than 14%" (D.C.M. Platt, "Foreign finance in Argentina for the First Half-century of Independence," *JLAS* 15, no. 1 [1983]: 16).

vided a strong impetus to the development of the early Argentine financial system.[52] Unfortunately the brief phase of prosperity was cut short by the outbreak of the Argentine-Brazilian war of 1826–28.

The financial policies of two nations should be noted here. Brazil and Haiti reached independence by routes different from those of their Spanish-American brethren. The separation of Brazil from Portugal came peacefully with the proclamation of Don Pedro I (son of the Portuguese monarch) as constitutional emperor of the new Brazilian nation. Two large loans issued in London in 1824 and 1825 had the specific purpose of smoothing the way to Portuguese recognition of Brazilian independence by liquidating debts and providing generous monetary compensation to the former mother-land.[53] In the case of the republic of Haiti, the objective of a 30,000,000 franc (£1,2000,000) loan was to win France's recognition of the independence of its former colony in exchange for indemnity payments to the several hundred plantation owners who had abandoned the island after the revolution of 1790s. Negotiations took place in June 1824 between Haitian President Jean-Pierre Boyer and French Admiral Baron Mackau, in the course of which the former capitulated to the demands of the government of Louis XVIII. British merchants were incensed about the terms of the agreement, because it called for an increase in import duties on British manufactured goods, placing them at a considerable disadvantage with respect to the French traders. Despite the protests, three Haitian agents set sail for France, where they soon reached an agreement with several Paris banking firms for the issue of the bonds.[54]

In summary, the objectives of the first foreign loans of Latin America were varied because the political and military priorities of the nascent states differed substantially. For this reason it is unwise to evaluate all of them with exactly the same criteria. Only a case-by-case study (using the abun-

---

52. For a detailed analysis of the 1824 loan and its links to programs of financial reform, see Samuel Amaral, "El empréstito de Londres de 1824," *Desarrollo económico* (Buenos Aires) 23, no. 92 (1984): 559–588.

53. N. M. Rothschild & Sons led the placement on the 1825 loan. According to the the *London Times*, the monarchical character of the Brazilian government was apparently the principal reason Rothschilds participated in the Brazilian loan. For additional information, see Gustavo Barroso, *Brasil, colonia de banqueiros: história dos empréstimos de 1824 a 1934*, 6th ed. (Rio de Janeiro, 1937).

54. The *Annual Register, 1825*, p. 146, went so far as to affirm: "It is impossible to doubt but that Boyer betrayed the trust reposed in him, and that henceforth he must be regarded as a French viceroy, rather than as the head of an independent nation." The 30,000,000 franc loan was intended to be the first installment on a total indemnity payment of 150,000,000 francs (£6,000,000), a fabulous sum for the age. On the Haitian loan, see Benoit Joachim, *Les racines du sous-développement en Haiti* (Port-au-Prince, 1979), p. 181, and Pierre Benoit, *Cent cinquante ans du commerce extérieur, 1804–1954* (Port-au-Prince, 1954).

dant but little-explored materials in the financial archives of each nation) could determine whether the money was obtained on reasonable terms, whether it was invested as originally planned, and whether repayment was feasible in the long run. Nevertheless, while the loans did place a heavy burden on the respective national treasuries, Latin American leaders used a substantial portion of the foreign funds to further fundamental goals: the consolidation of independence and the construction of new states and armies.

FINANCIAL AGENTS AND BANKERS

Latin American politicians played a critical role in launching the loan boom of the early 1820s, but they were not the only actors involved in these complex transatlantic transactions. Diplomats, financial agents, contractors, bankers, brokers, and investors all participated at different stages of what can be described as the life cycle of each loan. Indeed, once the issue of the foreign bonds had been authorized, the loan operation passed from the hands of the politicians into those of a heterogeneous collection of agents who served as intermediaries between the Latin American governments and the European bankers. At this point the loan proposals began to undergo a process of metamorphosis, changing from planks of local economic legislation into instruments of international financial diplomacy and finally into complex business transactions. After negotiations were under way, the borrowing governments frequently found they could no longer determine the trajectory of the financial proceedings. A broad range of external factors, including the skill and honesty of the agents, the tactics of the bankers, and the state of the stock markets, could modify the expected results.

The gradual process of amalgamation of public goals and private aims is illustrated by the role of the financial agents. The Latin American envoys sent to Europe had an official mission to fulfill, but in numerous instances they also desired to make a personal profit. It goes without saying that the negotiation of international loans offered considerable opportunities to realize pecuniary gains in the way of fees, shares in bond sales and other mercantile advantages. But who precisely were these intermediaries? Because in the early 1820s the Latin American governments had not yet developed stable diplomatic corps,[55] in some cases the first official representative was a high government functionary sent on a special mission, as was the case with Vice-president Zea of Gran Colombia, who negotiated the

55. The best case-study of the role of the early Latin American diplomats is found in the biography of Vicente Rocafuerte by Rodríguez O., *El nacimiento*, chaps. 5–6.

1822 loan. In other instances the agent could be a semi-official envoy charged with contacting various banking houses. For example, Chilean leader O'Higgins had the misfortune to rely on the services of a notably unscrupulous individual, Antonio José de Irisarri, who after arranging a government loan with Hullett Brothers used his contacts to further his speculations on the London Stock Exchange, including investments in a remarkable string of silver-mining companies.[56]

The head of the Peruvian government in 1822, General José de San Martín, proved equally hapless in his choice of envoys. He selected two singular adventurers, Juan García del Río and James Paroissien, to serve as minister plenipotentiaries in London. Pariossien's biographer notes: "They had been instructed to raise a loan on behalf of Peru, and in England in 1822, nothing could be easier."[57] The contract arranged at the "counting house" of Thomas Kinder in London provided for a loan of £1,200,000. We do not know whether the two agents personally participated in the subsequent intense speculation in Peruvian bonds, but they did simultaneously join financier Kinder and his cronies, the merchant Robert Staples and the previously mentioned Irisarri, in various Bolivian and Peruvian mining ventures.

There is an even more explicit instance of the private interests of the intermediaries in charge of the loan transactions in the arrangements made for the Argentine loan of 1824. The intermediaries were a small group of Anglo-Argentine merchants led by the Parish Robertson brothers. Working together with the prestigious banking firm of Baring Brothers, they netted a profit of £150,000, equivalent to almost 20 percent of the net proceeds obtained from the sale of the bonds. Later, they increased their gains by speculating in Argentine internal bonds and by buying and selling bills of exchange sent by Baring Brothers, all business derived from the foreign loan.[58]

56. "Though Guatemalan by birth, Antonio José de Irisarri (1786–1868) was Chile's second envoy to the Court of Saint James. Following explicit but unsigned instructions drafted by Bernardo O'Higgins, Irisarri proceeded to raise a £1,000,000 loan through the London firm of Hullett Brothers. . . . When the news reached Chile, the government reacted strongly against it. . . . But it was too late . . . the Chilean bonds had been selling briskly in the London market for several months" (Véliz, "Egaña," pp. 637–638).

57. Humphreys, *Liberation*, p. 121. Subsequently the Parish Robertson brothers assumed the old contract (held by Kinder) and transferred it to the banking firm of Frys & Chapman, which issued £750,000 of Peruvian bonds in 1824 and another £616,000 in 1825.

58. Argentine historians devoted much attention to the 1824 Baring loan. See Armando O. Chiapella, *El destino del empréstito Baring* (Buenos Aires, 1975); Ernesto Fitte, *Historia de un empréstito: la emisión de Buenos Aires de 1824* (Buenos Aires, 1962); Juan Carlos Vedoya, *La verdad sobre el empréstito Baring* (Buenos Aires, 1971); and Amaral, "El empréstito de 1824."

A more blatant case of fraud practiced by a loan agent is found in the activities of Borja Mignoni, a merchant long resident at London who handled the first Mexican foreign loan issued in 1824. Borja Mignoni established a secret pact with the banking firm of B. A. Goldschmidt & Company with the objective of manipulating the sale of the bonds for personal profit. Together they arranged a contract by which they paid the Mexican government only 50 percent of the nominal value of the bonds and later sold them off at 80 percent in the London Stock Exchange.[59]

The most outlandish piece of extortion, however, was carried out not by any of the Latin American government agents but by an extraordinary English soldier of fortune named Gregor MacGregor. Contemporary British investors were so ignorant with respect to Latin America that it was possible for MacGregor to present himself in London in 1822 as the representative of a fictitious kingdom in Central America called Poyais and to successfully market £200,000 worth of the spurious bonds of the nonexistent state. This Scottish adventurer had formerly been a general in Bolívar's army and later married his niece. He had subsequently quarreled with the South American liberator and began to operate as a self-styled privateer in the Caribbean. In 1821 he negotiated a treaty with the Miskito Indians of Nicaragua, who awarded him the honorary title of "Prince of Poyais." On his return to England, MacGregor began selling land in his nonexistent kingdom to gullible Scotch farmers and artisans. At the same time, he proceeded to sell the Poyais bonds. But when news reached London that most of the colonists who had sailed for the Central American paradise had perished on the malaria-ridden coast of Nicaragua, MacGregor was forced to flee England.[60]

Despite such scandals, the rage to invest in foreign securities continued on the Royal Exchange, reaching a peak in the years 1824–25. By this time the British and United States governments were in the process of extending diplomatic recognition to the majority of the Latin American states. As a result, the Latin American governments began to send abroad envoys who were men of a different stamp from the earlier financial agents. In the years 1823, 1824, and 1825 there arrived in London a number of distinguished diplomats who were not only well-known intellectual and political figures but also scrupulous guardians of their nation's financial patrimonies. Among them stood out Andrés Bello and José María Hurtado, ambassadors

59. The bonds were initially sold at 58, the lowest quotation of all Latin American bonds issued in the 1820s. After a variety of "expenses" charged by the bankers, the Mexican government received net proceeds equal to only 42.5 percent of the nominal value of the bonds. See Bazant, *Historia de la deuda*, p. 27.

60. For details, see Victor Allan, "The Prince of Poyais," *History Today*, January 1952, pp. 53–58.

for Colombia, Vicente Rocafuerte and José Michelena for Mexico, and Mariano Egaña for Chile.[61] It is not surprising that during their tenure the loan operations conducted with the London bankers proved most productive for the borrowing nations.

Nevertheless, the sale of the Latin American bonds depended less on the character of the government agents than on the stock market cycles and the corresponding strategies adopted by the merchant bankers. The bankers were interested in the loans for three basic reasons. First, they stood to receive substantial commissions by assuming responsibility for the promotion, issue, and sale of the bonds. Second, they could play the market by selling the securities as prices rose, buying them back as they fell. Third, they could extend their traditional merchant-banking business by using loan proceeds to finance the export of manufactured goods from Great Britain.[62]

The bankers usually had an interest in selling as many bonds as possible, because greater sales produced larger commissions. These ranged from 4 to 8 percent of the nominal value of the loan, depending on the contract clause. Such rates were not considered abnormally high in the 1820s because of the considerable risks involved in issuing bonds for foreign states at a time of marked political instability on both sides of the Atlantic. As far as the bankers were concerned, such financial quotas did not represent windfall profits, but simply were intended to cover generously the risk and cost of promotion. In many instances, however, the rates were blatantly extortionate. For example, B. A. Goldschmidt cleared more than £200,000 by charging an 8 percent commission on the first Mexican loan. Similarly, the firm of Herring, Powles & Graham, together with that of Barclay, Herring, Richardson & Company grossed almost £500,000 on commissions and other charges on the two Colombian loans, an astonishing figure for the age.[63]

But commissions were only one kind of profit derived from the loans. In some cases speculation on price swings of the Stock Exchange brought equivalent or larger returns. The financial manipulation began as early as 1822, when the first Latin American bonds came on the market. The *Lon-*

61. Much information on these diplomats can be found in D. Waddell, "Las relaciones," in Alberich et al., *Bello y Londres*, as well as in other essays in the same volume.

62. The firm of Barclay, Herring, Richardson & Co., e.g., used a part of the proceeds of the 1825 Mexican loan to finance a 1,300,000 peso arms shipment for the Mexican army (Liehr, "La deuda exterior," p. 426).

63. It is not always possible to make a precise estimate of bankers' profits on bond sales, but there is enough published information to make some broad comparisons. On the Argentine loan of 1824, the contractors earned 15 percent of the nominal value of the bonds. On the Mexican loan of 1824, the profits approached 30 percent. In contrast, the bankers' "spread" on the Brazilian loans of the period was only 3–5 percent of the nominal value of the securities.

don Times described the agitation that took place on the Royal Exhange when the first Peruvian loan was offered for sale. The crowd of brokers and investors protested against the contractor, Thomas Kinder, who attempted to fix the price of the securities.

All were indignant at the supposed backwardness of the contractor to take the offers made him; and pressing round him in still greater numbers, he and his agents were forced by the multitude to the opposite corner of the exchange where the Swedish merchants assemble. Here the brokers became so exasperated, being still unable to come to terms with the agents that they forced the whole party off the exchange, out at the north gate, opposite to Bartholomew lane.[64]

The rigging of bond prices was common in the case of the earliest Latin American loans, issued in 1822, but subsequently it tended to diminish. By the time of the bull market of 1824–25, relatively little manipulation was required by the bankers to obtain high quotations on the securities they wanted to sell. In the case of the second Mexican loan, which was issued by the Barclay financial house at 86, there was no difficulty finding buyers: the rival firm of B. A. Goldschmidt immediately subscribed the whole package of £3,000,000 worth of bonds and proceeded to unload them among investors at 89 and a fraction.[65]

The demand for Latin American bonds during this short-lived but intense period of speculation was stimulated by the abundance of surplus capital that flowed to the stock market. But the mercantile and banking firms also worked hard to create a market for the new securities. They had good reason to do so, because they expected to reap benefits not only from the sale of the bonds but also from the positive effects the loans could have on their extensive mining and mercantile ventures.

A brief review of the firms responsible for issuing the loans underscores the close-knit nature of this key group of cosmopolitan capitalists who played a decisive role in restructuring the international economic relations of Latin America in the years immediately following independence. In the case of Argentina, we have already noted the singular role of the Parish Robertson brothers in the River Plate trade, in the negotiation of the 1824 loan, and in mining and agricultural ventures. Their close rapport with San Martín and later with Bolívar allowed them to extend their activities further

---

64. The text, from the *London Times*, is cited in the *Annual Register, 1822*, pp. 193–194.

65. Contemporary British journals argued that the demand was closely related to the higher profits to be made on the Latin American loans. "We see that the positive amount of interest from the South American securities is more than double that which is offered to the English capitalists in continental loans" (*American Monitor* 2, pt. 4 [1825]: 140). On the specifics of the bidding for the Mexican bonds of 1825, see *London Times*, February 8, 1825, and Rodríguez O., *El nacimiento*, pp. 155–156.

to Peru, where in 1825 they became contractors for a foreign loan.[66] The success of the Parish Robertsons was linked to their alliance with the powerful banking house of Baring Brothers. The latter were initially not enthusiastic about the Latin American ventures, but by 1824 they were not only selling Buenos Aires bonds in London but also taking shares in Mexican mining enterprises and ranching estates.[67]

Like Baring Brothers, the London firm of Hullett Brothers did not limit itself to operating in one republic. It took responsibility for the Chilean foreign loan of 1822, but it was also engaged in trade at Buenos Aires and in mining ventures in western Argentina. Equally diverse were the activities of the less well known house of Thomas Kinder, which sold Peruvian bonds, shares in Bolivian mining companies, and stock in Mexican silver companies.

But the real banking bulls who worked the Latin American market most vigorously were Goldschmidt, Barclay, Herring, Richardson, Powles, and Graham. While in principle they were rivals, they tended to collaborate in order to sustain the financial frenzy. The banking firm of Barclay, Herring, Richardson & Company issued loans for the governments of Mexico, the Federation of Central America, and Gran Colombia, but did not therefore neglect its rousing business in war provisioning and in silver mines. Their rivals—Herring, Powles & Graham—marketed Colombian bonds, supplied Bolívar's army with arms, and invested in mines in South America. B. A. Goldschmidt & Company showed equal imagination and daring. They sold Mexican and Gran Colombian bonds on a grand scale during the years 1824 and 1825, financed much Latin American trade, and helped launch several silver-mining companies.[68]

The degree of monopolization of the Latin American business was striking. The three merchant banking firms—Barclay, Herring, Richardson & Company, B. A. Goldschmidt & Company, and Herring, Powles & Graham—were directly responsible (in alliance with immediate associates and allies) for the sale of slightly more than 60 percent of the total Latin American government bonds issued between 1822 and 1825 (see Table 1), and they did not hesitate to stoke the market until it had reached the bursting point. More cautious was the attitude of the premier banking firms of London, Baring Brothers, and Rothschild & Sons, which limited themselves to taking relatively small commissions on the Argentine and Brazilian loans they sold.

66. According to the British consul at Lima, "In 1823 the house of J. and P. Robertson had eight ships en route for Lima with goods to the value of £600,000" (Humphreys, *British Consular Reports*, p. 116).

67. On the Barings in Mexico, see Liehr, "La deuda exterior."

68. For precise information, see sources cited in footnotes 35, 36, 44, and 46, above.

As later experience demonstrated, prudence in such financial ventures was no liability. Barings and Rothschilds made little money on the loan transactions of the early 1820s, but they survived and eventually became the foremost foreign bankers of Latin America. Other less-judicious banking firms reaped greater short-term benefits from the bull market yet were swallowed up by the financial panic that was soon to grip the London money market.

Indeed, as the speculative frenzy subsided in the summer and fall of 1825, and as international trade weakened, the imminence of a major crisis—which threatened to flail the economies of both Great Britain and Latin America—could no longer be ignored. The brief postwar cycle of prosperity faded, and with it the first Latin American loan boom drew to a close.

CHAPTER 2

The Crash of 1825

Such a state of panic had scarcely ever before existed among us.

—Alexander Baring (1826)

The history of loans in Mexico is the same as in all parts: a history of usury, of immorality, of fortunes suddenly improvised, and of certain ruin for the nation.

—Manuel del Rivero (1842)

B Y THE END of the 1820s the Latin American states were in the grip of a grave debt crisis. The first government to default had been the last to win its independence: Peru suspended payments in April 1826, barely a year after the battle of Ayacucho. Then a few months later, Gran Colombia, having exhausted its resources after a decade and a half of war, suspended payments on its debt. The other republics continued to meet their obligations with the British bondholders for a year or two, but by mid-1828 all the Latin American nations, with the exception of Brazil, had defaulted.

The deterioration of economic conditions was unexpected. The trade boom, the silver-mining frenzy, and the wave of foreign loans that took place during the early 1820s had activated the Latin American economies and lent credence to the belief that political liberty would bring economic prosperity. Such illusions were soon shattered by economic crisis, social upheaval, and the outbreak of civil and regional wars. But domestic conflicts were not alone in unloosing the tempest. External factors also contributed decisively. More specifically, the European commercial and banking crisis of 1825–26, which abruptly reduced transatlantic trade and upset the money markets.

The first Latin American debt crisis was thus sparked by a European financial debacle that included the collapse of several important banking houses engaged in the international loan business. As a result, the market for foreign bonds weakened and capital exports dried up. To make things worse, the deficits of the Latin American governments increased after 1825, making it impossible for them to remit interest and amortization payments. Hence default was not only inevitable but also virtually irreversible. During a span of several decades most of the Latin American states did not and could not renew payments.

The causes and consequences of the string of Latin American defaults are the subject of this chapter. We shall begin with the external factors that interrupted the cycle of prosperity and provoked a widespread international economic recession.

THE EUROPEAN CRISIS OF 1825–26

The signs of an approaching financial storm could be discerned in England by October 1825. The London stock market was in the doldrums, the prices of such basic commodities as cotton, coffee, sugar, tin, and iron had begun a sharp decline, and several country banks were on the verge of collapse.[1] In November the failure of a number of leading cotton-trading firms was accompanied by severe credit restrictions on the part of the Bank of England, and by the end of the month London private banks, as well as many provincial commercial houses, were calling in their bills in order to shore up their reserves. Some contemporary observers anticipated a crisis, but almost none suspected the severity of the imminent crash.

On December 9 the *Times* reported the failure of Wentworth, Chalmer & Company, a financial firm of London closely linked to several Yorkshire country banks. Four days later the same newspaper announced the collapse of Peter Pole, Thornton & Company, "among the most considerable of London" and agent for some forty-seven country banks. At this point, distress became panic. Financial men from all points rushed to the capital:

An extraordinary number of country bankers from all parts of England were in town yesterday, either for the purpose of procuring specie and bank notes as a protection against a run upon them, or to ascertain by their own observations the state of affairs among their London friends. Several of them were to be seen in most of the leading banking houses, anxiously awaiting their turn for an interview with the principals. . . . The gloom within doors, and the events which produced it, were sensibly felt at the Stock Exchange.[2]

During the week that followed another four London banking concerns as well as some sixty country banks collapsed.[3] The drain of notes and specie

1. For statistics on price fluctuations between 1821 and 1826, see A. Gayer et al., *Growth and Fluctuation*, 1:174–181.

2. The full quotation is in T. Tooke and W. Newmarch, *A History of Prices and of the State of Circulation from 1792 to 1827* (London, 1827–58), 4:336.

3. On the country banks in 1825, see I. Bowen, "Country Banking, the Note Issues, and the Banking Controversy of 1825," *Economic Journal* (Economic History Supplement) 3, no. 13 (February 1938): 68–88. For what is still perhaps the best case-study of the relations between country bankers and London private bankers in the late eighteenth and early nineteenth centuries, see R. S. Sayers, *Lloyd's Bank in the History of English Banking* (Oxford, 1957). Also useful is L. S. Presnell, *Country Banking in the Industrial Revolution* (Oxford, 1956).

to the provincial financial houses was prodigious, "post chaises" arriving every hour to Lombard Street, stationing them as near as possible to the doors of the Bank of England in order to obtain the much-sought-after gold sovereigns and official bank notes. In the bank's discount department, clerks worked overtime to meet demands, and there was even greater activity at the counters of the bullion office, which were "beset by a multitude of persons awaiting to convert bank-notes into sovereigns."[4] So great was the crowd that special scales were set up to weigh the piles of gold coins, thereby avoiding the need to count them out one by one.

The state of agitation could not last indefinitely. On December 16 the *Times* reported that the run on the London banks had ceased. Communications also came from Nottingham, Leicester, Derby, and York banks that the panic was subsiding. At the same time, 700 leading merchants of London met at the Mansion House to sign a declaration stating their confidence in the underlying solvency of the financial system.[5]

In the months that followed, only a few additional banking houses collapsed, yet the overall economic picture did not improve. The financial crisis brought in its wake the bankruptcy of hundreds of mercantile and industrial firms, which toppled like ninepins through the winter, spring, and summer of 1826. The majority of the banks had saved themselves, but they did so by demanding repayment on all outstanding debts and, as the eminent banker Baring caustically observed, "by screwing almost to destruction every farmer, manufacturer and other customer in the country from whom they could get their money."[6]

As a result, tens of thousands of workers lost their jobs. In January and February, riots among weavers at Norwich were put down by the military. The situation turned equally critical for the spinners, weavers, and calico printers of the numerous factories of Lancashire. In April the weavers of Blackburn, Preston, Rochdale, and Manchester "broke into tumultuous rioting, destroying all the power looms within reach." In May there were revolts and attacks on factories at Bradford, and great distress was reported in Dublin.[7]

What had begun as a financial debacle at London soon became a full-scale economic depression. But its repercussions did not limit themselves

4. For an excellent description of the activity at the Bank of England, see the money market article in the *London Times*, December 15, 1825.

5. A long and detailed report on the Mansion House meeting and the merchants assisting is in the *London Times*, December 15 and 16, 1825.

6. *Annual Register, 1826*, p. 12.

7. These are numerous articles on worker discontent during the winter and spring of 1826 in the the *London Times*. See, e.g., articles on unemployment in Manchester and Glasgow in the February 27 and 28 issues.

to England.[8] The crisis soon spread across the Channel, a fact that reflected the delicacy and complexity of ties that linked the leading trading and banking firms in ports and cities throughout Europe.

The collapse of the Berlin banking concern of Benecke and of the Leipzig house of Reichenbach created grave difficulties at Frankfurt, the great German money capital. There the powerful firms of Bethmann and Gontar successfully weathered the storm, but that of Herts went bankrupt, apparently because of its close ties to B. A. Goldschmidt & Company.[9] The upheaval was also felt in Amsterdam, Saint Petersburg, and Vienna. In the latter city, the house of Fries—one of the four leading merchant banks of the Austro-Hungarian Empire—collapsed in the spring of 1826; its senior partner, the flamboyant David Parish, threw himself into the Danube in despair.[10] In Italy several financial firms of Bologna and Rome failed in May 1826. At the same time, the recession struck France.[11] The principal banks of Paris lost large amounts of money, but they managed to pull through. Less fortunate were numerous metallurgical enterprises in northern France, which entered a prolonged phase of depression.

According to most nineteenth-century economists, the crash of 1825–26 was the first of the great cyclical crises of modern capitalism. It is interesting to note that such eminent theorists as Sismondi, Tooke, and Juglar believed that the roots of the economic collapse were in the overtrading and overspeculation caused by the Latin American mining and loan ventures of the early 1820s. For example, Sismondi argued that the opening up of the Latin American markets had produced a sudden rush by British industrialists to get rid of their surplus production. He added that the trade boom was financed largely by the numerous loans issued by British banks for the new governments.[12]

8. Most historical works on the 1825–26 crisis focus on England, but a detailed study on international ramifications is needed. On effects in continental Europe, see Gille, *Histoire de la Maison Rothschild*, 1:133–157.

9. Ibid., 1:161.

10. On the extraordinary career of David Parish, who had been involved in the fantastic Mexican silver scheme of 1805 (jointly with the Barings and Hopes), see Stuart Bruchey, *Robert Oliver, Merchant of Baltimore, 1783–1819* (Baltimore, 1956), chap. 6; and Vincent Nolte, *Fifty Years in Both Hemispheres; or, Reminiscences of the Life of a Former Merchant* (New York, 1854), chap. 4.

11. The French government kept a close watch on events transpiring in the London money market. On effects of the crisis on French banks and industries, see Bertrand Gille, *La Banque et le crédit en France de 1815 à 1848* (Paris, 1959), pp. 301–329. On the textile depression in Mulhouse in these years, see M. Lévy Leboyer, *Les Banques europeénnes et l'industrialisation international dans la première moitié du XIXe siècle* (Paris, 1964), pp. 466–473.

12. J.C.L. Sismondi, *Nouveaux Principes d'economie politique* (Paris, 1827), vol. 2, book 2, chap. 4. This interpretation was subsequently cited uncritically by numerous economists. See Rosa Luxemburg, *Die Akumulation der Kapitalen* (Dresden, 1912), chap. 30. Similar

But how important was Latin American independence in stimulating an artificial expansion of British industrial production? The statistics indicate that the Latin American economies increased their consumption of British goods from approximately £3,000,000 in 1820–21 (8 percent of total British exports) to well over £6,000,000 in 1825 (16 percent of total exports).[13] Yet in spite of this commercial impulse, the *total* annual exports of the British economy barely increased during this period. Commerce with most European nations remained stable, and in some cases—for example, France, Germany, and Holland—it declined. Thus the new Latin American markets did not provoke overtrading, but rather compensated for the fall in trade with continental Europe.

If as the commercial statistics suggest, Latin American trade constituted a stabilizing rather than a destabilizing influence on the British economy, what was the effect of investment in Mexican, Brazilian, Peruvian, and Colombian bonds in spurring the crisis of 1825–26? The large volume of bonds sold did stimulate speculation, but in all the Latin American loans of 1822–25 the issuing bankers had taken the precaution of using a substantial portion of the proceeds to form short-term sinking funds. With these resources, held in London, interest and amortization payments were covered during the first two or three years after the sale of the bonds. Thus, when the crisis broke out in December 1825 there was no default on the Latin American loans; debt service payments were still being met regularly.

In summary, the crisis did not originate in Latin America. On the contrary, it began in Great Britain in late 1825 and moved across the Atlantic in early 1826. The economic catastrophe battered Argentina, Chile, Peru, Mexico, and the other nations of the subcontinent with particular force in three different spheres: international trade, silver mining, and government finance.

The Crisis in Latin American Trade and Mining

The depression in Europe caused an immediate and abrupt decline in trade with Latin America. British industrial exports to the region fell by 50 percent in 1826, and French and German shipments also dropped precipi-

---

views that overemphasize the importance of Latin American trade and financial transactions in provoking the crisis of 1825 include Tooke and Newmarch, *History*, 2:145–150; Clement Juglar, *Des Crises commerciales et de leur retour périodique en France, en Angleterre, et aux États Unis* (Paris, 1889), pp. 332–241; Michel Tougan Baranowsky, *Les Crises industrielles en Angleterre* (Paris, 1913), pp. 32–53; and Jenks, *Migration*, pp. 53–58.

13. For global and regional statistics on British exports, see Porter, *Progress of the Nation*, pp. 479–481, and Humphreys, *British Consular Reports*, pp. 344–351.

FIGURE 2.
BRITISH EXPORTS TO LATIN AMERICA, 1820–1830.

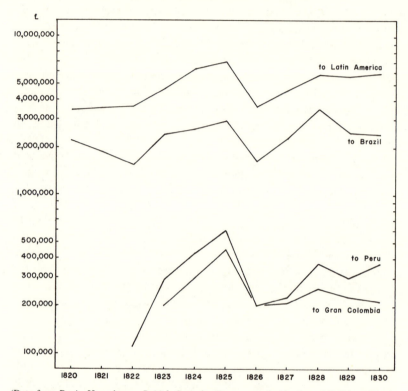

(Data from R. A. Humphreys, *British Consular Reports on the Trade and Politics of Latin America, 1824–1826* [London, 1940], Appendix 1, pp. 346–349.)

tously.[14] The commercial slump was widespread, although its effects were felt more acutely in some nations than in others (see Figure 2). Peru and Gran Colombia witnessed an especially severe reduction in their international transactions. British trade with both nations fell by almost 70 percent between 1825 and 1826. For example, the value of British exports to Peru approached £600,000 in 1825, but fell to less than £200,000 in the following year.[15] Exports to Gran Colombia were cut in half by the crisis and did

14. According to one estimate, British exports to Latin America dropped from approximately £6,400,000 in 1824 to £3,200,000 in 1826 (Gayer et al., *Growth and Fluctuation*, 1:182). Compare with the different data in the sources listed in footnote 13 of this chapter.

15. For Anglo-Peruvian trade statistics, see Heraclio Bonilla, *Gran Bretaña y el Perú: los mecanismos de un control ecónomico* (Lima, 1977), 5:159.

not recover for years. The trade of other Latin American nations also declined after the crisis of 1825–26. The peak in Anglo-Argentine mercantile activity came in 1824; it remained at a high level in 1825, but fell precipitously afterward, not to return to former levels for almost two decades.[16] In Mexico the trade recession advanced more slowly; total imports slid from 19,000,000 pesos in 1825 to 15,000,000 in 1826 and 14,000,000 in 1827, reaching a low point of 10,000,000 pesos only in 1828. In the case of Mexico, French and United States exports plunged abruptly, whereas the sale of British commodities did not decline substantially until the end of the decade.[17]

There was one exception in Latin America to the overall pattern of commercial distress—namely, Brazil. The large and constant volume of sugar exports from Recife, Aracaju, and Salvador, combined with the growing number of coffee shipments from Rio de Janeiro, helped pay for a large volume of imports, especially cotton textiles. The result was that British exports to Brazil did not drop below a level of £2,500,000 at any time during the 1820s, the 1830s, or the 1840s. Following the crisis of 1825–26, in fact, Brazil became the market for 50 percent of total British shipments to Latin America; in the 1830s it still took more than 40 percent; and in the 1840s it took 35 percent. Moreover, the stability and strength of its trade explains why Brazil was the only Latin American state able to meet debt payments on a fairly regular basis during this period, and the only state in a position to negotiate several *new* loans with the London banking community.[18]

The overall decline of Latin American trade can be directly linked to the financial debacle in the money centers of the Old World. The failure of important European banking and mercantile houses meant that industrialists, and in particular British manufacturers, could no longer obtain credit to finance the export of their commodities.[19] In late February 1826, the *London Times* underlined the dramatic consequences of the bankruptcy of one major financial firm. ''The downfall of Goldschmidt's house in London is the severest blow that Glasgow has yet met in the present calamitous

16. On Anglo-Argentine trade, consult Halperín, *Guerra y finanzas*, pp. 283–284.

17. Statistics on Mexican trade with Great Britain, France, and the United States are in Bernard Kapp, ''Les relations économiques extérieures du Mexique (1821–1911) d'après les sources françaises,'' in *Ville et Commerce* (Paris, 1974), pp. 58–67. see also Inés Herrera Canales, *El comercio exterior de México* (Mexico, 1977), pp. 26, 34, 82, 161.

18. For data on Brazilian trade, see Porter, *Progress of the Nation*, pp. 483–486; and Platt, *Latin America*, table 1, p. 30.

19. Approximately one dozen London merchant banks collapsed, including three that had been heavily engaged in Latin American loans: B. A. Goldschmidts and Herring, Powles & Graham failed in the spring of 1826, while Barclay, Herring, and Richardson & Co. failed in early 1827.

times. A large portion of the remittances for goods sent to South America consisted of draughts upon the Messrs. Goldschmidt.''[20]

The European credit squeeze also restricted the activities of trading concerns with branches in Latin America, because they were no longer able to acquire the bills of exchange required to finance their formerly flourishing import business. Many of these firms went bankrupt as a result of the difficulties they faced in cashing drafts that were theoretically guaranteed by government issues but in practice had little value, having been peddled like so much speculative paper by influential but reckless financial houses.

Among the casualties were scores of British firms that had set up shop in the boom days of 1820–25. In Lima, Consul Charles Ricketts reported that at the end of 1826 there were 2,000,000 pesos in outstanding debts due to British merchants established in the Peruvian capital, and he added, ''The recovery is most tedious and in great part, I fear, doubtful.'' Even such strong houses as Antony Gibbs & Sons could not entirely escape the maelstrom that wrecked their smaller brethren; Gibbs had about £45,000 (225,000 silver pesos) locked up in its Lima branch house in 1826.[21]

Other well-known British firms also suffered the impact of the crisis. The Hylsops trading company of Jamaica and Cartagena, for instance, cracked when Goldschmidt, the Colombian loan contractor, went bankrupt in February 1826. The Hylsops ''were caught short with dishonored bills and their affairs had to be put in to the hands of trustees.''[22] In Mexico the once-prominent establishment of Robert Staples & Company found itself submerged in difficulties, and despite its close links to the powerful bankers, Baring Brothers, it soon disappeared from the register of the Mexican mercantile community.[23]

In Buenos Aires another close associate of the Barings, the firm of William Parish Robertson, met its end in 1827. Although the partners had earned substantial fees on the Argentine loan of 1824, they lost large sums on an ill-advised mining venture and on an unrealistic and expensive colonization scheme. Furthermore, the trading activity of the Parish Robertsons, like that of all Anglo-Argentine merchants, was sharply curtailed by the outbreak of the naval war of 1826–28 between Argentina and Brazil, which closed the harbors of the River Plate to most traffic.[24]

20. *London Times*, February 27, 1826. According to Gille (*Historie de la Maison Roths-child*, 1:159–161), Goldschmidt's had £400,000 in unpayable bills on a total debit sheet of £1,200,000.

21. Platt, *Latin America*, p. 51.

22. Humphreys, ''British Merchants,'' p. 121.

23. On the joint investments of Francis Baring and Robert Staples in Mexico in 1824, see Liehr, ''La deuda exterior,'' pp. 427–429.

24. In 1825 ninety-five British ships had entered Argentine ports; in 1826 there were just

By the end of the decade the once-thick ranks of British trading firms in the Latin American ports had been drastically thinned. As Platt notes, "the future pattern of a few strong, diversified houses sharing out the limited market between them was already established."[25] Platt uses the term "limited market" advisedly, for the Latin American consumption of British manufactured goods remained virtually stable for almost twenty years. Not until the 1850s did a new trade boom allow for a new conquest of regional markets by foreign merchant houses.

While the crisis of 1825–26 produced a harvest of failures among mercantile firms, its effects on other spheres of the economy were equally dramatic. Most significant, the suspension of European capital exports interrupted development of an important source of national wealth on which the Latin American leaders had pinned their hopes for rapid economic recovery: the famous silver and gold mines.

Paradoxically, it was precisely in early 1826—as the European crisis reached its apogee—that a number of the British engineers sent to Latin America finally succeeded in putting their mining enterprises on a solid footing. They had won concessions to the key silver districts, begun drainage operations, and expected to process the precious metals with the new machinery they had brought across the Atlantic. But they needed a continuing flow of investments to get their enterprises rolling. The financial panic cut short their hopes of doing so, and soon most of the intrepid engineers were forced to lay off their workers and close down operations.

Contemporary observers in London were quick to conclude that these failures were due to unscrupulous mine promoters who had enormously exaggerated the mineral wealth of Latin America and squandered the funds of hundreds of hapless investors. This view, later adopted by many historians, suggests that the shutdown of the mines preceded and indeed contributed to the international crisis of 1825–26. But as Chilean scholar Claudio Véliz demonstrated recently in a brilliant revisionist essay, the reverse was true.[26] The British mining companies in Chile did not fail before the crisis, they failed after. It was the banking and stock exchange collapse in London that severed the flow of investments to the overseas mining enterprises and condemned them to bankruptcy. Meanwhile, many native-owned mining firms increased their production (despite their reliance on antiquated tech-

seven and in 1827 only one ship managed to weasel its way into the Buenos Aires harbor. The blockade caused a panic among the local community of British merchants, who in the first half of 1827 smuggled out more than 500,000 pesos of their capital from Buenos Aires. See Ferns, *Britain and Argentina*, pp. 164–165.

25. Platt, *Latin America*, p. 51.

26. Véliz, "Egaña," pp. 637–663.

nology), and by the 1830s Chile and other Latin American nations were again relatively important exporters of minerals.[27]

In the case of Mexico, several foreign-owned mining enterprises collapsed, but others survived. Between 1826 and 1828 the Real de Catorce, Tlalpujahua, and Guanajuato associations folded, but the United Mexican Mining Company operated throughout the nineteenth century, and the Bolaños mining concern paid profits consistently until 1849. Similarly, the story of the largest foreign-owned enterprise, the Real del Monte Company, demonstrates that in spite of serious obstacles local mining ventures could hold their own if sufficient capital were employed: British investors put more than £700,000 into the firm between 1825 and the late 1830s, helping to make it the most modern mining establishment in the nation.[28]

In the different context of the Argentine society, the experience of the early British mining enterprises was one of unrelieved failure. The directors of the companies discovered that capital and technology were not the only instruments required for economic success. Bitter political and business rivalries also played a decisive role and ultimately jeopardized their ambitious plans. The Río de la Plata Mining Association and the Famatina Silver Mining Company disputed rights to the same silver districts. The mines soon closed, and the value of the company stocks dropped precipitously. Political struggles on a local level and cutthroat competition between merchants and financiers of both Buenos Aires and London thus proved to be the undoing of early mining speculations in the Río de la Plata region.[29]

The checkered tale of the British mining firms reflected the complex and uncertain process of reaccommodation of the Latin American nations to the Atlantic economy during the 1820s. Most companies were swept away by the powerful undercurrents generated by the international mercantile and financial crisis, but a few survived and joined the numerous, native-owned mining concerns that participated in the restructuring of production in the mineral-rich districts of such countries as Chile and Mexico. Nonetheless, the progress realized proved to be more difficult than originally anticipated, a fact that reflected the damage caused successively by war and crisis to the once-famous pillars of precious metals that had sustained the colonial economy for almost 300 years.

27. On contemporary Chilean copper and silver production, see Pierre Vayssière, *Un Siècle de capitalisme minier au Chili, 1830–1930* (Paris, 1980), pp. 114–115, 269.

28. According to Randall (*Real del Monte*), the mining firm was eventually a financial failure for the British investors, but the technical innovations introduced in the years 1824–40 contributed to the technological transformation of the Mexican mining industry.

29. On the Argentine mining failures, see Francis Head, *Report Relating to the Failure of the Río de la Plata Mining Association* (London, 1827); and Galmarini, *Negocios y política,* chap. 5.

While the decline in trade and the collapse of many silver-mining firms was in good measure the result of the crash in London, what can be said of the suspension of loan payments by the Latin American states? Did the defaults precede or follow the European panic? Traditional interpretation suggests that the disruption of the London money market was provoked at least in part by the news of financial insolvency of the foreign states that had been lent large sums. In fact, however, no Latin American nation suspended its debt service until after the outbreak of the monetary chaos in Europe.

The Peruvian government was the first to default, in April 1826.[30] The failure of the Goldschmidts two months earlier had been a major blow, for though they were not official bankers to Peru, they had provided several short-term loans to finance outstanding debts. The Lima authorities were hard-pressed to pay off the anxious creditors of the bankrupt firm. Furthermore, they lacked sufficient resources to cover the April 15 dividend due on the foreign debt. The Mexican, Colombian, and Argentine ambassadors in London urged their Peruvian counterpart, José Joaquín de Olmedo, to take advantage of a short-term loan offered by the Paris branch of the Rothshchild banking family. The Peruvian envoy, however, refused the offer on the grounds that it would prolong the agony but not solve the penury of his government. Olmedo wrote from London to Bolívar, lamenting the difficulties that confronted both the Peruvian state and the bondholders: "If the failure of the government to pay is censurable in all circumstances, it is particularly so in the present situation when so many families depend upon the interest payments, when there have been over 600 bankruptcies, and money scarcely circulates, and no one knows how he will survive."[31]

The bankruptcy of Peru appeared symptomatic of the widespread financial malaise. Yet default was not inevitable, at least in the short run. The Colombian government, beset by equally trying circumstances, managed to avoid temporarily a suspension of payments. Hurtado, the Colombian ambassador in London, appealed to his Mexican colleague Vicente Rocafuerte to assist the sister republic by providing a loan to cover the upcoming April interest payment on the external debt. In a generous act of inter-American solidarity, Rocafuerte acceded to this request and ordered the Barclay banking company to transfer £63,000 of Mexican funds into the Colombian accounts.[32]

30. On the Peruvian default, see Rodríguez O., *El nacimiento*, pp. 169–170.
31. Ibid., p. 169, n. 36.
32. The Colombian authorities expected to pay back the Mexican loan with part of a 2,000,000 peso credit they had previously provided to the Peruvian government. After the

The remaining Latin American nations experienced little difficulty in fulfilling their current monetary obligations because they all held substantial funds on deposit with their respective bankers in London: the Argentine government with the firm of Baring Brothers; the Chileans with Hullett Brothers; the Central American and Mexican authorities with Barclay, Herring, Richardson & Company; the Brazilians with Rothschilds. The damage, however, had been done, and as soon as the news spread that the Peruvian treasury was insolvent, the bond quotations of the other Latin American nations dropped ten to twenty points on the London Stock Exchange.[33]

During 1826 the Mexican ambassador, Rocafuerte, made strenuous efforts to sustain the credit rating of the foreign bonds. He argued that by applying some of the loan reserves to the acquisition of the securities on the open market it might be possible to drive prices upward. He pressured his bankers to do this, but they refused. Shortly thereafter, Rocafuerte learned that the Barclay financial house—which now served simultaneously as agents for the Mexican, Colombian, and Central American debts—faced increasing problems as a result of its close relations with the bankrupt firm of Herring, Powles & Graham. A senior partner of the latter company, John Powles, had been involved in the Goldschmidt speculations and lost heavily on mining ventures.[34] These losses, which undermined the firm of Herring, Powles & Graham, proved doubly serious because Charles Herring was also heavily engaged in the merchant bank of Barclay, Herring, Richardson & Company.

The interdependency of the most audacious and reckless London bankers involved in Latin American finances now proved to be both their undoing and the cause of acute problems for the debtor governments. In June 1826 Rocafuerte urgently requested instructions from the Mexican finance minister to allow for the transfer of funds held at Barclay's to the safer hands of the Bank of England. The authorization never arrived. As a result, when

---

Peruvian bankruptcy this became impossible. Nonetheless, the Colombians offered Mexico two new warships recently purchased from the United States in order to cancel the debt. The offer was not accepted by Mexico, and the loan was not finally liquidated until the early 1850s. See Rodríguez O., "Rocafuerte y el empréstito a Colombia," *Historia Mexicana* 1969, pp. 485–515; Joaquín Ramírez Cabañas, *El empréstito de México a Colombia* (Mexico, 1930); and Ornán Roldán Oquendo, *Las relaciones entre México y Colombia, 1810–1862* (Mexico, 1974), pp. 98–134, 233–244.

33. The Mexican bonds dropped from 70 to 60, while the Argentine securities fell from 70 to 55. On the former, see Rodríguez O., *El nacimiento*, pp. 168–169; on the latter, see source cited in our Figure 3.

34. Rodríguez O., "Rocafuerte," p.507. This Powles was the same individual who hired Benjamin Disraeli to write favorable tracts on the Latin American silver-mining companies (Véliz, "Egaña," p. 639).

Barclay's suspended payments in early August, the Mexican treasury lost more than £300,000 of the sinking fund it had deposited with those bankers. On August 10, the *Times* reported that as a result of this banking failure a panic had erupted on the exchange, with investors trying to sell off Mexican and Colombian bonds for whatever price they could obtain.[35]

The situation was initially not as bleak as some bondholders were led to believe. Although Colombia and Chile defaulted in September, Mexico was able to transfer its agency and to pay the half-year interest payment due. Similarly, the Brazilian, Argentine, and Central American governments continued to cover their external obligations. Several months later, however, the financial situation worsened. By mid-1827 all but one of the Latin American states had defaulted, and in most cases they were not to resume remittances for twenty years or more.

THIRTY YEARS OF DEBT RENEGOTIATIONS

For more than a quarter of a century the unresolved dilemma of the foreign debt projected a dark shadow over Latin American government finance. Despite repeated efforts by envoys of European bondholders to recover their monies, all governments (with the exception of Brazil) systematically refused to resume payments. They did so for a simple reason: The national treasuries had barely enough cash to cover the regular expenses of the civil and military administrations, and almost no gold, silver, or foreign currency. Without the latter it was useless to promise remittances when only paper money (which clearly would not be accepted by foreign creditors) could be sent abroad.

The Latin American fiscal and monetary crises, which became manifest after the European crisis of 1825–26, deepened in years following. To begin with, customs revenues dropped steadily as a result of the trade depression.[36] The situation was aggravated by the increasing scarcity of silver and gold, most of which went to foreign merchants or was hoarded by the native propertied classes. The lack of currency contributed to the fragmentation of local economies and intensified regionalist political tendencies. Political separatism and economic disarticulation weakened attempts to forge na-

35. Rodríguez O., *El nacimiento*, p. 171.

36. Chilean ordinary revenues fell from an average of 2,000,000 pesos a year in 1820–24 to 1,600,000 pesos in 1825–32 (*Resumen de la hacienda pública en Chile desde la independencia hasta 1900*, Dirección general de contabilidad [Santiago de Chile, 1901]). Customs duties provided 80 percent of Argentine government revenues in 1822–24 but only 21 percent in 1825–28 (Halperín, *Guerra y finanzas*, pp. 190–191, 195). Mexican customs revenues reached a peak of 15,000,000 pesos in 1826, falling to 11,000,000 by 1829. See Tenenbaum, *Politics of Penury*, table 4, p. 26.

tional unity. And to this situation must be added the heavy debts that weighed on most Latin American governments.

The internal economic, social, and political problems were so grave that the foreign creditors could hardly have expected a favorable reception for their claims. The associations of bondholders directed their persistent and wearisome pleas to the British Foreign Office, but the latter did not generally assume direct responsibility for their demands. Of greater importance to the British authorities was the state of commercial relations with the nations across the Atlantic. Overly aggressive policies on behalf of the bondholders could undercut British trade relations, thereby benefiting rival French, German, and United States merchants. Nonetheless, the British authorities did not abstain from using military power to confirm their intention of defending the interests of merchants and creditors. The ships of the Royal Navy represented a constant threat for all the Latin American nations because they were in a position to impose blockades and even to support direct military intervention, as eventually occurred in the case of Mexico.[37]

During the 1830s, limited progress was made in restructuring the Mexican and Colombian debts. Formal agreements were reached with the representatives of the bondholders, but no new payments were forthcoming. The situation was no better in other Latin American countries. Between 1836 and 1839, Chile clashed with the Peruvian-Bolivian Confederation in a bloody struggle that drained their respective treasuries and made payment of the foreign debt an impossibility. In Argentina the naval blockade undertaken by French warships between 1838 and 1840 temporarily eliminated the government's principal sources of revenue and provoked an escalation in local military expenditures.

During the 1840s most Latin American nations continued to be plagued by bitter political and military conflicts. At Buenos Aires the Rosas regime confronted the rebellions of dissident provinces, a situation aggravated by a new blockade of the port between 1845 and 1848 by the combined British and French fleets. In Mexico, civil strife intensified as a result of the invasion by several thousand United States troops, who occupied the Mexican capital in September 1847. In Peru, civil war raged from 1842 to 1845, and throughout the rest of the subcontinent political instability, separatist movements, and popular insurrections ravaged land and society.

The degree of internal and external conflicts in most Latin American

37. Platt argues that the Foreign Office did not systematically use force to "force British trade down Latin American throats" or "to promote the interest of British finance." The first part of this argument is misleading because the active role of British warships throughout the region was intended to protect British merchant vessels engaged in both lawful trade and contraband trade. See D.C.M. Platt, *Finance, Trade, and Politics: British Foreign Policy, 1815–1914* (Oxford, 1968), chap. 6.

societies of the age meant that most governments had to give priority to maintaining their armies. As Tulio Halperín demonstrated in his study of Argentine finances during the first half of the nineteenth century, the state was to a large degree a militarized institution. This being the case, it was not surprising that the bulk of public funds went to pay salaries of officers and soldiers, to pay for such local provisions as flour, rice, meat, coffee, sugar, horses, and mules, and to cover the contracts for supplies that had to be imported—arms, munitions and uniforms.[38] These military requirements clearly had priority over the claims of the distant bondholders.

The quotations on Latin American bonds remained depressed on the London Exchange, because the prospects of repayment were bleak. These securities became merely speculative paper with little intrinsic value. Many of the original bondholders sold their holdings at rock-bottom prices to stockbrokers and merchants who played the market in accord with the sharp fluctuations in the political evolution of the debtor states. (See Figure 3 for the trends in Argentine foreign bond quotations.)

The 1840s marked the beginning of an important change, at least for a few fortunate countries. The rising European demand for primary products and raw materials ushered in a period of export-led growth in some nations, such as Chile and Peru. Growing prosperity brought increased revenues and therefore renewed opportunities for a settlement of the long-standing claims of British bondholders (see Table 2).

The first durable agreement was signed with the Chilean authorities in 1842. The government of Chile proposed resumption of regular payments on the debt as well as capitalization of the arrears of interest dating back to 1826. It is not surprising that the Committee of Spanish-American Bondholders quickly ratified the terms offered.[39] After years of haggling, a second round of negotiations between the bondholders and another important borrower, the Peruvian state, reached a successful conclusion.[40] The expansion of guano (fertilizer) exports in the 1840s provided the Lima treasury with new and considerable resources. The Peruvian authorities resumed interest payments in 1849 by channeling approximately half the income of the state guano monopoly to the foreign creditors.

In the rest of Latin America, circumstances were not yet ripe for similar

38. Halperín provides a detailed analysis of Argentine government expenditures during the 1830s and 1840s in his *Guerra y finanzas*, chap. 4.

39. C. Fenn, *Compendium of the English and Foreign Funds* (1883 ed.), p. 390.

40. Mathew notes that such firms as A. Gibbs & Sons, which had inside information on the progress of the negotiations, made large profits by buying up the bonds at low prices before publication of the debt arrangement. He adds, "It would seem fair to conclude that the bondholders desired a settlement for reasons which were essentially speculative" ("The First Anglo/Peruvian Debt," p. 98).

FIGURE 3.

PRICE TRENDS OF ARGENTINE 1824 EXTERNAL BONDS ON THE LONDON STOCK EXCHANGE,
1825–1860.

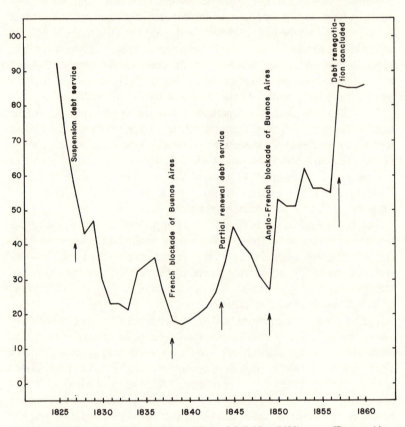

(Data from Pedro Agote, *Informe del Presidente del Crédito Público* . . . [Buenos Aires, 1887], vol. 4, pp. 96–98.)

pacts. In Argentina, initial conversations between a British agent and Governor Juan Manuel de Rosas allowed for a monthly remittance of 5,000 silver pesos to the bondholders in 1844, but this flow ceased abruptly as a result of the foreign blockade of the Buenos Aires port in years following.[41] In Colombia the treasury officials made polite overtures, but no concrete

41. According to one report, Rosas, the Argentine head of state, went so far as "to offer to cede the Malvinas Islands, seized by the British ten years before, in settlement of the debt," but there is no firm evidence to confirm such a view. See Harold E. Peters, *The Foreign Debt of the Argentine Republic* (Baltimore, 1934), p. 21.

TABLE 2
DEFAULTS AND RENEGOTIATIONS OF LATIN AMERICAN LOANS OF THE 1820s

Country	Nominal Value of Bond Issues (£)	Date of Default	Renegotiation and Settlement
Argentina	1,000,000	July 1827	*1857*: Payment of interest resumed on principal, and £1,500,000 in new 3% bonds issued for arrears of interest.
Chile	1,000,000	September 1826	*1842*: Payment of interest on principal resumed, and £756,000 in new 3% bonds issued for arrears of interest.
Mexico	6,400,000	October 1827	*1831 and 1836*: Preliminary conversions not fulfilled. *1850*: Principal and interest recognized at £10,200,000. *1854–63*: Interest payments suspended, then partially renewed in *1863–67*; default follows until final arrangement in *1888*.[a]
Peru	1,816,000	April 1826	*1849*: Interest payments on principal renewed, and £1,800,000 of new 3% bonds issued for arrears of interest.
Gran Colombia	6,750.000	September 1826	
Gran Colombia debts were reapportioned in 1834.[b]			
Colombia	50.0% of total debt		*1849*: Preliminary arrangement with bankers not implemented. *1861*: £775,000 new 3% bonds issued for arrears of interest. *1872*: Reduction of debt to £2,000,000.
Ecuador	22.0% of total debt		*1856*: £1,800,000 in new bonds issued to cover principal, arrears of interest paid with land certificates.
Venezuela	28.0% of total debt		*1859*: £1,700,000 in new bonds issued to cover principal, and £770,000 in 3% bonds issued for arrears of interest.

[a] The 1888 Anglo-Mexican debt arrangement provided for the issue of £13,000,000 in new bonds in recognition of principal and arrears of interest on the loans of the 1820s.

[b] After 1834 the Federation of Gran Colombia was gradually dissolved, and the outstanding external debt was redistributed according to the percentages indicated in the table.

TABLE 2 (*cont.*)

Country	Nominal Value of Bond Issues (£)	Date of Default	Renegotiation and Settlement
Federation of Central America	113,600[c]	February 1828	
Federation debts were reapportioned in 1838.[d]			
Costa Rica	8.3% of total debt		*1844*: Pays off principal at 85% of par.
Guatemala	42.0% of total debt		*1856*: Issues £150,000 in new 5% bonds.
Honduras	16.6% of total debt		*1867*: Issues £90,075 in new 5% bonds.
Nicaragua	16.6% of total debt		*1874*: Pays off principal at 85% par.
El Salvador	16.6% of total debt		*1860*: Pays off principal at 90% par.

SOURCES: Corporation of Foreign Bondholders, *Annual Reports* (London, 1873–85); C. Fenn, *Fenn's on the Funds* (London, various editions, 1838–83); J. F. Rippy, *British Investments in Latin America, 1822–1949* (Minneapolis, 1959). Other useful sources on country debts include the following: on the Argentine debt, H. Ferns, *Britain and Argentina in the Nineteenth Century* (Oxford, 1962), chaps. 5–6; on the Peruvian debt, W. M. Mathew, "The First Anglo-Peruvian Debt and Its Settlement, 1822–1849," *Journal of Latin American Studies* 2 (May 1970): 81–98; on the Central American debts, Robert Smith, "Financing the Central American Federation, 1821–1838," *Hispanic American Historical Review*, November 1963, pp. 483–510; and on the Mexican debt, Jan Bazant, *Historia de la deuda exterior de México, 1823–1946* (Mexico, 1968).

[c] The actual value of bonds sold was £113,600, but as of 1828 some £163,000 were claimed by bondholders as the sum of the principal and partial arrears of interest.

[d] In 1838 the Central American Federation was dissolved, although Guatemala did not formally recognize the fact until 1849.

results were forthcoming. In Central America the various small republics reapportioned their old 1825 debt and promised payment, but only the government of Costa Rica had sufficient resources to remit a small amount of hard cash.

An overall review of the debt renegotiations of the Latin American states indicates that the periods of defaults generally lasted between fifteen and thirty years. As already indicated, the nations that reached accords with the European creditors most quickly were Chile, Peru, and Costa Rica in the 1840s, largely because of the rise in their export earnings. In contrast, Argentina, Ecuador, Venezuela, and Guatemala took longer to stabilize their public finances and therefore did not renegotiate until the late 1850s. Even slower in coming to terms with the bondholders were Colombia, Honduras, and El Salvador, because they did not reinitiate debt payments until the mid-1860s and even then they made payments on an irregular basis.

The most complex and ultimately explosive of the Latin American debts was that of Mexico. The frustration and antagonism spawned by drawn-out and always tense negotiations aggravated the relations between the Mexican government and the European powers and ultimately led to a full-scale military invasion. The pernicious consequences of foreign indebtedness could not have been demonstrated more bluntly or more bloodily.

DEBTS AND FOREIGN INTERVENTION IN MEXICO

At the time of independence, Mexico had the reputation for being the wealthiest land in all of Latin America. The silver mines of Mexico were the richest in the world, and Mexico's agricultural and ranching wealth were well known. Mexico City had long been the largest city in the Western Hemisphere and the most important seat of Spanish imperial power. After independence, both foreign bankers and Mexican politicians judged that the prospects for economic recovery and growth were promising. But such beliefs were mere illusions. The economy stagnated, and the Mexican government entered into a vicious circle of deficits and debts from which it could not break out.

The deficits, which arose from the enormous military expenditures, were covered initially by the two loans taken in London in 1824 and 1825. By 1827, however, these funds had been exhausted. Tax revenues fell so sharply that interest payments on the loans had to be suspended. The government did not want to default, but there were few options. The national treasury simply did not have sufficient resources to cover its expenses. In 1828, ''when President Guadalupe Victoria instructed the Treasury Minister to renegotiate the British debt, Alexander Baring of Baring Brothers advised that Mexico first alter its fiscal system substantively before it promised to honor commitments previously broken.[42]

There were only two possible solutions to the fiscal crisis. The first was to carry out tax reforms. But Mexico had recently and radically restructured its entire fiscal system, eliminating many old colonial levies. The new tax system—based largely on import duties—was inefficient, there being much corruption and contraband. Yet Mexican leaders could hardly expect to win political support if they attempted to impose additional economic burdens on the population. The second alternative was to seek loans to cover the deficits. Following the default on the foreign debt, the financial authorities

42. See Tenenbaum, *Politics of Penury*, p. 29, which is the best source on nineteenth-century Mexican finance.

had no choice but to seek *local* sources of credit. As a result, after 1827 the government came to rely on the wealthy Mexico City moneylenders, a close-knit and increasingly powerful financial mafia.

For years the camarilla of loan sharks of the Mexican capital, led by such agile speculators as Manuel Escandón, Cayetano Rubio, Gregorio Martínez del Río, and Manuel Lizardi, among others, increased their fortunes by supplying the always desperate finance ministers with short-term loans in exchange for control over the state tobacco monopoly, salt works, the government mints, transport concessions, army supply contracts, and even the customs offices of various ports on the Gulf and Pacific coasts.[43]

In exchange for providing usurious loans, such moneylenders as Escandón were given free rein to consolidate their personal economic fiefdoms. In 1834 Escandón and his associates obtained a contract to repair roads from the nation's capital south to Cuernavaca and north to the rich agricultural and mining region of the Bajío. As recompense, Escandón's company received rights to collect taxes on the most heavily traveled commercial route of the nation, running from the Gulf port of Veracruz to Puebla and Mexico City.[44] Another lucrative contract was obtained by the Martínez del Río merchant firm in the early 1840s as a result of their government loan business. These merchants took over majority control of the Empresa del Tabaco, the largest of the state-owned tobacco factories, and ran it for private profit.[45]

Despite the financial difficulties and the rapidly growing internal debt, Mexican leaders did not despair of finding a solution to the external debt. The distinguished intellectual Lucas Alamán, who was minister of foreign affairs in the early 1830s, repeatedly urged that negotiations with the British bankers and bondholders be pursued. In September 1831 a first agreement was signed, stipulating that the 7,900,000 pesos owing in back interest be reduced to 5,500,000 pesos. Furthermore, the interest payments due between 1832 and 1836 were to be suspended, after which it was expected that the Mexican government would have accumulated sufficient monetary reserves to renew remittances on a regular basis.[46]

---

43. In exchange for lending cash to the government, the moneylenders often received customs certificates, which could be used to pay import taxes. As a result, the revenues of the customs offices were effectively mortgaged to the moneylenders. On the credit mechanisms used, see the essays by Barbara Tenenbaum and Rosa María Meyer in *Banca y poder en México, 1800–1925*, ed. Leonor Ludlow and Carlos Marichal (Mexico, 1986), pp. 75–118.

44. Margarita Urías, "Manuel Escandón: de las diligencias al ferrocarril, 1833–1862," in *Formación y desarrollo de la burguesía en México, siglo XIX*, ed. C. Cardoso (Mexico, 1978), pp. 25–56.

45. David Walker, "Business as Usual: The Empresa del Tabaco in Mexico, 1837–1844," *HAHR* 64, no. 4 (November 1984): 675–706.

46. On the 1831 arrangement see Joaquín D. Casasús, *Historia de la deuda contraída en Londres* (Mexico, 1885), pp. 122–140.

Repayment of the London loans was scheduled to begin in 1836, but in March of that year the Texas settlers issued their declaration of independence from Mexico. The war that ensued created a new fiscal crisis. The bulk of government funds went to pay for the army, which had marched north led by General Santa Anna. As a result, the firm of Baring Brothers renounced its position as financial representative of the Mexican government. The agency was then assumed by the firm of M. Lizardi & Company, which drew up the blueprint for a new settlement with the bondholders. In early 1837 the Mexican Congress approved the terms for renegotiation. The basis of the proposal was ingenious and could have been a feasible solution if not for the conflicts with the United States. The Mexican government recognized a total debt of £10,800,000 (a huge sum for the period), but it instructed Lizardi to convert half this sum into "Land Warrants on the vacant lands in the departments of Texas, Chihuahua, New Mexico, Sonora and California at the rate of four acres per each pound sterling."[47]

The idea of exchanging land certificates for the bonds was not unrealistic because Mexico possessed vast, sparsely populated territories in the northern sections of the nation. But military conflicts with United States colonists made realization of the land-selling schemes improbable. The British bondholders met at the City of London Tavern on September 14, 1837, to discuss the terms and to propose a series of modifications. They insisted on retaining the old bonds (worth approximately £6,400,000), although they accepted the possibility of exchanging interest payments due for "deferred bonds," which in turn could be used to buy land certificates. Few certificates were actually bought by the bondholders, but through this arrangement the Mexican government was able to avoid having to pay interest on its external debt during almost a decade.[48]

Meanwhile, the Mexican financial agent at London, Manuel Lizardi, proceeded to carry out a series of unorthodox transactions that had a negative effect on the market quotations of the bonds. Because he was not paid his commissions regularly, Lizardi took more than 1,000,000 pesos in unsold Mexican bonds and placed them among speculators, keeping the proceeds for himself.[49] Such maneuvers provoked acrimonious debate and criticism in Mexico. As a result, the agency was transferred in 1845 to the firm of John Schneider & Company of London.[50] Anticipating more favorable treatment, the bondholders pressed for a new agreement. They were encouraged by the results of the recent Chilean debt renegotiations, which

47. Copy of April 12, 1837, decree in Archivo de la Secretaría de Relaciones Exteriores, Mexico City (hereafter ASRE), file LE-1230, "Deuda de México a Inglaterra, 1822–1844."
48. For details, see ASRE, file LE-1231.
49. There is abundant correspondence on the Lizardi transactions in ASRE, file LE-1230.
50. The correspondence between Schneider and the Mexican government is in ASRE, files LE-1230 and LE-1231.

had increased the value of Chilean bonds on the London Stock Exchange. On July 30, 1845, the *London Times* noted that Chilean bonds were quoted at 100 to 103 whereas Mexican bonds remained at 36 to 38.[51]

The hopes of the bondholders dissipated as a result of the outbreak of the war between the United States and Mexico in early 1846. To finance the war effort, the Mexican treasury ministers relied heavily on local money-lenders. These capitalists contributed to the defense of the nation during the years of conflict, but once the armistice talks had commenced they began to exercise pressure on the government in order to collect their debts. Their formidable international connections put them in an excellent position. One leading moneylender was Ewen Macintosh, who served simultaneously as British consul at Mexico City and as representative of the foreign bondholders. Another wealthy *agiotista* (as the moneylenders were known), Cayetano Rubio, had for years been agent for Lizardi and at the same time maintained close ties to the Spanish minister at the Mexican capital. The firm of Barron/Forbes at Tepic, on the northern Pacific coast, also had broad international ties; William Forbes and Eustaquio Barron served respectively as United States consul and Spanish consul at the same port.[52]

The moneylenders demanded that the Mexican government use a large part of the indemnity payment from the United States government to pay both internal and external debts. The indemnity funds, totaling $15,000,000 paid by the United States for the territories of Texas, New Mexico, most of Arizona and California, represented an enormously attractive bait for both native financiers and foreign bondholders. It is curious that many Mexican politicians were not averse to complying with these claims, especially those of the British bondholders. As one historian recently argued, "Both Conservative Lucas Alamán and Liberal Valentín Gómez Farías welcomed British influence in Mexico as a counterweight to that of the United States."[53] Finally, in October 1850, a new debt accord was signed with the bondholders by Finance Minister Manuel Payno. Mexico acknowledged a foreign debt of 51,000,000 pesos (£10,240,000) and promised to pay 5,000,000 pesos to cover interest due, half to be paid with the indemnity funds and half with customs revenues. In exchange the bondholders accepted a reduction of interest rates from 5 percent to 3 percent.[54]

51. *London Times*, July 30, 1845.

52. On these financial houses based in Mexico, see Barbara Tenenbaum, "Merchants, Money, and Mischief: The British in Mexico, 1821–1862," *The Americas* 25, no. 3 (1979): 317–339. D.C.M. Platt, "Las finanzas británicas en México, 1821–1867," *Historia Mexicana* 32, no. 2 (October-December 1982): 226–261; and Jean Meyer, "Barron, Forbes y Cia.: El cielo y sus primeros favoritos," *Nexos* 4, no. 40 (April 1981): 22–36.

53. Tenenbaum, *Politics of Penury*, p. 99.

54. The negotiations were complex. There is a detailed description in Casasús, *Historia de la deuda*, pp. 219–243.

Despite the favorable 1850 arrangement, the Mexican government could not escape the ominous specter of indebtedness and potential bankruptcy. After 1856 the authorities found it necessary to suspend interest payments because of the outbreak of civil war. The already critical situation was complicated by claims of the Mexico City moneylenders. To protect themselves from government insolvency, many of these local capitalists asked the European powers—Great Britain, France, and Spain—to back their claims on the Mexican exchequer. To legitimize such procedures, the moneylenders had recourse to so-called diplomatic conventions, which allowed for conversion of a large part of the internal debt into a species of external debt. These maneuvers might appeared to have been less than orthodox, but the representatives of the foreign powers were hardly squeamish. Robert Wilson, a contemporary American traveler in Mexico, observed, "The best way to collect a debt in Mexico is to convert it into a foreign debt, if possible, and then, if there is a resident that stands high with his minister, the matter meets with prompt attention. He that can buy a foreign ambassador at Mexico has made a fortune."[55]

In the years 1851–53 the British Foreign Office succeeded in obliging the Mexican government to recognize a total of 5,000,000 pesos (one silver peso was equal to one silver dollar) in claims of this nature. Concurrently, the Spanish and French authorities did their utmost to browbeat various finance ministers until they accepted similarly dubious claims, totaling almost 10,000,000 pesos.[56] But the most notorious and irregular arrangement was the Jecker contract of 1859, by which the penniless Miramón administration promised to pay a well-known Swiss moneylender of Mexico City, Juan B. Jecker, 15,000,000 pesos in bonds in exchange for less than 1,000,000 pesos in hard cash. With characteristic flexibility the French ambassador extended diplomatic protection for Jecker and his associates and subsequently proceeded to press for reimbursement.

The Jecker contract accentuated political and financial conflicts in Mexico. In the spring of 1861 the liberal forces, led by Benito Juárez, took power and refused to recognize the legitimacy of the moneylenders' claims, going so far as to suspend payments on all outstanding foreign debts. Retaliation was swift and brutal. On November 15 the British foreign secretary, Lord John Russell, joined the Spanish and French ministers, Francisco Javier Istúriz and Count Flahaut de la Billarderie, in signing a convention that authorized the military occupation of the principal Mexican ports.[57] The results of this unsavory blend of financial and diplomatic ma-

55. Tenenbaum, "Merchants, Money, and Mischief," p. 336.

56. On the "diplomatic conventions," see William Wynne, *State Insolvency and Foreign Bondholders* (New Haven, 1951), 2:14–19.

57. The British authorities were at first reluctant to intervene on behalf of the bondholders, but when the Mexican government formally suspended payments on the foreign debt in July

neuvers came in 1862 with the invasion and occupation of Mexico by the combined forces of France, Great Britain, and Spain.

Conditions were ripe for such an imperial expedition. The United States—embroiled in the Civil War—could not intervene, and the Mexican army was in shambles and therefore unable to offer significant resistance. The British and Spanish troops were soon withdrawn, but a large contingent of French soldiers remained on Mexican soil for five years. With the support of Napoleon III, a peculiar form of colonial administration was hastily set up in Mexico, headed by an Austrian prince, Archduke Maximilian. During a period of three years, Maximilian occupied a makeshift throne at Chapultepec Castle, ruling with the support of a clique of Mexican conservative politicans and of the 30,000-man French occupation army.[58] Eventually, however, Maximilian was overthrown and the French troops were defeated as a result of the successful campaign of the liberal forces led by Juárez.

The European invasion of Mexico in the 1860s represented the final and bitter climax of decades of financial insolvency. The bankruptcy of the Mexican state, which had commenced shortly after the crisis of 1825–26, became a permanent specter, haunting the efforts of dozens of officials who headed the national Ministry of Finance during the first three-and-a-half decades of independent government. As in the rest of Latin America, harrowing political and military developments outstripped official expectations and made fiscal stability more of an illusion than a practical reality. With few exceptions, the construction of the new nation-states proved to be an infinitely more difficult and complex task than had been anticipated in the optimistic days of the early 1820s.

Yet from another perspective the efforts of the early Latin American republics to sustain their political and economic independence were not altogether unsuccessful. Despite numerous naval blockades, repeated threats of intervention, and two major military invasions, this heterogeneous collection of nations resisted and survived.[59] Furthermore, during a quarter of a century most of them maintained an effective moratorium on their external debts, which indicated an appreciable degree of economic autonomy

1861, British Ambassador Wykes began to advocate military intervention. For the British diplomatic correspondence on Mexico, see Gloria Grajales, ed., *México y Gran Bretaña durante la intervención, 1861–1862* (Mexico, 1974), esp. pp. 75–81, 107–110.

58. A balanced study of Maximilian's reign, emphasizing financial and military questions, is needed. For an engaging but antiquated biography of the emperor, see C. Conte Corti, *Maximilano y Carlota* (Mexico, 1944), which is based principally on materials in the Austrian archives.

59. The two full-scale military invasions were the United States' invasion of Mexico, 1846–48, and the Anglo-Spanish-French invasion of Mexico in 1862.

from the great powers of the day. The price paid for such autonomy was undoubtedly high, but it is questionable whether any contemporary alternatives were possible or indeed could have proven less costly.

Recapitulating, then, no Latin American state, with the exception of Brazil, received any new loans between 1825 and the late 1850s, a period during which private foreign direct investment also evaporated almost totally. After mid-century circumstances began to change. When the Chilean, Peruvian, and Argentine governments—among others—decided to renegotiate their foreign debts, they did so in the firm belief that a new economic and political era had commenced, an era in which the attractions of expanding international trade and finance appeared to outweigh the potential and already well-known dangers of accumulating voluminous foreign debts.

CHAPTER 3

The Rediscovery of Latin America, 1850–1873

Nations like England and France can think twice about taking foreign loans . . . ;
but poor and sparsely populated countries have no cause to hesitate.

—Juan Bautista Alberdi (1858)

BY MID-CENTURY a new and powerful economic wind had begun to
sweep throughout Latin America, ushering in a prolonged phase of
expansion that gained velocity and momentum until it broke on the formidable barrier of the Great Depression of the 1870s. The main force gener-
ating new growth trends was foreign trade. The export of agricultural and
ranching commodities as well as mineral products surged dramatically:
guano from Peru, copper and wheat from Chile, wool from Argentina, coffee from Brazil, sugar and tobacco from Cuba, silver from Mexico. The
rapid rise in export income simultaneously spurred a boom in imports of
manufactured goods as the Latin American propertied classes bought increasing quantities of British cotton textiles, French silks and liqueurs, German hardware, and Spanish wines and sherries.[1]

With the growth and diversification of trade came a new wave of foreign
merchants and entrepreneurs who established themselves in Latin American ports and in many inland towns and cities. In cooperation with local
capitalists, they contributed to the establishment of the first local joint-stock
companies: banks, insurance firms, steam navigation enterprises, and,
most important, railroads. The number and size of these concerns tended
to be small, but their creation marked a critical juncture in the incipient
process of capitalist transformation of the Latin American economies.

The expansion of trade meant increased income for local and foreign
merchants and bankers, for landowners, and for the urban middle classes
throughout the region. It also meant greater revenues for governments as a
result of the rise in import-export taxes. Fiscal prosperity, in turn, stimulated a period of major reforms during the 1850s, 1860s, and early 1870s

1. The basic secondary source on British–Latin American trade during the nineteenth cen-
tury is Platt, *Latin America and British Trade*. There are few monographs on trade between
Latin America and *other* major trading partners, such as France, Germany, and the United
States. An exception is Kapp, ''Les relations économiques extérieures du Mexique (1821–
1911),'' pp. 11–93. For additional information, see Bonilla, *Gran Bretaña y el Perú*; Ferns,
Great Britain and Argentina; Richard Graham, *Britain and the Onset of Modernization in
Brazil, 1850–1914* (Cambridge, U.K., 1972).

destined to restructure state bureaucracies, modernize armies, and promote ambitious public works programs.[2] Many of these reforms were covered with internal funds—basically those derived from customs duties—but some were financed with foreign loans.

The new ties between Latin American finance ministers and European merchant bankers contributed to a gradual increase in credit transactions with the outside world, thereby bringing to a close the three decades of financial hibernation that had followed on the crisis of 1825. Indeed, the transfer of foreign capital accelerated with such speed that by the late 1860s most of the nations of the subcontinent were once again in the grip of a billowing loan cycle.[3] At the prodding of European banks, the governments of Argentina and Brazil, Peru and Chile, and even small states such as Honduras, Costa Rica, or Paraguay sent agents to hawk their bonds in the money markets of London, Paris, and Amsterdam.

Nonetheless, the Latin American loan boom of the 1860s and early 1870s was neither autonomous nor singular in scope and character. On the contrary, it formed the tail end of a broad and powerful phase of capitalist expansion that had begun in the early 1850s in Europe and the United States and continued accelerating until the mid-1870s. This "long wave" of growth, as some economists have described it, had its dynamic axis in the industrializing nations of the North Atlantic, whence the great economic pulsations pressed outward: the export of consumer and capital goods, the incessant current of emigrants, and a growing stream of direct investments and loans.[4]

Once again, therefore, the bull market in Latin American stocks and bonds must be seen as a product of an expansive phase of the international economy. However, the volume and value of loans taken by the Latin American governments in the 1860s far surpassed those of the earlier loan cycle of 1820–25. This fact can be attributed to the growing vigor of capitalism on a global scale after mid-century.[5]

2. For the important political and social reforms implemented the Latin American nations during the 1850s, see Tulio Halperín Donghi, *Historia contemporánea de America Latina* (Madrid, 1969), chap. 4.

3. Although there is no overall historical study of Latin American foreign loans in period 1850–73, an excellent introduction to contemporary international finance can be found in Jenks, *Migration*, chaps. 7–10.

4. The literature on "long waves" of economic activity is abundant. See K. Barr, "Long Waves: A Selected Annotated Bibliography," *Review* 2, no. 4 (1979): 675–718. For a historical interpretation of the different concept of "long swings" in the United States and the Atlantic economies during the nineteenth century, see Jeffrey G. Williamson, *American Growth and the Balance of Payments, 1820–1913* (Chapel Hill, N.C., 1964).

5. For a perceptive and provocative synthesis of the international boom of the 1850s and

For our present purpose it is worth highlighting three key aspects of this process that had a major impact on the internationalization of the Latin American economies. First, it is essential to observe that the creation of an effectively integrated world market now became a reality; this development was forcefully impelled by such events as the gold rushes of California and Australia in the early 1850s, which caused a remarkable intensification of economic exchange between Atlantic and Pacific. A second key factor was the multiplication of dynamic poles of industrial growth. Great Britain continued to be the world's industrial leader, but other nations—for example, France, Germany, and the United States—emerged as major rivals, competing for new markets, such as those of Latin America. Finally, special attention must be devoted to the great transport revolution of the age, the most visible symbol of which was the triumph of the railway on an international scale. The construction of railways advanced most rapidly in the maturing industrial economies of the North Atlantic, but in other regions— Latin America, for instance—the steam locomotive soon also became the undisputed symbol of economic progress.[6]

The fact that a large percentage of the foreign loans taken out by the different Latin American states during the 1860s and early 1870s were intended to finance construction of such public works as railways is indicative of the new economic strategies adopted on a regionwide scale. The basic aim of the national elites was to obtain foreign capital in order to promote modernization. They formulated ambitious "development" projects, solicited loans abroad to finance these programs, and arranged contracts with engineering firms to carry them out. In short, they used the financial resources of their states to impel an early stage of capitalist growth, albeit highly dependent on foreign sources of technology, capital goods, and finance.

According to the much-cited view of one historian, the increasingly close ties forged between the regional elites and the European merchants and bankers can be defined as a new "colonial pact," based on the international division of labor between producers of raw materials and producers of manufactured goods.[7] Despite the underlying cogency of this argument, it tends to place the emphasis on the impact of external rather than internal factors. The growth of foreign trade and the renewed flows of foreign capital did impel adoption of a new model of economic growth, but the ruling groups

---

1860s, see Eric Hobsbawm, *The Age of Capital, 1848–1875* (New York, 1975), chaps. 2 and 7.

6. For international railway statistics and much else, see Paul Bairoch, *Commerce éxterieure et développement économique de l'Europe au XIXe siècle* (Paris, 1963), pp. 31ff.

7. Halperín, *Historia contemporánea*, p. 214.

in each Latin American nation decisively influenced how the model was formulated and implemented.

In this chapter the emphasis is on the role of the Latin American elites in using government loans to accelerate the process of capital accumulation. The analysis of the foreign loans of the period suggests that the financial policies adopted by governments played a decisive role both in determining the size, type, and number of operations undertaken and in shaping the way the loan proceeds were invested. Particular attention will be paid to the experience of the larger Latin American debtors of the day: Chile, Peru, Argentina, and Brazil. In each of these cases we shall begin with a review of the impact of the foreign trade cycle on the local economy. This is followed by a description and evaluation of the loan policies adopted by the respective national elites to promote economic and political modernization. But before delving into the details of the case studies, it is worthwhile to review the principal factors that sparked the international expansion of trade and finance after mid-century. In the case of Latin America it was a fortuitous event—the discovery of gold in California—that proved to be the turning point.

The Gold Rush and the Latin American Trade Boom

Among historians of the United States, the discovery of gold in California in 1849 is viewed as a milestone in the expansion of the national economy, but Latin American historians do not tend to view the gold rush in the same light. The reasons are not difficult to determine. First, the California boom is seen as a direct consequence of the defeat of Mexico in the 1846–48 war with the United States. Had the war not taken place, Mexico rather than its northern neighbor would have benefited from the discovery of the precious metals. Second, there is evidence that as a result of the renewed interest of foreign powers in Latin America as a strategic crossroads between Atlantic and Pacific, the entire region became subject to an intensification of imperial pressures.[8]

Whether such a view is altogether justified or not, the fact is—as Tulio Halperín suggests—that the gold rush did mark the beginning of a broad phase of economic expansion that lasted for almost a quarter of a century.[9]

8. The acquisition of 1,000,000 square miles of Mexican territory by the United States was the most blatant example of foreign expansionism in Latin America at mid-century, but additional events—e.g., the European intervention in Mexico (1862–67), the Spanish naval incursions in the Caribbean and on the Pacific coast (1864–66), and the aggressive tactics of citizens and enterprises of the United States and Great Britain in Central America, particularly in Panama, Nicaragua, and Honduras—testify to the vigor of imperialist tendencies.

9. Halperín, *Historia contemporánea*, p. 208.

But the immediate impact of the massive migration of people and goods was limited mainly to regions located on or near the two great maritime routes that fed on the gold traffic.[10] The case of Chile is illustrative of the economic and social repercussions caused by the sharp rise in traffic along the Cape Horn shipping route, which initially took the bulk of passengers and supplies bound for California. In the 1840s an annual average of 1,400 vessels from Europe and the United States put in at Chilean ports, but by 1850—at the height of the mining craze—more than 3,000 did so.[11] Moreover, it should not be forgotten that a large number of the famous "forty-niners" were Latin Americans; in fact, more than 20,000 Chileans joined the immense cosmopolitan throng of prospectors who flocked to San Francisco in the halcyon days of the gold boom.[12]

While the increase in the southern Pacific trades broadened the channels of international exchange, an equally important development was the abrupt expansion of passenger traffic across Central America. From 1849 onward, tens of thousands of adventurers, lured by the distant gleam of California treasures, made their way to Panama, Nicaragua, and Tehuantepec.[13] In all three cases, the journey through fever-ridden tropical jungles and across uncharted valleys and mountains was difficult and full of perils. But the persistence of the great human tide soon generated pressure for introduction of more-efficient methods of trans-isthmian transport. Construction of the Panama railway between 1850 and 1855 represented a major advance, although the death rate among the workers who built the road was staggering. Thousands of workers were brought from the nearby Magdalena River valley in Colombia, as well as smaller numbers of recruits from Jamaica and even from as far away as China and India. They toiled

10. Contemporary Latin American politicians and ideologues were acutely aware of the dramatic implications of the gold rush. Argentine intellectual Juan Bautista Alberdi observed in his classic study *Bases para la organización política* (Santiago, 1852): "California, an improvisation of barely four years, has transformed fable into reality, and revealed the true law of the formation of the new states of the Americas, bringing from abroad great masses of people and integrating them into the body of the nation."

11. For details, see Claudio Véliz, *Historia de la marina mercante de Chile* (Santiago, 1961).

12. The literature on the impact of the gold rush throughout the region is scattered. There are many useful references in R. A. Humphreys, *Latin America: A Guide to the Literature in English* (Oxford, 1960), pp. 111–178.

13. On the Panama route, see Gerstle Mack, *The Land Divided: A History of the Panama Canal and Other Isthmian Canal Projects* (Stanford, 1947), and David McCullough, *The Path between the Seas: The Creation of the Panama Canal, 1870–1914* (New York, 1977). On the Nicaraguan route, consult David Folkman, "Westward via Nicaragua: The United States and the Nicaraguan Route, 1826–1869" (Ph.D. diss., University of Utah, 1966). On the Tehuantepec route, an illuminating eyewitness report is that of Charles Brasseur, *Viaje por el istmo de Tehuantepec, 1859–1860* (Mexico, 1981).

and perished as they laid down the iron tracks through jungles rife with insect plagues and tropical fevers.[14]

Before completion of the railway, a new and redoubtable actor entered the stage. Cornelius Vanderbilt, king of the steamship lines on the eastern coast of the United States, could hardly overlook the enormous profits his rivals were reaping from the Panama traffic. He moved swiftly and surely, wresting from the Nicaraguan government a concession that allowed him to open a competing route to be run by his American Atlantic and Pacific Ship Canal Company.[15] Despite his failure to build the canal, Vanderbilt continued to run his paddlers up and down the San Juan River and across Lake Nicaragua for several years, until an outburst of political and military conflicts disrupted the traffic. The intervention of a modern-day buccaneer from the United States, William Walker, who attempted to set up a personal dictatorship in Nicaragua, provoked a series of regional wars. By the end of 1856, the North American soldier of fortune fled to the United States, and shortly thereafter the Nicaraguan passenger route was definitively closed.[16] In the years following, the greater part of the international flow of passengers and goods returned again to Panama. But the boom generated by the gold rush gradually faded, and when the Civil War broke out in the United States, shipping on the Caribbean run to the isthmus dwindled to a trickle.

While the California mining frenzy provided a dramatic if brief stimulus to the Latin American economies, more durable and sweeping was the subsequent surge in trade with the industrial regions of northern and central Europe. This commerce involved a broad range of agricultural, ranching, and mineral commodities. The textile and shoe factories of England, France, Belgium, and Germany consumed increasing quantities of cotton, wool, and leather—raw materials essential to the manufacture of the coarse and fine cloth, hats and jackets, belts and boots, and rugs and blankets that came churning out of the mills. Inevitably, European industrialists looked far afield to meet their needs, turning to the United States, Egypt, and India for cotton but also—on a smaller scale—to the plantations of Brazil and of coastal Peru. They bought wool from Australia and South Africa, yet they

14. On this, one of the earliest railway companies in Latin America, see Joseph L. Schott, *The Story of the Building of the Panama Railroad, 1849–1855* (New York, 1967); and J. F. Rippy, *Latin America and the Industrial Age* (New York, 1944), pp. 18–23.

15. Vanderbilt attempted to enlist the support of London bankers Rothschilds and Barings for his company. Reference to Barings' refusal to support the project can be found in Ralph Hidy, *The House of Baring in American Trade and Finance: English Merchant Bankers at Work, 1763–1861* (Cambridge, Mass., 1949), p. 596, n. 147.

16. On the nefarious exploits of Walker, see W. O. Scroggs, *Filibusters and Financiers: the Story of William Walker and His Associates* (New York, 1916), and Folkman, "Westward via Nicaragua."

were also soon acquiring large quantities from Argentina and Uruguay. They placed orders for leather hides from the United States and Russia, but also increasingly from the cattle, sheep and horse ranches of Venezuela and the Río de la Plata region.[17]

Factories were not the only consumers of Latin American commodities. The rapid growth in population of European cities also created new markets for a variety of tropical foods and goods that were not produced domestically. Most important in terms of volume and value were sugar, coffee, and tobacco, the bulk coming from Brazil and the Caribbean, while a smaller flow originated in Peru, Colombia, Ecuador, and Central America. The demand for such items was stimulated by the rising consumption of the new and prosperous European bourgeoisie as well as the lower-middle and working classes in the industrial metropolises of London, Manchester, and Glasgow, naturally, but also of Paris, Lyons, Brussels, Antwerp, Frankfurt, Munich, Milan, and Barcelona. It was at this time that coffee and sugar became staples on the breakfast and dinner tables of both wealthy and poorer households throughout central and southern Europe. As the income and size of the urban populations rose, the demand for these exotic yet increasingly indispensable products mounted year by year.

By the 1860s most of Latin America was in the throes of an unprecedented trade boom, which continued unabated until the international crisis of 1873. The growth rate of mercantile transactions was phenomenal. Precise statistics for the whole of Latin America and its trading partners are not available, but the British data is illustrative of overall trends.[18] Between 1850 and 1873, British imports from Latin America rose by almost 300 percent, and exports to the region multiplied by some 400 percent (see Figures 4 and 5). French exports also climbed steadily, from 150,000,000 francs in 1848 to more than 600,000,000 francs in 1860. French silks, woolens, glassware, wines, and liqueurs had their largest markets in Argentina and Brazil, although luxury goods from Paris and Lyons could now be found in elegant shops in all the Latin American capitals.[19]

17. Two especially illuminating studies on the expansion of Latin American exports should be mentioned: on leather, see the classic article by Tulio Halperín Donghi, "La expansión ganadera en la campaña de Buenos Aires, 1810–1852," in *Desarrollo económico* (Buenos Aires) 3, nos. 1–2 (1963): 57–110; and on wool, see the recent article by Hilda Sabato, "Wool Trade and Commercial Networks in Buenos Aires, 1840s to 1880s," *JLAS* 15, no. 1 (1984): 49–81.

18. The annual statistics of British trade with each Latin American nation are summarized in Platt, *Latin America*, appendix I–II, pp. 316–323.

19. In 1860 Argentina and Brazil together were responsible for 45 percent of total French trade with Latin America. The precise data can be found in the reports published by the Direction generale des Douanes et des Contributions Indirectes, *Tableau générale du commerce de la France avec ses colonies et les puissances étrangères* (published yearly from 1827).

FIGURE 4.
LATIN AMERICAN EXPORTS TO GREAT BRITAIN, 1855–1880.

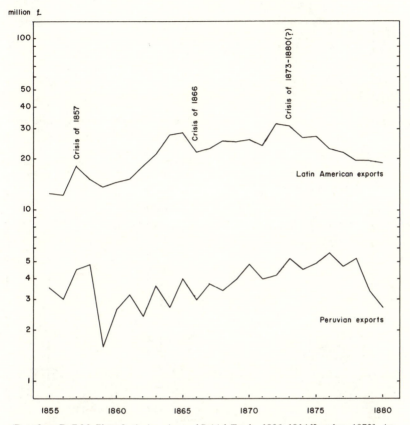

(Data from D.C.M. Platt, *Latin America and British Trade, 1806–1914* [London, 1972], Appendix 2, pp. 320–321.)

A number of other mercantile rivals began to make their mark as traders from the United States, Germany, Italy, Spain, Belgium, and even the Scandanavian countries expanded their activities in markets throughout the region. For example, United States exports to Brazil increased from $3,000,000 in 1850 to more than $6,000,000 in 1860. Imports from that country rose more rapidly, increasing from $9,000,000 in 1850 to $20,000,000 in 1860 and to more than $30,000,000 in 1870.[20]

20. International Bureau of the American Republics, *Handbook of the American Republics* (Washington, D.C., January 1891), bulletin no. 1, p. 103.

FIGURE 5.
BRITISH EXPORTS OF CAPITAL AND MERCHANDISE TO LATIN AMERICA, 1855–1880.

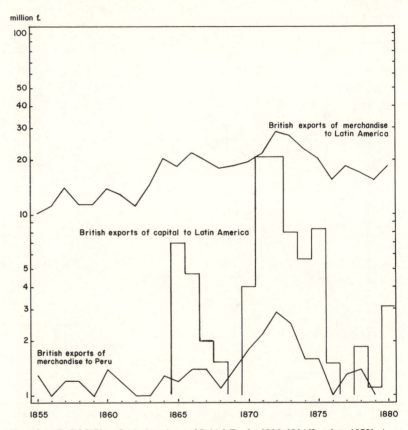

(Data from D.C.M. Platt, *Latin America and British Trade, 1806–1914* [London, 1972], Appendix 1, pp. 316–317; and Mathew Simon, ''The Pattern of New British Portfolio Investment, 1865–1914,'' in A. R. Hall, *The Export of Capital from Britain, 1870–1914* [London, 1968], pp. 39–40.)

In summary, the expansion in trade reflected the transformation of the most dynamic sectors of the Latin American economies. But there were limits to the economic and social changes. They did not lead to the formation of national bourgeoisies comparable to those in the more-advanced industrial countries, for industrial production in Latin America was not yet significant. Instead, the most important trend of the period was an increasing mercantilization of rural production. It is not surprising that this process led to a strengthening of the two most traditional and important sectors of

76

the propertied classes: the landowners and the merchants. Nonetheless, the increasing accumulation of capital in the hands of these groups, together with the renewed flows of foreign investments and loans, indicates that important features of capitalism had begun to take root in Latin American soil.

THE FINANCIAL CONSEQUENCES OF THE TRADE BOOM

If trade was the vehicle of Latin American economic expansion, finance greased the wheels of international exchange on both the Atlantic and the Pacific coasts of the hemisphere. Without credit and loans, commerce on a large scale could not be sustained. Initially, the main supply of commercial credit was that provided by European merchants and merchant bankers engaged in both the import and export trades. From the mid-1850s, additional sources became available. The creation of deposit banks in many Latin American cities and ports, the establishment of a variety of joint-stock companies linked to the export complex, and the negotiation of foreign loans by national governments put a great deal of money capital into circulation. The financial expansion, in turn, stimulated the trade boom.

Numerous historical studies have emphasized the role of foreign capital in this phase of the takeoff of the export economies.[21] In the first place, foreign merchants extended credit on a large scale in order to facilitate commercial transactions. A substantial portion of these short-term funds were obtained from London merchant-banking houses—for example, Baring Brothers, N. M. Rothschild, and Antony Gibbs—which were engaged in financing the trade in various commodities, such as hides from the Río de la Plata, coffee from Brazil, and guano from Peru.[22] French banking houses also participated in the financing of transatlantic trade, although they were not able to seriously challenge British preeminence in this field.[23] A similar situation prevailed in the field of direct investments; the bulk of

21. The two most complete studies are Rippy, *British Investments*; and Irving Stone, "The Composition and Distribution of British Investments in Latin America, 1865 to 1913" (Ph.D. diss., Columbia University, 1962).

22. The most useful studies shedding light on the role of London merchant bankers in the financing of transatlantic trade are Hidy, *The House of Baring*; Reber, *British Mercantile Houses in Buenos Aires*; William Mathew, *The House of Gibbs and the Peruvian Guano Monopoly* (London, 1981); and the various works of Platt previously cited.

23. No work on the role of French merchant banks operating in Latin America can compare with the magnificent study by David Landes on French bankers in contemporary Egypt, *Bankers and Pashas: International Finance and Economic Imperialism in Egypt* (Cambridge, Mass., 1958). Detailed case studies on the financing of German and United States trade with Latin America, the bulk of which was financed through London until the 1880s, are also needed.

the funds came from England. By 1875 a total of 77 companies operating in Latin America were selling their stocks and bonds on the Royal Exchange, including 25 railway firms, 11 mining enterprises, 6 overseas banks, and 7 telegraph companies.[24]

Foreign capitalists, however, were not the only entrepreneurs promoting new business organizations in Central and South America. Local merchants and landowners also participated actively in the formation of banks, insurance firms, gas companies, and railroads. In some instances, such as that of Chile, local stock markets came into existence and carried on a flourishing business in the securities of a broad range of these companies.[25] But most investment by the native propertied classes simply consisted in the plowing back of profits into ranches, plantations, haciendas, and mines. The importance of this local capital accumulation is difficult to ascertain because of the lack of quantitative studies, although reinvestment by native or resident merchants and landowners probably played an even more significant role in the process of economic growth than foreign direct investments did.

While both foreign and native entrepreneurs benefited from the trade boom of the 1850s and 1860s, the governments of most Latin American nations also increased their economic role.[26] To be more specific, many governments began to play a major role in the areas of transport and communications, financing construction of some of the first railways, telegraph systems, and port works in the subcontinent. The level of public investments was largely contingent on the trade cycle, for as commerce rose or fell, so did revenues. For example, an increase in trade and taxable income allowed finance ministers to expand the supply of paper money, the issue of treasury bills, and the sale of internal bonds. The multiplication of mon-

24. The nominal capital value of the British companies operating in Latin America in 1875 surpassed £45,000,000. There were twenty-five British-owned railway companies (worth £24,085,000), eleven mining companies (worth £2,456,000), six banks (worth £3,201,000), nine gas companies (worth £1,919,000), seven telegraph companies (worth £5,380,000), five steamship companies (worth £4,820,000), four tramway firms (worth £990,000), and ten other enterprises (worth £2,396,000). See Irving Stone, "The Composition and Distribution of British Investments in Latin America, 1865–1913" (Ph.D. diss., Columbia University, 1962), appendix B, pp. 229–247.

25. There are relatively few studies of the history of Latin American joint-stock companies and stock exchanges of the nineteenth century. Useful information for the case of Chile can be found in Robert Oppenheimer, "Chilean Transportation Development: The Railroad and Socio-Economic Changes in the Central Valley, 1840–1885" (Ph.D. diss., University of California at Los Angeles, 1976).

26. The annual reports of the respective finance ministries of the Latin American nations are among the most important sources of information available, but to date they have been studied in depth by few historians. The Library of Congress (Washington, D.C.) has a large collection of these documents.

etary instruments gave a powerful impulse to government spending and therefore to internal trade and production. In several instances, official or semi-official banks were set up to facilitate the financial operations of the state. Equally important, recourse was had to foreign loans, and these soon became one of the favored methods of raising money for government "development" programs.

There were basically three types of foreign loans during this period: loans for refinancing of old debts, loans for arms acquisitions, and loans for railway construction (see Table 3). The collaboration as well as the rivalry between foreign bankers, local entrepreneurs, and the government elites were reflected in these large and complex financial transactions.

The financing of state railways illustrates the symbiotic interests of the interest groups mentioned. For example, foreign merchants and bankers were interested in the issue of railway loans because they expected to obtain profits both from the sale of the securities and from the contracts to supply railway equipment to be paid with the loan proceeds. Local merchants and landowners also supported these projects because state railways promised to facilitate the transport and export of the commodities produced on the rural estates and therefore to stimulate economic growth. Finally, for politicians, the public works projects represented a way to increase the economic power of the state and to win the political support of constituencies by recourse to the pork barrel.[27]

The potential economic and political benefits of contracting foreign loans could be considerable, but the dangers in mortgaging state revenues to foreign bankers tended to be overlooked. The expansive economic cycle of the 1850s, 1860s, and early 1870s appeared to justify a sustained increase in government borrowing and spending policies. For the Latin American elites, the contracting of government loans appeared to offer a tremendously dynamic lever for capital accumulation. The most striking proof of confidence in this lever is the number of loans they authorized. All told, Latin American governments negotiated fifty important foreign loans between 1850 and 1873; most of them were issued in London, while a smaller but not insignificant number were placed in Paris and other European money markets (see Appendix A).

The contemporary loan business thus fed on a formidable array of interlocking factors: the rapidly increasing volume of foreign trade, the buildup of local financial and transport infrastructure, and the adoption of aggressive loan-seeking policies by the respective governments. To these must be

27. There are few detailed studies of the political and economic impact of foreign loans in Latin America during this period. The best single work is Heraclio Bonilla, *Guano y burguesía en el Perú* (Lima, 1974).

TABLE 3

FOREIGN LOANS TO LATIN AMERICAN GOVERNMENTS, 1850–1875

Country	Total No. of Loans	Nominal Value[a] (£ thousands)	Purpose[b]		
			Military (%)	Public Works (%)	Refinance (%)
Argentina	7	13,488	20	68	11
Bolivia	1	1,700	—	100	—
Brazil	8	23,467	30	13	57
Chile	7	8,502	37	51	12
Colombia	2	2,200	—	9	91
Costa Rica	3	3,400	—	100	—
Ecuador	1	1,824	—	—	100
Guatemala	2	650	—	77	23
Haiti	1	1,458	—	—	100
Honduras	4	5,590	—	98	2
Mexico[c]	2	16,960	70	—	30
Paraguay	2	3,000	—	80	20
Peru[d]	7	51,840	10	45	45
Santo Domingo	1	757	—	100	—
Uruguay	1	3,500	—	—	100
Venezuela	2	2,500	—	30	70

COMBINED SUBTOTALS BY SUBPERIODS

Years	Total No. of Loans	Nominal Value[a] (£ thousands)	Purpose[b]		
			Military (%)	Public Works (%)	Refinance (%)
1850–59	9	10,862	—	32	68
1860–69	20	56,705	41	12	47
1870–75	22	73,270	—	60	40

SOURCES: Corporation of Foreign Bondholders, *Annual Reports* (London, 1873–80); C. Fenn, *Fenn's on the Funds* (London, 1883); I. Stone, "The Composition and Distribution of British Investments in Latin America, 1865–1913" (Ph.D. diss., Columbia University, 1962). See also sources cited in Appendix A.

[a] This table gives the approximate nominal values of the foreign bond issues of the Latin American governments, but nominal values are not equivalent to actual sums realized by sale of the bonds. The proceeds received by the government were much less than the nominal value.

[b] These are approximate estimates based on the ostensible objectives as described in the loan contracts and/or loan prospectuses; they do not reflect real disbursement of the proceeds. Only a detailed study of each loan, using the financial archives of each Latin American government, would provide an approximation to the latter information.

[c] Not included here is the Mexican renegotiation of 1851 (recognizing approximately £10,000,000 of old debts) because its implementation was soon suspended. We do include the "Mexican Imperial" bond issues made by the government of Maximilian in 1864–65, although they were repudiated in 1867 by the Mexican government headed by Benito Juárez. All subsequent Mexican administrations considered that the "imperial bonds" were fraudulent insofar as Napoleon III used the loan monies to finance the invasion and occupation of Mexico.

[d] Missing here are a pair of Peruvian loans issued in the 1850s in Paris. See Appendix A for data.

added the participation of European bankers who pressured the local politicians, urging them to throw caution to the winds. After all, was not the
moment propitious? Interest rates in Europe were descending, and the issue
of external bonds was as easy as printing paper money.

Yet the precise combination of these personal and impersonal factors,
and their relative weight, varied from one nation to another, as did the
advantages, or alternatively disadvantages, of seeking financial assistance
abroad. In short, the Latin American loan boom of the third quarter of the
nineteenth century can be adequately understood only in light of the specific circumstances that governed the political and economic evolution of
each nation riding the exhilarating but perilous roller coaster of international finance.

BOOM IN THE SOUTH PACIFIC: CHILEAN TRADE, LOANS, AND RAILWAYS

Although the decade of the 1850s witnessed a substantial increase in the
foreign trade of Latin America, we should note that from a geographic and
economic perspective there were important intraregional differences. For
example, the foreign commerce of Mexico, Central America, and the Caribbean tended to be sluggish, with the exception of Cuba. In contrast, the
highest rates of growth were recorded in the South Atlantic—in Argentina
and Brazil—and in the South Pacific, in Chile and Peru. The dynamism of
these southern poles of economic growth helps explain the speedy advance
of local capital accumulation as well as the large volume of foreign investments and loans in these countries.

The case of Chile is of particular interest because it was there that the
new forms of capitalist organization of production and finance first took
root.[28] As already indicated, from the time of the gold rush the vitality of
the Chilean economy was closely linked to its role as southern bridge between the Atlantic and the Pacific. The rise of international shipping on the
Pacific coast of the Western Hemisphere stimulated trade between the various ports and regions along this now busy route. The hundreds of ships
carrying tens of thousands of seafaring gold prospectors also brought much
merchandise from Europe and the United States. At the same time, this
commercial movement stimulated an increase in exports of local produc-

28. The first railways of South America were built in Chile in the 1850s. Furthermore, as
of 1860 Chile had the largest merchant marine in Latin America, the largest number of copper
and coal mines, the greatest number of metal-smelting establishments, and the most active
stock markets. The Chilean economic model was much admired such by Argentine politicians
and intellectuals such as Domingo Sarmiento and Juan Bautista Alberdi, and its influence in
Peru was not less important, particularly in the field of railways.

tion. Chilean wheat was exported to California in growing quantities in exchange for gold. Chilean grain exports also went to Peruvian and Ecuadorian markets in return for the sugar, cotton, and cocoa produced on the coastal plantations of Arequipa, Trujillo, and Guayaquil.[29] Much of this trade was facilitated by the Pacific Steam Navigation Company, a new enterprise that operated out of Chile but had offices and depots for its steamers along the six thousand miles of coast from Valparaíso to San Francisco.[30]

Mercantile and shipping expansion did not limit itself to the coastal and California trades. The discovery of gold in Australia in 1850 spurred a parallel movement of people and goods from Europe, around Cape Horn, and out across the Pacific. As a result, for a few years Chile became a leading wheat-exporter to far-off Sydney and Melbourne. The already extensive European trade with the Far East brought renewed activity to the various western ports of South America as dozens of British schooners bound for India and scores of China clippers from Boston and Salem stopped yearly at Valdivia, Talcahuano, and Valparaíso for fresh water and provisions.[31] Many of the famous New Bedford whalers came also, bound to and from their hunting grounds in the South Seas.

By mid-century the Chilean economy was expanding with vigor. The agricultural production of the Central Valley, surrounding Santiago, increased steadily and allowed for a substantial volume of exports. Even more rapid was the advance of mining in the northern provinces of Coquimbo and Atacama. Production there progressed so swiftly that between 1840 and 1873 Chile became the world's foremost copper exporter.[32] Much of this relatively scarce metal was shipped to India, where it fetched high prices in the bazaars because it was in great demand among local artisans of fine copperware, while the rest was sold by British merchants throughout Europe.[33] Considerable amounts of silver were also sent from Chile to the Far East, where British traders in Calcutta, Bombay, Hong Kong, and Canton required the precious metal to carry on trade in tea, silks, and spices.

The prosperity generated by exports stimulated the formation of many new firms. Although most Chilean business enterprises were small and

29. The classic history of the Chilean wheat trade in the nineteenth century is Sergio Sepúlveda G., *El trigo chileno en el mercado mundial* (Santiago, 1959).

30. On the Chilean merchant marine, see Véliz, *Historia de la marina mercante*. On the history of the Pacific Steam Navigation Company, see Robert Greenhill, "Shipping 1850–1914," in *Business Imperialism*, ed. D.C.M. Platt, pp. 121–124; and A. C. Wardle, *Steam Conquers the Pacific* (London, 1940).

31. On the Pacific trades, see Véliz, *Historia de la marina mercante*, pp. 71–78 and passim.

32. Marcos Mamalakis, *The Growth and Structure of the Chilean Economy* (New Haven, 1976), p. 40.

33. On the role of one British merchant firm at Valparaíso involved in the export of copper to India, see Benjamín Vicuña Mackenna, *Los hermanos Clark* (Santiago, 1929).

technically quite backward, an appreciable number of joint-stock companies began to appear. By the early 1870s the shares of four banks, seven mining companies, three insurance firms, and seven railroads were traded regularly on the Santiago and Valparaíso exchanges.[34] These financial markets were among the most active in all of contemporary Latin America, and this was due in part to the proliferation of local banking firms. The earliest financial institutions, the Banco de Valparaíso (1855) and the Banco Nacional de Chile (1856) relied heavily on the support of English mercantile firms based at Valparaíso and Santiago, such as the houses of Graham, Rowe & Company and Antony Gibbs & Sons. Similarly, the British trading firm of Balfour, Williamson & Company bought shares in the Banco de Chile and the Banco Nacional de Chile, as well as in a leading insurance company, in the Coquimbo and Taltal railway companies, and in various nitrate mining establishments.[35]

But foreign merchants had no monopoly on new business ventures. Local merchants, moneylenders, miners, and landowners were also engaged in a variety of profitable activities. In fact, in most of the banks they held the bulk of the stock, and the same could be said of the other joint-stock companies. By 1865, according to one recent study, Chilean landowners held 49 percent of the shares in joint-stock enterprises, Chilean merchants held 16 percent, and foreign traders held the remaining 35 percent.[36] Such data suggests that it would be erroneous to consider the European merchants as a dominant neo-colonial group. In Chile, as in the rest of Latin America, foreign merchants who set up trading houses tended to establish close business, political, and social ties with the native-born elite.[37] In time they became virtually full-fledged members of the local propertied classes. They frequently bought landed estates and married into prominent families with old roots. The result was that during the nineteenth century the Latin

34. Between 1850 and 1875 approximately 270 stock companies were formed in Chile, with a capital of 210,000,000 pesos (Oppenheimer, "Chilean Transportation Development," p. 106). For additional information on the Chilean stock market, see William Sater, "Chile and the World Depression of the 1870s," *JLAS* 2, no. 1 (1979): 67–99.

35. See Manuel A. Fernández, "Merchants and Bankers: British Direct and Portfolio Investment in Chile during the 19th Century," *Ibero-Amerikanishces Archiv*, n.f. 9, nos. 3–4 (1983): 354. See also John Mayo, "Before the Nitrate Era: British Commission Houses and the Chilean Economy, 1851–1880," *JLAS* 2, no. 2 (1979): 282–302.

36. Data from Charles G. Pregger Roman, "Dependent Development in Nineteenth-Century Chile" (Ph.D. diss., Rutgers University, 1975), cited in Fernández, "Merchants and Bankers," p. 358.

37. "British merchants and other British nationals in Chile played a significant role in the long-term process of integration that the ruling class underwent during the nineteenth century" (Fernández, "Merchants and Bankers," p. 358).

American propertied classes became increasingly hybrid, in terms of national origin.

By 1860, however, the two wealthiest members of the Chilean elite were not merchants or landowners but railroad contractors—namely, Henry Meiggs and William Wheelwright, both North Americans resident in Santiago. The affluence of this pair of hard-driving if unscrupulous entrepreneurs had a simple explanation: Railway construction represented the largest business of the day in terms of total capital investment.

Wheelwright first consolidated his reputation and fortune by founding the Pacific Steam Navigation Company (1838), an enterprise destined to play a major role in Latin American trade for many decades. Subsequently he became interested in the silver and copper mines of Copiapó. In order to provide an outlet for their production, he built the first Chilean railway. But Wheelwright's goals were not limited to promoting small regional railways; as early as 1855 he projected a transcontinental railway line to connect the Argentine port of Rosario with the leading Chilean port of Valparaíso.[38]

Henry Meiggs began his railway activities somewhat later, winning contracts in the late 1850s for the construction of the two largest Chilean railways, both in the wheat-rich Central Valley. By the 1860s he had become the best-known railway contractor in South America.[39]

The success of Meiggs and Wheelwright as railway builders was closely linked to the Chilean government's adoption of a series of plans to promote public works. During the 1840s, the Ministry of the Interior invested 1,000,000 pesos in the construction and repair of roads.[40] In 1847 the Congress authorized a more ambitious plan: construction of a railway from the port of Valparaíso to the capital, Santiago, in the heartland of the main grain belt of the country. Although the government raised most of the money to construct this key line, several wealthy Chilean merchants and landowners also invested funds. In 1858, however, the financial authorities decided that a foreign loan was needed to finance further expansion and to acquire additional equipment (e.g., locomotives, passenger cars). Negotiations were quickly arranged with the house of Baring Brothers, which sold £1,554,000 worth of Chilean external bonds for this purpose.[41]

During the 1860s and early 1870s the increase in trade revenues stimu-

38. The best source on Wheelwright is still the eulogistic biography by Juan Bautista Alberdi, *The Life and Industrial Labors of William Wheelwright in South America* (Boston, 1877). This is a translation of the Spanish edition, *La vida y los trabajos industriales de William Wheelwright en la América del Sud* (Paris, 1876).

39. On Meiggs, the classic study is Watt Stewart, *Henry Meiggs: Yankee Pizarro* (Durham, N.C., 1946).

40. Oppenheimer, "Chilean Transportation Development," p. 64.

41. Ibid., pp. 144–145.

lated the Chilean state to continue with its ambitious public works plans, despite unexpectedly large military expenditures. Meiggs was contracted to build a second state-sponsored railroad that would connect Santiago with the south-central agricultural districts. Two large foreign loans totaling £3,000,000 were taken in 1870 and 1873, the funds being used for construction of new branches as well as for acquisition of shares of the railway companies that were still in the hands of private investors.[42]

Private capitalists were therefore not the only captains of economic development. The Chilean state eventually became the biggest entrepreneur of all, obtaining large sums from abroad and additional funds internally to finance its "development" projects. As Colin Lewis recently indicated:

State mileage eclipsed private initiative in central and southern Chile during the 1870's. By 1876 the government had spent 5.7 millions on railways, a figure which represented over 90% of the country's foreign debt, and on the eve of the War of the Pacific (1879) government-owned rails accounted for 58% of national trackage.[43]

In practice the Chilean government did not limit itself to issuing railway loans. During the 1860s it also contracted several "war loans" in Europe with the firm of J. S. Morgan & Company with the aim of modernizing the Chilean navy, then engaged in a series of sporadic battles with Spanish naval squadrons that had been sent to harass the Pacific ports of several South American nations. But apart from these military transactions, the main trend is clear: The Chilean state exercised an increasingly prominent role within the national economy, using trade revenues to obtain foreign loans that in turn could be used to finance major public works projects. In more ways than one, the Chilean experience was soon to provide a model for its neighbor Peru.

THE PERUVIAN LOAN FRENZY: GUANO AND RAILWAYS

Until the late 1840s the Peruvian government suffered from acute financial difficulties that can be attributed both to fiscal penury and to political and military conflicts. This situation changed dramatically with the discov-

42. The £1,000,000 loan of 1870 was issued by bankers J. S. Morgan & Co. on behalf of the state-run Chilean and Talcahuano Railway. The £2,276,000 loan of 1873 was issued by the Oriental Bank Corporation and the City Bank Ltd. to pay for construction of the railway between Curicó and Angol and the branch line to Los Ángeles. In that year, 1873, Oppenheimer notes that the government took over the entire stock capital of the Ferrocarril Santiago (Oppenheimer, "Chilean Transportation Development," p. 162).

43. Colin Lewis, "The Financing of Railway Development in Latin America, 1850–1914," *Ibero-Amerikanisches Archiv*, n.f. 9, nos. 3–4 (1983): 264.

ery of the great economic potential of guano, a natural fertilizer, which was in great demand in Europe. As a result of its monopoly over guano production, the Peruvian state became one of the richest in Latin America for the space of several decades. Paradoxically, it also became the most heavily indebted of all the nations of the region.

The unprecedented volume of income earned from the thousands of shiploads of guano sent abroad during the 1850s, 1860s, and early 1870s was a boost for the Peruvian economy.[44] It allowed the government to reform its entire administrative and financial structure and to launch a series of grandiose plans for railway and port construction. Prosperity so beguiled Peruvian politicans that they could not withstand the temptation to negotiate loan after loan on European money markets, until finally the debt burden became cyclopean and suffocated both the public and private sectors of the economy. Thus, the exceptional fiscal prosperity of the Peruvian state (no other contemporary Latin American government exercised *direct* control over exports) became the key factor that led the local elites to accumulate an excessive quantity of external financial obligations.

The main deposits of guano were located on a tiny archipelago, the Chincha Islands, just a few miles off the Peruvian coast. The government supplied a stream of ex-convicts, Chinese coolies, and other hapless laborers to mine what were literally mountains of dried bird dung and to transport the guano down to the ships anchored to a series of ramshackle piers. From there the fertilizer was sent to England, Belgium, and other European countries, where it was in great demand among farmers desirous of increasing yields at a time of rising food prices. British imports of guano skyrocketed from 2,000 tons in 1841, to 95,000 tons in 1850, and to more than 300,000 tons in 1858. This immense trade required the use of more than 3,000 ships in the decade 1850–60, practically all of them dispatched from Peru under consignment to the powerful guano contractors, Antony Gibbs & Sons.[45]

The guano business became a source of considerable profits for Gibbs, which charged a commission on sales and took a percentage on all insurance and ship contracts, but the bulk of the income actually went into the coffers of the Peruvian treasury. Nonetheless, the complementary if frequently strained relationship between the Lima government and the British merchant firm was not limited to the shipping and selling of the precious fertilizer. As principal international fiscal agents for the Peruvian state,

44. A classic and still-useful study on the guano trade is Jonathan Levin, *The Export Economies: Their Pattern of Development in Historical Perspective* (Cambridge, Mass., 1959), chap. 2. More recent and detailed studies are the works of Bonilla, *Guano y burguesía*, and Mathew, *The House of Gibbs*, previously cited.

45. W. M. Mathew, "Antony Gibbs and Sons, the Guano Trade, and the Peruvian Government, 1842–1861," in *Business Imperialism*, ed. Platt, p. 366.

Gibbs soon also found itself engaged in supplying an uninterrupted stream of short-term loans for the Lima Finance Ministry.[46] The latter required these funds to cover the costs of a ballooning civil and military bureaucracy because it was inevitable that a major consequence of the guano boom was that it provided Peruvian politicians and generals with the resources necessary to expand their power base. The provision of jobs and emoluments in the government and the army constituted an attractive instrument for gaining the support of the middle and lower-middle classes, especially in the capital. Yet the availability of fresh and apparently inexhaustible sources of hard cash also provoked intense conflicts among the ruling factions, culminating in the liberal revolution of 1856, which in itself consumed a large portion of the export income of the republic.[47]

During this agitated period, each of the various administrations in power sought to win the support of the popular classes as well as to ingratiate itself with the most important propertied sectors. In the first place, the guano revenues allowed for major fiscal and social reforms. These included the abolition of the traditional taxes paid by the Indian communities (*tributo indigena*) as well as the abolition of slavery.[48] The old slaveowners were paid off with government bonds and new sources of labor were provided by importing tens of thousands of Chinese coolies.[49] In the second place, the guano income was used to cancel a huge volume of internal debts held by local merchants and landowners, allowing them to exchange much worthless government paper for hard currency.[50]

The accumulation of wealth by the new Peruvian aristocracy was threatened by a sharp drop in exports in 1859. In order to mollify the propertied classes, the government authorized negotiation of two large loans with London bankers in the years 1862 and 1865 for a combined total of

46. In 1849 Gibbs paid an advance of £72,000 in dividends on the Anglo-Peruvian debt and supplied a 472,000-peso short-term loan to the Peruvian government. In 1850 the sums advanced totaled 1,442,000 pesos; in 1853 they totaled 1,460,000 pesos; in 1854 it was a total of 500,000 pesos plus a monthly subsidy of 200,000 pesos; and so on, until the termination of the Gibbs monopoly in 1862 (ibid., pp. 351–353).

47. The 1856 revolution cost approximately 40,000,000 pesos, equivalent to almost 40 percent of the total guano revenues between 1854 and 1862 (Julio Cotler, *Clases, estado y nacion en el Peru* [Mexico, 1982], pp. 79–82).

48. For an incisive survey of the policies adopted with respect to the taxes on the Indian communities in Peru and Bolivia, see Nicolás Sánchez Albornoz, "Tributo abolido, tributo repuesto: invariantes socioeconómicas en la época republicana," in his *Indios y tributos*.

49. The government helped finance the coolie trade, which brought almost 80,000 extra laborers to Peru between 1849 and 1874. See Watt Stewart, *Chinese Bondage in Peru: A History of the Chinese Coolie, 1849–1874* (Durham, N.C., 1951).

50. For analysis of these complex internal debt arrangements, see Bonilla *Guano y burguesía*, pp. 26–35; and Carlos Palacios Moreyra, *La deuda anglo peruana, 1822–1890* (Lima, 1983), chap. 3.

£14,500,000.[51] A large part of these funds were used to convert the internal debt into external debt, thus further contributing to the accumulation of money capital in the hands of native merchants, landowners, and speculators. But the Lima elites did not leave their funds idle. They soon were engaged in launching a variety of joint-stock enterprises, the most important of which were a half-dozen banks.[52]

By the mid-1860s Peru had acquired a substantial foreign debt. Yet this was only the beginning. Most of the gold from the previously mentioned loans quickly evaporated. The money was absorbed by the debt conversions as well as by the expenses incurred in the brief but bitter conflict with the Spanish navy, which raided several ports and seized the guano islands in 1865–66. After the termination of hostilities, the Lima elites again looked abroad for additional financial assistance, although now with the aim of fulfilling a different set of goals.

The extravagant dream that seized the imagination of the Peruvian ruling caste in the late 1860s was construction of a vast network of railways to connect the dynamic coastal regions with the almost impenetrable subsistence economies of the peasant communities of the Andean highlands. The motives that led contemporary politicians to promote the building of these mountain railways were various. Government leaders like Manuel Pardo, president of Peru between 1872 and 1876, were great enthusiasts of the "iron horse." Pardo wrote:

Who will deny that the railroad is today the missionary of civilization? Who will deny that Peru urgently needs such missionaries? Without railroads there cannot be material progress . . . nor moral progress, for material progress provides the masses with prosperity and eliminates their misery and ignorance.[53]

Such principles were unquestionably laudable, but the unanswered question is precisely why Pardo and other contemporary Peruvian politicians felt that building railways up into the Andes would prove more economi-

51. For a nominal total of £5,500,000, the 1862 loan was issued ostensibly to convert the old Anglo-Peruvian debts of the 1820s. The 1865 loan, which had a nominal value of £9,000,000, was placed by the London banking firm of J. Thomson Bonar & Co., which from 1863 had been named guano consignees in Great Britain and international fiscal agents by the Peruvian state. The 1865 loan was intended for conversion of the foreign debt, but it also served to cancel a large part of the internal Peruvian debt as well as to cover important military expenses. See Palacios Moreyra, *La deuda anglo peruana*, pp. 96–113.

52. In Peru, native merchants monopolized the premier banking concerns such as the Banco del Perú (1863) and the Banco de la Providencia (1863), largely excluding British merchants from this strategic branch of local business. On the first Peruvian banks, consult Carlos Camprubi Alcázar, *Historia de los bancos en el Perú, 1860–1879* (Lima, 1957).

53. Cited in Bonilla, *Guano y burguesía*, p. 58.

cally beneficial than building them along the coastal regions, where the export economy was booming. One explanation Pardo offered was political; it was necessary to incorporate the majority of the Indian population, which lived in the Andes, into the nation. A second may have been of a historical nature. The Andean region had not only been the seat of the Inca empire, it had also been the source of the silver wealth of Peru during the colonial period. Unfortunately, in the 1860s the silver mines were in disrepair and, even with railways it was doubtful that a new mining boom could take place, at least in the short run.

The Lima politicians, nonetheless, were bent on modernizing their nation. The task of building railways up and across the Andes was certainly formidable, but there were entrepreneurs that insisted it could be done. The daring capitalist who finally convinced the Peruvian authorities that such railways could actually be built was Henry Meiggs, who had already gained a reputation as a master railway promoter in Chile. Plying journalists with propaganda and liberally distributing bribes to dozens of public officials, Meiggs soon had the Balta-Pierola administration (1868–72) eating out of his hand. Although the price he was prepared to charge for such stupendous engineering feats was almost as redoubtable as the Andes, this did not deter the ministers at Lima, who were confident that their apparently inextinguishable guano deposits could withstand the challenge.[54]

In 1868 Meiggs initiated work on a railway line in southern Peru destined to link the port of Mollendo with the highland agricultural center of Arequipa. He brought 10,000 Chilean and Bolivian workers there to build 107 miles of track. Most supplies and equipment were also shipped in: hundreds of tons of flour from Chile to feed the workers; thousands of wood ties from Chile and from as far off as Oregon; bridgework, rails, and locomotives from Great Britain.[55] A second line, begun in 1870 to connect Lima with the Andean town of La Oroya, covered a distance of 138 miles through incredibly rugged terrain. In order to traverse the deep chasms and range after range of towering mountains, a total of 61 bridges, 26 switchbacks, and 65 tunnels were constructed, including the remarkable Galerna tunnel, which passed below the summit of Mount Meiggs (!) at more than 15,000 feet above sea level, making the Central Peruvian the highest railway on earth. In addition to Chilean, Bolivian, and Peruvian workers, a great mass

54. According to William Clarke, who was sent by the British bondholders to Peru in 1877 to study the railway contracts, "My idea of the whole affair was that the real ingenuity consisted in obtaining £40,000 per mile for its construction. Any American or even English railway engineer could have made a fortune out of it had the cost been restricted to one quarter of the amount per mile" (cited in Stewart, *Henry Meiggs*, p. 47).

55. For information on workmen, materials, and methods of construction, see ibid., pp. 111–165.

of Chinese were forcibly put to labor on the Andean lines; thousands perished in this titanic enterprise.

Such epic construction exploits required a constant stream of laborers and an increasingly large flow of funds. In order to fulfill their growing obligations, the Balta-Pierola administration signed an extraordinary contract with the French merchant firm of Dreyfus Frères in 1869.[56] According to this agreement, the Dreyfus syndicate was to buy a total of 2,000,000 tons of guano, subsequently to be sold throughout Europe. In exchange for the gross proceeds, the syndicate was to pay the expenses involved in the loading, shipment, and sales of the fertilizer as well as to provide the government with a variety of financial services linked to the payment of interest and amortization on the Peruvian external debt.

Dreyfus further promised to promote a major railway loan, issued simultaneously in England and France to the tune of almost £12,000,000 in 1870. The banking houses that led the placement were the powerful Société Générale concern of Paris and J. H. Schröder & Company, merchant bankers at London. Barely two years later the same financiers launched another and even greater loan for a grand total of £22,000,000, among the largest Latin American loan operations of the entire nineteenth century. Nonetheless, this gigantic transaction proved to be a failure, and most of the banking parties engaged were stuck with huge amounts of Peruvian bonds. Worse hit was the Lima treasury, because it received only a fraction of the nominal sum yet became responsible for what was now an immense external debt service. As a result, the specter of national bankruptcy soon cast a dark shadow over Peru. The days of the guano boom as well as the subsequent loan boom were over by 1873. The dilemma for the Peruvian government now lay in finding a way to pay back a mountain of debts with sharply reduced resources.

The Finances of Brazil and Argentina: War and Railways

If trade along the Pacific coast of South America advanced at a rapid pace during the 1850s and 1860s, the mercantile expansion of the south-central Atlantic coast was equally impressive. Commercial activity was

56. On the partners and Peruvian associates of the Dreyfus firm, see Ernesto Yepes del Castillo, *Perú, un siglo de desarrollo capitalista, 1820–1920* (Lima, 1972), pp. 85–87, nn. 27, 28, 29. For the text of the Dreyfus contract, see Republic of Peru, Ministerio de Hacienda y Fomento, *Memoria, 1870,* "Documentos de contabilidad general y crédito," anexo 3, pp. 99–103. Additional information based on French archival sources is in Bonilla, *Guano y burguesía,* pp. 85–116. For a still-useful overall survey of the same contracts, see Wynne, *State Insolvency and Foreign Bondholders* (New Haven, 1951), 2:107–196.

highest in the ports and hinterland of Rio de Janeiro and São Paulo in Brazil and of Buenos Aires in Argentina.[57]

Here too, economic growth was fueled by exports: wool from the ranching *estancias* of the Argentine pampas, and coffee and cotton from the slave plantations surrounding Rio de Janeiro and São Paulo. The export boom in turn stimulated urban modernization. A contributing factor was the rising population of many coastal towns and cities that absorbed several waves of European immigrants and a flow of migrants from the less-dynamic regions of the interior.[58] The construction of commercial and residential buildings, the multiplication of mercantile firms, the establishment of the first banks, and the initiation of port and drainage works were testimony to the vitality of the economic expansion.[59]

Few historians have devoted detailed attention to how this early phase of Argentine and Brazilian economic development was financed. Reinvestment of profits evidently provided much of the necessary capital, which was supplemented by the credit supplied by resident merchants and by the earliest banks.[60] The landlords of the province of Rio de Janeiro, for instance, obtained short-term funding at the peaks of the planting and harvesting seasons from a special breed of merchants called *commissarios*, or coffee factors. The latter, for their part, maintained close ties with the leading export houses in the city of Rio itself. Similarly, the ranchers of the province of Buenos Aires procured credit from a local circle of wool and leather trading firms and from the recently established and extremely dynamic Banco de la Provincia de Buenos Aires.

The greater part of the revenues of the Brazilian and Argentine governments throughout this period were derived from import taxes, which rose steadily as foreign trade expanded. With their coffers regularly replenished,

57. Accurate and complete commercial statistics are difficult to come by, but various published studies provide an idea of the major trends. Buenos Aires wool exports rose from 10,000 tons in the year 1855 to more than 70,000 tons in 1872. See Sábato, "Wool Trade," p. 51. In that same time period, Brazilian cotton and coffee exports to Great Britain jumped by 500 percent and 400 percent respectively (Graham, *Britain and the Onset of Modernization in Brazil*, p. 72).

58. The population of Buenos Aires rose from 91,000 in 1855 to 180,000 in 1872, and that of Rio de Janeiro rose from 186,000 in 1854 to 267,000 in 1872 (Richard Morse, ed., *Las ciudades latinoamericanas* [Mexico, 1973], 2:62, 82).

59. On the role of British entrepreneurs in promoting urban modernization and a variety of new economic enterprises, see Michael Mulhall, *The English in South America* (London, 1878), pp. 494–534 and passim.

60. For a fascinating description of the activities of the Brazilian "coffee factors," see Stanley Stein, *Vassouras: A Brazilian Coffee County, 1850–1890* (1958; reprint, New York, 1970), chap. 4. On Buenos Aires wool merchants and wool ranchers, see Sabato, "Wool Trade"; on the Banco de la Provincia, see N. Casarino, *El Banco de la Provincia de Buenos Aires, 1822–1922* (Buenos Aires, 1922).

the finance ministers at Rio and at Buenos Aires were not as inclined as the Peruvians to contract foreign loans to cover ordinary expenditures. Relations with foreign bankers were initially limited to the renegotiation and conversion of outstanding foreign debts. The house of N. M. Rothschild & Sons, for example, formally became the international bankers of the Brazilian empire in 1855, but its chief function was to roll over the loans of the 1820s, 1830s, and 1840s rather than provide significant transfusions of new capital.[61] The Argentine government established close ties with another British merchant bank, Baring Brothers, which in 1857 assumed responsibility for renegotiating the foreign loan of 1824. But again no new transfer of gold was involved; the operation was limited to an exchange of old bonds for freshly printed ones.[62]

In the year 1865 a new and unexpected event blew a gaping hole in both Argentine and Brazilian budgets. The outbreak of war against Paraguay (1865–70) absorbed huge expenditures. This war proved to be the bloodiest and most vicious of all military conflicts that took place in mid-nineteenth-century Latin America.

How did the Brazilian and Argentine governments finance the war? Some money came from abroad, but an overall analysis of public income and military spending indicates that internal sources of funds were more important than foreign loans. To finance the acquisition of arms and munitions, the Brazilian authorities negotiated a £7,000,000 loan with Rothschilds in 1865, but this large sum represented no more than 15 percent of the total expenses of the Rio treasury in the Paraguayan war.[63] In practice, the considerable task of maintaining the 50,000-man Brazilian army abroad during five years was achieved mainly by printing paper money, issuing internal bonds, and negotiating short-term loans with local banks or with merchants engaged in war-contracting.

In Argentina the rocketing costs of war impelled the government to send

61. Apart from placing three Brazilian refinancing loans (1852, 1859, 1863), Rothschilds also promoted two issues designed specifically for Brazilian state railways (1858 and 1860) totaling £2,800,000. For some interesting sidelights, see Gille, *Histoire de la Maison Rothschild*, 2:410–413, 458–460. For details on the contracts, see Valentim Bouças, *História da dívida externa da Uniao* (Rio de Janeiro, 1946).

62. For comments, see Ferns, *Britain and Argentina*, chap. 10, and Platt, "Foreign Finance in Argentina," pp. 32–35.

63. For a detailed survey of Brazilian finances during the war, see Liberato de Castro Carreira, *História financeira e oçamentaria do Império do Brasil* (Rio de Janeiro, 1889), pp. 381–432. According to a contemporary Buenos Aires newspaper, the five-year Paraguayan war cost the Brazilian government a total of £56,000,000 and resulted in a loss of 168,000 Brazilian troops (*Buenos Aires Standard*, October 1870). J. C. Herken Krauer, "La cobertura de la Guerra de la Triple Alianza por The Times," in *Todo es Historia*, no. 175 (Buenos Aires, 1981).

agents to Europe to solicit funds and to supervise the purchase of uniforms, cannons, and other military materiel. The net proceeds of a £2,000,000 loan, issued by Barings in 1866, proved disappointing. The merchant bankers attempted to sell the securities in the midst of a London financial crisis (sparked by the failure of the Overend Gurney bank) that obliged them to retain most of the Argentine bonds in order to avoid large losses. The final sale, effected in 1868, brought a price disadvantageous to the Argentine government.[64] Meanwhile, in Buenos Aires successive finance ministers managed to cover the huge military expenses with a series of loans granted by the Banco de la Provincia de Buenos Aires, as well as by issuing a flood of promissory notes to officers, soldiers, and purveyors. All told, foreign loans accounted for no more than 20 percent of the funds expended by the Argentine state in this protracted and wretched war.[65]

The enormous financial drain provoked by the military conflict caused a slowdown of most government-sponsored development projects in both nations. Railways suffered most. The first short lines had been built during the 1850s and 1860s by relying on a combination of private capital (mostly British) and state funds. But construction subsequently faltered, and as of 1870 Brazil could claim only a total of 740 kilometers of track in operation, and Argentina could claim just 730 kilometers. When compared with contemporary figures for Canada (4,200 km) or India (7,600 km), the backwardness of the largest South American nations was evident.[66] But after the war, rail construction resumed at a brisk pace. In Brazil most of the capital invested was raised by private capitalists. In Argentina the bulk of the ambitious public works programs undertaken during the Sarmiento administration (1868–74) were financed by the government with foreign loans contracted for this purpose. The money raised in Great Britain was used to construct several state-run railways and major waterworks in the city of Buenos Aires.

The rivalry among British merchant bankers to win a share of the lucrative Argentine business became so intense that the prestigious banking house of Baring Brothers temporarily lost its financial preeminence in the Río de la Plata region. The first and decisive blow was struck by the small

64. The bonds were sold at 72–74 percent of nominal value. For details on Baring's participation, see Platt, "Foreign Finance in Argentina," pp. 34–38.

65. On Argentine loans and war expenditures, see complete statistical charts in Republic of Argentina, *Memoria del Ministerio de Hacienda, 1876* (Buenos Aires, 1877), pp. xiii–xic, xciv–xcvi, ci–ciii.

66. For a comparative survey of Brazilian and Argentine railway development, as well as data on Canadian and Indian rails, see Eduardo Zalduendo, *Libras y rieles: las inversiones británicas para el desarrollo de los ferrocarriles en Argentina, Brasíl, Canadá e India durante el siglo XIX* (Buenos Aires, 1975).

but aggressive Anglo-Spanish financial firm of Cristobal de Murrieta & Company. In 1870 this London merchant bank sold £1,000,000 in external bonds of the provincial government of Buenos Aires. In 1871 it won the bidding on a large £6,000,000 "public works loan" for the national government. And in 1872–74 Murrieta capped its remarkable string of Argentine financial triumphs by convincing the Santa Fé and Entre Ríos provincial authorities that they should be named financial agents for two small but important foreign loans.[67]

In Brazil the firm of N. M. Rothschild kept a tight grasp on the international transactions of the imperial treasury. Rival bankers protested against this monopoly and criticized the *London Times*, denouncing it as the "Jew's-harp," because it boosted the Brazilian stock handled by Rothschilds.[68] But the Rio de Janiero financial authorities rarely complained, and with good reason. Their bond issues in London sold at higher premiums than any other contemporary Latin American securities.[69]

In summary, despite the flurry of international loans taken out by Brazil and Argentina in the early 1870s, their foreign obligations were not as unmanageable as the Peruvian external debt. As a result, the former nations were able to weather the depression of the 1870s without suffering a generalized economic or political collapse.

The Height of the Loan Frenzy, 1870–1873

A review of the international financial transactions of the Latin American states between 1850 and 1873 reveals three stages that have distinct characteristics (see Table 3). The majority of the loans of the 1850s were limited to conversion of old foreign debts (most dating from the 1820s) and therefore did not represent a transfer of new capital to the region. At mid-century, foreign bankers were not yet willing to risk much new money in Latin American ventures, whether public or private. They were intent basically on recovering their old outstanding debts. The only exceptions were two loans taken by the Chilean and Brazilian governments to finance state railways, and a series of small bond issues to finance private railways in Cuba.

67. The 1871 public works loan was used to finance the state-owned railway companies, the Central Norte and the Andino; the Buenos Aires provincial loans of 1870 and 1873 went to pay for the waterworks of the capital; and the two small provincial loans of Entre Ríos and Santa Fé were used to stabilize local finances. For details, see Carlos Marichal, "The State and Economic Development Policies in Argentina, 1868–1880" (Paper presented at the American Historical Association meeting, San Francisco, December 27–29, 1983).

68. Jenks, *The Migration*, p. 399, n. 42.

69. For a comparison of interest rates on Latin American bonds during the nineteenth century, see Carlos Marichal, "Perspectivas históricas sobre el imperialismo financiero en América Latina," in *Economía de América Latina*, no. 4 (Mexico, 1980), pp. 13–44.

During the 1860s the number of *new* Latin American external bond issues multiplied, there being a total of seventeen in this decade. A surprisingly large number were war loans. These included loans for the Chilean and Peruvian navies, then engaged in conflicts with Spanish forces; loans for the Argentine and Brazilian armies during the Paraguayan war; and two spurious loans taken by the empire of Maximilian in Mexico to finance the French occupation army during the years 1863–67.[70]

Finally, in 1870–73, a new and significant shift in Latin American loan operations took place as the bulk of the funds raised abroad were channeled into public works projects, particularly for state railways in Argentina, Chile, Peru, and Central America. The large volume of capital invested in these enterprises can be attributed in good measure to the availability of excess funds in European money markets, but it also mirrored the new "developmentalist" strategies that had become an integral part of the policies of virtually all Latin American governments.

The loans thus fulfilled a varied set of political and economic objectives, including the conversion of debts, the modernization of armies, and the promotion of public works. In this respect the Latin American experience may not have been too dissimilar from what took place in other regions of the world. The professionalization of the military forces was in itself a typical feature of the nation-building efforts of all nineteenth-century states. Similarly, the recognition and conversion of internal and external debts proved to be crucial to the consolidation of parliamentary regimes everywhere. To be more concrete, in Latin America the creation of a stable public credit system was an indispensable instrument to win the allegiance of the powerful merchant and landowning classes as well as to renew capital flows from abroad. Last, but certainly not least, the financing of railways and ports also constituted a key feature of government policies in many other nations—for example, Germany, Belgium, Russia, and Australia—during the second half of the nineteenth century.[71] In this sense the financial policies of the Latin American states reflected a series of broader worldwide trends.

The three years immediately preceding the international crisis of 1873 marked the climax of the loan-contracting business. Virtually all the Latin

---

70. For a stimulating essay on the French banks involved in Mexico, see Geneviève Gille, "Les Capitaux français et l'expédition du Mexique," *Revue d'Histoire Diplomatique* 79 (1965): 193–251.

71. Historical case studies of state intervention in various nations are in Hugh Aitken, ed., *The State and Economic Growth* (New York, 1959), esp. Neil Butlin's essay on Australia in the second half of the nineteenth century. A more general analysis of state investment policies in Europe is Barry Supple, "The State and the Industrial Revolution, 1700–1914," in *Fontana Economic History of Europe*, ed. C. Cipolla (London, 1973), 3:301–357.

American states—with the exceptions of Venezuela, Ecuador, and Mexico—negotiated important credits with the European bankers.[72] The crowd of Latin American agents who flocked to the financial districts of London and Paris were no longer limited to those of the larger, richer states; they now also included official and unofficial representatives of such small and relatively poor republics as Honduras, Guatemala, Costa Rica, Santo Domingo, Haiti, Bolivia, and Paraguay (see Appendix A). Most of the loans they negotiated were aimed at promoting railway construction. The next chapter shows how the misuse of a large portion of these funds played a fundamental role in leading to the bankruptcy of the smaller states after the crisis of 1873.

The desire of Latin American governments to stimulate material improvements was not the only factor responsible for the issue of close to £75,000,000 in external bonds during the early 1870s. An additional and compelling force behind the loan boom was the acute rivalry among European bankers for a share in this highly lucrative if speculative business. The circle of banking companies and speculators engaged in the Latin American loan operations broadened with remarkable speed to include a wide spectrum of British and French merchant banks.

The participation of Parisian bankers in Peruvian finances has already been mentioned. The most important houses engaged in issuing Peruvian bonds were the Société Générale and Dreyfus Frères, but a large number of allied firms also played a part in the huge loans of 1870 and 1872. In Central American finances the cosmopolitan firm of Bischoffsheim & Goldschmidt of Paris, Brussels, and London took a leading role. Meanwhile, in Mexico, under Maximilian, such leading Parisian banks as the Comptoir d'Escompte and the Crédit Mobilier helped Napoleon III with the financing of his military ventures.

Despite the intrusion of the Continental firms, the London merchant banks continued to dominate most of the Latin American loan transactions. The best known were such firms as Rothschilds, Barings, J. S. Morgan, Thomson/Bonar, J. H. Schröder, and Sterns (see Appendix D). They customarily took the largest issues, organizing broad-ranging syndicates in order to guarantee a rapid and successful placement. A secondary roster of financial firms included Murrieta, Knowles & Foster, Robinson, Fleming & Company, and Peter Lawson and Son, which generally had to content themselves with the discards of their more powerful brethren, but were occasionally able to win profitable business. Then there were the no-less-important individual gamblers, such as Edward Hartmont, Albert Grant, or

72. Venezuela defaulted in 1866, Mexico in 1867, and Ecuador in 1868. For additional information see Table 4 in Chapter 4.

Samuel Laing, who played high-stakes poker with any bonds they could lay their hands on.[73]

The activities of the more avaricious financiers tended to make the Latin American loan transactions increasingly speculative and dangerous as they pushed the smaller republics into the vortex of the international money game by providing generous bribes for high-level public officials while at the same time devoting their talents to the creation of artificial markets for the securities with enticing, if misleading, propaganda. The premier banking houses were habitually more conservative, preferring to negotiate with the wealthier, solvent governments, but even so the high profit rates and large commissions stirred competition to a high point.

In summary, all the Latin American states were besieged by the European moneylenders, who urged them into the financial fray. Under the circumstances, it was not surprising that few politicians or bankers took precautions to deal with a possible abrupt change in the international economic climate, so when a major crisis broke in late 1873, virtually all the participants in the debt contest were severely jolted. The golden days of the loan boom were over. A long, wintry decade of depression followed, during which most of the Latin American nations had no alternative but to default and hence to be ousted from the European capital markets.

73. On the activities of these international financial knaves, see W. R. Reader and J. Slinn, *A House in the City: Foster and Braithwaite, 1825–1975* (London, 1980), pp. 70–79, and César A. Herrera, *De Hartmont a Trujillo: estudio para la historia de la deuda pública* (Santo Domingo, 1953), chaps. 1–2.

The First World Debt Crisis

We shall be curious to see whether Bolivia will be more successful than Honduras, Santo Domingo and other of the South American Republics in meeting the interest on loans from which it has obtained no sort of benefit.

—*The Economist*, July 4, 1874

EW CLOUDS obscured the economic horizon of Latin America as the year 1873 began. Throughout the region the commercial and financial boom was still in full swing. Hundreds of sailing vessels and steamers jammed the harbors of Rio de Janeiro, Buenos Aires, Callao, and Valparaíso, swiftly disembarking their cargoes of emigrants from Europe—Italian and Spanish workmen, French and German artisans, British traders—and more slowly unloading crate upon crate of merchandise.[1] Merchant firms busied themselves with the traffic as their agents identified shipments at the customs houses, reviewed bills of lading, and paid fees to ship captains and taxes to port officials. The intense mercantile activity was complemented by bustling construction work: huge new piers and docks in the harbor of Callao, Peru; major drainage projects in Buenos Aires; new water and gas companies as well as port works visibly transforming Santos and Rio de Janeiro.[2]

But the press of business did not limit itself to the ports. Equally striking was the movement and activity generated by construction of the first railways in the hinterland. Across the Argentine pampas the 1870s saw thousands of Spanish and Italian laborers laying down the tracks of several competing companies. In the inland valleys of Brazil, even greater numbers of blacks, mulattoes and white peasants hammered ties and rails into the red clay soils of the coffee districts of São Paulo and Minas Gerais. Far to the west, on the towering Andes, tens of thousands of Chilean *rotos*, Bolivian *yanaconas*, and Peruvian *serranos*, toiled to complete the Oroya railway,

1. During 1870–73, Europeans emigrated in large numbers to Brazil, Chile, Uruguay, and above all to Argentina; the average yearly number of immigrants arriving at the port of Buenos Aires rose from 5,000 in the 1850s to 20,000 in the 1860s and to more than 40,000 in the early 1870s (*Extracto estadístico de la República Argentina* [Buenos Aires, 1916], pp. 589ff.).

2. On the Callao docks, the most important contemporary Latin American port works, see Mulhall, *The English in South America*, pp. 523–524. On the Buenos Aires waterworks of the early 1870s see ibid., pp. 521–522. On urban modernization in Brazil, see Graham, *Britain and the Onset*, chaps. 4 and 7.

the Juliaca-Cuzco route, and the Arequipa-Puno line. Even in the small states of Central America railway construction proceeded apace. In Honduras, British contractor Charles Waring pushed his iron road fifty-seven miles into the interior from the coastal town of Puerto Caballos, while in Costa Rica North American entrepreneur Minor Keith hired 2,000 Chinese coolies and Jamaican laborers to build the route from the Caribbean port of Puerto Limón to the highland centers of Cartago and San José.[3]

Yet like all cycles of prosperity, the Latin American boom was not destined to last indefinitely. The first news of an impending slowdown in the international economy came with the mail steamers that anchored in the Atlantic ports of the subcontinent in early June 1873; the newspapers from Europe spoke of the crash that had taken place on the Vienna Stock Exchange on May 8 and the subsequent spread of the financial panic to the principal money markets of Germany.[4] Preliminary reports were disquieting, but it was reassuring that neither the British nor the French exchanges had been seriously disturbed and that recent Latin American loan issues continued to sell briskly. Only in September—when word of a dramatic collapse of the New York stock market arrived—did fading optimism on both sides of the Atlantic completely dissipate.[5] It now became clear that a major international crisis had commenced.

Within a matter of months, trade between Europe and Latin America began to fall off. At the same time, the export of capital from England and France ceased as stock exchanges weakened and as banking houses began calling in their domestic and foreign bills. The commercial and financial retrenchment not only produced a harvest of mercantile failures in Latin America but also sharply reduced government income. As a result, a succession of states declared themselves bankrupt and suspended payments on their external debts.

3. On railway construction in Peru, Argentina, and Brazil, see previous references in Chapter 3, footnotes 39, 43, and 66. A description of Keith's railway-building activities in Costa Rica is in Watt Stewart, *Keith and Costa Rica: A Biographical Study of Minor Cooper Keith* (Albuquerque, 1964).

4. For a brief but illuminating evaluation of Vienna's financial development in the 1860s and 1870s, see D.C.M. Platt, *Foreign Finance in Continental Europe and the USA* (London, 1984), chap. 4. The number of failures that took place as a result of the Viennese crash was astonishing; between 1873 and 1878, half the Austrian banks closed, and 400 of the 800 Austrian joint-stock companies went bankrupt (M. Sokal and O. Rosenberg, "The Banking System of Austria," in *Foreign Banking Systems*, ed. H. Parker Willis [New York, 1929], pp. 106–109).

5. The most resounding banking failure in the United States was that of the firm of Jay Cooke & Company of New York and Philadelphia. For a vivid description, see Mathew Josephson, *The Robber Barons* (New York, 1962), pp. 93–96, 165–170.

The Causes of Depression

There seems to be no doubt that the commercial and financial upheaval in Latin America was triggered by external factors, but it is worth asking why this crisis was so widespread and intense. One answer is that by the 1870s the international monetary and banking system had become much more complex and closely interrelated. World finances were no longer under the sway of just one or two dominant money markets; they could now be better described as a constellation of various primary and secondary financial centers, all interdependent. Thus, in contrast to previous nineteenth-century financial debacles, which had been ignited by panic on the London or Paris money markets, the crisis of 1873 was triggered by distress in Central Europe and the United States. This development reflected the rapid process of integration of capitalism on a global scale. Severe banking problems in one corner of the world were now transmitted with considerable speed to distant financial centers, thus producing a generalized economic short-circuit.[6]

The steep decline in commodity and stock prices in most capitalist nations, as well as ensuing bank and industrial failures, inaugurated an era of deep and widespread economic troubles. In the United States the high rates of unemployment stirred up popular discontent, including numerous strikes and mass demonstrations. At the same time, the collapse of many large enterprises led to a restructuring of the major financial and industrial groups.[7] In Europe the crisis at first appeared to be less severe, but by the end of the decade it became clear that the recession had actually been transmuted into what historians have called the "Great Depression of 1873–96."[8]

Contemporary writers, as well as theorists of a later age, attributed the economic calamities of the 1870s to two principal factors. For Juglar, Kondratieff, and Lewis, the prime force underlying the breakdown was the de-

6. Kindleberger suggests that there was a close connection between the financial panics in Central Europe and the United States. See Charles Kindleberger, *Manias, Panics, and Crashes: A History of Financial Crises* (New York, 1978), p. 132. We do know that much German capital had been invested in American rails (e.g., in Cooke's favored Northern Pacific), but there is little documentary evidence on the presumed flight of capital back to Germany.

7. The argument that the collapse of Cooke & Co. opened the way for J. P. Morgan's assumption of the role as leading international banker of the United States from the 1870s onward is in Lewis Corey, *The House of Morgan* (New York, 1930), pp. 122–127.

8. The "Great Depression of 1873–96" has been extensively discussed in such classic articles as J. T. Walton Newbold, "The Beginnings of the World Crisis, 1873–1896," *Economic History* 2, no. 7 (January 1932): 425–441; and A. E. Musson, "The Great Depression in Britain, 1873–1896," *Journal of Economic History* 19, no. 2 (1959): 199–228. For a revisionist interpretation, see S. B. Saul, *The Myth of the Great Depression* (London, 1969).

cline of primary and industrial commodities on a world scale; this trend produced a drop in the profit rates of key economic sectors in both the more-advanced nations and the less-developed nations.[9] For Giffen, Schumpeter, and Rostow the ultimate cause of the crisis came from the slowdown in the most powerful and "internationalized" branch of economic activity—railway construction.[10] The advances achieved in the years preceding the crisis of 1873 had been nothing less than spectacular. In the United States, rail mileage had doubled since the end of the Civil War, from 55,000 to more than 100,000 miles; in Russia, more than 20,000 miles of railway, had been built from the late 1860s; and throughout Europe the railway mania continued to incite investors to pour their savings into dozens of new companies, both at home and abroad. Subsequently, the stock market slumps produced a dramatic fall in the companies' paper profits and an equally abrupt decline of investment in the field. As a result, railway magnates and contractors around the world froze construction in progress, laid off workers, and canceled supply contracts with metallurgical and mining industries.

But the downturn in commodity prices and the drop in railway construction were not the only catalysts of depression. The financial tidal wave caused by the Franco-Prussian War of 1870 also played a critical part. Following Bismarck's unforeseen and stunning triumph over the army of Napoleon III, the new French government headed by Louis-Adolphe Thiers had been obliged to pay a huge indemnity of 5,000,000,000 francs (£200 million) to Germany. The leading banks of both London and Paris organized a massive rescue operation, raised the money in a remarkably short time, and shipped the gold off to Berlin. These indemnity loans—the largest of all financial transactions of the nineteenth century—channeled a massive flow of capital into the economies of central Europe yet also spurred an unexpected degree of speculation, thereby destabilizing the financial markets of western Europe. As Newbold argued in a classic analysis: "Thus we can see that there is very strong ground for supposing that what started off the great crisis which commenced in 1873 was the ever more

9. Two classic studies that analyze the impact of the price fall of the 1870s are Juglar, *Des Crises commerciales*, pp. 390–433; and Nicolai Kondratiev, *The Long Wave Cycle* (New York, 1984), which is the first English translation of the original Russian edition published in Moscow in 1927. A more recent analysis is W. A. Lewis, *Growth and Fluctuations, 1870–1914* (Boston, 1978).

10. Giffen was one of the most respected contemporary financial writers. See Robert Giffen, "The Liquidations of 1873–76," in a volume of his essays entitled *Economic Inquiries and Studies* (London, 1904), 1:98–120. Schumpeter's views are in his much-cited *Business Cycles: A Theoretical, Historical, and Statistical Analysis of the Capitalist Process* (New York, 1939), 1:336–397. See also Walt W. Rostow, *The World Economy: History and Prospect* (Austin, 1978), pp. 153–156.

profound unsettlement of the short-term money markets by the movements of gold and the transfers of balances from France to Germany via London."[11]

In summary, a review of the major factors that sparked the financial storm of 1873 suggests that equal attention should be paid to the long-term forces that molded the dynamics of capitalism—such as the worldwide railway construction cycle of 1850–73—as well as to the short-term shocks that produced abrupt upheavals in international capital transactions, such as those arising from the Franco-Prussian War. Moreover, by the middle of the 1870s the crisis had spread to the less-developed nations of the capitalist "periphery," engendering a world depression of unprecedented severity.

THE BIRTH OF AN INTERNATIONAL DEBT CRISIS

Although the contemporary economic upheaval had its roots in the financial and commercial fluctuations of the industrial nations of the North Atlantic, its impact soon made itself felt with particular virulence in the non-industrialized regions of the Near East and Latin America. In these regions the depression of the 1870s can best be defined as a "debt crisis," because the overriding cause of the economic turmoil there stemmed from an excessive accumulation of foreign debts by governments. By 1876 the Ottoman Empire, Egypt, Greece, Tunisia, and eight Latin American states had defaulted, and the prospects of repayment appeared remote.[12]

The largest and most notorious of these debtors were Turkey (the seat of the Ottoman Empire) and Egypt, a semi-autonomous satellite of the former. By 1875 the Turkish sultan and the Egyptian khedive had each managed to saddle their respective administrations with external obligations approaching £100,000,000. Because no other nations outside Europe could boast an equivalent feat, this merits a brief commentary before proceeding to a more detailed analysis of the financial quandary of the Latin American states. Indeed, it was the simultaneous default of Turkey and Egypt that finally forced contemporaries to recognize the weighty and unpredictable consequences of the "foreign loan collapse."[13]

11. Newbold, "The Beginnings of the World Crisis," p. 439.

12. For two contemporary surveys of the international debt crisis, see Dudley Baxter, "The Recent Progress of National Debts," *Journal of the Statistical Society* 36 (March 1874): 1–20; and Hyde Clarke, "On the Debts of Sovereign and Quasi-Sovereign States Owing by Foreign Countries," *Journal of the Statistical Society* 41 (June 1878): 249–347.

13. Giffen wrote: "No doubt in 1873 . . . the collapse of the foreign loan financing had been foreshadowed; but the anticipatory events of that year were in themselves comparatively unimportant, so that down to 1875 what chiefly happened was a succession of monetary and commercial crises in countries dependent on England, but from which England by comparison escaped. In 1875 these crises were succeeded by a crisis in England itself of very great inten-

The implications of the international debt crisis took some time to sink in. During 1873 and 1874 the European financial press did not judge the situation of the Turkish treasury to be particularly disturbing, despite the signs of distress in the money markets. But by 1875 the Turkish bond market collapsed, and few British, French, or German bankers seemed disposed to throw more money after bad.[14] The day of reckoning had finally arrived. Jenks dramatically described the situation:

On October 7, 1875, the Turkish ministry, confronted with an indebtedness of 200 million pounds, incurred in only 20 years, beset by rebellion in Bulgaria, insurrection in Bosnia and Herzegovina, disorders in Crete, menaced with external war and palace revolution, listened to the disinterested [*sic*] advice of the Russian ambassador. It announced that for the next five years interest coupons would be paid one half in specie and one half in 5% bonds.[15]

The news of the Ottoman bankruptcy also provoked a precipitous decline in the price of Egyptian bonds on the London and Paris stock exchanges. To repay his creditors, the khedive drastically increased local taxes, pressing ever more brutally on the toiling Egyptian peasantry. At the same time, he sought new loans to pay for the old, and in late 1875 he determined to sell the Suez Canal for less than £5,000,000, a mere fraction of the original cost. Despite this extreme sacrifice, the Egyptian state remained in desperate straits, aggravated by the demands of the European powers that it repay all outstanding debts.[16] The bitter upshot of this contest came in 1882, when the British navy bombarded Alexandria, an event shortly followed by the military occupation of the entire country.

The collection of international debts had become a hopelessly complicated and indeed a bloody business. The European bankers had entangled the Near Eastern rulers into a financial web so intractable that the only options left to them lay either in soliciting new loans or in proclaiming outright default. When the latter option was actually adopted, the chancelleries and military establishments of Great Britain and France began to ap-

sity . . . the whole culminating in the financial disorders of the foreign loan collapses, which will probably form in after years the most conspicuous feature of the whole series of liquidations"(cited in Clarke, "On the Debts," p. 326).

14. A classic study on the Ottoman loans is David Blaidsell, *European Financial Control in the Ottoman Empire* (New York, 1929). See also Sevket Pamuk, "The Ottoman Empire in the Great Depression of 1873–1896," *Journal of Economic History* 44 (1984): 107–118.

15. Jenks, *Migration*, p. 320.

16. On contemporary Egyptian finance, the most illuminating work is Landes, *Bankers and Pashas*. Useful references are also in Jean Bouvier, "Les Intérêts financiers et la question d'Egypte, 1875–76," *Revue Historique*, no. 224 (1960): 75–104.

ply pressure to demonstrate that the bankers' bills would be backed up by guns.

In Latin America the crisis of the 1870s also caused extensive damage as a series of mercantile and financial squalls on a local scale were followed by a string of defaults. But in contrast to the situation in the Near East, there was no military intervention, a fact that may be attributed to Latin America's less important "strategic" role in European power politics. Hence the external coercion directed against the governments of the region was limited essentially to economic measures. The first response to the suspension of payments (which began in 1873 and multiplied in years following) was a sharp fall in the stock exchange quotations of the bonds of the defaulting nations. A second and more premeditated reaction on the part of the bankers was a freeze on new foreign loans, excluding the bankrupt states from foreign capital markets but not thereby forcing them to reimburse the angry bondholders. The third and inevitable step consisted in the launching of a series of aggressive campaigns by the bondholder committees to pressure the Latin American governments, the British Foreign Office, and the British Parliament for a favorable resolution to their claims.[17]

But not all Latin American states of the period defaulted. Several of the larger and more prosperous nations continued to meet their external financial obligations on a regular basis throughout the crisis years and, in some instances, even managed to raise new short-term or long-term loans. Therefore, a balanced analysis of the contemporary debt crisis requires us to distinguish between the degrees of financial penury afflicting the countries of the subcontinent.

ECONOMIC RECESSION AND DEFAULT IN LATIN AMERICA

The mercantile and financial crisis battered all the Latin American nations, yet its intensity and duration were not uniform. For some states, such as Peru and the Central American republics, the economic downswing led to a profound depression and subsequently to default and complete ostracism from foreign money markets. More fortunate countries, such as Brazil, Argentina, and Chile, suffered acutely but were able to weather the storm without suspending payments.[18]

The combined trade statistics of Latin America suggest the widespread

17. The complex and prolonged campaigns of the bondholders are documented in detail in the annual reports of the Corporation of Foreign Bondholders, published from 1873 (cited hereafter as CFBH).

18. For a comparative review, see Carlos Marichal, "La crisis de 1873 en América Latina: algunos comentarios sobre los casos de Argentina, Chile y Perú," *Iztapalapa, Revista de Ciencias Sociales* (Mexico) 3, no. 6 (1982): 59–90.

worsening of circulation and production. The data on trade with Great Britain—the region's most important commercial partner—indicate that exports from Latin America dropped by 37 percent between 1872 and 1878 and that imports fell just as sharply, by 37 percent in the years 1872–76 (see Figures 4 and 5).[19] In conjunction with the steady price decline of most primary and mineral commodities—for example, sugar, coffee, wool, copper, and silver—the drop in trade provoked numerous mercantile and banking failures, the collapse of dozens of recently established joint-stock companies, and a sharp reduction of government income.

The three wealthiest nations—Argentina, Brazil, and Chile—avoided default because of a relatively high level of export earnings. Even so, their respective finance ministries had to make severe adjustments. The impact of the crisis on these three countries was not synchronized, however.

In Argentina the European economic troubles caused a disruption of trade beginning in late 1873 and resulted in the downfall of a large number of Buenos Aires trading firms.[20] In 1874 two local banks, the Banco Belgo/Alemán and the Banco Mercantil, collapsed; the following year a pair of state-owned banks, the Banco de la Provincia de Santa Fé and the Banco Nacional, approached the brink of bankruptcy. By mid-1876 the private sector of the economy had begun to recover, but the government confronted a fiscal crisis as a result of the decline in import-tax revenues. The president of the republic, Nicolás Avellaneda, proclaimed that the Argentine people would willingly suffer privations and even hunger in order to sustain the international credit and reputation of the national government. The austerity program he methodically implemented was warmly applauded by the British financial community, as attested by an important short-term loan advanced by the London banking house of Baring Brothers.[21] This loan allowed the Buenos Aires Ministry of Finance to meet its scheduled payments on the foreign debt. Subsequently, rising export receipts provided sufficient surpluses of hard currency to meet commitments with European bondholders.

In Brazil the effects of the crisis proved barely perceptible during the years 1873–75, because foreign trade remained remarkably buoyant. Only

19. The statistical data is summarized in Platt, *Latin America*, appendix I–II, pp. 316–323.

20. In 1877 Mulhall affirmed that "in the River Plate alone more than 400 commercial houses failed in the last four years" (Mulhall, *The English in South America*, p. 528). For a recent analysis of the crisis of the 1870s in Argentina see José Carlos Chiaramonte, *Nacionalismo y liberalismo económicos en Argentina, 1860–1880* (Buenos Aires, 1971), pp. 91–120.

21. Information on the Argentine short-term loans negotiated abroad can be gleaned from government accounts with Baring Brothers and Murrieta & Co. published in the appendixes to Republic of Argentina, *Memoria del Ministerio de Hacienda*, for the years 1875 and 1876.

in 1876 did commercial depression shake Rio de Janeiro, Santos, São Paulo, and the other commercial centers of the vast nation.[22] In the contemporary Brazilian banking world, the most resounding failure was that of the powerful firm of the Baron de Mauá, which had offices throughout the nation as well as at Montevideo and London.[23] Yet Mauá's difficulties did not unleash a general financial panic. The stability of the imperial government continued to inspire the confidence of local and foreign capitalists, a fact underlined by the excellent relations maintained with its official bankers, the house of N. M. Rothschild and Sons of London.[24] Despite the depressed state of the markets, this influential banking concern managed to place a major Brazilian bond issue on the London Stock Exchange in 1875, an operation that guaranteed that the government would continue its service on its relatively large external debt without interruption.

In Chile the crisis wreaked greater havoc, successively battering agricultural production, industry, mining, and finally banking.[25] In 1874 cereal exports began to fall, provoking widespread hardship among the peasants employed on the haciendas of the Central Valley. The agrarian depression was accompanied by economic recession in the principal cities and in the mining districts of the north. As a result, many small commercial and manufacturing firms temporarily folded, and approximately twenty-five of the leading industrial, construction, and mining joint-stock companies collapsed. The weakening of local money markets and the decline of foreign trade simultaneously scorched the Valparaíso and Santiago banks, wrecking several of the smaller firms; in 1877 the Banco Thomas failed, and in 1878 the Banco del Pobre closed its doors. During 1878 the drain of gold became so acute that the bank reserves of the largest Chilean financial institution, the Banco Nacional de Chile, were wiped out and the government declared its bank notes inconvertible.

But the Chilean authorities did not respond passively to the turmoil. They quickly approved new tariff laws to reduce imports and to protect domestic manufactures and at the same time ratified a sweeping fiscal reform, including direct taxes on property.[26] The results were encouraging

22. Brazilian exports to Great Britain were estimated at £7,400,000 in 1875, £5,200,000 in 1876, £6,300,000 in 1877, and £4,700,000 in 1879. The 1875 figure marked the peak in Brazilian-British trade until the year 1905. See Platt, *Latin America*, appendix II, pp. 320–322.

23. On the Mauá failure, see Marchant, *Viscount Mauá*, pp. 202–203, 228–233.

24. On the role of the Rothschilds in Brazilian finance, see Bouças, *História da dívida externa*, and Gille, *Histoire de la Maison Rothschild*, 2:410–460.

25. The complex nature of the Chilean economic crisis has been described by Sater, "Chile and the World Depression," pp. 67–89.

26. Sater argues that the tax reforms would have inaugurated a new and more industrial phase in Chilean economic development, but that the acquisition of the rich Peruvian nitrate

but short-lived. The war that broke out in 1879 between Chile and Peru radically modified the preexisting political and economic situation. Paradoxically, the military conflict cut short the crisis in Chile by reactivating local agriculture and industry and above all by facilitating the conquest and exploitation of the rich nitrate fields that had formerly been under Peruvian jurisdiction. Indeed, for Chile this imperial victory inaugurated a decade of rapid mercantile, mining, and financial expansion, consolidating the nation's credit standing among international bankers and investors.

The picture was radically different in the smaller Latin American states that found themselves obliged to default: Honduras and Santo Domingo suspended payments in 1873, Costa Rica and Paraguay in 1874, Bolivia and Guatemala in 1875, and Uruguay in 1876. In all these cases perhaps the most important cause of economic disaster was the excess weight of external debts. In all probability the smaller Latin American republics would not have been so gravely affected by the world crisis of the 1870s had it not been for the great foreign loan operations that threatened to crush their respective treasuries.

Before the outbreak of the panic of 1873, most of the smaller countries mentioned had experienced significant improvements in their economic situation. Given such relatively promising circumstances, there existed some justification for European bankers and investors to believe that a few small foreign loans could be repaid in hard currency. On the other hand, there was no reason to expect that they could recover large loans or investments. Yet the London and Paris financiers were apparently interested less in security than in obtaining quick and voluminous speculative gains by the sale of large amounts of bonds. Nonetheless, by 1873 the bankers had managed to foist one or more large loans on each of these tiny republics. They therefore engaged them to cover a foreign debt service that annually represented between 50 percent and 200 percent of total export earnings and frequently was greater than the national budget.[27] The consequence could be none other than default.

A similar if somewhat less acute dilemma confronted nations that had suspended payments before the crisis: Venezuela, Ecuador, and Mexico.[28]

---

deposits (obtained as a result of the war conquests of 1878–82) once again lent strength to the old export model (ibid., pp. 98–99).

27. Precise fiscal data for each of the small Latin American nations is relatively hard to come by. In the case of Costa Rica, government revenues averaged approximately £500,000 in the crisis years of 1875–77, whereas the debt service (including interest and amortization) was about £250,000. In the case of Honduras, the debt service as of 1874 was almost 200 percent of total government revenues. See Fenn, *Compendium* (1883 ed.), pp. 404–410, 477–479.

28. The Mexican government had formally suspended payments in 1867 and did not renew

The only possibility of renewing payments on their external debts lay in a sustained increase in export income, but in the mid-1870s this appeared unlikely, given the international contraction of markets and prices.

The most spectacular financial collapse in Latin America during the 1870s was that of Peru, the nation with the largest foreign debt. For the British and French bankers, Peru had been an ideal client because it had not one but several valuable export commodities with which to pay the interest on its loans: guano, cotton, sugar, and nitrates. Furthermore, in contrast to many of its sister republics, Peru did not experience an extreme mercantile slump in the years 1873–75. Guano shipments did tend to decline, but the surge of production in the nitrate districts and on the sugar plantations compensated.[29] Thus, two years after the onset of the crisis abroad, this Andean nation appeared to be riding the financial storm with remarkable poise, a performance that reinforced the impression that it had managed to escape the worst effects of the international recession (see Figure 6).

The first clear-cut evidence of the grave difficulties soon to be confronted by the Peruvian economy came with an announcement on August 1, 1875, of the virtual bankruptcy of the Banco Nacional del Perú, a private institution with close ties to the government. The finance minister resolved to confer with the directors of the other leading banks of the capital, because all the banks suffered from similar if somewhat less severe problems. The most disturbing was the scarceness of gold and bills of exchange caused by the decline in guano exports.[30]

On September 10 the treasury officials and the bankers signed an agreement by which the government allowed the banks to increase their note issue by some 8,000,000 *soles* in exchange for lending this paper money to the government with the object of liquidating a number of outstanding internal debts. In addition, the banks were encouraged to assume a leading role in the new state program of nationalization of the nitrate business, which was expected to replace guano as the major source of public revenues. The pact established that the state would hand over bonds and certif-

remittances on the "English debt" until 1884. Venezuela suspended payments in 1866. Ecuador stopped payments in 1868.

29. The value of guano exports fell from £2,418,000 in 1873 to £1,631,000 in 1875. In contrast, nitrate exports rose from £3,679,000 to £5,113,000; sugar exports also climbed steeply, from £443,000 in 1873 to £1,273,000 in 1875. The real mercantile crunch came after 1876. For statistics, see Heraclio Bonilla, "La coyuntura comercial del siglo XIX en el Perú," *Desarrollo Económico* 46, no. 12 (1972): tables 1–2.

30. The finance minister's report of 1875 indicates that the Peruvian government believed it had short-term liquidity problems, not severe structural problems. For transcripts of the pertinent government documents, see Emilio Dancuart, *Anales de la hacienda pública del Perú: Historia y legislación fiscal de la República* (Lima, 1908), vol. 10 (1875–78), pp. 261–292, and vol. 11 (1877–79), pp. 9–81.

FIGURE 6.

MARKET PRICES OF PERUVIAN, ARGENTINE, AND BRAZILIAN EXTERNAL BONDS ON THE
LONDON STOCK EXCHANGE, 1870–1880. BASED ON MEAN HIGHEST AND LOWEST PRICES.

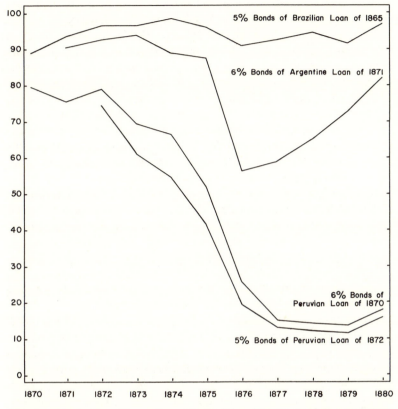

(Data from Charles Fenn, *Compendium of the English and Foreign Funds* [London, 1883],
pp. 354–385, 523.)

icates to the nitrate producers in exchange for their properties. Nationalization would be mitigated by allowing the Lima banks to serve as local
consignees of nitrate production, while several foreign firms—such as Antony Gibbs—handled the worldwide distribution of the precious mineral
fertilizer.[31] In practice, however, the credit crunch did not allow the Finance Ministry to take over the mines. As a result, most nitrate entrepreneurs did not sell out, but continued to administer their companies, selling

31. Robert Greenhill and Rory Miller, "The Peruvian Government and the Nitrate Trade,
1873–1879," *JLAS* 5, no. 1 (1973): 119–131.

109

the produce to the state. At the same time, the Lima banking firms assumed a key role in the administration of this quasi-public monopoly, which helps explain their survival until 1879.

In spite of these mercantile and financial reforms, the Peruvian government abruptly suspended service on its foreign debt in January 1876; it did not resume payments for more than a decade. The default was the result of two parallel developments. On the one hand, the Peruvian debt had increased astronomically in recent years; on the other hand, the main source of state income, guano revenues, had been subcontracted to the firm of Dreyfus Frères of Paris. Dreyfus promised to cover the debt service in exchange for the guano monopoly, but it warned the Lima ministers in July 1875 that the interest on the huge external debt would no longer be paid if guano sales remained depressed. Six months later the inevitable suspension took place. The foreign bondholders were informed that, because of differences among the guano contractors and the Peruvian authorities, no further payments would be forthcoming.[32] Consequently the London quotations of Peruvian bonds fell precipitously (see Figure 6). Various elaborate attempts were made to resolve the financial tangle, but none could revive prosperity.

THE SELECT COMMITTEE ON FOREIGN LOANS

The Peruvian default—coincident with the defaults of Turkey and Egypt—marked the climax of the world debt crisis. By the year 1876 fifteen non-European nations had suspended payments on almost £300,000,000 of foreign securities. The agitation of the bondholders now reached a peak, although since 1873 financial circles throughout Europe had been well aware of the potentially explosive denouement. Investors, however, initially paid greater attention to the news of financial disturbance in the smallest debtor countries of Latin America than to the more ominous if less perceptible evidence of potential bankruptcy in Turkey, Egypt, or Peru. They were not altogether mistaken, at least in the short run. After all, the first defaulters were precisely the little nations—Honduras, Santo Domingo, Costa Rica, and Paraguay—whereas the big international borrowers temporarily managed to steer clear of default by negotiating several huge rescue loans.

During 1874 and most of 1875, the British financial press spent a great deal of time arguing that the growing instability on Lombard Street had been caused by excess speculation in the bonds of a number of insolvent republics in Central and South America. The value of these bonds had begun to fall as a result of defaults in 1872 and 1873 (see Figure 7). The

32. There is a detailed discussion of the Peruvian default in Wynne, *State Insolvency*, 2:121–170; and in Palacios Moreyra, *La deuda anglo peruana*, chaps. 4 and 5.

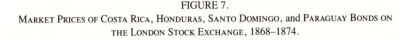

FIGURE 7.

Market Prices of Costa Rica, Honduras, Santo Domingo, and Paraguay Bonds on the London Stock Exchange, 1868–1874.

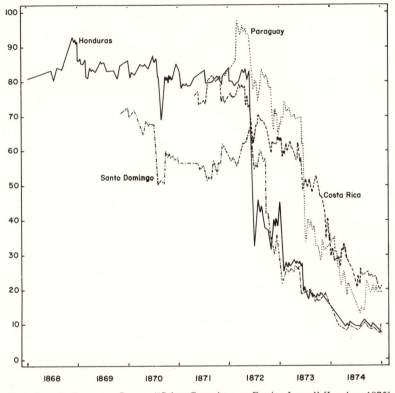

(Data from Parliamentary Papers, "Select Committee on Foreign Loans" [London, 1875], vol. 11.)

bondholder committees demanded an official inquiry into the matter, hoping for some kind of telling police action on the part of the Royal Navy in order to submit the offending governments to the established and presumably sacred norms of international credit transactions. But the British Foreign Office did not appear disposed to intervene, given the small economic stakes involved and the nonstrategic character of the states in default. Parliament proved more interested, apparently because several members of the House of Commons felt that a public airing of loan scandals might encourage legislation to supervise the operations conducted on the great London Stock Exchange.

In early March 1875 the Select Committee on Foreign Loans, organized

111

by the British Parliament, began hearings that continued through June. During this time a broad array of bankers, brokers, contractors, speculators, and even clerks were questioned in depth on the mechanics of the loan business.[33] By focusing on the bond issues of only four nations—Costa Rica, Honduras, Paraguay, and Santo Domingo (see Figure 7)—the committee avoided discussion of the largest financial scandals of the day, thereby eluding a confrontation with the most powerful members of the London banking community. But there is also no question that the voluminous parliamentary report shed much light on the mysterious ways in which foreign loans were managed and/or mismanaged.

The Latin American loans investigated were among the smaller financial affairs of the era; they had only a marginal impact on the world depression. As case studies, however, they are illustrative of the methods bankers, speculators, and politicians used to enrich themselves at the expense of the gullible if avaricious European bondholders and of the virtually defenseless peoples of the small debtor republics. A brief review of the practices disclosed provides an "inside" view of the conduct and motives of the principal actors involved in the international bond business.

From a general point of view, what does the report tell us about the protagonists of the loan deals? It demonstrates that there were four main groups engaged in these highly complex and cosmopolitan financial undertakings. The first group was composed of government officials of the Latin American states seeking funds abroad. In most instances the political elite sought foreign gold for what could be considered productive purposes, such as construction of local railways; this was the case with the Costa Rica and Honduras loans. In other instances the objective was simply deficit-financing, as occurred with the Paraguayan and Santo Domingo bond issues. But regardless of publicly advertised goals, politicians frequently intended to promote private aims by taking a percentage of the profits to be reaped from the securities abroad or, alternatively, by obtaining "gratuities" from the entrepreneurs engaged in the business contracts derived from the loans.[34]

The entrepreneurs, generally public works contractors, constituted a second group of individuals interested in the negotiation of foreign loans. Often they took the initiative in suggesting the opportuneness of raising money through the European capital markets in order to finance particular public works programs. For example, the railroad firm of Charles Waring (active in Honduras) and that of Henry Meiggs (operating in Costa Rica as

33. *Parliamentary Papers*, "Loans to Foreign States" (Reports from Committees), vol. 11, (London, 1875) (hereafter *Parl. Papers*, "Loans").

34. Some insights on political graft derived from the Latin American loans are in ibid., but in most instances it is difficult to document such practices. An exception is the Costa Rica loan of 1870, because President Guardia publicly acknowledged and defended his "commissions." See footnote 55 in this chapter.

well as Peru) used the proceeds of the bonds to cover construction costs on the railways they were building and to pay for importing expensive capital goods—steel rails, locomotives, and so forth. Such contractors usually concentrated on the engineering aspects of their business, but they were not averse to speculating in the sale of the same bonds with which they were paid.[35]

Nonetheless, the issuance and distribution of the securities remained the responsibility of the community of bankers and brokers at London and Paris. Their aim invariably was to collect commissions from client governments as well as to turn a profit on the "spread" between the price they paid for the bonds and the price at which they were able to sell them. Furthermore, in most nineteenth-century Latin American loans, an additional and frequently stupendous source of gain stemmed from the reception and disbursement of the loan proceeds by the bankers. The degree of fraud arising from the maladministration of these funds sometimes reached astonishing proportions, as the parliamentary investigation conclusively demonstrated. Premier banking houses like Barings and Rothschilds (which considered themselves above such unorthodox manipulations) attributed this to the activities of second-rate and unscrupulous firms.[36]

Finally, a fourth and large group of individuals directly involved were the investors who purchased bonds. Those acquiring Latin American securities formed a varied cast of characters, including wealthy capitalists as well as "country clergymen, widows, poor professional men and tradesmen who have got a little money to invest." After default the bondholders inevitably protested that the bankers had misled them into placing their hard-won savings in spurious stocks. Yet, as virtually all the witnesses before the Select Committee testified, the smaller Latin American loans were known to be highly speculative. As Charles Lewis, M.P., affirmed: "I have no hesitation whatever in saying, from what I know, that the public have made the Stock Exchange a great gambling house, especially in regard to transactions in unallotted stock and shares . . . and in all these South American Republic loans, the whole of the dealings have been gambling transactions, or for the purpose of rigging the market."[37]

The small investors, nevertheless, frequently did not have access to re-

35. Charles Waring, e.g., was paid for his railway work in Honduras with bonds he sold through the speculator Lefevre. Waring was also heavily engaged in the sale of Paraguayan bonds, even though he had no railway interests there. For Waring's testimony, see *Parl. Papers*, "Loans," pp. 74–82, 195–204.

36. Such arguments were not altogether misleading. The first witness called before the select committee was George Henry White, member of Baring Brothers for forty years and a specialist in foreign loans; he explained that Barings never took more than 2 percent as commission for the issue of the bonds and disbursement of the proceeds (ibid., pp. 1–4).

37. Ibid., pp. 210–211.

liable information on the real resources of the country issuing the bonds, and they were rarely privy to the specifics of the contracts drawn up between the issuing bank and the government. The bankers resolutely refused to divulge this information, because they feared, logically, that the market might be weakened if it became known that they were gouging the treasuries of the very foreign governments whose bonds they were promoting.[38] As a result, investors tended to act on the basis of alluring tips rather than on facts, thereby intensifying the speculative character of the bond deals. When asked to explain the cause of the speculative fever, no less an authority than Nathaniel de Rothschild, banker and member of Parliament, told the committee that the reason was deceptively simple: "I should say that the disease is the desire of people to get a high rate of interest for their money."[39]

These desires could be richly fulfilled with the 13 percent real interest rates offered, for example, by Honduras 1870 bonds. But what happened when the Central American government defaulted? As prospects for repayment evaporated, the bondholders asked what had become of their monies. The debtor states could usually justifiably answer that they had never seen more than a fraction of the original loan proceeds and that they were equally mystified.

A central question remains: who benefited and who lost from the loan transactions? The money did not simply disappear. Some went into the pockets of bankers; some went to a variety of financial speculators, agents, and politicians; and the remainder went to contractors and merchants who had extensive dealings with the state in question. The exact proportion of disbursement can be determined only through a case-by-case study of individual loans, and only a vast research effort can determine the precise circumstances attending all the Latin American loans of the 1870s. For the present and more limited purpose, it is sufficient to comment on some of the financial operations highlighted by the hearings of the Select Committee on Foreign Loans.

Two examples of highly speculative but partially productive issues were the Costa Rica and Honduras railway loans. In the case of Costa Rica, a tiny country with barely 145,000 inhabitants, two large bond transactions were pushed onto the London Stock Exchange in 1870 and 1872. The ostensible purpose of the loans was to finance a railway that would stimulate

---

38. The European financial press acted in collusion with the bankers. Cairncross notes: "The individual investor simply had not the information on which to base a sound judgement. . . . It was estimated that only 25 out of 186 financial journals had any claims to independence . . . and only 2 or 3 of these could be said to be thoroughly honest in their comments on new issues" (Alec Cairncross, *Home and Foreign Investment, 1870–1913* [Cambridge, U.K., 1953], p. 224).

39. *Parl. Papers*, "Loans," p. 266.

coffee exports. The Costa Rican president, General Tomás Guardia, contacted the famous railway builder Henry Meiggs, then resident at Lima, and asked him to take responsibility for the project. Meiggs accepted the task of building the line and soon dispatched his nephew, Minor Keith, to supervise the work.[40] A preliminary account of the financial results of both loans suggests that there was little mystery about the distribution of the funds. Of net proceeds, totaling approximately £1,920,000, some 45 percent went to the railway contractors, 12 percent went to the bondholders for interest charges during the years 1871–73, a total of 34 percent went to the bankers, and roughly 8 percent went to President Guardia.[41] Securing foreign gold this way proved to be extraordinarily costly for Costa Rica.

For Honduras, the successive loan deals of 1867, 1869, and 1870 were so outrageous that, by contrast, the Costa Rican transactions appeared positively judicious. Like their neighbors, the Honduras authorities were intent on stimulating economic progress through the construction of railways, but they had even more ambitious plans. In 1867 the government announced its decision to build a railroad to be pompously named the "Inter-Oceanic Railway Company," connecting Puerto Caballo on the Caribbean with the Bay of Fonseca on the Pacific. According to the prospectus, the new line would provide an alternate route for international traffic that could successfully compete with the profitable Panama railway. It was never made clear, however, why shippers or merchants should prefer a 230-mile route across mountainous territory to the short, flat 50-mile run across Panama.[42]

In any event, the rulers of Honduras did not hesitate to leap precipitately into the European loan circus; they launched four major bond issues in London and Paris within five years. An initial £1,000,000 loan—taken by the ubiquitous Bischoffsheim/Goldschmidt bankers—proved to be a failure on the London Stock Exchange. Despite this situation, the government resolved to press forward with the railway and advanced one-fifth of the bonds to the engineering firm of Charles Waring, with the promise that a

40. On Keith's activities, see Stewart, *Keith and Costa Rica*.

41. The main banking firm engaged in the Costa Rica loans was the Anglo-French firm of Erlangers, although they did not act alone. The 34 percent in profits was split among various participants in the syndicate, including such well-known firms as the International Financial Society, J. S. Morgan, Louis Cohen & Sons, Cristobal de Murrieta & Co., and Knowles & Foster (*Parl. Papers*, "Loans," p. 149). Nonetheless, Erlangers reaped extraordinary gains from the management of the loan proceeds, retaining £300,000 in cash and £250,000 in unsold bonds as a guarantee for several large overdrafts by the Costa Rica government (ibid., pp. 160–172).

42. The prospectus of the company painted a glowing picture: "Besides the trade of the countries above mentioned [the Central American republics], the Honduras Inter-Oceanic Railway will command a large proportion of the trade now going to the west coast of Mexico by the Panama railway and even a certain trade connecting South and Central America with California and China, Japan and Australia" (ibid., appendix 12, pp. 113–114).

market would soon be "made" for these little-known and unattractive securities. In 1869 a new and larger loan was floated in Paris through the offices of the banking company of Dreyfus, Scheyer et Compagnie which in spite of lack of success in obtaining subscriptions took 11,000,000 "firm," representing a little less than 20 percent of the total value of the bonds. Part of these funds went to the railway contractors, part went to Bischoffsheim in recompense for alleged outstanding debts, and another 3,000,000 went for the manufacture of nickel coin on behalf of the Honduras state treasury.[43]

By 1870 the enormous volume of unsold bonds from the 1867 and 1869 transactions led the European bankers concerned to propose a new loan for £2,700,000. Once again Bischoffsheim assumed formal responsibility for the issue. This house worked in alliance with a singularly mischievous speculator named Charles Lefevre who, it was later found, had a criminal record in France for fraudulent business dealings. Lefevre hired between fifty and one hundred agents to create an artificial market at London for the Honduras bonds and soon managed to sell off a large proportion of both the old and new loan paper at relatively high prices. According to an embittered former clerk in his financial house by the name of Gossip, Lefevre bought the cooperation of the Honduras minister in England with a gift of £4,000 in diamonds for his wife; at the same time, the financier remitted a gratuity of £10,000 to Rafael Medina, president of the Central American republic.[44]

But these perquisites were only the scraps of the enormous pickings enjoyed by Lefevre and the bankers on the Honduras loans. The net proceeds on the bond issues of 1867, 1869, and 1870 totaled £2,695,000. About one-quarter of this sum went to Waring for constructing fifty-seven miles of the projected railway, another 20 percent went to the bondholders to pay interest charges in advance, and 15 percent went to the Honduras treasury for sundry expenses. Yet almost £1,000,000 remained unaccounted for. According to the parliamentary inquiry of 1875, three-quarters of this huge sum constituted the booty of Lefevre (who apparently spent a great deal of it on racehorses), while the remainder went into the pockets of Dreyfus and Bischoffsheim.[45]

Although it might appear that the financiers would by now have satiated

43. Paradoxically, the nickel coins were not accepted by the Honduras public, and the operation was therefore a failure. The details of the Paris loan are reviewed in ibid., appendix 12, pp. 67–70.

44. Mr. Gossip added: "Immediately after the loan [of 1870] was issued . . . Mr. Lefevre began to astonish all his clerks by his lavish expenditure. . . . He purchased the most costly works of art by the greatest masters, some by Jérôme, the great French painter, . . . and he purchased racehorses to an enormous amount" (*Parl. Papers*, "Loans," p. 108).

45. The committee had considerable difficulty ascertaining the precise figures related to the Honduras loan proceeds and their disbursement, but the final report has a summary estimate (ibid., pp. xiii–xxvi).

their lust for riches, they were unrepentant. The gargantuan nature of their appetites was exemplified by the attempt of Lefevre and his cronies in 1872 to promote a gigantic £15,000,000 loan to finance what was proclaimed to be a revolutionary innovation in contemporary transport—the establishment of the Honduras Ship Railway Company.

According to the plan, the few miles of rails already built would be transformed by the marvels of modern engineering into a stupendous steel road capable of transporting oceangoing ships with a weight of 1,200 tons across the entire territory of Honduras. Two prominent British engineers publicly announced that they considered the project to be feasible, even though no such enterprise had ever been attempted and even though it required laying six parallel rails as well as construction of several immense "ship wagons" (weighing 700 tons), each of which would be equipped with 240 wheels.[46] The Honduras minister at London, an enthusiast of this mad scheme, attempted to justify it by proclaiming; "This gigantic, colossal, bold idea . . . could not be doubted . . . in an age which has seen electric cables stretched across the ocean, a passage for ships opened between the Mediterranean and the Red Sea across the isthmus of Suez, locomotives traversing the Alps after the perforation of an immense tunnel in Mount Cenis, and works prepared for opening another tunnel from England to France under the Channel."[47]

But enthusiasm could not guarantee success. The prestigious financial journal *The Economist* soon buried this crude stratagem under a mountain of abuse. The bonds were never sold and Lefevre shortly decamped to France.[48]

While the Honduras loans proved to be an instrument of prodigious fraud, at least a small percentage of the funds raised on the European money markets were actually used for building one-third of a small railway. On the other hand, two additional groups of loan transactions studied by the Select Committee on Foreign Loans—those of Santo Domingo and Paraguay—represented clear cases of larceny, with no tangible benefits to either state.

46. The two "distinguished" engineers were James Brunlees and Edward Woods, the latter president of the Society of Civil Engineers of England (*Parl. Papers*, "Loans," appendix 12, pp. 72–73).

47. Carlos Gutiérrez, simultaneously minister to both Costa Rica and Honduras, had formerly been a clerk in a commercial house at Liverpool. What his "percentage" was in all these financial transactions is a matter for speculation, but it must have been substantial. Gutiérrez published his defense in a pamplet entitled "Historical Account . . . ," which is reproduced in ibid., pp. 58–108.

48. Five days after the project was presented to the British investing public, news arrived in London of a revolution in Honduras followed by invasion by forces from Guatemala and El Salvador. These events caused the quotations of Honduras bonds to plunge abruptly and eliminated all possibility of issuing any new securities (ibid., pp. 116–120).

The Santo Domingo loan of 1869, nominally valued at £714,000, was an Anglo-American fabrication that included an attempt to annex the island to the United States, a series of real-estate speculations in which President Ulysses S. Grant, among others, was involved, and a sophisticated market-rigging operation in London. Among the bankers who took part were such prominent firms as Bischoffsheim, J. S. Morgan, and Morton, Rose & Company. They earned huge profits on the sale of the bonds by retaining almost all the proceeds. Santo Domingo received a net payment of only £38,000, approximately 5 percent of the value of the loan. It is not surprising that the legislative assembly of the Caribbean island soon repudiated the bonds.[49]

Finally, the history of the Paraguayan loans of 1871 and 1872 reveals the vilest characteristics of contemporary speculation. This small country had just barely managed to survive an extremely bloody war against Brazil, Argentina, and Uruguay (1865–70). Most of the male population had been wiped out, epidemic disease was rife, and food was scarce. Despite these catastrophic conditions, local politicians and London bankers contrived to launch two large foreign loans that the country clearly could not support. But the financiers insisted that they were innocent of fraud and that they had no knowledge of the true state of affairs in this remote South American nation.[50] For their part, the politicians of Paraguay were only too happy to get their hands on a substantial amount of gold, which they surreptitiously shipped out of Asunción and lodged in Buenos Aires bank accounts and Argentine real estate.[51]

A review of loans scrutinized by the Select Committee suggests that the

49. On the involvement of Grant and various North American politicians and financiers in this early annexation scheme, see the excellent account by Sumner Welles, *Naboth's Vineyard: The Dominican Republic, 1844–1924* (New York, 1928), vol. 1, chap. 5. The gallery of rogues involved in the 1869 loan included: Edward Hartmont, loan contractor and principal organizer of the fraudulent deal; the underwriters, Peter Lawson & Co., guano and seed merchants who subsequently went bankrupt; and financiers Julius Beer and Charles Morrison, as well as the bankers mentioned in the text. This group took the bonds at 55 and sold them at prices ranging from 65 to 70 in financial markets in England, France and Germany (*Parl. Papers*, ''Loans,'' pp. 130–135). For additional details see Wynne, *State Insolvency*, 2:199–206, and Herrera, *Las finanzas de la República Dominicana*, which has two chapters on the so-called Hartmont Loan of 1869.

50. The verbal exchange between the committee members and George Fleming of the merchant-banking firm of Robinson, Fleming & Co. during the parliamentary investigation illustrated the stupendous insolence of the financiers. It went as follows: *Question*: ''Did you know the state Paraguay was in at the time you issued the prospectus?'' *Answer*: ''It was perfectly peaceful.'' *Question*: ''Yes, very peaceful; did you not know that the population had been almost exterminated?'' *Answer*: ''No.'' (*Parl. Papers*, ''Loans,'' p. 188.)

51. Harris Gaylord Warren, ''The Golden Fleecing: The Paraguayan Loans of 1871 and 1872,'' *Journal of Interamerican Economic Affairs* (hereafter *IAEA*), no. 26 (1972): 11–13.

Latin American bonds of the day were nothing more than gambling chips in a transatlantic financial casino managed by avaricious scalpers. Yet not all Latin American governments were subject to such extortionist practices. The larger and more prosperous states could obtain foreign loans on relatively expensive but still payable terms. Furthermore, the disbursement and allocation of funds were carried out by the finance ministers of these nations with considerable fidelity to the objectives espoused, be they investments in public works, arms contracts, or refinancing operations. Thus, fiscal and financial restraint, in conjunction with a favorable debt-service/export-earnings ratio, allowed Argentina, Brazil, and Chile to avoid default.[52]

In summary, it is possible to argue that the European bankers adopted a substantially different behavior when dealing with the larger and more dynamic nations of Latin America than when arranging business deals with the smaller, poorer republics. The London and Paris financiers exercised greater prudence with their larger, stable clients, who provided them with profits and remittances on a regular basis. In contrast, the weaker countries were fair game for all kinds of speculators, whether established or newcomers, because the benefits to be reaped were expected to be extremely large, if short-lived. Once the bankers had harvested their golden crop, they abandoned the scene as soon as possible.

But investors, who saw that they had been left holding the bag, could not make a similarly profitable exit. They demanded reimbursement on their securities, however spurious. The result was a series of protracted conflicts between the private creditors and the debtor republics, the latter waging a successful battle in the late 1870s only to succumb in almost every instance during the 1880s.

TURNING THE SCREW: DEBT RENEGOTIATIONS

A detailed analysis of the prolonged and labyrinthine negotiations waged between European creditors and Latin American governments (of which eleven were in default by 1876) goes beyond the limits of the present study, but we should sketch out the common features of these financial and political struggles, which lasted in some cases ten, twenty, or even more years. (For comparative data, see Table 4.) The main contenders were the bondholders, who sought repayment of the bonds, and the Latin American finance ministers, who argued that such demands could not be met.

52. In all three cases the debt service averaged between 10 and 15 percent of total export earnings, a reasonable ratio according to modern-day debt-experts. In the Argentine case, precise estimates can be formulated on the basis of documents published in Republic of Argentina, *Memoria del Ministerio de Hacienda, 1876*, sec. v, "Deuda pública." My Brazilian and Chilean estimates are based on data in Fenn, *Compendium* (1883 ed.), pp. 380–403.

TABLE 4
DEFAULTS AND SETTLEMENTS OF LATIN AMERICAN LOANS FOLLOWING THE CRISIS OF 1873

Govts. Defaulting	Interest Rate and Original Date of Issue of Loans	Nominal Value of Unredeemed Principal (£ thousands)	Date of Default (day, mo., yr.)	Settlement
Boliva	6%—1872	1,654	1/1/1875	1880: Bondholders received £793,000 deposited in Bank of England.
Costa Rica	6%—1871 7%—1872	940 2,362	1/11/1874 1/4/1874	1885: £2,000,000 in new bonds issued to bondholders; state railways and land sold.
Guatemala	5%—1856 6%—1869	73 469	1/2/1875 1/4/1875	1882: Preliminary arrangement not accepted by Guatemala Congress. In 1887, £887,000 in new bonds issued to cancel old bonds.
Honduras	5%—1856 10%—1867 7%—1869 10%—1870	79 901 2,177 2,243	1/4/1873 1/1/1873 1/3/1873 1/1/1873	The entire Honduras external debt continued in default at the turn of the century.
Paraguay	8%—1871 8%—1872	957 548	15/6/1874 1/7/1874	1885: Debt reduced to £800,000, and 2,000,000 hectares of land given to bondholders.
Peru	5%—1869 6%—1870 5%—1872	265 11,142 21,547	1/1/1876 1/1/1876 1/1/1876	1890: British bondholders exchange bonds for stock in Peruvian Corp., now owner of state railways, lands, and mining concessions.
Santo Domingo	6%—1869	714	1/1/1873	1888: £770,000 in new bonds issued to bondholders.
Uruguay	6%—1871	3,165	1/8/1876	1879: Debt payments renewed.

Of the bondholders' organizations, the most important and vociferous were the British committees, although in several instances the French and Dutch associations also played a role in the discussions.[53] The bondholders usually could count on the informal support of their respective chancelleries, but in contrast to the situation in the Near East (where the European powers intervened directly to guarantee the repayment of debts), in Latin America armed force was used sparingly during the last quarter of the nineteenth century. There were calls by individual capitalists or by jingoistic newspapers to send the gunboats, but official response tended to be muted. Indeed, only at the turn of the century did military punishment for nonpayment of Latin American debts become common practice.[54]

The British and French bondholders of the 1870s generally had to limit themselves to seeking the support of a prestigious banking house that might be able to persuade a given Latin American government to renew payments on its debts. More effective were pacts worked out with public works contractors who brought private creditors and public debtors together to negotiate a settlement, as in the cases of Costa Rica and Peru.

Initially, all the Latin American ministers were leery of renegotiation, and this was understandable, considering that the commercial depression of the 1870s made it almost impossible for the debtor states to dispose of the resources required for service of their external debts. Moreover, the

---

TABLE 4 (cont.)

SOURCES: Corporation of Foreign Bondholders, *Annual Reports* (London, 1873–90, 1895, 1905); C. Fenn, *Fenn's on the Funds* (London, 1883); Hyde Clarke, "On the Debts of Sovereign and Quasi-Sovereign States, Owing by Foreign Countries," *Journal of the Statistical Society* (London), June 1878.

NOTE: Not included here are the defaults preceding the crisis of 1873: Venezuela (1866), Ecuador (1868), and Mexico (1867). Information on the partial resolution and settlement of these debts (by issue of new bonds) in the years 1885–88 is in the *Annual Reports* of the Corporation of Foreign Bondholders.

53. The British Corporation of Foreign Bondholders was established in 1868, but it began to publish annual reports regularly only from the year 1873, when it began to take an active role in international finance.

54. In 1875 Charles Waring suggested to the parliamentary committee that it might be expedient to send a gunboat to Paraguay in order to oblige the Asunción government to pay its debts (*Parl. Papers*, "Loans," p. 204). In 1876 a British warship was sent to the Argentine river port of Santa Fé to protest the closing of the local branch of the Bank of London and River Plate. For some time afterward the British authorities tended to be more circumspect in their use of direct military force in Latin America. On the Santa Fé incident, see Ezequiel Gallo, "El gobierno de Santa Fé versus el Banco de Londres y Río de la Plata: 1876," *Revista Latinoamericana de Sociología*, nos. 2–3 (Buenos Aires, 1971), pp. 146–173. On the militarist tactics adopted by the European powers to collect debts at the turn of the century, see Miriam Hood, *Gunboat Diplomacy, 1895–1905: Great Power Pressure in Venezuela* (London, 1975).

debtors could scarcely be expected to renew payments until a final resolution of the complex lawsuits could be reached. As far as the finance ministers were concerned, the longer the cases dragged on in the British courts, the better. The suspension of interest payments provided breathing room for the suffocating economies of the smaller countries of Central and South America.

Another factor that moved Latin American rulers to postpone resolution of the debt question was political. The meager benefits derived from the loans, as well as the corruption they had generated, provided excellent opportunities for opposition parties to attack governments. Finance ministers could hardly justify fulfilling engagements on foreign bond transactions that had frequently produced net returns equivalent to less than 50 percent of the nominal value of the securities. And for such politicians as General Guardia of Costa Rica, who had publicly acknowledged his acceptance of huge "presents" from the foreign financiers, it seemed less than expedient to insist on the discharge of great sacrifices by the local treasury in order to appease the bondholders.[55]

By the mid-1880s a new set of political and financial circumstances began to soften the intransigeance of Latin American ministers and presidents. The rise in exports of raw materials and primary commodities that took place at this time stimulated the regional economies and replenished the coffers of local governments. These circumstances renewed the interest of European investors in profitable enterprises in the region. The agents of the London bankers and of the bondholders insisted that if the old debt questions could be successfully untangled it might be possible to stimulate a new flow of investments from abroad. The arguments were plausible, but implementation was more difficult and costly for the debtor governments than they had anticipated.

The first favorable resolution obtained by the bondholders came as a result of a decision adopted by the British courts with respect to the Bolivian foreign debt. The judges announced that the £800,000 of the net proceeds of the Bolivian loan of 1872, which had been deposited at the Bank of England, should be returned to the bondholders. The railway contractors who had been hired by the Bolivian government to build a line from the

---

55. Guardia acknowledged receipt of large gratuities in a speech to the Costa Rica legislature and in a pamphlet entitled "Vindicación de Tómas Guardia, Presidente de la República en los Asuntos del Ferrocarril y Empréstito" (1871), in which he affirmed that Meiggs "by an act of pure generosity . . . put at my disposal . . . the sum of £100,000 in order that I should do with the sum what I thought best." The full text is reprinted in F. Nuñez, *Iniciación y desarrollo de las vias de comunicación y empresas de transporte en Costa Rica* (San José, 1924); the same text was printed in English in *Parl. Papers*, "Loans," pp. 153–155.

highlands of Bolivia to the plains of southern Brazil protested, but to no avail. They received almost no part of the funds.[56]

A second agreement that also proved favorable to the British bondholders was signed between the Guatemalan government and the bondholders' committee in December 1882.[57] Other agreements followed in 1885, when Costa Rica and Paraguay finally bowed to foreign pressure, making key economic concessions in exchange for what appeared to be long-term reductions of their outstanding external obligations. In the years 1886–88 the governments of Mexico, Ecuador, Santo Domingo, and Venezuela followed suit. Peru, in contrast, remained enmeshed in court battles in London and Paris until 1890, while the most impenitent debtor, the government of Honduras, continued with its lawsuits until well after the turn of the century (see Table 4).[58]

That the majority of the long-delayed financial accords should ultimately have benefited the creditors more than the debtors is not surprising. After all, the small Latin American states had no alternative but to make concessions if they wanted to return to the fold of creditworthy nations and to spur a new current of direct investments from abroad. Since none of the governments counted on abundant fiscal resources, they were obliged to adopt one of two possible solutions in order to placate the bondholders.

One solution was to issue a new set of bonds that would replace the old ones. This was the strategy adopted by the authorities of Guatemala, Mexico, Santo Domingo, and Venezuela. The extortionate nature of some of these agreements is luridly illustrated by the incredible contract signed by the Santo Domingo government. In 1888 the administration of Ulysse Heureaux (the Haitian ruler who had taken control of the entire island) agreed to issue £770,000 in new bonds to reimburse the bondholders of the 1869 loan that had originally netted less than £40,000 for the government. The negotiations took place through the offices of a mysterious Dutch firm, known as the Westendorp Corporation, which assumed effective control of the tax collection machinery of the nation. This neo-colonial financial solution was much applauded by the European bankers.[59]

A second and different possibility for Latin American governments that

56. An account of the Bolivian railway project can be found in Rippy, *Latin America in the Industrial Age*, chap. 6.

57. Because of a long-standing border conflict with Guatemala, the Mexican government attempted to torpedo the Guatemalan loan negotiations in London by publishing adverse articles in the financial press, but its efforts were unsuccessful. Details are in ASRE, file 51–1–16.

58. Details on all these renegotations are in the annual reports of the Corporation of Foreign Bondholders.

59. For details, consult Wynne, *State Insolvency*, 2:204–211.

wanted to restructure their foreign debts consisted in exchanging public properties for old bonds. In the case of Costa Rica, the entrepreneur Minor Keith persuaded the finance minister that he could reduce the foreign debt by selling the state-owned railway company to a private firm. The success of this proposal depended on the goodwill of the bondholders. They had to accept stock in the private railway enterprise in exchange for their bonds. In order to make the contract more attractive, a clause was added, stipulating that 600,000 acres of public lands would be donated to the new concern as an incentive to the construction of additional lines. Having won the approval of the San José elite, Keith sailed for Europe, where after two tedious years of negotiations he finally induced the bondholders to accept his plan. The latter received one-third of the stock in the railway company, but the Costa Rican government had to issue £2,000,000 in new bonds as additional recompense.[60] In the long run it was Keith who turned out to be most highly rewarded by the agreement. He used the railway and the land concession to lay the foundations of the famous, and infamous, North American firm known as the United Fruit Company.[61]

Bankers and politicians adopted similar measures to reduce the Paraguayan debt. In 1885 the Asunción government proposed a reduction in the value of bonds outstanding from £3,000,000 to £800,000 in exchange for 2,500,000 acres of public lands and forests, to be ceded to the Corporation of Foreign Bondholders. The British investors accepted the proposition and soon established the Anglo-Paraguay Land and Cattle Company, an enterprise destined to play a major role in the local economy for more than two decades.[62]

The complexities of debt resolution in the Peruvian case should also be noted. Renegotiation proved to be extremely difficult, a fact that was related to the enormous volume of interest in arrears on the Peruvian foreign bonds since the default of 1876. After years of litigation between the Lima government and the bondholders, an agreement was worked out. This pact, known as the Grace Contract of 1890, canceled most of the Peruvian external debt but gave the bondholders (now constituted as ''The Peruvian Corporation'') possession of all the state railways (approximately 770 kilometers of lines), 2,000,000 tons of guano, a concession for the operation of a

---

60. For data on the Costa Rican negotiations see, T. Soley Guell, *Historia económica y hacendaria de Costa Rica* (San José, 1947), 1:340–341; C. González Víquez, *Capítulos de un libro sobre historia financiera de Costa Rica* (San José, 1979), pp. 174ff.; Henry C. Bischoff, ''British Investment in Costa Rica,'' *IAEA* 7, no. 1 (1953): 40ff.

61. Some useful references are in Stacy May and Galo Plaza, *The United Fruit Company in Latin America* (Washington, D.C., 1958).

62. For details, see Warren, ''The Golden Fleecing.''

steamship line on Lake Titicaca, 5,000,000 acres of public lands, and rights to the development of the rich mines of Cerro de Pasco.[63]

Despite the generous terms obtained by the British bondholders, the court cases did not end. French bondholders had not been included in the accord, and they protested and demanded reimbursement, but met with less success than their British colleagues. Not until 1910 was the French Ministry of Foreign Affairs able to persuade the Peruvian Finance Ministry to renew payments due on £3,400,000 claimed by the firm of Dreyfus Frères. And it was not until 1926 that the last remittances were made on that half-century-old debt.[64]

In summary, the consequences of the debt defaults of the 1870s were both complex and protracted. In the short-term, the defaulting Latin American nations benefited from a unilateral grace period during which no interest or amortization was paid on the outstanding loans. But after approximately a decade of moratoriums, the majority of the governments shifted their position and resolved to settle their disputes with the bondholders. They hoped that a renewal of international credit transactions would inaugurate a new era of economic prosperity, although the price they were forced to pay was often exorbitant. In the long run the consequences of the depression of the 1870s spelled severe financial as well as political problems for many countries of the region. The first world debt crisis reflected the traumas and the contradictions that accompanied the spread of capitalism throughout Latin America—contradictions that sprang from the alternating and apparently inevitable cycles of boom and bust, of development and underdevelopment.

63. There are sharp differences of opinion with respect to the virtues and vices of the Grace Contract. Most Peruvian historians see it as an instrument of foreign economic domination. Rory Miller disagrees and defends the British-owned Peruvian Corporation against its critics (Rory Miller, "The Grace Contract, the Peruvian Corporation and Peruvian History," *Ibero Amerikanisches Archiv*, n.f. 9, nos. 3–4 [1983]: 319–348).

64. Wynne, *State Insolvency*, 2:169–170.

Loan Frenzy in the Río de la Plata, 1880–1890

With just one of these loans, we can carry out a thousand useful public works.
. . . Here we have Archimedes' lever with which it is possible to realize the
greatest economic revolution.

—Julio Roca, President of Argentina (May 1880)

THE WORLD DEPRESSION of the 1870s wreaked havoc on most of the
Latin American economies, but by the early 1880s a process of recovery had begun. The foreign trade of many nations in the region increased
and tended to become more diversified.[1] At the same time, the flow of
foreign capital resurged vigorously. By the late 1880s a new loan boom
was sweeping the financial markets of Europe.

Not all the Latin American countries benefited from the mercantile and
financial expansion, however. The pattern of economic development
throughout the region was markedly uneven, for while some nations sustained high rates of growth, others stagnated. For instance, the foreign trade
of Argentina, Brazil, Chile, Mexico, and Uruguay rose rapidly.[2] In contrast, during the same years the foreign trade of Peru and Colombia declined, and this discouraged European capitalists from investing funds
there.[3] Concurrently, in most of the smaller republics, mercantile activity
and agricultural production recovered gradually, but progress was slow.

While the effects of foreign trade on economic development were more
unsettling and haphazard than might have been expected, the renewed flow
of foreign capital to Latin America constituted a strong compensating tendency. In this respect, it is important to note that the 1880s were the first
decade in the history of the region when foreign *direct* investments (as op-

1. On the diversification of Latin American trade during the 1880s see Platt, *Latin America*,
chaps. vi–x.

2. Information on Latin American foreign commerce in this period is scattered. For statistical data on Argentine trade, see Vicente Vázquez Presedo, *Estadísticas históricas argentinas*, 2 vols. (Buenos Aires, 1971, 1976); on Mexico, see Kapp, "Les relations économiques"; on Brazilian exports, see Steve Topik, "State Autonomy in Economic Policy:
Brazil's Experience, 1822–1930," *Journal of Interamerican Studies and World Affairs* 26,
no. 4 (November 1984): 455.

3. On Colombian trade, see J. Rodríguez and W. McGreevey, "Colombia: comercio exterior, 1835–1962," in *Compendio de estadísticas históricas*, ed. M. Arrubla and M. Urrutia
(Bogotá, 1970); on Peruvian trade, see H. Bonilla, *Gran Bretaña y el Perú*.

posed to loans) began to arrive in large quantities. Now, not only British but also French, German, and North American firms moved aggressively to stake out positions in the traditional spheres of commerce and banking, as well as in railways, tramways, mines, sugar refineries, flour mills, gas works, and even some early electric and telephone companies.[4]

But once again it is essential to underline the uneven impact of this external economic influence. The data on foreign investments shows the skewed nature of their distribution. During the 1880s the bulk of total British direct investments went to just five countries: 37 percent to Argentina, 17 percent to Mexico, 14 percent to Brazil, 7 percent to Chile, and 5 percent to Uruguay.[5] Not surprisingly, it was in these nations that agricultural, ranching, and mining production, as well as railway construction and urban development, advanced most swiftly. By 1890, Argentina, Brazil, and Mexico could each boast a railway network of 9,000 to 10,000 kilometers in operation, while Chile had 2,700 kilometers of rails and Uruguay had 1,700. In contrast, through most of the rest of Latin America the impact of the railroad was still limited.[6] The overall picture is one of a handful of economically dynamic nations that had begun to outstrip the poorer republics of the subcontinent in terms of growth rates.

If attention is directed to the role of foreign loans in Latin America, the disparate distribution of resources becomes even more conspicuous than in the case of trade or direct investments. During the 1880s two nations—both bordering on the great Río de la Plata—were responsible for most of the international credit transactions undertaken by contemporary Latin American governments. Together Argentina and Uruguay secured almost 60 percent of the value of *all* loans negotiated by the states of the region in this era (see Table 5). In the brief span of ten years, Argentina took a total of

4. The nominal value of British-owned enterprises operating in Latin America rose from approximately £50,000,000 in 1880 to some £230,000,000 in 1890. During this period, French investments in the region also rose substantially; much French capital went into the Panama Canal Company, which issued almost 2,000,000,000 francs (£80,000,000) in stocks and bonds during the decade. French funds were also invested in such Latin American banks as the Banco Nacional de México (1884) and the Banco Francés del Río de la Plata (1889). German investments were still concentrated mainly in commercial and banking companies operating in various countries of the subcontinent. United States capital exports went primarily into Mexican railways and mining firms. For source materials, see the broad range of bibliographical references in Marvin Bernstein, ed., *Foreign Investment in Latin America* (New York, 1966), pp. 283–305.

5. Data from Rippy, *British Investments*, chap. 3, charts 7, 8, 9, 10.

6. Much statistical information can be found in what are still the most complete histories of railway development in Latin America: G. S. Brady and W. R. Long, *Railways of South America*, 3 vols., Bureau of Foreign and Domestic Commerce (Washington D.C., 1926, 1927, 1930); and W. R. Long, *Railways of Central America and the West Indies* (Washington, D.C., 1925), and by the same author, *Railways of Mexico* (Washington, D.C., 1925).

TABLE 5

FOREIGN LOANS OF FIVE LATIN AMERICAN STATES, 1880–1890

Country and Govt. Entity		No. of Loans	Nominal Value (£ thousands)
Argentina			
National govt.		13	39,223
Provincial govts.		27	32,505
Municipal govts.		10	6,257
	Subtotal	50	77,985
Brazil			
National govt.		4	37,164
Provincial govts.		2	1,050
Municipal govts.		2	700
	Subtotal	8	38,914
Chile			
National govt.		4	9,525
Mexico			
National govt.		3	19,200
Provincial govts.		1	250
Municipal govts.		1	2,400
	Subtotal	5	21,850
Uruguay			
National govt.		3	17,382
Municipal govts.		1	1,400
	Subtotal	4	18,782

SOURCES: Corporation of Foreign Bondholders, *Annual Reports* (London, 1880–91); Henry L. Shepherd, *Default and Adjustment of the Argentine Foreign Debt, 1890–1906*, U.S. Department of Commerce Trade Promotion Series, no. 145 (Washington, D.C., 1933); Carlos Marichal, "Los banqueros europeos y los empréstitos argentinos: rivalided y colaboración, 1880–1890," *Revista de Historia Económica* (Madrid) 2, no. 1 (1984): 47–82; Jan Bazant, *Historia de la deuda exterior de México* (Mexico, 1968), pp. 125–141; O. Onody, "Les invéstissements étrangers au Brésil," in CNRS, *Colloque International sur l'Histoire Quantitative du Brésil de 1800 à 1930* (Paris, 1971), pp. 302–307.

NOTE: The five states included in this table received close to 90% of the total Latin American foreign loans in this decade. Several small Latin American republics carried out refinancing operations in the 1880s—Costa Rica in 1886, Guatemala in 1887–88, Paraguay in 1886, El Salvador in 1889, and Santo Domingo in 1888—but these loans were essentially conversions of old bonds in default and did not surpass £5,000,000 in all.

Cuba negotiated two large loans during the 1880s, but they fit into a special category because they were guaranteed by the Spanish Crown. The two Cuban loans, in 1886 for £24,000,000 and in 1890 for £8,000,000, were issued in Spanish and other European capital markets.

fifty foreign loans (including national, provincial, and municipal issues), whereas only eight loans were taken by Brazil, five by Mexico, four by Chile, and two by Cuba. Less fortunate were Peru, Colombia, Venezuela, and most of the smaller republics of the subcontinent, because they were virtually frozen out of the European capital markets.[7]

The special role of Argentina, and to a lesser extent Uruguay, in the loan boom of the 1880s was not limited to the fact that it contracted the bulk of the foreign loans of the decade. It was also reflected in the objectives of the financial transactions that were markedly different from those of other Latin American states. The bulk of the Argentine issues of the 1880s were intended to accelerate economic development by financing the construction of state railways and ports, establishing public banks, and promoting urban modernization. In contrast, the loans taken by other Latin American nations were simply refinancing operations. For example, the great Brazilian £20,000,000 loan of 1889 was issued to convert the old bonds of the previous loans of 1865, 1871, 1875, and 1885. Similarly, the mammoth £10,500,000 Mexican loan of 1889 did not bring much new capital to Mexico; it was used basically to convert all the old 5 percent and 6 percent bonds circulating in Europe, a large number of them dating from as far back as 1825. Likewise, the largest Chilean financial operation, the £6,000,000 loan of 1886, was used to redeem the old bonds of 1858, 1867, 1870, 1873, and 1875. Finally, the great Cuban loan of £23,000,000 issued in 1886 by Baring Brothers in conjunction with Spanish banking concerns was used for refinancing purposes but not for the promotion of public works.[8]

The productive nature of the Argentine loans was not the only thing that distinguished them from those of other Latin American states. An additional and important feature is that the Argentine authorities allowed provincial and municipal governments, as well as several state enterprises and banks, to compete with the national government for loans in the international capital markets. This trend stood in marked contrast to the financial policies of Brazil, Mexico, and Chile, where central governments monopolized virtually all foreign loans.

During this period the principles of financial federalism were implemented in Argentina on a grander scale than in any other Latin American country.[9] Between 1880 and 1890, ten Argentine provinces negotiated

7. The smaller Latin American republics were able to obtain support from some European financial houses for refinancing some of the debts on which they had defaulted in the 1870s (see Table 5), but this did not imply the transfer of any new capital to them from Europe.

8. Although the Cuban bond issue was a Spanish foreign loan inasmuch as Cuba was a colony of Spain and the transaction was guaranteed by the Madrid treasury, the nineteenth-century financial operations of Cuba deserve greater attention from historians.

9. The only foreign loans issued by *local* entities of the other Latin American nations during

twenty-five loans in England, France, Belgium, and Germany for a total of almost £35,000,000 (U.S. $175,000,000) (see Appendix B). At the same time, five municipal governments—those of Buenos Aires, Rosario, Córdoba, Santa Fé, and Paraná—were able to obtain ten smaller loans abroad. Equally successful were several Argentine state companies and banks that created markets in Europe for their bonds. The Buenos Aires provincial railway company, the Ferrocarril Oeste, raised various loans in England in the early 1880s. The government-run Banco Nacional sold its bonds through a syndicate of British and German bankers. Similarly, the public mortgage banks (the Banco Hipotecario Nacional and the Banco Hipotecario de la Provincia de Buenos Aires) placed more than £30,000,000 of their mortgage bonds in primary and secondary financial markets throughout Europe.

The dominance of Argentina in the foreign loan activity of the 1880s would seem to contrast with the more widespread character of the previous loan boom of 1860–73, when almost every Latin American state had participated in the financial frenzy. But in the previous boom there was also one government that took the largest number of loans—the government of Peru. Nonetheless, the Argentine financial authorities of the 1880s did not take into account the lessons of the Peruvian experience—namely, that the contracting of foreign loans on a large scale could stimulate economic expansion but was also fraught with danger. The greatest debtor of the 1860s and 1870s, the Peruvian state, had become a major casualty of the international crisis of the 1870s. The greatest debtor of the 1880s, Argentina, would be the nation most severely battered by the crisis of 1890.

In this chapter we focus on why and how the Argentine and Uruguayan governments became the leading borrowers of the 1880s. Particular attention will be devoted to the programs and methods these states used to obtain European funds in order to accelerate the capitalist transformation of their economies. A second theme is the rivalry of the European bankers to obtain a share of the loan business in the Río de la Plata region. The rise in competition was closely linked to the ability of the most prosperous Latin American governments of the day to raise money on various markets simultaneously: London, Paris, Brussels, Berlin, and several less-important centers. These changes made the Latin American and particularly the Argentine loan business increasingly complex.

We begin with a review of the financial policies adopted by the Argentine

---

the 1880s were a Montevideo municipal loan, a Mexico City municipal loan, a loan for the provincial government of San Luis Potosí (Mexico), and a loan for the provincial government of Bahia (Brazil) (see Appendix B). The municipal and provincial foreign loans of all other Latin American nations thus totaled a mere four, compared with the thirty-five taken by Argentine provincial and municipal governments.

elites during the years 1880–86, which were aimed at promoting an active role for both national and provincial governments in the administration of several important economic enterprises. These policies were destined to make Argentina the largest Latin American debtor.

FINANCING RAILWAYS AND PORTS IN ARGENTINA, 1880–1886

The Argentine economy had been severely bruised by the crisis of 1873, which bankrupted numerous mercantile and banking firms at Buenos Aires, cut short the flow of immigrants and of foreign capital, brought railway construction to a virtual standstill, and pushed the government to the brink of insolvency. By the late 1870s, however, the recession came to an end as ranching, agricultural, commercial, and manufacturing activity rallied. Paradoxically, one cause of the renewed prosperity in the Río de la Plata region originated in the widespread crisis that had gripped European agriculture. Several bad harvests in the 1870s not only drove food prices sky-high but also impelled thousands of hungry European peasants out of the countryside and into the ports, where they soon boarded ships bound for the United States, Canada, Australia, and Argentina. The *Buenos Aires Standard* observed in late February 1880; "The distress in Europe, the loss in crops, and the misery of thousands tend to increase our appreciation of the rare blessings all enjoy in this favored country [Argentina] . . . Fifty thousand immigrants have settled on these shores in the past year."[10]

It was from 1880, therefore, that European commercial interests began to view the Río de la Plata region not only as a major wool-producing zone, which it already was, but also as a great potential meat and bread basket for the industrial economies of northern and central Europe. Like the United States and other "newly settled" nations, Argentina was blessed with vast open frontiers and extraordinarily rich soils, which needed only the arrival of men, threshers, and railways to become one of the most productive agricultural belts in the world. The *South American Journal* commented, "In fact, absolutely no limit can be put to the development in this direction, the extent of virgin soil suitable for wheat-growing being unlimited. . . . The number of sheep is nearly double that existing in the whole of the United States and is about on a par with the Australian continent and far surpasses it as far as cattle."[11]

The prospects for growth, however, depended not only on the abundance of natural resources but also on political and social conditions. In order to establish a stable national government, two fundamental problems had to

10. Cited in *South American Journal*, February 19, 1880.
11. Ibid., January 8, 1880.

be resolved. The first was expulsion of the Indian tribes from the rich lands of the pampas. During the years 1876–80 the Argentine army carried out a successful campaign to expand the western and southern frontiers, slaughtering thousands of Pampa Indians and driving the remaining tribes across the Río Negro (Black River). The second major obstacle to consolidation of a unified political system lay in the resolution of the regional-political conflicts. The divisions were so acute that in December 1879 the governor of the wealthiest and most populous province, Buenos Aires, launched a military revolt against the national authorities. Eventually the army succeeded in smashing the insurrection, but only at the cost of several thousand lives.[12]

Subsequently, national elections brought to power General Julio Roca, a man who had won fame as the main strategist of the Indian Wars. Roca immediately reduced the power of the provincial government of Buenos Aires by transforming its leading city into the federal capital of the republic and by working out a complex political pact with the ruling elites of the other Argentine provinces. The process of political unification made it possible for the national government to assume an active role in the promotion of economic growth.

But the Roca administration did not come up with a new development strategy. Most of the ambitious railway and port projects it sponsored had been initiated during Domingo Sarmiento's presidency (1869–74).[13] What it did do was seek an unprecedented degree of financial assistance from abroad to carry out and conclude these programs. The Argentine politicians and technocrats of the early 1880s spared no effort in their campaign to attract banking and industrial companies from Great Britain, France, Belgium, Germany, and even the United States to participate in the financing and construction of railways across the pampas, ports at Buenos Aires and La Plata, and other important public works.

Even though the Argentine authorities placed great emphasis on the promotion of state-run enterprises (financed with foreign loans), this does not imply that they were opposed to private enterprise. On the contrary, most politicians were themselves landowners or engaged in some kind of private

12. The rebellion was led by Governor Tejedor in order to impede General Roca from winning the presidency. The rebel militia actually forced the national government authorities out of the capital, but were subsequently defeated by the better-trained and more-disciplined troops of the national army. For an eyewitness account of the battles, see the synopsis in Ferns, *Britain and Argentina*, pp. 388–391.

13. Argentine historians have emphasized the originality of the economic policies adopted by the Roca regime; see Roberto Cortés Conde and Ezequiel Gallo, *Argentina, la república conservadora* (Buenos Aires, 1972). For a contrary view, see Carlos Marichal, "The State and Economic Development under Sarmiento and Avellaneda, 1868–1880" (Paper presented at the American Historical Association meeting, San Francisco, December 1983).

business, often in conjunction with one or more foreign-owned companies. However, the majority of the Argentine propertied classes believed that the state should play a key role in the administration of economically important enterprises, especially railways and ports. It was precisely this view that appeared to justify the negotiation of numerous external loans, because they would benefit the entire community by providing a major input of both foreign capital and technology.

⌊The first major loan negotiated by the Roca administration was taken in the year 1881 with the aim of concluding two important trunk lines: the Central Norte railway, running from the midwestern city of Córdoba northward to Tucumán and Jujuy; and the Andino railway which was to connect Córdoba with the western towns of Mendoza and San Juan, near the Chilean border. Together these lines were destined to form the skeleton of the modern transport system of the nation and hence to contribute to the double task of strengthening the political unity of the republic and of forging an incipient national market.

In mid-1881 the finance minister, Santiago Cortínez, began to sound out several British banking houses, including Baring Brothers, on the possibility of raising funds in London for construction of the state railways. But Roca intervened, ordering that the loan should be negotiated with a Parisian syndicate of banks that had offered greater security. In early June 1881 the Argentine ambassador at Paris wrote to Buenos Aires confirming the success of the issue: "The loan has been completely oversubscribed in France. . . . This is, in effect, a great triumph, for the unfavorable impression which had been caused by the loans [in default] of Mexico, Peru and Honduras made the present transaction uncertain."[14]

In years following, additional foreign loans were negotiated on behalf of the state railways by French bankers in a joint syndicate with the Anglo-Spanish banking firm of Cristobal de Murrieta & Company. The French financiers took advantage of these transactions to promote a set of commercial objectives. They used a part of the funds to arrange the sale of French-made rails and locomotives to the Central Norte line. And by financing railroad construction in Tucumán province they were able to expand their participation in the supply of machinery to modernize the sugar mills then being established in the region by immigrant-entrepreneurs, many of them of French origin.[15]

14. Letter from the Argentine ambassador at Paris, Mariano Balcarce, June 4, 1881, Archivo de la Deuda Exterior de la República Argentina, Ministerio de Economía, Buenos Aires (hereafter ADERA), folder 2088.

15. For additional information on the French role in financing Argentine railways, see Carlos Marichal, "Los ferrocarriles franceses en Argentina, 1880–1940," *Todo es Historia* 9, no. 105 (Buenos Aires, 1976): 38–54. See also Andrés Regalsky, "Las inversiones francesas

Both the Central Norte and Andino railways proved to be of great importance for the economic expansion of the central, western, and northern provinces of Argentina, and this appeared to justify the large loans used to finance the construction. In addition, these enterprises broadened the technical expertise of key branches of the government, such as the National Department of Engineers, which drew up the basic blueprints for the railways. Furthermore, it was in this department that the first generation of Argentine engineers received their practical training. These included men like Pompeyo Moneta, Guillermo Villanueva, Julio Lacroze, Knut Lindmark, and Luis Huergo, all of whom played a critical part in the introduction of new technology in the fields of railways, port works, roads, bridges, and urban development.[16]

The national government was not alone in promoting new economic enterprises. The provincial government of Buenos Aires already had considerable experience in this area, having promoted and financed the first Argentine railway, the Ferrocarril Oeste, from the late 1850s. This line, which ran through the most prosperous ranching and agricultural districts of the province, produced sufficient earnings to cover a large portion of the costs of construction of new branches. But after 1880, Governors Dardo Rocha and Carlos D'Amico accelerated expansion by taking several foreign loans to pay for additional capital equipment.

The principal banking firm engaged in the sale of the Buenos Aires railway bonds was an Anglo-Canadian merchant bank: Morton, Rose & Company.[17] This cosmopolitan firm used the money raised in London to finance a complex and sophisticated technological package that included the import of supplies from various countries—rails from the Schneider steel mills in France, carriages and bridge material from Cockerill & Company in Belgium, and powerful locomotives from the Baldwin Locomotives Company in the United States.[18] As a result, the Ferrocarril Oeste remained an efficient carrier throughout the 1880s, sustaining a volume of commodity and passenger traffic that was matched only by the British-run Great Southern Railway of Buenos Aires.

---

de transporte en el nordeste del país," in Academia Nacional de Historia, "Quinto congreso de historia regional" (Buenos Aires, 1982, mimeographed).

16. Information on the activities of the National Department of Engineers can be found in the annual reports of the Argentine Ministerio del Interior, *Memoria*, 1870–90.

17. Morton, Rose & Co. specialized in the financing of Canadian railways in the second half of the nineteenth century, raising money in London and using it to buy railway equipment in the United States which was shipped to Canada. For details, see Tom Naylor, *The History of Canadian Business* (Toronto, 1975), 1:chap. 8.

18. On the financing of the Ferrocarril Oeste, see Carlos Marichal, "Los banqueros europeos y los empréstitos argentinos: rivalidad y colaboración, 1880–1890," *Revista de Historia Económica* (Madrid) 2, no. 1 (1984): 72–77; Zalduendo, *Libras y rieles*, pp. 265–285.

If railways could be deemed the number-one priority of the economic development plans of the Argentine state in these years, urban modernization was clearly the second most important objective. In this period the Argentine elites first dreamed of making Buenos Aires the "Paris of South America," and they spent a great deal of money to do so. The mayor of the capital in the 1880s, Torcuato Alvear, who fancied himself a latter-day Haussmann (the famous French city planner of Napoleon III), launched a grand public works campaign to build broad avenues, spacious parks, and ostentatious government buildings. Alvear also supported a municipal company that built a modern water supply and drainage system for the rapidly growing metropolis.

The most ambitious of the urban development plans, and that requiring the largest foreign loans, was the building of a modern port to meet the demands caused by the enormous rise in international and local shipping at Buenos Aires. Because of the size and complexity of this project, the national government assumed responsibility for financing the construction. But the authorities had difficulty deciding which of two port proposals would prove most beneficial.[19]

One plan proposed by the engineer Luis Huergo consisted of deepening and widening the Riachuelo, a small river on the southern side of the city, transforming it into a secure deep-water port for oceangoing vessels. During the 1870s and early 1880s, Huergo managed to garner sufficient economic and political support to carry out the initial stages of his plan, but as of 1882 he began to face increasing opposition. His rivals were led by the wealthy entrepreneur Eduardo Madero, who was supported by the influential senator Carlos Pellegrini as well as by a powerful set of Buenos Aires merchants and British financiers. This group sponsored a scheme to build a series of docks and basins on the riverbanks of the downtown mercantile section of the city, next to the great square known as Plaza de Mayo.

Madero made several trips to London, where after arduous negotiation he succeeded in convincing Sir John Hackshaw, a leading British port expert, to serve as technical adviser. At the same time, Madero engaged the Baring banking house to provide financial assistance. In late 1883 the Argentine government authorized a large foreign loan for this purpose, but the issue on the London market was a failure.

The lack of success in marketing the Argentine bonds was due fundamentally to the outbreak of a financial crisis in 1884 in Great Britain. These circumstances caused a suspension of much government-sponsored construction throughout Argentina. In order to break the financial deadlock,

19. On port works projects in Buenos Aires during the 1870s and 1880s, see James Scobie, *Buenos Aires: From Plaza to Suburb, 1870–1910* (Oxford, 1974), chaps. 3 and 5.

President Roca decided to send his trusted lieutenant, Pellegrini, to Europe on a special mission. The goal consisted in fusing several public works loans into one gigantic £8,000,000 loan to be issued by a syndicate of British, French, and German bankers.[20] Although the Berlin financiers finally withdrew from the group, the bond sales were successful. As a result, a large portion of the funds became available to build what came to be known as the Madero Port of Buenos Aires, the largest and most modern port to be built in all of Latin America in the last decades of the nineteenth century.

While the national legislature spent several years squabbling over the merits of various port schemes for the capital of the republic, provincial deputies moved more swiftly, authorizing the building of a provincial capital at La Plata and a small port at the nearby town of Ensenada. The construction of La Plata, which involved several foreign loans, was one of the most ambitious urban development projects undertaken in South America in the 1880s, for it meant building a new city entirely from scratch. Some Argentines criticized the plan, which they denounced as a white elephant of gigantic proportions. Nonetheless, it would be incorrect to argue that the only criteria for the construction of the provincial capital were political.[21] Governor D'Amico (1882–86), for instance, did a great deal to promote the nearby port at Ensenada with a view to attracting part of the trade that went to Buenos Aires, as well as fostering establishment of several of the first modern meat-packing plants near the new city.[22]

In summary, during the years 1880–86 both the national authorities and those of Buenos Aires province carried out a series of state-run development projects that, in terms of size and cost, had few precedents in Latin American history. In the short run the expansionist policies of the Roca administration were unquestionably attractive, but in the long run they posed serious dangers. The flow of gold from across the Atlantic quickened the pace of railway and urban development in Argentina and attracted a great wave of immigrants. Yet even as this powerful engine of growth stimulated prosperity, it also loaded down the state treasury with an increasingly heavy and inflexible debt burden.

20. On Pellegrini's financial mission in Europe, see Charles Jones, "European Bankers and Argentina, 1880–1890," Working Paper No. 3, Business Imperialism Series (1972), Centre of Latin American Studies, University of Cambridge.

21. A summary of some criticisms can be found in John H. Williams, *Argentine International Trade under Inconvertible Currency, 1880–1900* (Cambridge, Mass., 1920), pp. 40–41.

22. A personal justification for the construction of La Plata and the Ensenada port is found in Carlos D'Amico, *Buenos Aires, sus hombres, su política, 1860–1890* (Buenos Aires, 1977), pp. 126–27, 162–68. (The first edition of this work was published in Mexico City in 1891.)

THE BANKING BOOM IN THE RÍO DE LA PLATA, 1886–1890

As General Roca's presidential term drew to a close, he began organizing a campaign to name his successor. Roca's personal choice was his brother-in-law, Miguel Juárez Celman, an influential landowner and governor of the province of Córdoba. In 1886, after what can only be described as fraudulent elections, Juárez Celman assumed the presidency. Most of his supporters probably expected him to follow the basic guidelines set down by his illustrious predecessor, but the new head of state unexpectedly decided to discard a number of Roca's key policies. Specifically, he decided to reduce the state's role in the administration of railways.

In early 1887 the Ministry of the Interior sold the trunk lines of both the Central Norte and the Andino railways to British capitalists.[23] Juárez Celman justified these measures, arguing that governments are by nature bad economic administrators and that the laissez-faire policies espoused by many European theorists should be adopted as the basic doctrine of the Argentine government.[24] Moreover, both the president and his finance minister insisted that the sale of the transport enterprises would provide the necessary gold to reduce the nation's foreign debt.

But the external financial obligations of the republic did not decline after 1886; they rose to fabulous new heights (see Figure 8). The explanation for this phenomenon is not at first self-evident, for it might be assumed that a government that reduced the issue of railway bonds abroad would lessen its dependency on the European financial markets. But the Argentine elites of the late 1880s did not reject all foreign loans. While they did stop issuing railway loans, they increased the number of external securities sold on behalf of state banks. In this they were extraordinarily successful, obtaining the support of both first-ranking and secondary financial houses in England, France, Belgium, and Germany, all of which channeled enormous amounts of capital into the Argentine banking network.

Between 1886 and 1890 the promotion of government-run banks (on both a national and a provincial level) became the fundamental instruments of the new administration's policies to stimulate economic growth. The public credit institutions included the Banco Nacional, the Banco de la Provincia de Buenos Aires, two state mortgage banks, and after 1887 the official banks of a dozen provinces. As one contemporary observer noted, "The administration has not remained content with the role of these insti-

23. On the sale of the state-owned railways, see Raúl Scalabrini Ortiz, *Historia de los ferrocarriles argentinos* (Buenos Aires, 1974), pp. 221–224, 232–241.

24. On the laissez-faire views of Juárez Celman, see Luis Sommi, *La revolución del 90* (Buenos Aires, 1957), pp. 27–31.

FIGURE 8.
BRITISH EXPORTS TO (A), AND CAPITAL ISSUES FOR (B), ARGENTINA, 1882–1902.

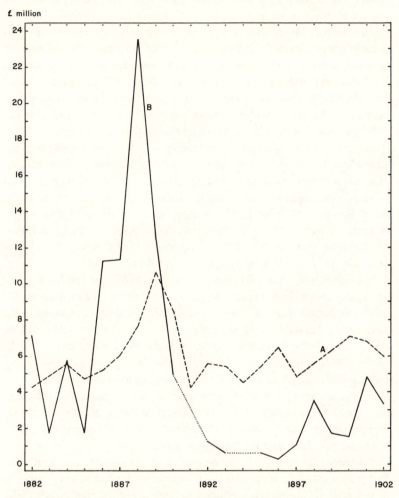

(Source: D.C.M. Platt, *Latin America and British Trade, 1806–1914* [London, 1972], fig. 5, p. 281. Used by permission.)

tutions [the official banks] as auxiliaries to commerce, industry and agriculture; it has converted them into the agents and initiators of all types of economic enterprise . . . having been induced in this error by the experience of the Banco de la Provincia de Buenos Aires."[25]

For more than thirty years the Provincial Bank of Buenos Aires, estab-

25. D'Amico, *Buenos Aires*, p. 107.

lished in 1854, had dominated Argentine finances.[26] Eventually its success provoked the envy and concern of many politicians and businessmen. In order to break its monopoly over note issue, the National Bank (Banco Nacional) had been set up in the 1870s, but not until the following decade did this bank begin to seriously challenge its provincial rival. The National Bank established branches in all the Argentine provinces and contributed to the creation of a unified national monetary and credit system. The bank's expansion was not only based on domestic growth. It relied increasingly on foreign business. The National Bank became the principal international financial agent for the government, servicing the foreign debt and negotiating new loans abroad. In 1886 the bank took the audacious step of issuing 10,000,000 gold pesos worth of its own bonds through a syndicate of German bankers. The following year it assumed responsibility for a similar transaction on behalf of the municipal government of Buenos Aires, and subsequently it multiplied its activities in the European money markets.[27]

An equally important factor in the banking boom of the 1880s was the expansion of the mortgage bank business. Here again the role of foreign capital proved critical. In 1886 the Argentine Congress approved a law creating the National Mortgage Bank, modeled on its provincial counterpart, the prosperous Mortgage Bank of the Province of Buenos Aires. During the years 1886–90 these two land banks issued the fabulous sum of 150,000,000 gold pesos (£30,000,000) in *cédulas* (mortgage bonds) on various European markets, including those of Belgium, Holland, France, England, and Germany.[28]

The mechanics of the sale of the mortgage bonds was one of the most efficacious instruments of speculation ever conceived. The large landowners of the pampa region and the real-estate operators at Buenos Aires (who were the main clients of these banks) received mortgage bonds in exchange for deeds to the specific properties on which the transactions were based.

26. In a speech to the Argentine Congress in 1890, Finance Minister López observed: "During a third of a century the Banco de la Provincia de Buenos Aires was the solid column upon which rested the prosperity of the province" (*Memoria del Ministerio de Hacienda, 1890* [Buenos Aires, 1891], p. lvi). For additional information, see Horacio Cuccorese, *Historia del Banco de la Provincia de Buenos Aires* (Buenos Aires, 1972).

27. The National Bank gradually replaced the Provincial Bank as the main agency for international financial transactions. It also temporarily displaced private Buenos Aires financial firms, such as E. Tornquist y Cía. and S. Hale y Cía. as intermediaries in the negotiations of loans with various European banking syndicates. An illuminating analysis of Argentine banking developments is in Williams, *Argentine International Trade*, chap. 5.

28. The *Money Market Review*, March 29, 1890, published an article entitled "Cédulas," in which it noted, "The great bulk of this paper is held in Europe and chiefly on the Continent. Some amounts were imported into England through certain London establishments, but the vast majority of the several issues passed into the hands of Continental investors through the banking establishments of Paris, Hamburg, Berlin, Amsterdam, Frankfurt and other financial centres."

These mortgage bonds were negotiable cash instruments that could be sold by financial agents on the Buenos Aires Stock Exchange or abroad.[29] Meanwhile, the individuals who held the mortgages were obliged to make regular payments to the banks so that the latter could in turn cover the interest charges on the bonds. But given the complex nature of the financial jugglery, the banks were rarely able to determine whether the money had been invested productively or whether it had been employed in speculative ventures. Moreover, because the mortgage banks were public institutions the government soon found itself trapped into servicing an immense number of private debts that had been generated by the spiraling prices of rural and urban properties.[30]

The number of fortunes built on the basis of mortgage-bond speculation during the later 1880s was legion and included a varied cast of characters: wealthy landowners, urban property owners, out-and-out speculators, politicians, and bank directors. The same could be said of the large crowd of individuals who benefited from the increasingly lax policies applied by the National Bank and the Provincial Bank. The corruption became so widespread that, according to one report, the unscrupulous governor of the province of Buenos Aires, Máximo Paz (1886–90), made it a daily habit to ask the director of the Provincial Bank to his home to provide him with a list of people who were to be granted financial favors on the following day.[31]

The pivot of the financial frenzy was located at Buenos Aires, but soon politicians and capitalists from the other Argentine provinces also began to take steps to profit from the real-estate and banking boom. It should be recalled that Juárez Celman and many of his closest collaborators came from the midwestern province of Córdoba, and that they had retained extensive business interests there. Until 1887, however, local banking capital was scarce, both in Córdoba and in other regions of the interior of the country, all of which relied heavily on Buenos Aires banks and merchant firms for credit.[32] In order to lessen this financial dependency, the national and

29. On the mechanics of the *cédula* sales, see Ferns, *Britain and Argentina*, pp. 370–371, 420–422; and Williams, *Argentine International Trade*, pp. 73–85.

30. In early 1891 the Mexican ambassador at Buenos Aires commented on the consequences of the speculation provoked by the *cédulas*: "In the days of prosperity of this Republic, the business fever became epidemic; the transactions multiplied and the real estate passed through the hands of eight to ten proprietors in a single week, increasing their value with each new sale. Thus the nominal price was much greater than the real value of the property. The banks gave credit on properties which in reality were not worth a tenth of the mortgage and issued mortgage bonds [*cédulas*] on the basis of the nominal value of the real estate" (ASRE, file LE-1678, letter from Juan Sánchez Azcona, minister at the Mexican Legation at Buenos Aires, March 23, 1891).

31. D'Amico, *Buenos Aires*, pp. 109, 180–183.

32. On the demands of Córdoba politicians for new sources of credit and for foreign loans,

provincial authorities agreed to ratify the so-called Free-Banking Law of 1887, which authorized any banking organization to issue bank notes, provided it purchase government gold bonds to the full amount of the notes to be issued.

As a result of this law, seven provinces that had no banks (Santiago del Estero, La Rioja, Mendoza, San Juan, Catamarca, San Luis, and Corrientes) were able to set up official credit institutions and to begin printing money quickly. At the same time, thirteen previously existing financial institutions also took advantage of the law to increase their issue; among these were the provincial banks of Córdoba, Santa Fé, Entre Ríos, and Buenos Aires.

With some modifications, the new legislation was an attempt to emulate the National Bank system of the United States.[33] Argentine businessmen and politicians were aware of the enormous expansion and multiplication of banks in North America and of the decisive contribution they had made to economic development there. But several important differences existed between the basic guidelines used in the Argentine and United States banking systems. One common point was assurance that each bank would guarantee its note issue with negotiable government bonds to be held as a reserve fund. In contrast to the United States, however, where almost all the banks were private, in Argentina a great number of the new credit enterprises were public provincial institutions. The Argentine regional banks raised most of their capital through negotiation of foreign loans that were guaranteed by state revenues.

In the years 1886, 1887, and 1888, Córdoba politicians authorized three successive bond issues in Europe, totaling 16,000,000 gold pesos. Similar measures were adopted by the authorities of almost all the Argentine provinces. As a result, the value of the external debts of these provinces had surpassed £30,000,000 by the year 1890 (see Appendix B). In theory, the bulk of these funds were to be used to strengthen the capital base of the provincial banks and to back up their bank notes. In practice, however, local state treasurers and bank directors channeled much of the foreign gold into private speculative ventures.[34]

In summary, the sweeping bank reforms did not strengthen the autonomy of the Argentine banking system, but rather weakened it by accentuating

---

see M. Candelari, M. González, and D. Roca, *Inversiones extranjeras en Córdoba, 1870–1900* (Universidad Nacional de Córdoba, 1975), pp. 22–39.

33. For parallels between United States and Argentine banking legislation, see Williams, *Argentine International Trade*, pp. 55–64.

34. According to an official investigation, the authorities in the province of Córdoba "managed to dispose in illegal ways of no less than 70 million pesos" (Williams, *Argentine International Trade*, pp. 63–66).

dependency on foreign money markets. At the same time, the finances of the national government were compromised by the irresponsible policies of the bank directors. All told, the national government delivered 200,000,000 gold pesos worth of bonds to the banks as a guarantee for a similar quantity of bank notes. But the banks paid less than 80,000,000 gold pesos for these securities. The national treasury thus found itself in the position of having to guarantee a huge sum of paper money with reserves equivalent to less than 40 percent of that sum. Depreciation of the paper money began almost at once, driving the gold premium upward by 130 percent between 1887 and 1890. As the inflation accelerated, various rings of gold speculators in Buenos Aires added fuel to the fire, causing havoc in currency markets, in the stock exchange, and in the real-estate market.[35]

FINANCIAL FRENZY IN URUGUAY, 1887–1890

The banking boom of the late 1880s was not exclusively an Argentine phenomenon. Similar developments took place in Uruguay, where following the financial reform of 1883 a rapid expansion took place in urban and railway construction, sheep ranching, real-estate speculation, and banking. Although Uruguayan capitalism was fueled fundamentally by domestic factors, a contributing element was the migration of capital and capitalists from Buenos Aires to Montevideo.

That Argentine entrepreneurs were interested in expanding their activities to the small republic on the northern banks of the Río de la Plata is no surprise. For more than half a century Montevideo had been a key commercial entrepôt, serving as intermediary for the trade of the Argentine river provinces of Entre Ríos, Santa Fé, and Corrientes as well as for the trade of the southernmost province of Brazil, Rio Grande do Sul. Already in the early 1850s audacious businessmen, such as Brazilian banker Baron Mauá, and his friend the speculator José de Buschental had grasped the nature of the advantages Montevideo offered for a broad range of financial and commercial transactions. Mauá established the first modern bank in Uruguay and remained active in the real-estate and financial spheres until 1875. Furthermore, during the years 1870–73 several groups of financiers from Buenos Aires staked out positions in the Uruguayan capital, participating in the first important foreign loan of the nation.[36]

35. On gold speculation in Buenos Aires, see A. G. Ford, *The Gold Standard, 1880–1914: Britain and Argentina* (Oxford, 1962), pp. 132–141.

36. On Mauá's activities in Uruguay, see Lidia Besouchet, *Mauá en el Río de la Plata: prólogo a la correspondencia política* (Buenos Aires, 1942), and Marchant, *Mauá*, pp. 151–154, 176–178. The Argentine firm that served as intermediary for the £3,000,000 Uruguayan

After 1880 the financial links between Argentina and Uruguay became stronger. In 1883, for example, the Buenos Aires financial firm of S. B. Hale y Cia. arranged a foreign loan for the city of Montevideo through the banking house of Baring Brothers. At the same time, the Bank of London and River Plate, which had formerly operated mainly in Argentina, intensified its operations in Uruguay. The president of the bank, George Drabble, took over the most important local transport firm, the Central Uruguay Railway, and obtained capital from Great Britain to build hundreds of miles of new branches.[37]

But the most spectacular example of the role of foreign capital in bringing Uruguayan finances to the boiling point can be found in the activities of the syndicate organized by Emilio Reus during the years 1887–90. Reus came to be considered the prototype of the speculator-banker in this age of unbridled financial furor. Born in Tarragona, Spain, he had settled in Madrid, gaining a widespread if brief notoriety as lawyer, politician, playwright, and editor. In 1885, after losing much money on the Madrid Stock Exchange, he emigrated to Argentina, presumably to escape his creditors. In Buenos Aires he obtained employment as financial chronicler in the newspaper *Patria*, and soon he was speculating heavily in the money market. Another spate of losses led him once again to seek greener pastures for his financial talents, and early in 1887 he turned to Montevideo.

At that moment a major banking boom was gathering strength at the Uruguayan capital. Two large private banks, the Banco Comercial and the agency of the Bank of London and River Plate, dominated the local credit market, although they faced increasing competition from a number of smaller financial firms. The president of Uruguay, General Máximo Tajes, did not oppose the proliferation of banks, but he wanted a strong credit institution that could serve simultaneously as a financial *point d'appui* for the government and as a source of funds for ranchers and farmers. Emilio Reus immediately seized the opportunity, organizing a syndicate of capitalists, including Argentine wool merchants and financiers Edward Casey, Thomas Duggan, Emilio Bunge, and Eduardo Agarragaray, who proposed to serve as the founders of a national bank. Shortly thereafter the Banco Nacional de la República Oriental del Uruguay was set up, with Reus as first managing director.[38]

---

foreign loan of 1871 was that of Lumb and Wanklyn, owners of the Banco Mercantil Argentino.

37. On Drabble's business interests in Uruguay, see David Joslin, *A Century of Banking in Latin America* (London, 1963), pp. 39–40, 133–139.

38. On Reus and his activities, see J. Ferrando, *Reseña del crédito público del Uruguay* (Montevideo, 1969), pp. 97–101; Carlos Visca, *Emilio Reus y su época* (Montevideo, 1963);

Although the aims of the Uruguayan National Bank were to stabilize official finance and promote rural development, its operations stimulated financial speculation and instability.[39] The first major transaction Reus pursued, in conjunction with the London banking firm of Barings, was acquisition of a large percentage of the internal bonds of 1886 at a low price. Barings negotiated a £4,000,000 foreign loan for the Uruguayan government by which the internal bonds were exchanged for external gold bonds, producing a huge profit for the insiders. A second project of Reus and his cronies lay in the creation of a large construction and real-estate firm to promote the development of two important suburban districts of Montevideo, both named after Reus.

In 1889, after having overextended himself, Reus had to liquidate most of his holdings. But once again, like the eternal phoenix, the audacious financier managed to raise enough capital to launch a last and formidable speculative venture. He created two new banks, the Sociedad de Crédito Argentino at Buenos Aires and the Banco Transátlantico at Montevideo. These enterprises lasted only a few months. Both were swallowed up by the crisis of 1890, and a year later Reus died in complete poverty in a small apartment in Montevideo.

Emilio Reus was not the only bankrupt of these years. In 1890 the Banco Nacional of Uruguay folded, producing a run on all the other local banks and creating a panic on the Montevideo Stock Exchange. At Buenos Aires the years 1890 and 1891 witnessed the fall of the Argentine National Bank, the collapse of the land mortgage banks, and the crash of the Provincial Bank of Buenos Aires. Hundreds of mercantile firms were swallowed up by the crisis. In addition, the Buenos Aires and Montevideo financial debacles exercised a critical influence in triggering the famous Baring Panic in London, an event that dramatically illustrated the degree to which the greatest European banking houses had become involved in the vicissitudes of the finances of the Río de la Plata.

THE EUROPEAN BANKERS: RIVALRY AND COLLABORATION

While there is no doubt that the expansionist policies of the Argentine and Uruguayan governments were largely responsible for the phenomenal loan boom of the 1880s, it would be misleading to neglect the role of the

---

and Raul Montero Bustamamnte, *El Banco Comercial y la época de Reus* (Montevideo, 1966).

39. Nonetheless, according to an informed study the Banco Nacional did contribute substantially, if ephemerally, to the expansion of many ranching and agricultural establishments (Bernardo Nahum and José P. Barrán, *Historia rural del Uruguay* [Montevideo, 1971], 2:460–472).

foreign banks. The large surplus of capital in European money markets encouraged bankers to channel funds to the Río de la Plata. During the early 1880s a steady flow of gold began, but as we have already seen, by the second half of the decade the stream became an uncontrolled torrent. In May 1887 the *Money Market Review* spoke glowingly of the boom in South American securities, describing Argentina as "the United States of South America," and as late as April 1889 the same journal could affirm: "Even at this hour what can an investor desirous of getting 4 or 5% interest (an increasingly difficult thing to accomplish) do better than spread it over a selection of the Argentine State and Railway Guarantees, throwing in a mixture of Brazil and Chili?"[40]

But why were the European investors so eager to invest their capital in Argentina? High profit rates on both private and public investments offer one important explanation, but there were additional reasons. Argentina and Uruguay were very good credit risks. In the 1880s their per capita foreign trade averaged £6 to £7 per year, whereas in most other Latin American nations the figures ranged between £1 and £2. According to the contemporary statistician Michael Mulhall, the per capita income of the inhabitants of Uruguay and of the eastern provinces of Argentina ranked on a level with those of Canada, the United States, and Australia.[41] Such a high level of prosperity could not be overlooked by foreign bankers, who fought for a share of the rapidly expanding financial business in the Río de la Plata.

Although the bulk of the money that flowed to Argentina and Uruguay originated in the London Stock Exchange, we should also note the parallel surge of capital that came from other financial centers of Europe. Most important in this respect was the role of Paris and Brussels as markets for Argentine government securities and mortgage bonds, but equal note should be taken of the growing participation of the Berlin and Frankfurt exchanges in this intoxicating financial merry-go-round. Inevitably, money attracted more money. The *Money Market Review* underlined the cosmopolitan character of the loan business:

Holders of Argentine securities may be invited to consider how vast and widespread are the interests which are concerned in upholding Argentine credit. Four or five of the greatest Banks and other Joint-Stock Companies are identified with her bond issues; and so likewise are the establishments at Paris, Berlin, and many other continental centres of finance. It is not as in the old days when the relations

40. *Money Market Review*, April 13, 1889.
41. See references to comparative per capita income in Michael Mulhall, *Handbook of the River Plate* (Buenos Aires and London, 1885), pp. 17, 19, 88.

of the Argentine government with Europe were conducted only through one or two channels.[42]

The Argentine railway loan of 1881 had marked the entrance of French bankers into the Río de la Plata bond business. Thereafter, several leading Paris banks—for example, the Comptoir d'Escompte, the Banque de Paris et des Pays Bas, and the Société Générale—took shares in another seven national government loans, while a number of lesser French financial firms participated in eight Argentine provincial loans. In the larger transactions the French financiers tended to act jointly with British banking houses, forming broad-based syndicates to guarantee the success of sales. Even so, the French participation represented an unmistakable threat to the former monopoly of the London merchant banks over South American finance.[43]

A more belated challenge to the British came from another quarter as two powerful German financial concerns, the Deutsche and Disconto banks, moved into private banking at Buenos Aires in the late 1880s. At the same time, they promoted international loans for the Argentine national government, for the National Bank, and for the city of Buenos Aires.[44] Some historians have linked this German financial offensive to Bismarck's new geopolitical strategy, but evidence suggests that strictly economic factors played a dominant role. German mercantile and industrial companies were actively pursuing the conquest of Latin American markets in the late 1880s. And German banks were becoming increasingly involved in the export of capital because of the growing abundance of money on the stock exchanges of Frankfurt and Berlin[45]

Despite the growing competition, the London financial firms continued to control the greater part of the capital exports that deluged the region of the Río de la Plata. In contrast to their French and German rivals, who invariably operated in groups or syndicates, the British bankers generally adopted a more individualistic strategy. There were at least a dozen important London merchant banks engaged in Argentine and Uruguayan loans. The best known were Stern Brothers, J. S. Morgan, Murrieta, Morton/ Rose, L. Cohen & Sons, Glyn/Mills, and of course Baring Brothers.

Each of these merchant banks tended to specialize in a particular sphere

42. *Money Market Review*, November 26, 1887.

43. On French loans to the Argentine national and provincial governments, see Marichal, "Los banqueros europeos," pp. 54–62, and Andrés Regalsky, "Inversiones francesas en empréstitos públicos nacionales, 1880–1890" (Paper presented at Asociación Argentina de Historia Económica, VI Jornadas de Historia Económica Córdoba, 1984).

44. On the participation of German bankers in Argentine finance, see Marichal, "Los banqueros europeos," pp. 63–68.

45. For data on the foreign bond activity on the German stock market, see Max Wirth, "The Crisis of 1890," *Journal of Political Economy* (London), March 1893, pp. 227–229.

of Argentine or Uruguayan financial business. For instance, Murrieta was heavily engaged in loans for the provincial governments of Entre Ríos and Santa Fé, as well as in the financing of the Central Norte railway. Morton, Rose & Company tended to specialize in the sale of bonds on behalf of the Buenos Aires state railway, the Ferrocarril Oeste. Cohen & Sons participated in the issue of foreign loans for the provinces of Corrientes, San Juan, and Tucumán. Glyn, Mills & Company was closely linked to various Anglo-Argentine railway firms. Stern Brothers took part in bond issues for San Juan and Buenos Aires. And Morgan participated in the 1886 public works loan and in financing a private railway firm.[46]

The most powerful house, Baring Brothers—which jointly with N. M. Rothschilds was considered to be the preeminent leader of the British merchant banking community—was engaged in activities more vast and more diverse than those of any of its rivals. It took charge of the Uruguayan government's foreign loans of 1883 and 1888. At the same time, it led most of the European banking syndicates selling bonds of the Argentine national government during the 1880s and also took a share in several Buenos Aires provincial and municipal loans.[47] Despite the breadth of Baring's ventures in the realm of public finance, these were less risky than its speculative plunges in the field of private finance.

Baring's participation in the wild speculations of Emilio Reus at Montevideo has already been mentioned. Equally audacious and imprudent was the attempt by Lord Revelstoke, leading partner of the merchant bank, to take over the state-owned Buenos Aires Water Supply & Drainage Company. British and Argentine critics of the operation accused Revelstoke of having bribed President Juárez Celman and Minister Eduardo Wilde with the huge sum of £180,000 for the concession.[48] But regardless of the veracity of the accusations, the waterworks scheme turned out to be a financial disaster for the bank because it overloaded the Baring portfolio with stock that proved to be unsaleable amid the financial turmoil of 1889 and 1890.

In summary, a great number of European financial firms became engrossed in Argentine and Uruguayan finances during these years, and as happens time and again in the banking world, the intense rivalry led the banks to take unwarranted risks, believing that if they did not participate in

46. Additional information on the operations of these banking firms in the Río de la Plata region can be found in Carlos Marichal, "Foreign Finance and the Argentine State, 1862–1890" (unpublished manuscript).

47. Barings led the European syndicates for the Argentine national loans of 1882, 1885, 1888, and 1889. For additional details, see Appendix B in this book.

48. British newspaper reports did not agree on the actual amount of the bribes paid; £180,000 was the low figure, £320,000 was the highest estimate (*Weekly Bulletin*, June 20, 1891, cited by M. Peña, *Alberdi, Sarmiento, el 90* [Buenos Aires, 1973], p. 12).

the loan boom they would lose profitable opportunities for business.[49] Yet by mid-1889 the majority of the foreign money managers had begun to think twice about advancing any more money to the Argentine or Uruguayan republics.

Almost alone, the directors of Barings, a firm that had a reputation for prudent, conservative practice in the handling of international business transactions, seemed oblivious to the waning of confidence in the financial markets. As late as the spring of 1890, they attempted to place £2,000,000 in newly minted Uruguayan bonds on the London market. Shortly thereafter came news of the banking and mercantile crisis at Montevideo (May 1890), of political revolution at Buenos Aires (July 1890), and of the possibility of a suspension of payments by the treasuries of both Argentina and Uruguay. To make matters worse, Barings itself was on the verge of bankruptcy and was therefore in no position to assist its South American clients. Once again, the transition from boom to bust undermined the most dynamic Latin American economies and shook the international banking community. The inevitable result was a new debt crisis.

49. For comments on the aggressive tactics of the European money managers and for information on the principal financial companies involved in Argentine speculation, see Horacio Cuccorese, "La versión histórica argentina sobre la crisis de Baring Brothers en 1890," in Academia Nacional de Historia, *Investigaciones y Ensayos* (Buenos Aires) 20, no. 2 (1976): 312–315.

The Baring Panic of 1890

The suspension of payments on the foreign debt [of Argentina] would have consummated the catastrophe of Baring; affected the Bank of England; and aggravated the perilous state of the London market.

—Speech by Vicente Fidel López to the Argentine Congress, May 5, 1891

O N THE MORNING of Saturday, November 8, 1890, three of the financial leaders of the City—Everard Hambro, Lord Revelstoke, and William Lidderdale—met privately to discuss the fate of what was perhaps the most prestigious London merchant bank. Revelstoke (E. C. Baring) informed Lidderdale (governor of the Bank of England) that he did not know whether his firm could continue operating or "whether we have to stop."[1] The implications were grim, for the bankruptcy of Baring Brothers threatened to unleash a financial panic and perhaps even a major economic depression.

On Monday, November 10, Lidderdale met with Viscount Goschen, the Chancellor of the Exchequer, to ask his support on two counts. The first consisted in persuading the Rothschilds to help transfer a large sum of gold from the Bank of France to the Bank of England as speedily as possible. The second lay in putting pressure on the Argentine government to cover its outstanding debts with Barings. By Wednesday, £3,000,000 in gold arrived from Paris; at the same time, the Bank of England managed to raise another £1,500,000 by selling Exchequer bonds to the financial agent of the Russian government. Although it had been presumed that these measures could stave off or at least slow down the panic, the volume of Baring bills that began to pour into the Bank of England for discount was greater than expected. As a result, Lidderdale moved to unite the entire London banking community in a sophisticated rescue operation. Between Friday and Saturday he succeeded in convincing the cream of the merchant banks—Rothschilds, Glyn/Mills, C. J. Hambro & Son, Raphael, J. S. Morgan, Antony Gibbs, Smith Payne & Smith, Brown/Shipley, and Robarts—as well as the leading joint-stock banks, to pool resources totaling £17,000,000 in order to back up Baring.[2] In the weeks that followed, a

---

1. John Clapham, *The Bank of England: A History, 1797–1914* (Cambridge, 1944), 2:328.

2. Ibid., pp. 332–333. For additional data, see Republic of Argentina, *Memoria del Ministerio de Hacienda, 1890*, pp. xix–xxi.

large portion of Baring's liabilities were liquidated, and by the beginning of 1891 the English financial market had begun to stabilize.

As in previous crises, European financial journalists were quick to look for a scapegoat. In this instance the culprits could be easily identified. The firm of Baring Brothers had unsettled the financial world by overextending itself in a variety of South American ventures, having been beguiled by Argentine and Uruguayan politicians into rash but potentially profitable speculations.[3]

But how decisive were this bank's financial commitments in the Río de la Plata in unleasing the turmoil? The *South American Journal* defended Barings, arguing:

The unfortunate circumstances which together conspired to bring the great house in Bishopsgate Street to a sudden halt did not only relate to its vast commitments in South America, but to the general disturbance of the finance markets throughout the world. Its transactions in North America and all the countries of Europe were even on a larger scale than those identified with the River Plate, and the prolonged depression of North American bonds must have had a most embarrassing influence upon its business.[4]

The powerful merchant bank had extensive interests: in Canada, Barings had long been involved in the financing of railways; in the United States it participated (through allied firms) in the great reorganization of the railway monopolies that took place in the late 1880s; and in France it was engaged in the resolution of the fantastic copper corner that caused the collapse of the powerful Paris bank the Comptoir d'Escompte in 1889.[5]

But regardless of the breadth of the Baring holdings, there is no question that by November 1890 the bank's balance sheet showed that the firm had overburdened itself with Argentine securities totaling some £5,700,000. In principle these stocks and bonds were assets that could be used to liquidate a substantial portion of Baring's £21,000,000 in outstanding liabilities.[6] But the Argentine paper could not be easily transformed into hard cash.

3. The financial press criticized European bankers as a whole, but the brunt of their fire was directed against Baring Brothers and the Argentine state banks. See, e.g., W. R. Lawson, "Gaucho Banking," *Bankers Magazine* (London) 51 (January 1891): 33–52.

4. *South American Journal*, November 22, 1890.

5. On the Baring interests in Canadian railways, see Naylor, *History of Canadian Business*, 1:267–275. On the French copper corner of 1889, see Max Wirth, "The Crisis of 1890," *Journal of Political Economy* 1 (March 1893): 220–222; and Claudio Jannet, *Le Capital, la spéculation, et la finance au XIXe siècle* (Paris, 1892), pp. 322–331.

6. According to the *South American Journal*, June 13, 1891, the Baring portfolio contained £5,700,000 in Argentine securities, £2,100,000 in Uruguayan bonds, and £1,100,000 in bonds of other Latin American governments as of November 1890.

The suspension of debt service payments by the Banco Nacional at Buenos Aires, six months earlier, had caused a steady decline in the market value of Argentine external bonds. If Barings attempted to sell off these securities on the Royal Exchange, it would not only suffer enormous losses but further disrupt stock transactions and possibly precipitate a full-scale collapse. Thus it was in the interests of the entire financial community at London to shore up the old merchant bank at the same time as they moved to restructure the Argentine foreign debt.

The Baring Panic of 1890 was an intense but relatively short-lived crisis. It reflected a temporary weakening of commercial, industrial, and banking activity in different parts of the world, but it was not the harbinger of a prolonged international depression like that of 1873. In this sense, economic historians are probably correct in arguing that the financial storm of 1890 can be defined essentially as an Anglo-Argentine crisis.[7] Nonetheless, several aspects give this debt crisis a broader significance and demonstrate the growing complexity of the relationship between the debtor states of Latin America and their European creditors.

First, in contrast to previous debt crises, which were triggered by recession in the industrial nations of the North Atlantic, that of 1890 was unleashed fundamentally by the crash of the Argentine economy. More than any other factor, it was the bankruptcy of the Argentine state banks and of the government itself that led to the downfall of Baring Brothers. Such consequences were vivid testimony to the growing weight of the Latin American nations in the world economy.

Second, the Anglo-Argentine crisis of 1890 dramatically underlined the risks of the international loan business. The effects of the panic were soon felt in other nations of Latin America, because the panic provoked a marked reduction in the flow of foreign capital. During the 1890s, European bankers were reluctant to extend more new loans for the governments of the region, fearing that they would be burned as badly as Barings had been. In fact, it was not until after the turn of the century that capital flows to Latin America were renewed on a large scale.

But the freeze on foreign loans was not the only important consequence of the crisis. The price that Argentina, in particular, had to pay for having adopted overly ambitious policies of financial expansion was ominous. The restructuring of the Argentine foreign debts took more than a decade to complete. It proved to be the most complex of all financial negotiations in Latin American history to that date, and it was extremely costly for Argen-

---

7. In a classic study, Lauck argued that the 1890 crisis was basically an Anglo-Argentine financial debacle and not therefore the cause of the more widespread depression of 1893 (W. J. Lauck, *The Causes of the Panic of 1893* [Boston, 1907], chaps. 1 and 5).

tine society. It led to the imposition of unpopular austerity measures, a striking reduction in real wages, and the sale of state enterprises to foreign bankers. It implied, in short, capitulation to the dictates of the international banking community in almost every sphere of the economy. The collapse of the Argentine boom bespoke the dangers of promoting economic growth by relying on foreign sources of capital.

On the other hand, for European creditors the events of 1890 reflected the extent to which a political and economic crisis in one Latin American country could affect the money markets of the most powerful capitalist nations. It mattered little now that Buenos Aires was 8,000 miles from London. The staccato telegraph message that told of political revolution and financial turmoil in the Río de la Plata region had an almost immediate impact on the transactions in the Royal Stock Exchange.

FINANCIAL AND POLITICAL TURMOIL IN ARGENTINA

The crisis at Buenos Aires had a prolonged gestation period that spanned the year preceding the Baring collapse. Violent flutuations of the gold premium and of stock prices on the Argentine market, as well as of urban and rural property values, undermined the economy. These circumstances provoked increasing social agitation that finally exploded in a virulent if brief political upheaval.[8] In spite of the symptoms of growing disorder, the Juárez Celman administration did not react decisively, but instead continued its dangerous balancing act between boom and bust. Until early 1890 the bulk of the Argentine propertied classes—wealthy ranchers, urban property owners, merchants, bankers, and politicians—remained engrossed in a fantastic speculative carnival, oblivious to the signs of impending catastrophe.

The vigor of the economic boom appeared to justify the behavior of both Argentine and foreign capitalists in playing the market to the hilt. During the year 1889, property sales had surpassed 300,000,000 pesos, ten times more than in 1886.[9] Scores of new companies were registered on the local stock exchange where total transactions reached as much as 1,000,000,000 paper pesos.[10] Much of the buying and selling represented speculative ven-

8. The classic study on the revolution of 1890 in Buenos Aires is Luis Sommi, *La revolución del 90* (Buenos Aires, 1957).

9. The real-estate transactions at Buenos Aires during these years have been studied by O. Yujnovsky, "Políticas de vivienda en la ciudad de Buenos Aires, 1880–1914," *Desarrollo Económico* 18, no. 54 (July–September 1974): 330–361.

10. See, e.g., Ferns, *Britain and Argentina*, chap. 14, and A. G. Ford, "Argentina and the Baring Crisis of 1890," *Oxford Economic Papers*, n.s. 8, no. 2 (June 1956): 127–150. A contemporary novel that described the stock market speculations of the late 1880s in lurid terms is Julián Martel, *La bolsa* (Buenos Aires, 1898).

tures, but the flood of bank notes and mortgage bonds issued by the official banks ensured that the financial whirlwind would continue. By late 1889 the state banks had put into circulation almost 200,000,000 pesos of their notes, and the mortgage banks had sold *cédulas* to the tune of 350,000,000 pesos.

The boom in banking, real estate, and joint-stock companies did not have only a local origin. Foreign capitalists, as already noted, played an important role. The greater part of the Argentine mortgage bonds were bought by investors in Belgium, France, Germany, and Great Britain, and during 1889 European and especially British financiers invested more than 100,000,000 pesos in a variety of private enterprises in the South American country: railroads, tramways, electric firms, gas works, banks, import-export companies, and ranches.[11]

Not all social classes were deceived by the illusions of economic grandeur. The rapid depreciation of the Argentine currency began to corrode the real income of rural and urban workers. In August 1889, mass strikes took place among port workers in Buenos Aires. In September there were strikes by the employees of various railway companies, and in October thousands of construction workers at the capital carried out a series of demonstrations and walkouts. The authorities responded by jailing several union leaders, but did not go so far as to outlaw the strikes. As the newspaper *El Nacional* argued in an editorial published on October 4, 1889: "The working class movement has a logic of its own and there is no need to force it out of its path into a class war which would be prejudicial to all."[12]

By early 1890 the patience of both workers and middle-class opponents of Juárez Celman evaporated as the phenomenal rise in the premium of gold undercut the value of the peso and produced an equally sharp decline in real wages and property values. In February the gold premium reached 218, in March it was at 240 and in April it reached a peak of 310. Meanwhile Juárez Celman and his ministers ratified a succession of unorthodox monetary and financial reforms that only made things worse. To begin with, the suspension of gold transactions on the stock exchange (decreed in March 1889) spawned a huge black market in foreign currencies and precious metals. In order to defend the peso against further devaluation, Minister Rufino Varela ordered the National Bank to begin selling its gold reserves, a measure that succeeded only in further undermining the value of the national currency. To make matters worse, the government authorized national and provincial banks to continue issuing a huge volume of bank notes and mortgage bonds.

11. For statistical series on foreign investments in Argentina in this period, see Williams, *Argentine International Trade*, chap. 6.

12. Cited in Sommi, *La revolución del 90*, pp. 105–106.

The excess issue of paper money, the government deficits, the gold drain, and the large number of bad bank loans were a vicious combination. The situation became so critical that by March 1890 the national treasury, the National Bank and the Provincial Bank, of Buenos Aires were virtually bankrupt.[13] The government made a last-ditch attempt to raise funds by selling the profitable state railways, including the Ferrocarril Oeste and the remaining branches of the publicly owned Andino and Central Norte lines, to syndicates of British investors. These measures provoked a resounding outcry by the opposition parties and press, who declared that the government had betrayed the nation by selling off its hard-won economic patrimony to foreign capitalists.[14]

On April 13 the opponents of the Juárez Celman regime organized a series of protest meetings throughout the capital, sowing the seeds of the broad-based social and political movement destined to overthrow the president. By June the political movement known as the Union Cívica Radical, which included substantial numbers of workers but was led by members of the propertied classes, had gained such momentum that its spokesmen proclaimed their intention to oust the corruption-ridden executive authorities. On July 26 a revolution headed by several prominent army officers and politicians, broke out at Buenos Aires. But the rebels failed to take advantage of their initial military superiority, and after several days of heavy fighting they were obliged to surrender. Shortly thereafter the Argentine National Congress forced Juárez Celman to resign, replacing him with Vice-president Carlos Pellegrini, who promptly formed an emergency cabinet, including General Roca as minister of the interior and the venerable Vicente Fidel López as minister of finance. These changes placated the opposition forces temporarily but did not bring a definitive peace.

In February 1891 the agitation continued to run strong. The Mexican ambassador at Buenos Aires reported:

Since my arrival official circles are in a state of constant alarm. . . . Every night the garrison troops are placed on a state of alert and numerous brigades patrol the streets. . . . There is little confidence in the economic situation. The number of unemployed increases day by day and the emigration of workers begins to be alarming. . . . Over 20,000 have left recently from Buenos Aires to Montevideo. . . . Among the signs of public discontent I must report a recent and grave

13. It appears that Juárez Celman was oblivious to the dangers of bankruptcy, but a recent revisionist study suggests that the policies adopted by this administration during 1887–89 actually presupposed an audacious financial strategy intended to oblige foreign capital to carry the burden of Argentine economic development. See Tim Duncan, "La política fiscal durante el gobierno de Juárez Celman: una audaz estrategia financiera internacional," *Desarrollo Económico* 23, no. 89 (April–June 1983): 11–34.

14. *La Capital*, March 20, 1890.

event. General Julio Roca, Minister of the Interior, was almost assassinated last evening, and everything suggests that the crime is the doing of a group of unemployed men. . . . Since it is thought that Minister Roca is the soul of the administration in power, all criticisms are directed against him.[15]

A major factor that contributed to the persistence of political instability was the failure of the Pellegrini government to gauge the full extent of the financial crisis that had engendered the social conflicts. This is not to say that it responded passively. In two important fields—fiscal reform and the foreign debt—the administration acted firmly. Minister of Finance López, an aged but lucid politician and intellectual, introduced new fiscal policies that he hoped would increase revenues and reduce deficits. López hiked up customs duties and introduced new taxes on exports and on sales of tobacco, beer, and sugar. He also levied a series of taxes on all foreign banks operating in Argentina. The tax reforms were accompanied by efforts to maintain the international credit of the government and to implement a policy of reconciliation with the European banks in order to avoid default on the enormous foreign debt of the republic. But in the sphere of banking, the authorities responded with less firmness, and as the Argentine banking system crumbled the crisis deepened.

THE BANKING CRISIS AT BUENOS AIRES

The initial steps taken by the Pellegrini administration decelerated but did not halt the economic crisis. The authorities had most difficulty dealing with the gradual but inevitable collapse of the state banking network. The contradictory tactics adopted by the ruling elites to save the public credit institutions reflected their reluctance to recognize the degree of failure of the financial policies that had been adopted in the 1880s.

During the regimes of Roca and Juárez Celman, a large part of the Argentine propertied classes had come to believe that the state banks constituted not merely the symbol but also the chief instruments of economic progress itself. They thought that the demise of the state banks would bring total anarchy to the economy. While their fears ultimately proved to be unwarranted, this attitude delayed adoption of the measures necessary to restructure the banking system and weakened the position of the Argentine government in its renegotiation of the foreign debt.

As early as March 1890 it had been suspected that the most important financial institutions, the Provincial Bank of Buenos Aires and the National Bank, were on the verge of bankruptcy. In order to avoid such a denouement, the governor of the province of Buenos Aires ordered that the funds

15. ASRE, file LE-1678, letter from Minister Sánchez Acona, February 20, 1891.

obtained from the sale of the state-owned railway, the Ferrocarril Oeste, be deposited in the Provincial Bank. At the same time, Finance Minister José Evaristo Uriburu proposed that 60,000,000 pesos of treasury bills be issued to support the National Bank, on the condition that the much-criticized bank president should resign. But Juárez Celman refused to take the latter measure. Instead, in an abrupt about-face he asked for the resignation of Minister Uriburu. Meanwhile, the Argentine president authorized a series of clandestine note issues by various public banks, to be backed up by three short-term loans negotiated with French and Belgian bankers.[16]

After the ouster of Juárez Celman, Pellegrini and López again confronted the prospect of an imminent collapse by the National and Provincial banks. Pellegrini decided to carry out Uriburu's old plan, issuing 60,000,000 pesos in treasury bills to bolster bank reserves. This stabilized financial operations for several months, but in November the unexpected news of the Baring collapse came. At the instigation of the governor of the Bank of England and of Lord Rothschild, the Argentine government agreed to transfer 43,000,000 pesos of the treasury notes held by the National Bank to pay short-term debts in Europe, a large portion consisting of acceptances due to Barings.[17] As a result, the once-powerful Argentine state banks found themselves moving again toward financial disaster.

In early January 1891 Pellegrini received news of an imminent run by depositors on the Provincial Bank of Buenos Aires. In response he instructed the already weak Banco Nacional to transfer a part of its reserves to the former institution. To raise additional funds, he imposed a 2 percent tax on all deposits held by foreign-owned banks, as well as a 7 percent tax on their profits. The executive branch justified the latter action, arguing that private firms—such as the Bank of London and River Plate—were run by heartless, avaricious managers who refused to recognize the wisdom of helping the public banks in their darkest hour.[18] These nationalistic measures won Pellegrini political support but did not solve the banking crisis.

The managers of the Bank of London and River Plate, as well as those of other private banks, had good reason to protect themselves—building up their gold reserves and restricting credits, rather than helping the state banks. They were aware that the Buenos Aires banking system was about

16. These short-term loans totaled 11,000,000 gold pesos and were obtained through L. R. Cahen d'Anvers et Cie. and the Bank of Antwerp (Williams, *Argentine International Trade*, p. 117, n. 3).

17. For details on the transfer of the treasury bills by the Banco Nacional to European creditors, see Republic of Argentina, *Memoria del Ministerio de Hacienda, 1890*, pp. xxiii–xxv, and "Anexos" 1 and 2; see also ibid., *1891*, pp. 169–170, 172.

18. See the bitter attack by Minister López against the private banks in ibid., *1890*, pp. xxxix–xli.

to collapse.[19] On March 6, after being informed that the leading state institutions were once again on the verge of suspending payments, Pellegrini and López declared a banking holiday. Four days later they asked the financial and merchant community of Buenos Aires to save the public banks by subscribing to a "patriotic loan" of 100,000,000 pesos. The capitalists took 40,000,000 pesos of the bonds, but this was not enough. As a result, on April 4, the National Mortgage Bank suspended payments on its *cédulas*, and on April 7 both the National Bank and the Provincial Bank announced a ninety-day moratorium on all transactions. The Buenos Aires newspaper *El Diario* noted: "While the news [of the bank moratorium] has made a large impression on commercial circles, it has provoked great alarm among the working classes and the small depositors subject to the impact of street rumors. . . . On Florida Street the agitation was intense among the circle of stockbrokers and merchants."[20]

At this point it became clear that the entire public banking system would have to be dismantled. Pellegrini's close friend Vicente Casares, who had been conducting an investigation of the financial state of the Banco Nacional, issued a withering report on the extraordinary degree of corruption in this banking institution.[21] Pellegrini and López had no alternative but to close the Banco Nacional.

In the months that followed, the economic situation worsened. On July 6, 1891, the *Buenos Aires Standard* observed with considerable bitterness:

Business is almost at a standstill. . . . Hundreds of the working classes are starving and soup kitchens are crowded by hungry applicants. Nevertheless, the display of carriages and Russian horses at Palermo Park last Thursday was really superb, quite equal to what one sees at the Bois de Boulogne of Paris. The people who own the carriages are evidently living in a fool's paradise, ignorant of the volcano on which we stand.

The volcano did not explode. The leading private banks survived a run by thousands of depositors in June.[22] Gradually the economy stabilized. By September the government reported that there would be a large trade surplus, the first in a decade, and that railway and urban construction had

19. Joslin, *A Century of Banking*, pp. 125–127.

20. *El Diario*, April 8, 1891.

21. The report prepared by Casares was published in full by the *Buenos Aires Standard* on April 29, 1891. For comments, see J. E. Hodge, "Carlos Pellegrini and the Financial Crisis of 1890," *HAHR* 50, no. 3 (August 1970): 517–518.

22. Not all the private banks escaped unscathed, however. For example, the Banco de Italia y Río de la Plata was obliged to close its doors temporarily after the drain of 12,000,000 pesos by fearful depositors. For a vivid description of the run on the Bank of London and River Plate, see Joslin, *A Century of Banking*, pp. 127–129.

begun to pick up. A month later the National Congress passed a bill authorizing creation of a new state credit institution, the Banco de la Nación.[23]

It can be argued that the Pellegrini administration was ultimately successful in its efforts to resolve the banking crisis, but the impact of the financial damage should not be underestimated. The breakdown of the Argentine banking system (the most highly developed national banking network in Latin America during the 1880s) reflected three serious failures on the part of the Argentine ruling classes.

The first error may be considered a technical fault. The extraordinarily rapid growth of the state banks had taken place without maintenance of a reasonable level of gold or silver reserves with which to back up the issue of paper money. This was not only inflationary but also dangerous for the banks. A comparison of the national bank balances of twenty-four of the most economically advanced nations in the world in the year 1889 reveals that the specie ratio of the Argentine banks ranked lowest on the list.[24] In other words, the managers of the Argentine banks adopted extremely risky policies.

The second major failing, which should be defined as a sociopolitical rather than a technical problem, stemmed from the propensity of national and provincial politicians to use bank funds and reserves for outlandish speculation. The issue of loans to friends, relatives, and political allies came to be considered legitimate practice, and most of the money extended in this fashion went into risky but lucrative real-estate operations. Public funds thus became a favored instrument for private accumulation.

The third and most complex failure sprang from the involvement of the state banks in the international loan business. Since the early 1870s the Argentine government had adopted a policy of financing major public works projects and other economic development programs with money raised abroad. As long as the inflow of foreign capital surpassed the outflow, such policies appeared justifiable. But by 1890 the debt service produced a gold drain of ominous proportions.[25] The institutions affected most were the state banks, because they were responsible for assuring the pay-

23. The Banco de la Nación later became the leading bank of Argentina and still holds that position today. An excellent official history is *El Banco de la Nación en su cincuentenario* (Buenos Aires, 1941).

24. The ratio of specie reserves to bank note issues was 357 percent in Australia, 128 percent in the United States, and 70 percent in Great Britain, but only 10 percent in Argentina and 20 percent in Uruguay (Michael Mulhall, *The Dictionary of Statistics* [London, 1892], p. 76).

25. According to one estimate, the debt service for 1890 was equivalent to 60 percent of total Argentine export revenues (Ford, *Gold Standard*, p. 141).

ment of interest and amortization on national and international public debts. The state treasury was unable to provide the credit institutions with the required funds, and it forced them to sell off their gold reserves in order to pay the foreign creditors. When the banks had exhausted all sources of foreign exchange, they faced bankruptcy. Because the banks were in effect government agencies, the whole edifice of public finance was jeopardized. The once-coveted blessings of foreign financial dependency had become a curse.

RENEGOTIATING THE ARGENTINE FOREIGN DEBT, 1891–1893

As a result of the domestic financial crisis and the simultaneous drop in capital flows from abroad, the Argentine government found it impossible to cover the entire external debt service. During 1890 the foreign trade balance produced a deficit of 41,000,000 gold pesos, which if added to the 15,000,000 due in debt service created a gap in the balance of payments that surpassed 50,000,000 pesos.[26] Despite the grave implications of these figures, President Pellegrini insisted that Argentina would not fail its foreign creditors. On receiving news of the Baring Panic, he spelled out his position to a correspondent of the Buenos Aires newspaper *La Nación*: "If the customs revenues are insufficient . . . I shall ask for authorization to sell the properties of the state. . . . Rather than suspend service on the debt, I would prefer to renounce the presidency."[27]

In practice, however, both Pellegrini and López had already begun to sound out the European bankers on a series of rescue measures that they hoped would tide the treasury over the crisis. In September 1890, two months before the Baring collapse, they had sent an experienced financial technocrat, Victorino de la Plaza, to London to open discussions with the leading merchant bankers of the City. He was urged to argue that the Argentine Finance Ministry could not continue to remit payments to Europe without buying large quantities of gold on the Buenos Aires market. But such action threatened to produce even greater agitation among the gold speculators and to debilitate the Argentine currency further.[28]

---

26. Williams, *Argentine International Trade*, p. 136.

27. Cuccorese, "La version histórica argentina sobre la crisis de Baring Brothers en 1890," p. 290.

28. Finance Minister López observed, "The principal aim of the mission [of De la Plaza] was to avoid having to go into the market to buy gold [for the payment of the debt service]" (Republic of Argentina, *Memoria del Ministerio de Hacienda, 1890*, p. xii). Williams adds that the speculators, "knowing when the half-year remittances of interest came due, laid their plans accordingly. By 'rigging the market' they ran up the price of gold in preparation for the great event . . . so that the government found itself forced to pay a higher price" (Williams, *Argentine International Trade*, p. 124).

The group of London bankers in charge of supervising the Baring liquidation, known as the Rothschild Committee, met with De la Plaza on November 27, 1890.[29] Soon there was an agreement that stipulated that the Argentine authorities should temporarily overlook their own financial problems and assist Barings by ordering the Banco Nacional to remit money to liquidate short-term debts and by canceling Barings' obligations to pay its last installment on the notorious Water Supply & Drainage Company transaction.[30] In exchange, the London banking community agreed to arrange a large bond issue to cover the service on the Argentine external debt. This would impede a drop of the bond quotations and protect both the bankers and the government. Baron Rothschild explained the nature of the measures in a public letter to the Bank of England: "The recent severe crisis . . . has disclosed that there are very large financial interests engaged in the Argentine Republic, and has made it clear to those who joined together in facilitating the liquidation of the Barings' affairs that the result of this liquidation is dependent upon the future value of Argentine securities and obligations."[31]

The Argentine Funding Arrangement, as it came to be known, was in fact a moratorium that relieved the Buenos Aires authorities of having to make full payments in cash on their debts during a period of three years. In exchange the Argentine state would print a set of new bonds (with a value equivalent to the interest due) that would be handed over to the bondholders.[32] The banking houses were amenable to this arrangement because many of them—including not only Baring, but also Murrieta, Glyn/Mills, Stern, Morton/Rose and others—held large amounts of Argentine securities and wanted to avoid the catastrophic fall in quotations that would surely follow on default.

The unstable situation on the London money market made it difficult to

29. The committee was headed by the banker Rothschild precisely because he was not engaged in Argentine business. Additional members included partners of Antony Gibbs, Hambros, J. S. Morgan, and Glyn/Mills. Two other important participants were Charles Goschen, brother of the Chancellor of the Exchequer, and George Drabble, president of the Bank of London and River Plate.

30. The last installment to be paid by Barings was for 7,000,000 gold pesos (approximately £1,200,000) (Republic of Argentina, *Memoria del Ministerio de Hacienda, 1890*, p. xvii).

31. The full text of the letter is in H. L. Shepherd, "Default and Adjustment of the Argentine Foreign Debt, 1890–1906," U.S. Department of Commerce Trade Promotion Series, no. 145 (Washington, D.C., 1933), pp. 29–32.

32. A total issue of 15,000,000 gold pesos in new bonds was authorized, but only 7,000,000 pesos actually went onto the market. Details on the funding arrangement are in Jose Peña, *Deuda Argentina, recopilación de leyes, decretos, resoluciones, notas y contratos* (Buenos Aires, 1907), document 85, pp. 527–540. Additional information is in ADERA, folder 2103, "Antecedentes de empréstitos argentinos—Empréstito de Consolidación de 6% de 1891."

decide which bank should underwrite the new bond issue. Finally, the powerful Anglo-American house of J. S. Morgan & Company decided to assume responsibility for the transaction. Why that firm took this bold step has not been explained by historians, but one important reason was the alliance with its sister branch of J. P. Morgan & Company of New York, already the leading investment bank in the United States. Proof of the importance of the American connection came in the spring of 1891, when J. P. Morgan sailed for England to assume control of J. S. Morgan & Company following the death of his father. While in London, the New York financial magnate was able to preside over the final negotiations for the issue of the Argentine bonds under the Funding Arrangement.[33]

Not all the creditors of the Argentine government were satisfied with the moratorium loan. The German and French bankers were especially critical of the way negotiations had been conducted with De la Plaza. They tended to be more sanguine than their British colleagues, arguing that a respite of six months would be sufficient for the Argentine economy to recover. After that, they expected Finance Minister López could raise the funds necessary to renew interest payments. Furthermore, the German bankers felt that they had not been fairly treated by the London merchant banks in charge of the negotiations.

The director of the Disconto Bank, Von Hansemann sent a memorandum to Finance Minister López in March 1891, noting that several of the loans in which German investors had interests were not guaranteed by the Rothschild / De la Plaza arrangement. Moreover, he added, the favoritism of the British committee had been clearly demonstrated by the disclosure that the only Argentine loan to receive 100 percent interest payments was the 1886 Port Works Loan, an operation that was in the charge of none other than the house of Morgan.[34]

In order to answer these charges and to assure the success of the agreement on the European continent, de la Plaza promised to go to Berlin in early 1891. But on receiving news of the intransigeance of the heads of the Deutsche and Disconto banks he canceled his trip. He wrote to Carlos Calvo, the Argentine ambassador at Berlin, criticizing the German financiers and adding that their fears with respect to the British bankers were groundless.[35] The financial wrangling went on for more than a year, but by early 1892 De la Plaza was finally able to sign an accord with bankers at Berlin and Paris.

Although Pellegrini and his associates appeared to have maintained the

---

33. *South American Journal*, March 28, 1891.
34. The text of Von Hausseman's memorandum is in ADERA, folder 2156.
35. The letters of De la Plaza on this subject are in ibid.

credit standing of the government, the costs were heavy—so heavy that, only a few months after authorization had been given for the Morgan loan, officials at Buenos Aires were having second thoughts about its virtues. Popular protests at Buenos Aires revealed widespread anti-British sentiments.[36] The *Buenos Aires Standard* observed on June 5, 1891:

The bankers and millionaires of London can have no idea of the bitter feelings that have been engendered by the unfortunate Moratoribus-Rothschild loan. They were apparently under the impression that they were conferring a great favor on Argentina by preventing the financial bankruptcy of Baring Brothers. But the whole business had been viewed here in a very different light. . . . The English flags in Plaza Victoria were torn down by well-dressed Argentines. . . . and the recent run on the London Bank was cheered and applauded in many circles that never before showed us any ill will.

In October 1892 a new president, Luis Saenz Peña, replaced Pellegrini, and a new finance minister, Juan José Romero, took over the task of dealing with the foreign creditors. Romero sent another financial agent to Europe to cancel the old Morgan loan and to negotiate a new agreement with the bankers.

The minister's instructions were peremptory: The funding loan was a national disaster, having placed an enormous and unacceptable burden on the treasury.[37] A new solution was indispensable. Moreover, Romero added, the collusion between De la Plaza and the Morgan bankers had been notorious. In order to avoid further misunderstandings, Romero requested Baring Brothers, which was now back on its feet, to send a representative to Buenos Aires to discuss terms. The agent, a Mr. Read, accepted most of the demands of the finance minister, and in mid-1893 a new moratorium was arranged, known as the Romero Arrangement. Payments on the sinking fund of the Argentine external debt were suspended for a decade, and interest payments on fourteen loans were reduced substantially over a period of five years. After that date, full interest payments were to be resumed.[38]

The advantages of the new pact for the Argentine government were considerable. In the first place, no more new Morgan bonds would be issued, thereby arresting the increase of the nominal value of the external debt. The

36. Much criticism was directed against the Bank of London and River Plate. The local managers of the bank became so anxious that they asked the British government to intervene militarily to protect their interests. However, the secretary of the Foreign Office, Salisbury, refused to intervene (Ferns, *Britain and Argentina*, pp. 465–467).

37. The correspondence of Romero is in ADERA, folder 2103, "Antecedentes de Empréstitos Argentinos-Arreglo Romero."

38. On the negotiations with Read and on the final settlement, see ibid., folder 2110.

Morgan bonds had merely constituted an expedient by which the arrears in interest were immediately capitalized and added to the already mammoth financial burden of the Argentine treasury. In the second place, Romero succeeded in obtaining a reduction of interest rates without causing a drop in the quotations of the bonds. The Barings, who were responsible for this result, were probably pleased with themselves; they had managed to regain control over Argentine international finance, displacing their rivals of the house of Morgan.[39]

The Long-term Consequences of Financial Dependency

While the debt arrangement of 1893 provided substantial relief for the Argentine national treasury, the drain of capital from Buenos Aires to Europe continued. The net outflow of capital caused by the external debt service and by remittances of foreign companies totaled approximately 160,000,000 gold pesos between 1891 and 1900. This sum represented more than 80 percent of the export surplus obtained by the Argentine economy during the decade.[40] As a result, after 1890 Argentina became a *net capital exporter*, in striking contrast to its condition as a great *capital importer* during the 1880s. The flow of funds now went back to Europe, rather than vice versa.

Despite the large payments remitted from Argentina, the foreign debt of the national government did not decline. In fact, between 1891 and 1900 it rose from 204,000,000 to 389,000,000 gold pesos. This huge increase did not come from fresh loans as such, but rather from a series of conversions of previous debts. Specifically, the Argentine national government assumed responsibility for all existing debts of the provincial governments and the municipalities.[41] The method used to convert these debts consisted in providing the foreign bondholders with new national bonds in exchange for the old provincial and municipal ones. In addition, the treasury issued a huge volume of new bonds to liquidate the so-called railway guarantees, which were held by a dozen British railway companies operating in the country.[42]

39. Barings was reorganized in 1891 as Baring Brothers & Company Ltd. After paying off its debts, it again resumed its role as a leading London merchant bank.

40. Based on data in J. H. Williams, *Argentine International Trade*, pp. 136, 152.

41. The total value of new Argentine gold bonds issued for debt settlements between 1891 and 1900 was equal to approximately 190,000,000 gold pesos. Provincial loan-restructuring absorbed 93,000,000; gold pesos; 40,000,000 were issued to convert municipal debts of various kinds, and almost 60,000,000 gold pesos were issued to cancel the railway guarantees. A detailed chart of all outstanding Argentine securities is in CFBH, *Annual Report, 1892*.

42. On the railway guarantees, see Raúl Scalabrini Ortiz, *Historia de los ferrocarriles argentinos* (Buenos Aires, 1974), pp. 176–177, 254–256, 308–311, 322–323; and Carlos Mari-

These complex financial arrangements had important political consequences. By assuming the debts of the provinces and municipalities, the
national government centralized financial control and power in its hands.
The federalist tendencies that had gained strength in the late 1880s were
thus dealt their death blow. The trend toward political and financial cen-
tralization at the nation's capital gained strength, setting a course that was
progressively accentuated during the twentieth century.

Because the Argentine debt renegotiations of the 1890s (Table 6) were
among the most complex ever undertaken by a Latin American nation, it is
necessary to analyze the different settlements separately. We begin with the
restructuring of the provincial external debts.

A survey of the rise in the foreign debt during the 1890s indicates that
50 percent of the total increase was due to the conversion of the provincial
debts. These provincial securities had been sold in the 1880s throughout
Europe. We cannot make an accurate estimate of foreign holdings, but we
can say that approximately 10 percent were held in Germany, 10 percent in
Belgium, Holland, and Switzerland, 30 percent in France, and perhaps 50
percent in Great Britain.[43] Thus the number of creditors of the Argentine
provincial governments was large and widespread. Generally speaking, the
bonds had been sold by second-rank financial firms that had less political
influence than the big banking houses that handled the bonds of the Argentine national government, so in the early stages of debt renegotiations
(1891–93) little attention was paid to the demands of the holders of the
provincial bonds and they received almost no payments on their investments. It is not surprising that the bondholders accused the big banks and
national financial authorities of Argentina of collusion. Yet it was also a
fact that the provincial governments did not have the funds with which to
pay.[44]

At first the national government was reluctant to accept responsibility for
the tangled finances of the ten provinces with outstanding foreign debts.
But finally, in 1896, it took a decisive first step, assuming the task of reorganizing the external loans of the province of Buenos Aires. It offered
the provincial bondholders £6,700,000 in national gold bonds in exchange
for approximately £7,000,000 in old provincial bonds. This agreement
paved the way for similar conversions of the bonds of the provinces of
Catamarca, Córdoba, Corrientes, Entre Ríos, Mendoza, San Juan, San

chal, "British and French Investments in Argentina, 1880–1940" (Ph.D. diss., Harvard University, 1977), pp. 53–54.

43. Based on data in Marichal, "Los banqueros europeos y los emprestitos argentinos,"
table 2, pp. 58–59.

44. There is abundant information on the demands of the various committees of British
bondholders of the Argentine provinces in CFBH, *Annual Report, 1890–1897.*

TABLE 6
ARGENTINE FOREIGN DEBT RENEGOTIATIONS , 1890–1906

Year	Category and Value of Debt Renegotiated	Objective	New Bonds Issued (£)	Bankers	Comments
1891	National govt. bonds, £40,500,000	Payment of interest	5,060,000	J. S. Morgan	Known as Morgan Loan; contract canceled 1893.
1893	National govt. bonds of 14 loans, £44,100,000	Reduction of interest, 1893–99, to lump sum of £1,500,000 per year	No new bonds[a]	Baring Bros.	Known as the Romero Arrangement. Full debt service renewed in 1899.
1896	Railway guarantees[b]	To cancel railway guarantees	10,422,626	Baring Bros.	New bonds given to foreign-owned railway companies.
1896–99	Provincial bonds, £22,000,000	To convert provincial bonds to 4% national bonds	17,778,813	London and Paris banks[c]	Represented loss of £6,000,000 for bondholdes.
1897	Municipality of Buenos Aires bonds, £1,221,400	To convert municipal bonds to 4% national bonds	1,527,778	Baring Bros.	New bonds exchanged for old bonds.
1899	Municipality of Córdoba bonds, £779,000	To convert municipal bonds to 4% national bonds	779,500	Baring Bros.	New bonds exchanged for old bonds, but interest due 1890–99 canceled.
1900	Municipality of Rosario, £2,200.000	To convert municipal bonds to 4% national bonds	1,853,317	Baring Bros.	New bonds exchanged for old, but capital and interest reduced.

[a] The old bonds continued to remain valid and received the same interest rates and sinking-fund payments after 1899, as originally contracted.

[b] The railway guarantees were subsidies given to numerous private railway companies, mostly British-owned. The companies claimed payment for subsidies in arrears from 1890 and requested an additional lump sum in bonds for cancellation of the guarantees.

[c] A great variety of London and Paris banks, as well as some German and Dutch banks, were involved in the original issue of the provincial bonds and in the renegotiations (see Appendix B).

TABLE 6 *(cont.)*

Year	Category and Value of Debt Renegotiated	Objective	New Bonds Issued (£)	Bankers	Comments
1905	Municipality of Santa Fé, £260,000	To convert municipal bonds to 4% national bonds	300,000	Baring Bros.	Part of interest in arrears canceled.
1906	Cédulas-Banco Hipotecario Provincia Buenos Aires	Conversion to 3% bonds	11,160,980		Investors lose approx. one-third the nominal value of securities.

SOURCES: Jose B. Peña, *Deuda argentina, recopilación de leyes, decretos, resoluciones, notas y contratos*, 2 vols. (Buenos Aires, 1907); Henry Shepard, "Default and Adjustment of Argentine Foreign Debts, 1890–1906," Department of Commerce, Trade Promotion Series 145 (Washington, D.C., 1933).

Luis, Santa Fé, and Tucumán. A total of £17,778,000 of new national bonds were exchanged for some £22,000,000 in outstanding provincial debts. These conversions freed the provinces from their foreign financial commitments, but at the same time reduced their political and economic autonomy. The price they were forced to pay was subordination to the increasingly centralized fiscal and financial machinery of the national government.

It might be presumed that the national authorities would have paid less attention to the external debts of the Argentine municipalities than to those of the provinces, but this was not the case because the bulk of the municipal debts were those of the federal capital, the city of Buenos Aires. The national government had important political reasons to press forward with a major reform of the capital's fiscal and financial system.

The first step in restructuring the municipal finances of Buenos Aires took place in early 1891. The National Congress approved a law stipulating that the Buenos Aires Water Supply & Drainage Company would be bought back from Baring Brothers.[45] Originally this company had belonged to the city, but in 1887 negotiations to transfer it to the British financiers were initiated. After the crisis, however, the London bankers pressed Pellegrini to nationalize the enterprise. They calculated that reimbursement of the water company stock could be a key instrument in the liquidation of the huge volume of Baring liabilities. Some Argentine deputies were not

45. On the recision of the waterworks contract, see ADERA, folder 2156.

pleased with the salvaging of Barings. As Deputy Olmedo noted: "The bankers who negotiated the concession [of the Water Supply & Drainage Company] have been the first in suggesting the need to rescind the contract in order to lift this enormous weight from on top of Barings, which fell, as is well-known, as a result of this ruinous transaction."[46]

With the new law in hand, Finance Minister López transferred 31,000,000 gold pesos in new bonds to the Rothschild Committee, which was in charge of liquidating Barings' debts. The waterworks of the city of Buenos Aires were now once again public property, but the costs of the related financial operations left a large debt on the hands of the national treasury.

Less extortionate but equally complex was the renegotiation of the Buenos Aires municipal bonds of 1888 and 1889. Most of these bonds had been sold in Europe through the agency of the Banco Nacional. When the latter went bankrupt in 1891 the foreign bondholders panicked, but there was little they could do. Interest payments were temporarily suspended, although subsequently the city renewed service by paying in paper pesos. The big London banks were not predisposed to include these debts in the Morgan or Romero arrangements. In September 1897 a final solution was reached by which the national government issued £7,000,000 in gold bonds in exchange for the old securities.

The advantages of the Buenos Aires settlement were not lost on the bondholders of other Argentine municipalities. By exchanging their old bonds (which were now quite worthless in terms of stock market quotations) for new national gold bonds (which were quoted at par), the European investors recovered their capital. Nevertheless, in some instances they were forced to accept substantial sacrifices of interest payments in arrears. For instance, the Rosario bondholders lost more than £300,000 and those of Santa Fé and Córdoba also lost large sums (see Table 6).[47]

The resolution of the provincial and municipal debts thus became an essential part of the broader plan of the Argentine authorities of the 1890s to restructure and stabilize the financial machinery of the state. The final arrangements were not satisfactory to any of the parties concerned because the national government was forced to increase its foreign debt while the provincial and municipal governments lost power. Nevertheless, the various administrations in charge of the renegotiations argued that the stabilization of public institutions was more important than the sacrifice of federal principles.

46. *Diario de Sesiones, Cámara de Diputados* (Buenos Aires), January 23, 1891, p. 966.

47. On the municipal loan arrangements, see Shepherd, "Default and Adjustment," pp. 56–58.

The motives of the Argentine political elites were quite different when it was decided to include the demands of the British-owned railway companies as a part of the global debt settlement.[48] By bowing to the demands of the European bankers and railway magnates, the Argentine authorities opened the door to increasing penetration of the nation's economy by foreign capital. The strong state role in the economy, which had been promoted by the administrations of Sarmiento, Avellaneda, Roca, and even Juárez Celman, was reversed. After 1890 the state would continue to fulfill certain supervisory economic functions, but it was not allowed to compete with private companies, and foreign firms in particular, in the running of *profitable* railway and/or port enterprises.

By including the railway guarantees in the larger debt package, the Argentine financial authorities guaranteed that the railway managers and shareholders would be protected from the negative impact of the economic depression of the early 1890s. In effect, the Argentine elites transferred a huge volume of public resources into the hands of a group of private firms—which, it should be added, were the largest capitalist enterprises in the country.

The links between the railways and the external debt became manifest from the outbreak of the crisis in 1890. In that year the executive authorities of the republic decided to sell off the remaining state railroads to several British concerns with the object of reducing the foreign debt. Protests against these measures were led by Deputy Osvaldo Magnasco, who argued that it would be a mistake to auction off these valuable public properties.[49] But his criticisms were to no avail. Pellegrini and López argued that the crisis offered no other alternatives because the sale of the state enterprises guaranteed a possible method of reducing debts.

In later years the British railroad firms pressed for additional concessions. Most of these companies had been established during the 1880s with large annual subsidies paid by the government that were better known as "railway guarantees." In order to encourage construction of new branches, the government provided a yearly subsidy equal to between 5 and 7 percent of the nominal capital value of each company.[50] It is not surprising that in 1890 these payments were abruptly suspended.

48. For the text of the railway guarantee bond issue, see J. Peña, *Deuda argentina*, document 96, pp. 557–561.

49. Magnasco both criticized the sale of the state railways and opposed the early government proposals to redeem the railway guarantees because they would benefit the British railway companies (*Diario de Sesiones, Cámara de Diputados*, September 11, 1891, pp. 660–661).

50. For details, see R. Scalabrini Ortiz, *Historia de los ferrocarriles*, pp. 173–175, 239–242, 318–323.

The railway managers complained, but until 1896 they received no satisfactory reply.[51] It was then that they were able to convince the weak-willed Argentine president, Uriburu, to bow to their demands. Uriburu agreed to issue a grand total of 60,000,000 gold pesos in new government bonds (approximately £10,000,000) to be transferred directly to the company coffers. The injection of this huge amount of capital allowed the British-owned firms to use these funds to consolidate their control over the entire national railway network of Argentina, establishing four great monopolies that dominated the principal cattle, wheat, sugar, wine, and quebracho producing regions.

Once again several nationalistic deputies protested, arguing that the government was regaling the companies with enormous sums in exchange for the dubious privilege of canceling the railway guarantees.[52] They noted that most of the transport firms were already profitable enterprises and that they no longer had need for subsidies. The guarantees could simply be annulled, saving the government an enormous amount of money. But such arguments made little headway in the Congress or in the executive branch. The "railway lobby" already had accumulated more influence at the highest levels than the small circle of opposition parties.

The acquiescence of the Argentine government with respect to the British railway companies marked a striking and fundamental reversal of the 1870s and early 1880s, when state-run enterprises had been favored. Now laissez-faire became the recognized ideology of the state, and foreign capitalists were encouraged to expand their interests throughout the nation without restrictions. These concessions were, in effect, the bitter and final legacy of financial dependency.

In summary, the crisis of 1890 subjected the Argentine state to the dictates of the international banks that imposed severe financial conditions on both the national and the provincial governments in order to guarantee that they would recoup their loans and to assure the profitability of allied enterprises, such as the British railway firms. At the same time, the European bankers took advantage of the failure in 1890 of numerous Argentine-owned enterprises, public and private, to further consolidate the dominant position of foreign capital in key spheres of the Argentine economy. And after the turn of the century they promoted a renewed burst of capital ex-

---

51. The British bankers who had issued railway bonds also complained. See, e.g., the letter from J. S. Morgan & Co. to the Argentine minister of finance in early 1894, in which the financiers denied the extortionate nature of the tariffs charged by the railway companies and demanded payments of the guarantees (ADERA, folder 2110, letter dated January 3, 1894).

52. See speeches by deputies Almada and Varela in *Diario de Sesiones, Cámara de Diputados, 1895*, pp. 1013–1087.

ports to the Río de la Plata region, coordinating their strategies closely with commercial, railway, and industrial magnates interested in expanding their interests there. This trend was common to many other Latin American nations as international bankers promoted a new and powerful wave of loans and direct investments that continued to run strong until World War I.

Dollar Diplomacy and the Loan Boom of the 1920s

It would be delightful if loans to such countries could be made on the same credit basis as we make loans to England and Germany. But until we remold the world closer to our heart's desire, this cannot be the case.

—Henry K. Norton, U.S. economic expert (1928)

B Y 1914, Latin American governments had accumulated foreign debts valued at more than $2,000,000,000. Half this sum originated from loans taken during the nineteenth century that were still being paid off. The other half had been contracted more recently in the midst of the financial frenzy of the prewar era. The new loan boom of 1904–14 marked the apogee of European financial influence and power over the Latin American states.[1]

While the London merchant banks continued to play a most important role—Rothschilds remained the official bankers to Brazil and Chile, while Barings were the main financiers of Argentina and Uruguay—they were confronted with rivals that threatened to undermine and possibly break British financial predominance in Latin America. In Mexico, for instance, German bankers seized control of the international loan business as early as 1888, although by the first decade of the twentieth century they were forced to share this lucrative business with United States and French financiers. The German banks were also active in the promotion of loans for Chile and Argentina, working closely with industrial firms to stimulate trade.[2]

The French banks were just as active. In Brazil and Argentina, for example, French banks assumed a leading role after the turn of the century. Powerful firms such as the Crédit Mobilier and the Banque de Paris et des Pays Bas, provided numerous loans for national and provincial govern-

1. Statistics on European investments in Latin America in this period are in United Nations, Economic Commission for Latin America, *El financiamiento externo de América Latina* (New York, 1964), pp. 5–17; Rippy, *British Investments*, pp. 66–83; Jacques Thobie, *La France imperiale, 1880–1914* (Paris, 1982), pp. 214–227.

2. The Disconto and Deutsche banks, in particular, used loans to promote German industrial exports—e.g., railway equipment and cannons from the Krupp factories, and turbines and electrical supplies from the giant industrial establishments of Siemens and AEG. On the role of German banks in Argentina, see Luis Sommi, *Los capitales alemanes en la Argentina* (Buenos Aires, 1945); on their influence in Mexico, see Friedrich Katz, *The Secret War in Mexico* (Chicago, 1982), chap. 2.

ments and became engaged in a variety of economic enterprises, including the Rosario port works, railways in Santa Fé and Buenos Aires, port modernization in Pernambuco, and state railways in Minas, Goyaz, and Bahia.[3]

The United States banks were slower in moving south of the Río Grande than their European counterparts, but already by 1910 they had become engaged in several international financial syndicates that provided loans to Argentina, Mexico and Cuba. The most powerful of the New York banking firms—for instance, J. P. Morgan & Company and the National City Bank—recognized the possibilities for expanding business in Latin America, but in most instances they did not yet dare to strike out alone. The New York financiers relinquished the front seat to the European bankers in joint loan issues, not only because they felt that their colleagues from the Old World had superior experience in this field, but also because the North American investing public was much more reluctant than that of Europe to invest money in foreign government bonds.[4]

The increasingly cosmopolitan character of the Latin American loan activity reflected the intense economic rivalry that characterized this age of "high imperialism." But foreign capitalists were not only interested in loans. They had equal interest in obtaining control over the production, transport, and commercialization of the natural resources of Latin America. During this era, British, French, German, and United States private enterprises (many of them forerunners of the modern multinational corporations) invested an unprecedented volume of capital in railways, tramways, mines, and agricultural companies throughout the subcontinent.[5] The intense rivalry among the imperial powers thus stimulated a great burst of speculation in Latin American bonds and stocks, which continued unabated until 1914.

The outbreak of war in Europe caused an abrupt suspension of capital exports and threatened to dislocate the financial structures of all the Latin American economies. Yet in spite of the temporary breakdown of the international trade and credit machinery, the governments of most nations of the region continued to adhere to the gold standard as well as to sustain regular

3. On the role of French banks in Latin American provincial and municipal loans, see Fredrick Halsey, *Investments in Latin America and the British West Indies* Department of Commerce Special Agent Series, no. 169 (Washington, D.C., 1918), pp. 124–139.

4. Until 1914 the United States remained a net importer of capital from Europe. The only Latin American bonds placed in New York were those of Cuba (1904, 1909), Mexico (1904, 1912), and Argentina (1909). Even in these few cases, a substantial portion of the securities were sold in Europe by allied banking firms.

5. For the early history of U.S. multinationals in Latin America, see Mira Wilkins, *The Emergence of Multinational Enterprise: American Business Abroad from the Colonial Era to 1914* (Cambridge, Mass., 1976), chap. 9.

payments on their external debts. For the first time in Latin American history a major loan boom was not followed by widespread defaults.

Traditional explanations for the remarkable resiliency of the Latin American economies during World War I emphasize the role of United States banks in replacing the European financial institutions as suppliers of credit.[6] Such a view, however, is misleading on several counts. In the first place, during 1914–18 the majority of the Latin American governments were able to do without financial assistance from abroad. As recent historical studies demonstrate, they overcame the obstacles posed by the drastic reduction in European loans by relying on two different sources of funds: They used their large export surpluses to pay the service on foreign debts, and they covered government deficits by utilizing internally generated funds, such as local bank loans, by issuing treasury bills, and by printing considerable quantities of paper money.[7]

In the years immediately following the war (1918–20) there was an increase of United States direct investments in several countries of the region, especially Cuba, Mexico, and Chile, but there were no long-term loans for governments.[8] This situation changed after the international commercial crisis of 1921.

The violent and unexpected impact of the crisis of 1921 convinced Latin American leaders that they had no alternative but to seek the financial support of the United States. From that date, several Latin American governments began to explore the possibility of floating long-term loans on the New York Stock Exchange. Despite the initial opposition of authorities in Washington, D.C., to foreign loans, and the unreceptive attitude of North American investors toward foreign bonds, a number of New York banking firms took steps to prime the market with Latin American government securities. The speculation increased rapidly, reaching its apex during 1925–28, when United States bankers sold more that $1,500,000,000 in Latin American bonds. This "dance of the millions," as the financial furor came to be known in such countries as Colombia, dramatically illustrated the nature and impact of the financial relations that now linked the budding

6. Although the United States played an increasingly important role in Latin American trade after 1914, its ascendancy in the financial field did not come until the 1920s. For a restatement of the traditional view, see *Latin America in the 1930s: The Role of the Periphery in World Crisis*, ed. Rosemary Thorp (New York, 1984), p. 3.

7. Much of the following discussion on the evolution of the Latin American economies during 1914–18 is based on the manuscript of Bill Albert, "Latin America and the First World War," which he kindly allowed me to consult in a preliminary draft.

8. The best sources on United States investments during this period are Max Winkler, *Investments of United States Capital in Latin America* (Boston, 1929); and Cleona Lewis, *America's Stake in International Investments* (Washington, D.C., 1938).

money markets of Havana, Bogotá, Buenos Aires, and Rio de Janeiro to the enormously dynamic financial machinery of Wall Street.

The sudden triumph of the North American financial offensive in Latin America provoked the astonishment of contemporaries and spawned a considerable body of journalistic and academic literature that baptized the 1920s as the age of "dollar diplomacy."[9] This expression was intended to convey the idea of the coming-of-age of the United States as a preeminent economic power in Latin America. Implicitly it also suggested that the New York bankers and Washington diplomats were well on their way to becoming the proconsuls of a burgeoning empire. This was true in some of the smaller countries of the subcontinent, but not so in the larger nations.

In this chapter we argue that the transfer of control over Latin American finances from European banking centers to those of the United States was not as sweeping or unequivocal as traditionally supposed. Furthermore, while the United States bankers were fundamental protagonists of the great loan boom of the 1920s they did not act alone. Other key actors who played an important role included the Latin American politicians; in some instances, the latter were able to arrange the financial transactions with a certain degree of autonomy. The analysis of the finances of Brazil (the most prodigal borrower of the decade) suggests that the authorities at Rio de Janeiro and São Paulo were responsible for the formulation and implementation of a strikingly original loan policy. In addition, the Brazilian experience indicates that important ties with leading European banking houses were maintained throughout the loan boom. The New York bankers participated, but they did not control.

Quite different was the situation in the smaller republics—for example, Haiti, Santo Domingo, Nicaragua, and Cuba. Powerful financial groups of the United States imposed a tight grip over fiscal and monetary policy as well as over the public and private financial machinery of each of these nations. In this they were assisted by military force and by pressure brought to bear by the State Department. "Dollar diplomacy" was here equivalent to a symbiosis of financial and military colonialism.

In short, the experience of the smaller countries was quite different, and more tragic, than that of the larger nations of Latin America in this era. But before entering into a discussion of the loan boom of the 1920s, we return briefly to the year 1914.

---

9. Journalists coined the term, but a series of academic studies sponsored by the American Fund for Public Service provided empirical data to sustain this view. Among these excellent studies, see Leland Jenks, *Our Cuban Colony: A Study in Sugar* (New York, 1928); Margaret Marsh, *Our Bankers in Bolivia* (New York, 1928); and Melvin Knight, *The Americans in Santo Domingo* (New York, 1928). J. F. Rippy, *The Capitalists and Colombia* (New York, 1931); and C. Kepner and J. Soothill, *The Banana Empire* (New York, 1935).

LATIN AMERICAN DEBTS AND WORLD WAR I

The impact of World War I on the Latin American economies was contradictory. At first, transatlantic commerce and finance were severely disrupted, but later the economic situation tended to improve. During 1914 and early 1915 both exports and imports dropped, provoking mercantile failures and banking panics in many Latin American republics. Yet by the end of 1915 Latin American exports had rebounded. This explained why there were no major defaults on foreign debts, with the exception of Mexico.

The decline in trade, which took place at the beginning of the war, led to large public deficits because almost all governments depended heavily on customs revenues as their main source of income (approximately 50 percent in most cases). The time-worn solution of asking for bridge loans from European banks to allow for temporary relief could not now be implemented since the foreign banking houses were entirely absorbed in the problems of war finance. Only Brazil—because of its special relationship with Rothschilds—was able to extract a large long-term loan from Europe in 1914.[10] The rest of the Latin American states were obliged to seek different expedients for their financial worries.

During the war years Latin American finance ministers were concerned fundamentally with two interrelated problems: maintainance of regular payments on foreign debts, and financing of public deficits. The continuation of the debt service could be guaranteed only if the balance-of-payments situation improved. Such an improvement made itself felt from the end of 1915 as a result of the wartime export boom (see Figure 9). As exports rose and imports declined, most of the Latin American states accumulated large reserves of gold and foreign currencies. The trade surpluses provided sufficient foreign exchange to cover payments on foreign debts on a regular basis.

Nevertheless, the volume of funds required to satisfy foreign creditors was enormous. It was necessary to provide service not only on the public foreign debts (totaling some $2,000,000,000) but also on private foreign investments (totaling approximately $7,000,000,000). During 1914–18 the Latin American economies remitted interest and dividends on these sums to all its major creditors—England, France, Germany, Belgium, and the United States—and therefore became a *net capital exporter*. It can be estimated that, as a whole, Latin America transferred perhaps $2,000,000,000

---

10. This Brazilian loan of £14,000,000 (U.S. $70,000,000) was issued by Rothschilds to guarantee payments of interest on the outstanding foreign debt of the national government. Albert Kimber, *Kimber's Record of Government Debts, 1934* (New York, 1934), p. 253.

FIGURE 9.
LATIN AMERICAN EXPORTS TO ALL NATIONS, 1910–1929.

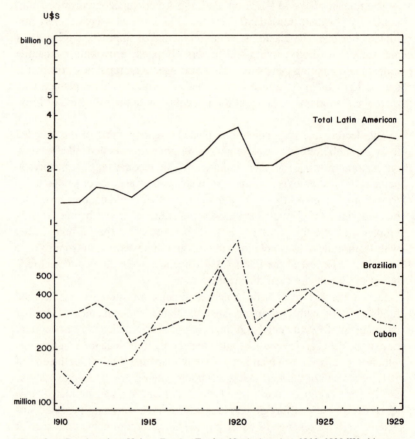

(Data from Pan American Union, *Foreign Trade of Latin America, 1910–1929* [Washington, D.C., 1931], pp. 1–53.)

in such payments, almost half of the $4,000,000,000 accumulated in the way of export surpluses during the war.[11]

Honoring foreign debts imposed severe strains on the public finances of many Latin American states. To begin with, the debt service provoked an increase in government financial expenditures. To make matters worse,

11. Calculating an annual return of 5 percent on foreign public debts and 4 percent on foreign direct investments, it can be estimated that total annual transfers from Latin America surpassed $400,000,000. Rippy calculated that the average annual return on British investments in Latin America in 1914 was close to 4.7 percent (see Rippy, *British Investments*, pp. 72–64). For additional data on foreign investments in Latin America in 1914, see footnote 1 of this chapter.

overall state income tended to decline as a result of the drop in import taxes. The combination of growing expenditures with declining revenues inevitably engendered mounting deficits. In order to resolve this dilemma, each Latin American government adopted a somewhat different solution.

The case of Argentina illustrates the effects of adopting conservative fiscal, monetary, and financial policies. The Argentine authorities were bent on complying with their foreign creditors. According to Bunge's calculations, the public debt service absorbed an astonishing 45 percent of government revenues during the war years.[12] This was made possible by recourse to a combination of short-term loans from London and New York bankers during 1914–16, an increase of 500,000,000 pesos in the internal debt, and a large flow of local bank loans to the government. Meanwhile, import revenues dropped approximately 30 percent between 1914 and 1918. Argentine financial officials responded by raising excise taxes and relying on bank credit rather than printing money to cover deficits. The result was that the government had to reduce its investments in economic development, education, and public health programs. At the same time, the private sector was starved of capital, because foreign funds were no longer available and because much local bank credit was siphoned off by the government. Such policies allowed the treasury to accumulate large gold reserves but did not stimulate balanced economic growth.[13]

The more flexible and heterodox monetary and financial policies adopted by Brazil stood in contrast to those of Argentina. To begin with, the Brazilian government suspended amortization payments on most of its foreign debts between 1914 and 1920. Interest payments continued to be made and represented close to 25 percent of total government expenditures, but it was clear that the financial authorities at Rio de Janeiro felt less obliged to comply with foreign bankers than the authorities at Buenos Aires did. They also had less confidence in the virtues of the gold standard and the maintenance of a strict monetary policy. On the contrary, in order to meet the growing deficits, which sprang from the decline in customs receipts, the Brazilian treasury officials tripled the issue of paper currency during 1914–18. But this did not affect the exchange rate, as the value of the Brazilian currency remained stable. Moroever, the flexible monetary strategy served to stim-

12. Alejandro Bunge, "Deuda pública," Informe No. 6, serie F, no. 2, Dirección General de Estadística de la Nación (Buenos Aires, December 1923), p. 9.

13. Because of its conservative monetary policies, the coffers of the Argentine treasury were so flushed with foreign currency reserves that the government was able to lend money to the European powers. In 1917 and 1918, Argentine credits totaling $200,000,000 were extended to England and France for the acquisition of grain. For the first time, a Latin American nation was able to change its condition from international debtor to that of international creditor.

ulate the economy, allowing for a large volume of public investments and pushing local banks to adopt expansive lending policies.[14]

The Chilean government found itself in a more auspicious situation, mainly because it relied primarily on export taxes for the bulk of its income. The boom in nitrate exports during 1914–18 provided the state with funds sufficient to cover all its expenditures without increasing the internal debt or printing money. In addition, the export surpluses allowed the value of the external debt to be reduced by 12 percent. Thus the war boom helped the Chilean authorities lessen the degree of external financial dependency.

The economic situation in the majority of other Latin American nations was not as favorable. The most complex situation was that of Mexico, which was immersed in revolution and threatened by the intervention of United States military forces. The Mexican government had continued to pay its debt service until 1913, and was even able to raise a large loan in Europe in that year.[15] Subsequently, however, the revolutionary struggles intensified and debt payments were suspended. In 1914 several battalions of U.S. Marines occupied the port of Veracruz to protect the properties of several large North American oil companies. The foreign bankers also demanded protection for their loans, but they could hardly expect to obtain any money from a nation engulfed in tremendous social and political upheaval.

Following the armistice in Europe, most Latin American nations benefited from the continuing rise in international prices of raw materials and primary products. The years 1918–20 were characterized by extraordinary speculation in all export commodities. In Argentina, for example, prices of wool, meat, and cereals reached a peak of 200 percent of their 1910 levels. Prosperity made it possible to continue covering the debt service as well as the large volume of profit remittances by British, French, and United States companies that operated in the various countries of the subcontinent.[16] But by mid-1920 the postwar boom came to a shattering end.

14. Albert sums up these policies: "The Brazilian government seems successfully to have defied prevailing financial orthodoxy, and although its policies might be seen as a blow against foreign domination, in effect they represented no more than an attempt to strengthen the export sector and the links with the world economy in a way consistent with the extreme conditions of the period" (Bill Albert, "Latin America and the First World War," ms. section "Brazilian Finances," p. 18).

15. Bazant, *Historia de la deuda exterior*, pp. 174–176.

16. The best information on the balance of payments of any Latin American nation during the war years is that on Argentina. Between 1914 and 1920, Argentina annually remitted an average of $150,000,000 on its public and private foreign debts. The total net export of capital by Argentina was equal to almost exactly $1,000,000,000. Its trade surplus during 1914–20 was equal to $1,400,000,000. The service on its private and public debts therefore absorbed

The international economic crisis of 1920–21 caused an abrupt decline in prices of most export commodities produced by Latin America. Exports plunged from an all-time high in 1920 to prewar levels the following year (see Figure 9). Meanwhile, imports tended to remain stable. As a result, many nations began to experience balance-of-trade deficits, and both public and private finances rapidly deteriorated. Indeed, from both a commercial and a financial perspective, the crisis of 1920–21 was one of the most severe ever suffered by the Latin American economies.[17] Furthermore, it was this crisis that pushed Latin American political elites into the arms of the bankers from New York.

THE BELATED FINANCIAL OFFENSIVE OF THE NEW YORK BANKS

Before World War I, the bulk of the new loans taken by Latin American governments had been provided by European bankers and investors. A small portion also came from the United States, but a rough estimate suggests that not more than 10 percent of the total Latin American bonds sold abroad between 1904 and 1914 were placed in American markets.[18] Bankers from the United States traditionally had been inclined to rely on British merchant bankers for the financing of most trade with Latin America. Similarly, the volume of United States *direct* investments was substantially less than that realized by the British, French, and German companies operating in Latin America.

An important exception was the case of Mexico, where United States investors acquired important railway and mining properties from the 1880s on.[19] Generally speaking, however, North American bankers and entrepreneurs did not begin to show a marked interest in Latin America until the end of the Spanish-American War of 1898. As a result of that war, the United States acquired two new valuable properties in the Caribbean: Puerto Rico and Cuba. Success in these early imperial ventures led United States bankers and politicians to advocate further expansionism.

The bellicose financial and military strategy of the United States in the early twentieth century, was directed not against the larger and stronger

an astonishing 70 percent of its export surplus. See Vernon L. Phelps, *The International Economic Position of Argentina* (Philadelphia, 1938), chart 7, p. 115, and table 1 of the appendix.

17. Only a few historians of Latin America have studied the impact of this crisis. For details on the effects of the drop in sugar prices on the Cuban economy, see Jenks, *Our Cuban Colony*, pp. 206–217; on the drop in meat prices in Argentina, see Peter Smith, *Politics and Beef in Argentina: Patterns of Conflict and Change* (New York, 1969), chap. 4.

18. For details, see Lewis, *America's Stake*, chap. 16.

19. Nicolau d'Olwer, "Las inversiones extranjeras," in D. Cosío Villegas et al., *Historia moderna de México. El Porfiriato. Vida económica* (Mexico, 1974), pp. 973–1185.

states of Latin America, where European bankers had major stakes, but against the smallest and weakest republics. The imposition of United States control over Cuba and Puerto Rico was followed by expansion into Panama and by intervention in Santo Domingo (1916–24), Haiti (1915–33) and Nicaragua (1912–25). In each case the New York bankers worked closely with the Marines.[20] The bankers involved in Santo Domingo loans were headed by the New York firm of Kuhn, Loeb & Company.[21] In the case of Haiti, the dominant financial force was the aggressive firm of the National City Bank, which ran the Banque Nationale d'Haiti.[22] Meanwhile, in Nicaragua a different set of buccaneering bankers was active, led by the blue-chip firms of Brown Brothers and J. and W. Seligman & Company.[23]

During World War I, therefore, the United States consolidated its financial and military grip over various small but strategically located nations in the Caribbean and in Central America, but it had not yet made major inroads in the rest of Latin America. On the contrary, the kind of gunboat diplomacy that was effective in the banana republics could not be applied successfully in the larger nations of South America. States like Brazil, Argentina or Chile, not only had relatively powerful military forces, but also counted on the support of important European economic interests. And few United States financial groups were predisposed to provoke a full-scale economic battle with the British and French banks and industrial corporations that had interests in those countries.

The only large New York financial firm that did challenge the European banks in South America was the National City Bank. From 1914 it began opening branch offices in various countries of the region, a policy facilitated by the Federal Reserve Act of 1913, which removed many constraints on the overseas activities of United States banks. The National City Bank also promoted formation of a large trade-finance association, which included several leading United States industrial companies engaged in the

20. In a recent study based mainly on military archives, Langley argues that the U.S. Marines played a dominant role in shaping imperial policy and practice in the Caribbean during the first third of the century. This is an important corrective to historical interpretations that argue that the State Department had a coherent policy in this field. On the other hand, Langley underestimates the importance of private economic interests in furthering political and military expansionism. See Lester Langley, *The Banana Wars: An Inner History of American Empire, 1900–1934* (Lexington, Ky., 1984).

21. On U.S.-Dominican relations, see the ponderous but detailed work by Welles, *Naboth's Vineyard*, and the more agile and critical Knight, *Americans in Santo Domingo*.

22. On United States economic interests in Haiti, see Scott Nearing and Joseph Smith, *Dollar Diplomacy: A Study in American Imperialism* (1925; reprint, New York, 1966), pp. 133–150; and Lewis, *America's Stake*, pp. 344–345.

23. On the United States role in Nicaragua, see Amaru Barahona Portocarrero, "Breve estudio sobre la historia contemporánea de Nicaragua," in *América Latina, historia de medio siglo*, ed. P. González Casanova (Mexico, 1984), 2:377–387; and Nearing and Smith, *Dollar Diplomacy*, pp. 151–168.

South American trades.[24] The bank's president, Frank Vanderlip, force-fully advocated the need for closer collaboration between United States banks and industries to conquer foreign markets. He repeatedly cited the example set by the German banks, noting that "the connection between industries pushing their goods in foreign markets and the German banks has had much to do with the institution of long credit in South America."[25]

Vanderlip advocated the extension of more bank credit for Latin America because he believed it was the essential instrument that could allow United States firms to capture regional markets from their rivals. As a result of the war, the European-owned railway companies, tramways, and electrical firms in Argentina, Brazil, Chile, Peru, and other countries could not ob-tain sufficient industrial supplies from Europe. If the leading New York banks seized the opportunity and provided them with loans, these firms would place orders in the United States, and American industry would ben-efit. As Charles Muchnic, vice-president of the American Locomotive Sales Corporation, argued in 1915:

The railways, mines, municipal and public utilities in South America are financed almost entirely by European capital, and the bankers in furnishing the funds have invariably stipulated . . . that the materials to be purchased by the proceeds of the loans . . . should come from the country that furnished the capital. . . . If we are to remedy this situation, we must insist upon our bankers taking a more active part in the development of South American railways.[26]

While the National City Bank pushed the expansion of commercial cred-its for private companies, it did not extend any long-term loans for Latin American governments during 1914–20. Why it adopted this policy is not difficult to explain. First, Latin American governments did not demand many loans during this period. Second, there was little surplus capital in United States capital markets for Latin American loans. Most of the avail-able funds were absorbed by the wartime domestic boom and by the Euro-pean allied governments. Furthermore, the most powerful investment banking houses of New York, like J. P. Morgan, did not favor Latin Amer-ican bond issues, which they judged to be the traditional prerogative of the London merchant banks.[27]

24. The American International Corporation was founded in 1915 with a capital of $50,000,000. For a complete list of the shareholders, see National City Bank, *The Americas*, November 1915, pp. 1–3.

25. On the views of Vanderlip and other officials of the National City Bank on economic expansion in South America, see the bank's journal, *The Americas*, esp. Vanderlip's articles in the October 1914, November 1914, and January 1919 issues.

26. *The Americas*, April 1915, pp. 29–30.

27. Parrini argues that the two dominant financial powers in New York at this time were Morgan, the greatest investment bank, and National City, the most dynamic commercial bank,

The international crisis of 1920–21 obliged the New York banks to re-formulate their Latin American financial strategies. At first, the abrupt drop in trade forced a reduction in commercial credits. Between 1920 and 1924 the number of foreign bank branches in Latin America declined from seventy-two to forty-five. One author recently argued, "The decrease in branch banks temporarily undermined the attempt on the part of National City and its affiliates to make New York the world center for the exchange of short-term dollar acceptances."[28] But this did not eliminate other possibilities for making profits in Latin America. Paradoxically, while trade declined the government loan business increased, opening up new avenues for the overseas expansion of the New York banks. After 1922 they focused their attention on the realization of lucrative gains by providing money at expensive rates to the governments of Uruguay, Brazil, Chile, Colombia, and other states of the region.

It was then that the two most powerful New York banking groups, Morgan and National City, began to forge a common strategy, working together in the issue of large Latin American loans, particularly for the governments of Argentina and Cuba. At the same time, other New York investment banks fought for a share of the bond business, each carving out its own sphere of influence: Dillon Read issued the bulk of the national loans for Brazil and Bolivia; J. and W. Seligman specialized in Peruvian bonds; Kuhn Loeb had a predilection for the gold bonds of the Chilean Mortgage Bank; Hallgarten and Kissel/Kinnicutt dominated the sale of Colombian government securities (see Appendix C).

The number of United States investment firms and banks engaged in these loans was large, and in several instances competition was keen, as with the Colombian departmental loans for which literally dozens of the smaller financial houses fought like so many sharks. But the big banks generally set the trend and created a market for the Latin American bonds.[29] In all, between 1922 and 1928 the United States banking community sold almost $2,000,000,000 in Latin American bonds to North American investors. (See Figure 10 for trends of dollar loans to Latin America.) As a result, New York displaced London as the money mecca to which all the

---

and that they made an effort to respect each other's spheres of influence. He adds: "Morgan and associates opposed rivalry with the British world banking system" (Carl Parrini, *Heir to Empire: United States Economic Diplomacy, 1916–1923* [Pittsburgh, 1969], p. 55).

28. Joan H. Wilson, *American Business and Foreign Policy, 1920–1933* (Boston, 1973), pp. 102–103.

29. On Latin American bond sales, see Charles C. Abbot, *The New York Bond Market, 1920–1930* (Cambridge, Mass., 1937); Ilse Mintz, *Deterioration in the Quality of Bonds Issued in the United States, 1920–1930* (New York, 1951); and Lewis, *America's Stake*, appendix E.

FIGURE 10.
UNITED STATES EXPORTS AND LOANS TO LATIN AMERICA. 1915–1931.

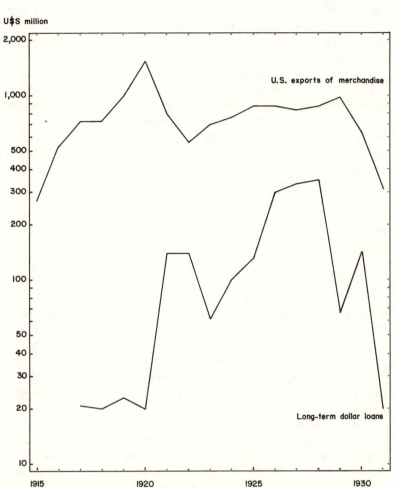

(Data from U.S. Department of Commerce, *Statistical Abstract of the United States* [Washington, D.C., 1926, 1930, 1933]; and Cleona Lewis, *America's Stake in International Investments* [Washington, D.C., 1938], pp. 617–634.)

governments of the region looked for financial assistance. "Dollar diplomacy" had now reached its apogee.

On the political side, it should be noted that many of the loans served to consolidate the power of dictators like Augusto Leguía in Peru (1919–30), Carlos Ibañez in Chile (1927–31) and General José María Orellana in Gua-

183

temala (1922–26), as well as to maintain neo-colonial regimes in Nicaragua, Santo Domingo, Haiti, Honduras, and Cuba. The alliance between bankers and authoritarian chiefs of state provoked acid criticisms, the brunt of which were directed against the corruption that the loan business stimulated among the ruling circles of the debtor states. As Seligman's agent in Peru observed, "The President was a dictator, and he spent what he chose and borrowed what he chose. The people had no way of checking."[30]

The New York financiers could reply that they also provided loans to the more-liberal administrations of Brazil, Argentina, and Colombia. This was true, although it did not absolve them of responsibility for backing up authoritarian and corrupt regimes. In any event, United States financial expansion was not a one-way street. The Latin American elites also played an important role in the formulation of loan policies during the 1920s. In order to understand the degree of financial influence exercised by the United States banks, therefore, it is necessary to review the nature of the financial strategies adopted by the Latin American governments during the 1920s.

LATIN AMERICAN LOAN POLICIES IN THE 1920S

Between 1921 and 1930 the majority of Latin American governments embarked on a foreign loan splurge, authorizing the issue of a total of some fifty national, forty provincial, and twenty-five municipal loans. The biggest borrower was Brazil, which increased its foreign debt by more than $600,000,000. Other big spenders included Argentina, Chile, and Colombia, although in per capita terms the nations that assumed the largest debt burdens were Cuba, Bolivia, and Uruguay. (See Table 7 for data on loans by country.)

While each country sought money abroad for different purposes, it is possible to single out two main reasons that impelled them to seek foreign funds during this period. The first decisive factor was the impact of the crisis of 1920–21. As previously suggested, the crisis gave rise to large public deficits and balance-of-payments problems. To overcome these difficulties recourse was had to "refinancing" loans. A second circumstance that spurred the loan frenzy was the widespread conviction among Latin American elites that they could carry out new public works and urban modernization projects with cheap money from New York. This urge led them

30. The quote is from testimony by Dennis published in United States Congress, Senate Committee on Finance, *Sale of Foreign Bonds or Securities in the United States* (Washington, D.C., 1932), p. 1601 (hereafter, U.S. Congress, *Sale of Foreign Bonds*). The hearings as a whole are a singularly revealing source on the collusion between New York bankers and Latin American politicians during the 1920s.

TABLE 7
FOREIGN LOANS TO LATIN AMERICAN GOVERNMENTS, 1920–1930

| Country and Govt. Entity | No. of Loans | Nominal Value (U.S. $ thousands)[a] | Purpose[b] | | |
			Public Works	Refinance (U.S. $ thousands)[a]	Other
Argentina					
National govt.	10	288,800	38,100	233,700	17,000[c]
Provincial govts.	8	102,601	58,878	47,601	2,122
Municipal govts.	7	28,017	28,017	—	—
Bolivia					
National govt.	3	66,000	43,000	23,000	—
Brazil					
National govt.	5	219,077	75,000	144,077	—
Provincial govts.	21	343,939	110,212	87,744	145,983[d]
Municipal govts.	10	78,302	62,302	15,000	—
Chile					
National govt.	10	228,788	176,696	52,092	—
Municipal govts.	3	23,750	23,750	—	—
Mortgage Bank of Chile	5	90,000	—	—	90,000[e]
Colombia					
National govt.	2	60,000	60,000	—	—
Provincial govts.	8	67,350	66,100	1,250	—
Municipal govts.	6	27,585	20,085	7,500	—
Colombian Mortgage Bank	5	21,840	—	—	21,840[f]
Costa Rica					
National govt.	3	10,990	9,800	1,190	—

[a] All bond issues in currencies other than U.S. dollars (e.g., pounds sterling, pesetas, or francs) have been converted into U.S. dollars according to contemporary exchange rates, but the figures given here are simply the published estimates of the nominal values of the bonds issued; they do not necessarily reflect the precise amounts sold. This would require a detailed loan-by-loan study, using documents from government and bank archives.

[b] These are approximate estimates based on the ostensible objectives as described in the loan contracts and/or loan prospectuses; they do not reflect real disbursement of the proceeds. Only a detailed study of each loan, using the financial archives of each Latin American government, would provide an approximation to the latter information.

[c] A 100,000,000 peseta bond issue in 1927 for acquisition of armaments.

[d] Bonds issued on behalf of the São Paulo Coffee Institute for the coffee valorization scheme.

[e] Mortage bonds of the National Bank of Chile, ostensibly for agricultural development.

[f] Bonds of the Agricultural Mortgage Bank of Colombia, ostensibly for agricultural development.

TABLE 7 (*cont.*)

Country and Govt. Entity	No. of Loans	Nominal Value (U.S. $ thousands)[a]	Purpose[b]		
			Public Works	Refinance (U.S. $ thousands)[a]	Other
Cuba					
National govt.	5	155,973	40,000	79,000	36,973[g]
Dominican Republic					
National govt.	2	20,000	15,000	5,000	—
El Salvador					
National govt.	3	21,609	—	21,609	—
Guatemala					
National govt.	3	9,465	4,950	4,515	—
Haiti					
National govt.	2	18,634	—	18,634	—
Panama					
National govt.	2	20,500	4,500	12,000	4,000[h]
Peru					
National govt.	5	105,814	57,366	48,448	—
Provincial govts.	1	1,500	1,500	—	—
Municipal govts.	1	3,000	1,500	1,500	—
Uruguay					
National govt.	3	55,081	55,081	—	—
Municipal govts.	2	15,307	15,307	—	—

SOURCES: A. Kimber, *Kimber's Record of Government Debts* (London, 1929 and 1934); Corporation of Foreign Bondholders, *Annual Reports* (London, 1928–35); Foreign Bondholders Protective Council, *Annual Reports* (New York, 1934, 1936).

NOTE: This table includes only long-term external bond issues by Latin American government entities. It does not include short-term and medium-term issues (1–5 years maturity).

[g] Sugar stabilization gold bonds issued in 1930 with the guarantee of the Cuban National Sugar Exporting Corporation.
[h] Gold bonds issued to bolster the reserves of the Banco Nacional de Panamá.

to contract a great number of "development" loans during the years 1925–28.

An adequate explanation of the forces that contributed to the multiplication of these two different types of loans requires at the very least a summary analysis of the economic context that shaped the views of the politicians who were responsible for formulating financial policy. We shall begin with a discussion of the reasons that the crisis of 1920–21 compelled so many Latin American leaders to look to the United States for refinancing loans.

The international commercial upheaval of 1920–21, as already noted, triggered a sharp drop in export revenues and therefore caused a crisis in Latin American public finances. The decline in foreign trade reduced the volume of customs revenues and obliged governments to cut spending. But some expenditures could not be easily reduced, the most important being the service on the foreign debt. The payments on these debts, as well as the remittances abroad of profits by foreign-owned companies, required an abundance of foreign exchange or of gold. But the commercial crisis eliminated the possibility of obtaining much foreign exchange. As a result, the burden of the foreign debts threatened to provoke a massive hemorrhage of the gold reserves that had been accumulated between 1915 and 1920.

The most serious structural problem confronting Latin American finance ministers in the early 1920s was maintenance of a steady flow of funds abroad to cover interest on loans and profit remittances. The bulk of these payments went to investors in Europe—England, Germany, France, Belgium, and Holland—because they were holders of most Latin American bonds as well as of shares in a great number of private enterprises operating in Brazil, Argentina, Chile, and the other countries of the region. On the basis of a rough estimate, we can calculate that between 1920 and 1929 Latin America transferred a total of approximately $5,000,000,000 abroad to cover the foreign debt service and the remittances by foreign-owned enterprises. During this period Latin America accumulated an export trade surplus of some $3,000,000,000. As a result, $2,000,000,000 was needed to cover the difference. It was therefore, not surprising, that during the same period the Latin American states should have contracted foreign loans for the sum of $2,000,000,000, mostly in the United States.[31]

The loans negotiated with New York bankers were crucial to the equilibrium of the Latin American balance of payments during the 1920s and to maintaining fluid financial and commercial exchanges between the triangle of Latin America, Europe and the United States. This relationship was recognized by the bankers. A certain Mr. Dennis, employed by Seligman Brothers of New York for negotiation of several Peruvian loans, explained the nature of the trade-off between European commercial and war debts and United States loans to Latin America:

It so happened, after the war, that England and France, and the creditor countries of Europe had to pay for a heavy surplus of imports from America. Where were they to get the necessary dollars? They got them very largely from South America and other fields in which they had invested capital. They drew their income from

31. For data see sources, Cleona Lewis, *America's Stake in International Investments* (Washington, D.C., 1938), pp. 617–634.

investments in Latin America in dollars, and they used those dollars to pay the United States for an excess of imports from this country and also on war-debt payments. . . . We loaned the money to Latin America and thus Europeans acquired dollars to pay us. . . . It was a triangular movement.[32]

From a macroeconomic perspective, the loans of the 1920s contributed to smoothing the operations of the capitalist economy on an international scale, allowing Latin America to pay off its European creditors with funds obtained from money markets in North America. On the other hand, from the viewpoint of the Latin American finance ministers, each of these loans was a key tool for covering deficits or promoting ambitious public works that they could not carry out with regular revenues.

The demand for these dollar credits became go great that numerous Latin American governments asked financial experts from the United States to help them in reorganizing their system of public finance with a view to winning the confidence of the great New York banks. It was believed that the banks might prove amenable to the granting of loans if these were designed to help implement a series of fiscal and financial reforms based on North American models.

The most famous of the financial experts contracted by Latin American governments was Edwin Kemmerer, a Princeton professor of economics, who became widely known as the "international money doctor." He led financial missions to Colombia (1923), Guatemala (1924), Chile (1925), Ecuador (1926–27), Bolivia (1927), and Peru (1931).[33] Kemmerer adopted a similar strategy in each case, taking with him a small team of experts, who studied various aspects of the local financial system in order to propose key reforms. Generally speaking, the missions recommended that a more-sophisticated public accounting system be established, that budgets be carefully balanced, that sufficient gold reserves be maintained in order to continue with adherence to the gold standard, and that central banks be created along the lines of the Federal Reserve Bank of New York.

The Kemmerer missions were not officially sponsored by the State Department, but rather were paid for by the Latin American governments that requested the financial advice of the "experts." But, it is clear that the role of the Princeton professor and his associates was considered useful by United States diplomats and bankers. Furthermore, many members of these

32. U.S. Congress, *Sale of Foreign Bonds*, pp. 1606–1607.

33. On the Kemmerer missions see, Robert Seidel, "American Reformers Abroad: The Kemmerer Missions in South America, 1923–1931," *Journal of Economic History* 32, no. 2 (1972): 520–545. For a detailed analysis of Kemmerer's role in Ecuador, see Linda A. Rodríguez, *The Search for Public Policy: Regional Politics and Government Finances in Ecuador, 1830–1940* (Berkeley, 1985), pp. 133–162.

missions were directly involved in programs designed to extend United States control over the fiscal structure of various Latin American nations. An example was that of Thomas R. Lill, member of the mission to Colombia, who stayed on afterward as technical adviser to the government at Bogotá. Another was William Roddy, who served on the Kemmerer mission to Peru, as director-general of customs in Ecuador (1927–30) and as adviser of customs in Colombia (1931).[34]

The establishment of United States control over customs receipts in several Latin American nations—in Cuba, Haiti, Santo Domingo, and Nicaragua during the entire decade of the 1920s, in Peru between 1921 and 1924, in Ecuador, Honduras, and Bolivia in the late 1920s—was closely linked to foreign loan policy. By arranging for appointment of North American advisers to supervise taxes, budgets, and public credit in foreign nations, the State Department gave comfort to bankers and investors engaged in buying and selling Latin American bonds. The advisers were effectively financial proconsuls who used their positions to ensure that United States bondholders would get their money back.

The leaders of the Latin American nations mentioned were not opposed to this foreign intrusion in the management of the finances of their states because they believed that the presence of the advisers might help attract new loans and investments from abroad. The acceptance of foreign advisers did not guarantee that a flow of foreign capital would begin immediately,[35] but by the mid-1920s there was such an abundance of capital in United States money markets that virtually all the Latin American elites were able to obtain large sums for their economic projects.

As in previous loan booms, the construction projects for railways and ports were major priorities of government development plans. But now more money was invested in urban modernization, including the building of schools and hospitals, the establishment of gas works and electrical plants, the construction of modern drainage systems, and the paving of streets and avenues. In rural areas the building of highways received much attention.

34. Information on the wide-ranging role of these "experts" can be found in Seidel, "American Reformers," pp. 528–532, 537, 542.

35. For example, the dictator of Peru, Agustin Leguía, accepted the State Department's recommendation that a financial expert be appointed to reform government finances and the national banking system. The individual chosen, William Cumberland, remained at Lima between 1921 and 1924 and played a key role in establishing the Peruvian Central Bank. Paradoxically, Cumberland's presence did not help Leguía obtain loans from the New York bankers in the short run. Not until 1927 did Peru manage to jump on the foreign-loan bandwagon. For details, see Frank Mackaman, "United States Loan Policy, 1920–1930: Diplomatic Assumptions, Governmental Politics and Conditions in Peru and Mexico" (Ph.D. diss., University of Missouri, 1977), 2:596–651.

The public works projects served a variety of purposes. Politicians, bankers, and contractors all had a finger in the pie. The politicians used public works as instruments to consolidate their power, expecting that they could win the support of their constituencies by stimulating economic growth. This did not mean, however, that the projects were viewed as humanitarian instruments to improve the lot of the working classes or the peasants. The contracts were intended fundamentally to produce political and economic profits for the ruling elites. Indeed, the less-scrupulous leaders, such as Leguía, the Peruvian dictator, or Gerardo Machado, the authoritarian Cuban president, had few qualms about using a substantial portion of the loan funds to line their own pockets.[36]

The contractors had a strictly economic interest in the public works. The most prominent were several large United States construction companies that used the loan proceeds to finance development projects in which they had a stake. Warren Brothers, for example, built roads in Chile, Colombia, Cuba, and Guatemala. Ulen & Company, which worked in conjunction with the National City Bank, won electrical contracts in Brazil, Peru, and Argentina and took charge of irrigation works in Chile and port works in Colombia. The Foundation Company was responsible for waterworks and street paving in Lima, Peru, as well as for additional building projects in Argentina, Bolivia, and Chile. And Snare & Company won the contracts for modernization of Peruvian ports.

These firms charged exorbitant prices and reaped enormous profits on their Latin American business, but government officials did not protest. After all, many of them were being paid handsome commissions to allow the North American entrepreneurs to bloat the contract bills. Furthermore, a large number of urban property owners in cities like Lima, Rio de Janeiro, São Paulo, Havana, and Montevideo were making enormous sums from the phenomenal boom in real-estate values.[37]

The New York bankers who provided the loans for the public works collaborated closely with politicians and contractors. In Peru, for example, the principal bankers involved, J. and W. Seligman & Company of New York, were aware that the loans did not contribute to financial stability, but rather fueled a tremendous wave of speculation in local real-estate markets and

36. On payoffs to Leguía, see Mackaman, "United States Loan Policy, 1920–1930," 2:646–677. On Machado's personal relations with the Chase Bank, see Raymond Buell et al., *Problems of the New Cuba*, Report of the Commission on Cuban Affairs of the Foreign Policy Association (New York, 1935), pp. 389–391.

37. An excellent case study of the relationship between urban-development loans and real-estate speculation is in the chapter on the Montevideo loans of the 1920s in Carlos Zubillaga, *El reto financiero: deuda externa y desarrollo en Uruguay, 1903–1933* (Montevideo, 1982), pp. 142–155. Abundant information on the U.S. construction companies and their Latin American ventures can be found in U.S. Congress, *Sale of Foreign Bonds*; see also Lewis, *America's Stake*, pp. 378–379.

banking circles. However, Seligmans was more interested in obtaining high commissions for selling the external bonds and in arranging lucrative public works contracts than in maintaining conservative and prudent fiscal and monetary programs.[38]

The loans of 1925–28 therefore had a purpose different from that of the foreign financial transactions which followed the crisis of 1920–21. "Development" now took priority over "refinancing" goals. The ways in which each government carried out their financial programs, however, varied substantially. To underline the differences, we shall compare Cuban loan policies, which were virtually designed by the United States banks, with the more independent policies implemented by Brazilian government authorities.

CUBAN LOANS AND NEW YORK FINANCIAL GROUPS

By the mid-1920s United States bankers and industrialists had invested more money in Cuba than in any other Latin American nation. From 1902 to 1924 their investments in sugar plantations and refineries rose from $50,000,000 to $600,000,000, to which must be added an additional $400,000,000 in railways, electric power plants, telephones and telegraphs, tramways, banks, and numerous commercial firms. In addition, United States businessmen wielded decisive control over the foreign trade of the island; at its apex the United States supplied 73 percent of Cuban imports and took 84 percent of its exports.[39]

Economic control was complemented by political and military intervention in the internal affairs of the republic of Cuba. During the years 1899–1902 and 1906–9, two different United States governors were in charge of the island government. Thereafter various instruments were used to maintain what can only be described as a neo-colonial regime. These included strict fiscal control, supervision of all elections, and the training and arming of the Cuban Rural Guard. As a further guarantee, frequent recourse was had to the Platt amendment, which sanctioned military intervention to guarantee political stability. In 1912 and 1917 the U.S. Marines were sent to Havana to quell working-class protests, and early in 1919 General Enoch Crowder was sent to Cuba to supervise the national elections, staying on afterward as a kind of American viceroy.[40]

While United States interests focused on consolidating their control over

38. See testimony of Mr. Dennis, employee of Seligmans, U.S. Senate, *Sale of Foreign Bonds*, pp. 1583–1609.

39. On U.S. interests in Cuba, see Jules P. Benjamin, *The United States and Cuba: Hegemony and Dependent Development, 1880–1934* (Pittsburgh, 1977), pp. 14–21.

40. On Crowder's involvement in Cuban finance, see Robert Freeman Smith, *The United States and Cuba: Business and Diplomacy, 1917–1960* (New York, 1960), chap. 6.

Cuban sugar production and trade, they did not disdain the considerable profits to be made in local banking. In the years preceding 1920, several banking subsidiaries were set up by powerful New York groups, including the Trust Company of Cuba (controlled by the Morgan interests), the American Foreign Banking Corporation (controlled by the Chase Bank), several branches of the National City Bank, and the Mercantile Bank of the Americas (closely linked to the huge Cuban Sugar Cane Corporation). But these banks did not operate alone. Two large Cuban-owned banks, the Banco Español and the Banco Nacional de Cuba, built up a large network of branches throughout the island and came to control much of local financing. As Leland Jenks notes in a classic study: "It is worth recording that there developed in Cuba between 1917 and 1920, under indigenous control, most of the phenomena of speculation, industrial combination, price-fixing, bank manipulation, pyramiding of credits and over-capitalization, which we are accustomed to regard as the peculiar gift of the highly civilized Anglo-Saxons."[41]

Then came the crash in the autumn of 1920. Sugar prices had climbed from 9 cents a pound in February to a high of 19 cents in June. Thereafter they began to decline. In September they fell sharply to 9 cents and continued downward, reaching bottom at 4 cents in December. On October 11 a bank moratorium was declared to save the banks from collapse. During the following year a Bank Liquidation Commission was set up, but it proved to be ineffective; in spite of its support, eighteen local banks failed. At the same time, a Sugar Export Committee was established to help stimulate a recovery in international sugar prices; it was more successful, but even so the majority of the Cuban-owned sugar companies were sold to large United States conglomerates.[42]

The National City Bank was one of the financial groups that moved most quickly to absorb local sugar plantations and mills. By 1925 it owned ten *centrales* and controlled financially another twenty. Other important New York groups that also took major shares in sugar firms included J. P. Morgan & Company, the Chase Bank, and the investment firms of J. and W. Seligman and Brown Brothers.[43] The expanding role of the banks in Caribbean agro-industrial enterprises reflected the increasingly complex strategies of United States finance capital in Latin America. These were complemented by aggressive promotion of loans for the Cuban government.

In late 1921 the Cuban president, Alfredo Zayas, appealed to J. P. Morgan & Company to provide a loan in order to cover the huge deficits that

41. Jenks, *Our Cuban Colony*, p. 207.
42. On the Cuban response to the crisis of 1920–21, see ibid., pp. 237–239.
43. On the United States financial groups involved in the Cuban sugar business, see Oscar Pino Santos, *La oligarquia yanqui en Cuba* (Mexico, 1975), pp. 96–106.

were a result of the commercial crisis. The New York bank immediately dispatched one of its senior partners, Dwight Morrow, to Havana; he was accompanied by Norman Davis, who had recently left the State Department to take over the direction of the Trust Company of Cuba. After consultation with the State Department, the financiers agreed to provide a $5,000,000 advance to the Cuban treasury as the first tranche of a larger $50,000,000 bond issue. But before proceeding to issue the bonds, Morrow and General Crowder submitted to President Zayas a program of wide-ranging fiscal, budgetary, and banking reforms that they expected the Cuban Congress to ratify. To assure success for the plan, Crowder pressured Zayas to revamp his entire cabinet, naming a set of new ministers who would favor the reform program.[44]

The 1923 Cuban loan can be considered a clear example of collaboration between New York bankers and Washington politicians to control the financial policies of a Latin American nation. It certainly revealed the close ties that existed between leading United States banks and the State and Commerce Departments. Nevertheless, it should not be considered a paradigm of foreign loan activity in the 1920s, for in most other bond issues the bankers did not make a major effort to obtain the support of authorities at Washington, D.C.[45] And even in Cuba, after the successful sale of the 1923 bonds, President Zayas began to adopt a more-independent financial policy.

The other large foreign loan negotiated by the Cuban government in this period was the public works loan of 1927. The new president, Gerardo Machado, undertook an elaborate program of public works, including construction of a central highway running the length of the island. Machado, who was personally in charge of the contracts, hired a Boston construction company, Warren Brothers, to build the highway. At the same time, he opened bidding on a large loan to finance the public works. The competition among the National City Bank, Morgan Guaranty, and the Chase Bank was intense. Chase finally won, helped perhaps by the fact that Machado's son-in-law was an employee of the local subsidiary of the bank and that Machado himself received several large personal loans from the Chase office in Havana. In any event, the bonds sold briskly in United States capital markets, and the Cuban government was soon proudly touting its development projects. According to the loan contract, 45 percent of the funds were to go to the highway, 20 percent to the building of a huge new capitol building at Havana, 10 percent for drainage and pavements, and 10 percent

44. Jenks, *Our Cuban Colony*, pp. 257–261; and Smith, *The United States and Cuba*, chap. 6.

45. This point is argued in detail by Mackaman, "United States Loan Policy, 1920–1930."

for hospitals and schools. In practice, the highway and the capitol building absorbed most of the money, while the public health and social programs were sacrificed. It is not surprising that there were reports of enormous graft on the contracts.[46]

A few years later, following the panic of 1929, Machado turned again to the Chase bankers, requesting their help to save his government from financial collapse. In early 1931, in the midst of the depression, the financiers advanced another $20,000,000 to the unscrupulous Cuban president. Shortly thereafter he was forced to leave office, and in 1934 the Cuban government temporarily suspended payments on the public works loan, linking it to the unethical nature of the financial arrangements. An advisory commission of lawyers concluded that the Chase loans had been illegally contracted and should therefore be repudiated.[47] In fact, there was no long-term default on the Cuban foreign debt, but the influence of the New York bankers over the finances of the island had been seriously shaken.

Brazil's Independent Loan Policy

Not all the Latin American nations were compelled to accept the tutelage of Washington politicians or the patronage of New York bankers. Indeed, during the 1920s some republics found space to negotiate what can be defined as a relatively independent loan policy. The Brazilian case illustrates the possibilities of implementing such a strategy, a fact that is doubly significant because Brazil was the largest borrower of the decade (see Table 7).

The formulation of Brazilian loan policies was inscribed within a complex financial structure. There were three tiers to this structure, including the national, provincial, and municipal governments. Each of these had a considerable degree of autonomy, as demonstrated by the fact that provincial legislatures and city councils could negotiate foreign loans without asking for authorization from the national government at Rio de Janeiro. Between 1920 and 1930 the national authorities took five large loans abroad, provincial governments twenty-one loans, and the municipalities took ten loans. This kind of financial federalism meant that no one public entity was responsible for designing the international loan programs of Brazil. As a result, the 1920s witnessed extreme competition to obtain funds abroad among the various government agencies. They were all remarkably successful.[48]

46. Buell, *Problems of the New Cuba*, pp. 386–393.

47. Republic of Cuba, Secretaría de Hacienda, Comisión Especial de Investigación de las Obligaciones Contraídas con The Chase National Bank, *Los empréstitos de obras públicas* (Havana, 1935).

48. The success of the financial strategies of the Brazilians was surprising for several rea-

The most unique of the Brazilian foreign loans were those negotiated by the state government of São Paulo on behalf of the powerful landed and mercantile interests involved in coffee production and trade. These loans demonstrated that, in contrast to the case of Cuba, the Brazilian ruling classes had a considerable degree of independence from United States political and banking interests.

The finances of São Paulo had long been closely linked to the fortunes of the coffee trade. From the turn of the century the state authorities had collaborated with the federal government in the promotion of a complex price-support program known as the coffee valorization scheme. Together they bought up a large part of bumper crops in 1906, 1911, 1913, and 1921, financing these transactions with loans raised in London. By removing surplus coffee from the market, this policy helped maintain stable, high prices for the most important Brazilian export commodity. But after 1921 the federal government refused to continue participating in the coffee valorization program. This blow to the coffee interests was compounded by the impact of the international commercial crisis, which produced a calamitous drop in international prices in coffee, from 24 cents per pound in 1920 to 9 cents in 1921.[49]

To avoid a collapse of this sophisticated price-defense mechanism, the Paulista plantation elites worked out a new solution. In 1924 the São Paulo Coffee Institute was set up with the specific purpose of buying up excess coffee stocks, storing them in warehouses, and selling them when prices rose. In order to finance the institute, the state authorities asked the New York banking firms of Dillon, Read & Company and Speyer & Company to help by issuing a foreign loan. But the United States government stepped in to block the operation. Specifically, the secretary of commerce, Herbert Hoover, denounced the Brazilian plans to defend coffee prices, arguing that it would be prejudicial for American consumers: "If European financiers were willing to enter into a gamble to hold the price of coffee at a point which curtailed consumption and stimulated production to a point where today we have a world surplus, that was a matter of their own responsibility

---

sons. The Brazilian economy had benefited less than other Latin American economies from the export boom of 1915–20. During this period the national government had actually been forced to suspend amortization payments on its foreign debts and had simultaneously adopted a series of inflationary monetary policies that were anathema to foreign bankers. Furthermore, the crisis of 1920–21 undermined what was already an unstable financial and commercial situation. The rubber export boom faded, sugar production faltered, and coffee, a traditional mainstay of the Brazilian economy, suffered from the steep fall in international prices.

49. On the coffee valorization schemes, see Thomas H. Holloway, *The Brazilian Coffee Valorization* (Madison, 1975); Stephen Krasner, "Manipulating International Commodity Markets: Brazilian Coffee Policy," *Public Policy* 21, no. 4 (1973): 493–523; and Celso Furtado, *The Economic Growth of Brazil: A Survey from Colonial to Modern Times* (Berkeley, 1971), pp. 195–202.

. . . but that if they did, it was better that it be done by some outsider than done by American bankers against the interest of the American public.''[50]

The banking firm of Dillon/Read protested, arguing that such a policy would allow European bankers to reassume their control over Brazilian finances.[51] But to no avail. The Washington politicians would not brook the financial independence of the São Paulo authorities. The latter were not stymied. They turned to the powerful London merchant banking firm of Lazard Brothers, which was a key player in international coffee markets. And in 1926 Lazards arranged the issue of a £10,000,000 loan (U.S. $50,000,000) in order to provide the Coffee Institute with the necessary funds for its operations. The London merchant bankers had no difficulty finding a market for the São Paulo bonds, selling 80 percent of them in Great Britain and 20 percent in Switzerland and Holland.[52]

During the rest of the decade the British bankers continued to support Brazilian coffee programs, much to the mortification of United States government officials. In 1927 and 1928 Lazards arranged new loans for the Bank of the State of São Paulo, which was in charge of administering the funds of the Coffee Institute. However, the success of the price-boosting mechanisms eventually proved counterproductive. By early 1929 an enormous quantity of unsold coffee had accumulated in the warehouses, and when international prices collapsed in the latter part of the year, São Paulo found itself on the brink of bankruptcy.[53] On this occasion another group of London merchant bankers, led by J. H. Schröder & Company, Baring Brothers, and N. M. Rothschilds stepped in to save the day, although they were now also assisted by a syndicate of New York banks led by Speyer & Company. In 1930 the British firms sold more than $60,000,000 in São Paulo gold bonds, placing them in markets in London, Amsterdam, Stockholm, Milan, and Zurich. At the same time, Speyer sold $35,000,000 worth of the bonds in New York. The specific purpose of this operation— the largest of all contemporary Latin American loans—was to liquidate 16,000,000 bags of coffee that sat unsold in warehouses throughout the state of São Paulo.[54]

The coffee valorization loans represented a sophisticated attempt by the coffee planters of Brazil to use foreign finance to sustain a century-old export model of growth. But the coffee aristocrats did not monopolize Brazilian financial policy. On the contrary, it can be argued that the 1920s

50. Wilson, *American Business*, p. 172.
51. Ibid., pp. 172–173.
52. Kimber, *Kimber's Record, 1934*, pp. 330–331.
53. Joseph Love, *São Paulo in the Brazilian Federation, 1889–1937* (Stanford, 1980), pp. 250–251.
54. Kimber, *Kimber's Record, 1934*, pp. 334–335.

actually witnessed a diversification of financial resources to the benefit of the nonexport sectors. This was demonstrated by the remarkable urban expansion that took place during these years, the substantial advance of industrialization, and the progress achieved in construction of such infrastructure as railroads, roads, port works, and electrical power plants.[55]

It was, in fact, the dynamism of the *domestic* economy of Brazil that helped overcome the effects of the crisis of 1920–21 and attain high growth rates in subsequent years. In this respect it should be noted that foreign commerce played a less-significant role in the Brazilian economy than ordinarily presumed. A comparison of the per capita value of foreign trade in several Latin American nations illustrates this point. In 1920, for example, Brazil had a foreign trade of $26 per head, as contrasted with $120 in Chile, $210 in Argentina, and close to $400 in Cuba.[56] Such data suggest that the economy of Brazil depended on external factors much less than did the economy of the other nations mentioned.

In the early 1920s the federal government contributed to the domestic recovery by adopting several policies that helped keep up production and employment. These included a sustained expansion of government spending to maintain consumption levels, a liberal credit policy by the Banco do Brasil, and the issue of two large foreign loans to finance a series of ambitious public works programs. The public works programs promoted by the administration of President Epitacio Pessoa (1918–22) were financed with two large loans taken in 1921 and 1922. The principal object of the 1921 loan was to build dams, irrigation works, and roads, to make the drought-ridden region of northeastern Brazil more habitable, and to prevent the periodic exodus of the population. The goal of the second loan was to electrify the Central Railroad of Brazil and to make other transport improvements. Because these public works programs were carried out during a severe commercial crisis, they can be seen as countercyclical measures to lessen the impact of the economic downturn.[57]

The state and municipal governments of Brazil were also active in the negotiation of loans to carry out public works, seeking the funds in both

55. Even in the case of São Paulo, many foreign loans went for purposes not directly linked to coffee valorization, including railways, conversion of previous debts, and the promotion of immigration (Love, *São Paulo*, p. 248).

56. Based on data from Pan American Union, *The Foreign Trade of Latin America, 1910–1929* (Washington, D.C., 1931).

57. On the other hand, after 1922 the administrations of Arturo Bernardes (1922–26) and Washington Luis (1926–30) did not negotiate any more foreign credits for productive purposes. They limited themselves to authorization of several refinancing loans through a coalition of New York and London banks. An interesting contemporary critique of Brazilian monetary and debt policies is Waldemar Falcao, *O empirismo monetario no Brasil: ensaio de crítica financeira* (São Paulo, 1931).

New York and London. They solicited the foreign gold in order to build railways and ports, but above all to promote urban development. The 1920s were a period of dramatic and rapid modernization of the leading cities of Brazil, as was the case in many other Latin American nations. The construction of broad avenues, the building of attractive residential districts for the middle and upper classes, the introduction of the automobile, the spread of the department store, and the universalization of electric lighting for both home and industry were all testimony to the enthusiasm and energy devoted to the transformation of city life.[58]

In almost every Brazilian state, large amounts of public funds were spent to transform the local capital city into a showhouse of progress. For example, the southern ranching state of Rio Grande do Sul issued two state and three municipal loans abroad to modernize the city of Pôrto Alegre; the funds were invested in harbor works, sanitation, and drainage, the construction and paving of new streets, and a new electric light system. In the northern sugar state of Pernambuco the goals of the local political elite were similar; they contracted loans to finance the building of wharves, docks, warehouses, and other public works at the port of Recife, an old colonial city that aspired to enter the turbulent world of the twentieth century. In Minas Gerais the loans of 1928 and 1929 went to finance electric light and power facilities in the city of Belo Horizonte and to provide funds for improvements in neighboring municipalities.[59]

The largest loans were taken by the two most important Brazilian cities—São Paulo and Rio de Janeiro. The dynamism of São Paulo was evinced in the extraordinary expansion of its population, which rose from 500,00 inhabitants in 1920 to more than 1,000,000 in 1930, as well as in the expansion of its construction and manufacturing industries. By 1930, São Paulo had the largest industrial "park" in South America.[60] The growing metropolis required a large amount of money to provide the basic infrastructure for economic expansion. In 1922 and 1927 the city authorities

58. An excellent study of urban development in this period is Warren Dean, *The Industrialization of São Paulo, 1880–1945* (Austin, 1969). Nonetheless, Dean considers that in these years industry did not grow as rapidly as in the first decade of the twentieth century. Other authors made a strong case for the rapid expansion of industry during the 1920s. See Flavio Robelo Versiani, "Before the Depression: Brazilian Industry in the 1920s," in *Latin America in the 1930s*, ed. R. Thorp, pp. 163–187.

59. There is a wealth of information on the state finances of Brazil in François Conty, *L'Indépendance financière des états fédérés du Brésil* (Paris, 1926). A large amount of data can also be found in Kimber, *Kimber's Record, 1934*, pp. 263–431. Another important source is Valentim Bouças, *Finanças do Brasil: história da dívida externa estadual e municipal* (Rio de Janeiro, 1942).

60. Alfredo Ellis, *A evoluçao da economia paulista e suas causas* (São Paulo, 1937), pp. 260–261.

turned to several United States investment houses, including Blair & Company and the First Boston Corporation, to provide loans to help finance construction of streets, tunnels, and municipal markets. Not to be outdone, Rio de Janeiro, the nation's capital, also resorted to New York bankers for assistance with its ambitious renovation plans. The city issued loans worth more than $30,000,000 to build avenues, to construct a municipal slaughterhouse, to remove Morro Castello (a large hill in the center of the business section), and for a variety of additional public works.[61]

The foreign loans negotiated by the national, state, and municipal governments contributed to an expansion of the state's role within the economy. By 1930 the federal government owned close to one-third of all Brazilian railroads, half the merchant marine, and the largest bank.[62] The state governments also became public entrepreneurs, using foreign loans to assume control of local railways and ports. Similarly, municipal governments used foreign funds to become chief promoters of the electrical power industry, there being more than 400 municipal lighting companies by the 1920s.

By promoting these and other enterprises, the Brazilian state accelerated the process of capitalist accumulation at both the national level and the provincial level. But this process did not benefit the mass of the Brazilian population. The benefits of a large volume of foreign capital were reaped fundamentally by the urban and rural propertied classes, which profited from the rise in the value of real estate and from a great boom in the construction industry.

The foreign loans of the 1920s had a dual and in some respects contradictory economic and social impact. They instilled new life in the traditional coffee-producing sector, which had constituted the basis of the Brazilian economy during the nineteenth century. But the loans also provided impetus for building cities and development of a series of young industries that were to be the axis of economic growth in future decades. The contradictions between these two models of growth would intensify as a result of the world crisis of 1929.

The impact of foreign loans was also contradictory in many other Latin American nations. The flow of capital from abroad spurred economic activity in the major cities without weakening the landed oligarchies or the export economy. On the contrary, by tying loans to foreign trade, financial

61. Data from Kimber, *Kimber's Record, 1934*, pp. 308–310, 339–340.

62. For an illuminating discussion of the expanding economic role of the Brazilian state, see Steven Topik, "State Interventionism in a Liberal Regime: Brazil, 1889–1930," *HAHR* 60, no. 4 (1980): 593–616; and by the same author, "A empresa estatal em um regime liberal: O Banco do Brasil, 1905–1930," *Revista Brasileira do Mercado do Capitales* 7, no. 19 (January 1981): 70–83.

dependency lent strength to the traditional power structure based on the alliance of merchants, landowners, and foreign capitalists. Meanwhile, other social sectors—including an incipient industrial bourgeoisie in such countries as Argentina, Chile, and Brazil—benefited from the rapid process of urban expansion and therefore offered little opposition to financial policies that progressively submitted the national economies to the dictates of the New York and London bankers. As long as the money flowed, the conflicts between different sectors of the propertied classes could be patched over.

But after 1929, as international trade fell and foreign loans dried up, social and political tensions escalated. The old model of the export economy increasingly came under fire. Furthermore, all Latin American nations now confronted an inescapable dilemma: either they suspended payments on their foreign debts and adopted a more autonomous path of economic development, or they continued to pay their creditors in the hope that prosperity would somehow return.

The Great Depression and Latin American Defaults

The government has the right to suspend payments [on the debt] when the nation is threatened with political and economic slavery.

—Cuban Government Commission on Foreign Loans (1934)

THE THUNDEROUS CRASH of the New York Stock Exchange on October 24, 1929, was heard around the world. It announced the end of a decade of prosperity and the beginning of the Great Depression of the 1930s. Black Thursday on Wall Street confirmed the severity of the economic catastrophe, but there had been numerous earlier signs indicating the ominous instability of the international economy.

In Latin America the downturn was felt at least two years before, as a result of the gradual decline in prices of several important export commodities.[1] Financial conditions in Latin America also began to deteriorate before the onset of the panic. In the latter part of 1928 the foreign loan boom waned, and during 1929 only $67,000,000 in Latin American bonds were sold in the United States, barely one-fifth of the average amounts placed in the previous three years.[2] Direct foreign investments also tended to dwindle, largely as a result of the diversion of capital by the wild speculation on the New York stock market. The economic upheaval that followed, therefore, was shocking but not entirely unexpected.

By the first months of 1930 the collapse of international trade and finance had seriously undermined almost all the Latin American economies. The fragility of the traditional export model of development became evident as the principal commodity markets in the United States and Europe closed their doors to the sugar, coffee, beef, wool, copper, tin, silver, and petro-

1. Bolivian tin prices began to fall in mid-1927 and then plunged 25 percent the following year. The prices of crude oil, on which Mexico and Venezuela depended for much of their export income, slid downward from 1927. Cuban sugar and Peruvian cotton values dropped by 20 percent between 1928 and 1929. For data on Mexico, see E.V.K. Fitzgerald, "Restructuring through the Depression: The State and Capital Accumulation in Mexico, 1925–1940," in *Latin America in the 1930s*, ed. R. Thorp, pp. 245–246. For statistical data on price trends of key Latin American commodities in this period, see Joseph Grunwald, *Natural Resources of Latin American Development* (Baltimore, 1970), table B-2, pp. 49–51.

2. During 1926–28, the value of Latin American bonds placed in United States capital markets averaged slightly more than $300,000,000 a year. For exact data, see Lewis, *America's Stake*, pp. 617–634.

leum that came from Central and South America and from the Caribbean.[3] Furthermore, the economic downturn generated enormous social and political tensions throughout the subcontinent. In the space of two years, virtually every state in the region suffered a coup d'état or revolution.

The first signs of the impending political turmoil in South America came from the highlands of Bolivia. On May 28, 1930, President Hernando Siles was overthrown as a result of the discontent caused by the economic depression, which led to closing of many tin mines and to widespread labor protests. A military junta temporarily took power in La Paz. Three months later the political unrest spread to Peru. On August 25, following a revolt led by several army colonels, dictator Augusto Leguía was forced to resign. Barely ten days later, on September 6, General José F. Uriburu led a coup d'état against Argentine President, Hipólito Irigoyen, who was forced out of office at gunpoint. A month later a great revolt broke out in the southern provinces of Brazil and spread quickly throughout the vast nation. By the end of October 1930, Getúlio Vargas, former governor of Rio Grande do Sul, had assumed power as Brazilian head of state, a post he was to hold without interruption until 1945. Finally, Chile's dictator-president, Carlos Ibañez, desperately attempted to stay in power in the face of a catastrophic economic situation, but social conflicts intensified. On July 24, 1931, a general strike brought down Ibañez, who fled into exile. A year later a group of radical military officers set up a socialist-oriented government that, although short-lived, presaged the Chilean Popular Front regime of the late 1930s.[4]

The political and social turmoil also swept through Central America and the Caribbean. In early 1930, President Vázquez of the Dominican Republic was forced to step down as a result of a revolt led by army officer Rafael Trujillo, who set up an authoritarian regime that harshly repressed all opposition parties. In January 1931 a revolution overthrew the government of Panama. In the same year General Jorge Ubico seized power in Guatemala and there was a coup in El Salvador. Meanwhile, civil war raged in Nicaragua between the revolutionary forces led by Augusto Sandino and the U.S. supported government troops. At the same time, social turbulence built up in Cuba, where sugarcane workers, white-collar employees, and railroad laborers organized strike after strike. On August 12, 1933, the army forced President Machado out of office, facilitating establishment of a nationalist administration under the direction of Ramón Grau San Martín.

3. On commodity trends, see charts and sources in the various country studies in *Latin America in the 1930s*.

4. An informative source on South American political developments during the 1930s is the collection of country studies in *América Latina, historia de medio siglo*, ed. González Casanova (Mexico, 1977), vol. 1.

The provisional government soon fell, but the Cuban revolution of 1933 shook the status quo in the island and weakened United States influence in the Caribbean.[5]

Despite the critical economic situation and the acute social and political tensions, the Latin American nations maintained full service on their foreign debts throughout 1929 and 1930. In addition, the national treasuries and state banks provided the exchange required to pay outstanding commercial credits and to allow foreign-owned companies to remit profits abroad. As a result, by 1931 the gold reserves of Latin America had fallen by approximately $1,000,000,000. [6] Once again, as had been the case during World War I, the region became a *net capital exporter*, transferring large sums to European and United States banks at a time of crisis.

But the financial sacrifice that the Latin American economies were forced to make had limits. The sustained fall in international trade, which reached its nadir in 1931–32, slashed public revenues and made it increasingly difficult to honor commitments with foreign creditors. Defaults were therefore unavoidable.

In January 1931, Bolivia became the first Latin American state formally to declare a unilateral moratorium on its foreign debts. It was followed by Peru in May and by Chile in July.[7] Then, in October, the largest Latin American debtor, Brazil, announced a partial suspension of payments on its debts (see Table 8). The government promised to remit scrip instead of gold to the bondholders, but indicated that it would take the necessary measures to renew payments in hard currency as soon as possible.[8] Such promises were not hollow, but the financial situation in Brazil and the rest of Latin America was destined to get worse before it became better.

During 1932 there were new defaults, including the partial suspension of payments on the foreign debts of Colombia and Uruguay. The Colombian government made strenuous efforts to continue meeting its obligations with its foreign creditors, but by 1935 the Bogotá treasury was empty and default could no longer be avoided.[9] Uruguay was more fortunate; it paid interest

5. On politics during the Great Depression in Central America and the Caribbean, see essays in ibid., vol. 2.

6. United Nations, ECLA, *Economic Development of Latin America* (New York, 1950), table 7, p. 31.

7. On the Bolivian and Peruvian defaults, see Ernesto Galarza, "Debts, Dictatorship, and Revolution in Bolivia and Peru," *Foreign Policy Association Reports*, May 13, 1931, pp. 101–119.

8. On Brazilian national, provincial, and municipal debt arrangements, see Kimber, *Kimber's Record, 1934*, pp. 230–341.

9. R. Thorp and C. Londoño, "The Effect of the Great Depression on the Economies of Peru and Colombia," in *Latin America in the 1930s*, pp. 96–97.

irregularly during several years, yet later returned to the good graces of the foreign bankers by renewing its full debt service.[10]

Meanwhile, in the Caribbean and Central America the debt situation became increasingly unstable. The governments of Costa Rica and Panama defaulted in 1932. The same year, the dictator of the Dominican Republic, Trujillo, froze payments on the sinking fund of his government's debt while at the same time continuing to remit interest to the New York bankers who were supporters of his regime. In Cuba the provisional government of Carlos Mendieta (1934) suspended service on the notorious 1927 public works loan, although it maintained payments on the rest of the external debt. In Haiti, Honduras, and Nicaragua no suspension took place. United States banks systematically collected a percentage of the customs duties in those countries and sent the sums to the bondholders.[11]

In summary, several of the smaller Latin American republics were able to avoid default, but most of the larger nations could not do so. The only exception among the latter was Argentina, which maintained interest and amortization payments on all national loans without interruption until their final liquidation.[12] Yet even in the Argentine case, negotiations with the foreign bankers were necessary. Throughout the 1930s and much of the 1940s all the Latin American governments were involved in complex readjustments of their debts with United States and European banks and bondholders. In this chapter we shall focus on the different approaches adopted by the three largest Latin American debtors—Argentina, Brazil, and Mexico—to resolve their respective financial quandaries. But before discussing these three cases, we shall review the nature of the international forces that unleashed the wave of Latin American defaults between 1931 and 1933.

THE CAUSES OF LATIN AMERICAN DEFAULTS

Events moved so rapidly in the first years of the depression that contemporaries had difficulty understanding the structural determinants of the economic cataclysm. As in previous crises, the first instinct was to look for

10. On the Uruguayan debt adjustments, see Juan Ferrando, *Reseña del crédito público del Uruguay* (Montevideo, 1969), vol. 1, chap. 9.

11. In Haiti, e.g., the American-appointed financial adviser during the 1930s was Sydney de la Rue, who in conjunction with the finance minister played a major role in planning the budget and supervising the customs. For this information I am indebted to Professor Guy Pierre, who kindly allowed me to consult his forthcoming study on the impact of the depression of the 1930s in Haiti.

12. However, there were several Argentine provincial and municipal loans on which payments were temporarily suspended between 1933 and 1935. In the latter year the Argentine government took measures to pay the interest in arrears by issuing national gold bonds to the creditors.

FIGURE 11.
MARKET PRICES OF LATIN AMERICAN GOLD BONDS ON THE NEW YORK STOCK EXCHANGE,
1930–1936. BASED ON HIGHEST PRICES OF THE YEAR.

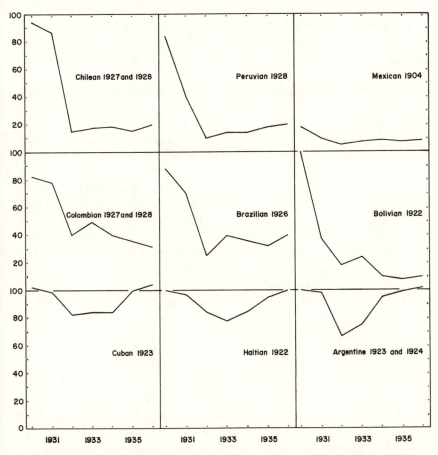

(Data from Foreign Bondholders Protective Council, *Annual Report, 1936* [New York, 1937]).

individual scapegoats. Hence it was not surprising that, following the first
Latin American defaults in 1931, which caused a steep drop in the market
prices of the bonds of Chile, Peru, Brazil, Bolivia and other nations (see
Figure 11), a large number of distressed bondholders in the United States
began to organize a campaign to demand a congressional investigation of
banker malpractice in the issue and sale of the bonds.

The bondholders believed, with some reason, that the New York investment houses had not adequately informed them of the political and eco-

nomic risks involved in acquiring Latin American government securities. A number of powerful Washington, D.C., politicians agreed with them, and in December 1931 the United States Senate opened hearings on the subject. Over four months an impressive roster of New York bankers was publicly cross-examined. The financiers called to Washington included patrician Thomas Lamont of the house of Morgan, the flamboyant Charles Mitchell, president of the National City Bank, Clarence Dillon of the blue-ribbon firm of Dillon/Read, Otto Kahn of Kuhn, Loeb & Company, James Speyer of Speyer & Company, and many others. These individuals denied any wrongdoing and affirmed that by selling the bonds they had simply been pursuing the expansion of United States trade. As Charles Mitchell affirmed, "That the banking interests of this country have floated foreign loans in America is something which should have the praise rather than the criticism of any body of men."[13]

Some senators did not appear to be convinced by this argument. Senator Tom Connally said to Mitchell, "With reference to foreign bonds, you are like the saloon keeper who never drank. His whiskey was made to sell, not to drink."[14] Connally's intention was to suggest that the financiers enticed the investors to buy the bonds without informing them of the dangers the transactions might entail. The bankers insisted they were innocent, but a number of lower-level employees of the banks divulged much information that revealed the degree of cupidity and amorality of both North American bankers and Latin American politicians. In many respects, the arguments put forth were similar to those presented before the British Parliament in its investigation of Latin American loans held in 1875. The bankers were judged to be unscrupulous businessmen who did not have the interests of the average investor at heart. Their duplicity had covered up the menace of a Latin American financial crisis so that it had not been forseen.

Despite the withering criticisms vented in the United States Senate and in the North American press against the bankers and politicians who had inflated the Latin American loan bubble, the defaults were caused not so much by speculation as by the depression itself. The single most important factor that undermined the capacity of Latin American governments to pay was the drastic decline in foreign trade revenues (see Figure 12). Without sufficient hard currency receipts from international commerce, few states could meet financial commitments abroad.

In order to defend their foreign trade and financial positions, Latin American governments rapidly instituted a variety of reforms. These included establishment of exchange controls, reduction of public spending, and spe-

13. U.S. Congress, *Sale of Foreign Bonds*, p. 64.
14. Ibid., p. 81.

cial measures to save the principal export-sectors from total collapse. Nonetheless, the impact of the depression was devastating.

The case of Chile illustrates well the difficulties encountered in responding to the crisis. According to economists, no other country in the world suffered as much as Chile from the trade depression. By 1932, Chilean exports had fallen to a mere one-sixth of their 1929 level; at the same time, government revenues dropped by more than 75 percent.[15] In spite of this calamitous situation, the Santiago treasury continued to service the foreign debt during most of 1929–31, transferring $90,000,000 to creditors in the United States and Europe. These remittances represented one-quarter of total government expenditures, a figure that suggests the magnitude of Chile's external financial commitment.[16]

As the economic crisis intensified, the Santiago authorities began to question the wisdom of continuing to cover the debt service. There were certainly other more pressing needs. The new Chilean Nitrate Company, COSACH, which had been set up in 1930 by the government to buy and sell nitrate stocks in order to stabilize prices, required a great deal of financial assistance. Similarly, several important public works projects—initiated by strongman Ibañez in the late 1920s and continued after the crash in order to mitigate unemployment—absorbed much local credit. The maintenance of trade and employment also had priority over the claims of the distant bondholders. By mid-1931 the Chilean government had decided it was necessary to suspend payment on its external debt.

In neighboring Bolivia, which also relied heavily on mineral exports, the effects of the depression were equally severe. The drop in tin prices shattered the brief but fragile boom experienced by the Bolivian economy in the late 1920s. Attempts were made to reduce tin stocks after 1930 by means of an international cartel of the leading tin producers of the world. But the damage was done—by 1931, Bolivia was bankrupt.[17]

The economy of Peru also suffered from the decline in prices of raw materials. The dollar value of Peruvian exports dropped by 72 percent between 1929 and 1932. This was due, in large measure, to the closing of foreign markets as a result of defensive action by the United States as well as by the United Kingdom and France, the latter subsidizing copper companies in their colonial territories.[18] The protectionism of the powerful in-

15. Gabriel Palma, "From an Export-led to an Import-substituting Economy: Chile 1914–1939," in *Latin America in the 1930s*, pp. 64, 73.

16. Republic of Chile, Dirección General de Estadística, *Sinopsis geográfico-estadístico de Chile* (Santiago, 1933), pp. 297–298.

17. For details on the evolution of the Bolivian economy, see Galarza, "Debts, Dictatorship, and Revolution in Bolivia and Peru," pp. 101–110.

18. Rosemary Thorp and Geoffrey Bertram, *Peru, 1890–1977: Growth and Policy in an Open Economy* (London, 1978), p. 156.

dustrial nations thus had a distinctly negative impact on the weak and dependent economies of such nations as Peru.

By 1930 the Peruvian debt service was absorbing one-third of the now-scarce export revenues. The burden was excessive. Financial officials at Lima could not continue to gratify foreign bankers and bondholders indefinitely. They abandoned the gold standard, set up rigorous exchange controls, and devalued the national currency. They also suspended the debt service. As Rosemary Thorp points out, the default was inescapable: "It is important to bear in mind that devaluation and default are closely interconnected; once devaluation occurred, the incidence of external debt service on internal revenues in domestic currency became so high that there was a strong incentive to at least partial default."[19]

The effects of the trade depression were not limited to the Andean nations; throughout Latin America, commerce dropped to pre-1914 levels (compare Figures 9 and 12). Few finance ministers could view such developments without apprehension. The trade catastrophe made suspension of payments on debts a logical defensive measure.

The second major factor that made defaults inevitable was the international banking crisis that took place in 1931. As already noted, during 1929 foreign banks had sharply reduced their lending to Latin America. Nevertheless, the negative impact of this reduction forced both European and United States banks to reconsider their policies, and in 1930 they made an effort to assist the Latin American governments in order to avoid a suspension of payments on their debts. For example, the Chilean government, was able to sell 60,000,000 francs in bonds in 1930 through various Swiss, French, and Dutch banks.[20] At the same time, Rothschilds and other influential London merchant banking firms helped the Brazilian government raise $35,000,000 in London, New York, and Paris as well as an additional $100,000,000 for the São Paulo Coffee Institute. Other Latin American republics also obtained emergency funds abroad: The Cuban government raised a large loan in New York through the Chase Bank, while Guatemala and Bolivia obtained two small credits through none other than the Swedish Match Corporation.[21]

So the international banking community did not completely abandon Latin America in the initial stages of the depression, but eventually the bankers were obliged to shut down all foreign loan transactions as a result of a major banking debacle. The first signs of a weakening of the banking system came from the United States as a run on banks in the Southeast

19. Thorp and Londoño, "The Effect of the Great Depression," p. 95.
20. Kimber, *Kimber's Record, 1934*, pp. 562–563.
21. Ibid., pp. 227–229, 893–894.

FIGURE 12.
LATIN AMERICAN TOTAL EXPORTS, 1928–1938.

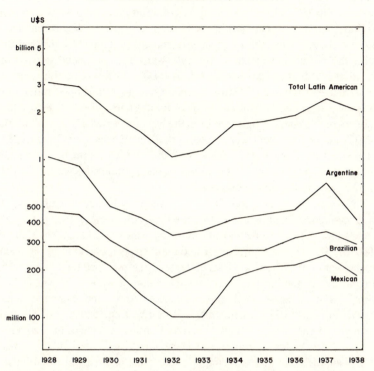

(Data from U.S. Tariff Commission, *The Foreign Trade of Latin America* [Washington, D.C., 1942], Report 146, 2d series, part 1, p. 17; part 2, pp. 14, 80, 186.)

almost provoked a national panic in mid-1930.[22] The weakest link of the international financial structure, however, was not in the United States but in Europe. The crisis exploded in May 1931, when the great Credit-Anstalt bank of Vienna collapsed. The run then shifted to Germany and provoked the fall of the even larger Danatbank. By late July the London money market had begun to crack under the strain, and on September 21 Britain went off the gold standard. Another twenty-one countries followed the British example, and exchange controls were established by the governments of thirty-one nations around the world.

22. Two recent essays dealing with the banking crisis in the United States are Eugene N. White, ''A Reinterpretation of the Banking Crisis of 1930,'' *Journal of Economic History* 44, no. 1 (March 1984): 119–138; and Elmus Wilkins, ''A Reconsideration of the Banking Panic of 1930,'' *Journal of Economic History* 40, no. 3 (September 1980): 571–583.

In order to shore up the European and especially the German banks, the major powers resolved to gather at an international economic conference in Lausanne in 1932. At this meeting the countries entitled to war reparations payments from Germany (which originated from World War I) renounced further claims when the German government assumed a much-reduced sum; the nominal value of Germany's war debt was pared down from $31,000,000,000 to less than $1,000,000,000. At the same time, the nations that had renounced German reparations now demanded relief from their own financial obligations to the United States. The so-called Allied debts (which also had originated from the war) surpassed $10,000,000,000. Of this total, 42 percent were owed to the United States by Great Britain, 34 percent by France, 16 percent by Italy, and 4 percent by Belgium.[23] Under great pressure the United States financial authorities accepted a debt holiday with a duration of one year.

Politicians in Washington, D.C., believed they had acted generously to save the international financial structure from collapsing, although they expected the sacrifice to be short-term. They were mistaken. At the end of 1932 the British Exchequer requested another postponement of payments on the war debts. The United States Treasury sidestepped the issue, preferring to avoid making public pronouncements on what it judged to be a "hot" political issue. Payments remained frozen, and there the matter rested until early 1934, when Senator Hiram Warren Johnson of California managed to push a law through Congress limiting the sale of foreign bonds in the United States. European monetary authorities interpreted this piece of legislation as an untimely and aggressive act of financial isolationism. On June 4, 1934, Great Britain unilaterally suspended all future payments on the war debts with the United States, and this act was soon followed by France, Italy, and Belgium.

The banking crisis of 1931 thus led to bitter transatlantic financial conflicts. The contradictions between the major powers offered a new set of opportunities for Latin American governments to justify default. Finance ministers at Mexico, Rio de Janeiro, Lima, and Santiago instructed their ambassadors at Washington and London to sound out discretely the possibilities of obtaining special treatment for their debts, such as that conceded to Germany at the Lausanne conference.[24] Moreover, the suspension of the

23. An excellent summary of the war debt negotiations is found in "Report of the Committee of the Chamber of Commerce of the United States on War Debts," published in *New York Times*, November 27, 1932. Another useful source is Maxwell Stewart, "The Inter-Allied Debt: An Analysis," in *Foreign Policy Association Reports*, September 28, 1932, pp. 172–183.

24. The Mexican ambassador in Washington, Campos Ortiz, followed these financial developments carefully and reported back to his superiors, suggesting that the new situation

gold standard provided attenuating circumstances insofar as Latin American finance officials could now justify payment of their debt service in national currencies instead of gold, dollars, or sterling.

But, again, not all Latin American states had suspended payments on their external debts. In 1934 seven republics were still paying part, if not all, of their foreign obligations. As already noted, Haiti, Nicaragua, the Dominican Republic, and Honduras were pressured by the United States to maintain payments. Cuba interrupted remittances on a portion of its debts in 1934 but eventually reimbursed the bankers. Brazil, the biggest debtor, paid part of the interest on the federal and São Paulo loans, although it suspended service on additional provincial and municipal debts. And the Argentine government, which never even considered a moratorium, met its foreign financial commitments with what may be described as Swiss punctuality. On the other hand, Mexico, Chile, Peru, Bolivia, Colombia, and six other states continued in complete default (see Table 8).

The strategies adopted by the Latin American nations to deal with the debt crisis were diverse. In all cases, financial rescue programs were the result of complex and prolonged negotiations with bankers and politicians in Washington, London and Paris. In several instances the debtors won major concessions that helped soften the blow of the Great Depression. In other cases the conditions obtained were less favorable. To illustrate the complexity of the international financial adjustments, we shall review the different solutions negotiated by the three largest debtors—Argentina, Brazil, and Mexico. In each case, international and political factors played as important a role in the ultimate resolution of the debt dilemma as did strictly economic factors.

ARGENTINA: THE FOLLY OF A LOYAL DEBTOR

Prior to the Wall Street panic of 1929, the prices of the key Argentine export commodities—beef and cereals—had begun to weaken in international markets. By mid-1930, discontent had become rife among local cattle ranchers, wheat producers, merchants, and bankers. The resentment was soon transmitted to the top ranks of the Argentine army, and when General Uriburu carried out a swift and bloodless coup against the aging but still popular president of the republic, Hipólito Irigoyen, there was little opposition on the part of the ruling Radical party or of other parliamentary groups.

The demise of the seventy-year-old Argentine parliamentary regime was

---

might influence the renegotiation of the Mexican debt (ASRE, file III–1325–5, letter from Ortiz, December 29, 1932).

TABLE 8
STATUS OF LATIN AMERICAN DEBTS AND DEFAULTS, 1931–1950

Country	Date of Initial Default	Funded External[a] Debt in 1933 (U.S. $)	Renegotiations
Argentina	No default	864,000,000	Interest and amortization paid regularly until final liquidation of foreign debt in 1946.
Bolivia	January 1931	63,000,000	Default continued until 1948, when negotiations began to cancel interest in arrears but not capital.
Brazil	October 1931 (partial default)	1,239,000,000	Renegotiations in 1933, 1940, and 1943. By last agreement, a portion of capital reduced in value.
Chile	July 1931	343,000,000	During several years, partial resumption of interest payments. In 1948, settlement with bondholders.
Colombia	February 1932 (partial default)	164,000,000	Partial payments until 1935; Subsequent total default. Renegotiations in 1940, 1942, 1944, and 1949 for reduction of interest payments.
Costa Rica	November 1932	21,000,000	In 1933, funding bonds offered to cover interest in arrears. In 1935, new default, which continues until 1946.
Cuba	1933–34 (partial default)	153,000,000	Interest payments on part of external debt suspended 1933–34 but renewed thereafter.
Dominican Republic	October 1931 (partial default)	16,400,000	Only the sinking-fund payments were suspended; interest payments continued regularly.
Ecuador	July 1931	23,000,000	Debt remains in total default until mid-1950s.
El Salvador	January 1933	4,000,000	Renegotiation in 1936 for renewal of part of interest payments. In 1946, final settlement, by which 50% of interest is canceled.

[a] Includes long-term external bonds still unredeemed. Does not include short-term or "floating" external debts.

TABLE 8 (*cont.*)

Country	Date of Initial Default	Funded External[a] Debt in 1933 (U.S. $)	Renegotiations
Guatemala	February 1933 (partial default)	14,000,000	Partial default on sinking fund, but interest payments continue. The 1946–51 entire debt is liquidated by redemption.
Haiti	No default	13,000,000	Sinking-fund and interest payments continue regularly under U.S. supervision and control.
Honduras	No default	4,000,000	Payments met regularly under supervision of National City Bank (N.Y.).
Mexico	1914	684,000,000	Renegotiation of debt in 1930, but terms not fulfilled. Final settlement of national external debt in 1942 and of national railway company debt in 1946. By these accords, capital and interest reduced by 90%.
Nicaragua	No default	21,000,000	Sinking-fund payments reduced, 1932–46, but interest payments continue in full.
Panama	January 1932	16,000,000	Renegotiation in 1933, but partial default continues until 1946.
Paraguay	June 1932	3,000,000	Debt service renewed in 1938.
Peru	May 1931	114,000,000	In 1934–37, renewal of part of interest payments. In 1947 Peru offers settlement on basis of reduced interest payments. Final readjustment plan in 1951.
Uruguay	January 1932 (partial default)	98,000,000	Sinking fund temporarily suspended, but interest payments continue.
Venezuela	No default	—	Had extinguished external debt by 1933.

SOURCES: A. Kimber, *Kimber's Record of Government Debts* (London, 1934); Corporation of Foreign Bondholders, *Annual Reports* (London, 1930–52); Foreign Bondholders Protective Council, *Annual Reports* (New York, 1934, 1936–50).

NOTE: The information in this table should be complemented by additional data from the primary sources cited as well as in secondary literature.

213

not lamented by United States bankers. Only a month after Uriburu took power he received offers for a $50,000,000 short-term loan from the influential investment bank of Brown Brothers, ostensibly with the goal of stabilizing the finances of the new administration. The signing of the loan suggested the possibility of a rapprochement between the Argentine military and the United States that might even lead to a weakening of the traditional Anglo-Argentine alliance.[25] But such was not to be the case.

In 1932 Uriburu was replaced by General Agustín Justo, who had been elected president by the Conservative party in one of the most fraudulent elections in the history of the republic. Justo was less intent on negotiating with the United States than he was on strengthening the old political and economic ties between Argentina and Great Britain. His administration was dominated by representatives of the powerful cattle-ranching interests, which wanted to conserve the all-important British markets for their products. The ranchers were acutely concerned with the results of the Ottawa Conference of 1932, the purpose of which had been to propose a common defensive strategy for all the member nations of the British Commonwealth. As a nonmember, the Argentine government feared that it might be excluded from British markets and also lose access to the London money market in the future. In order to obtain favored treatment, such as that gained by Canada and Australia, Justo sent Vice-president Roca to London in 1933 to negotiate a wide-ranging commercial and financial accord with the British authorities.

The agreement, subsequently known as the Roca-Runciman Treaty, provided for concessions by both nations. Argentine beef exports were guaranteed a fixed and large portion of the British market,[26] and in exchange, the powerful British commercial and railway firms operating in the Río de la Plata were now offered the possibility of remitting dividends to stockholders in England. From 1930 these remittances had been frozen by the Argentine treasury in so-called blocked sterling accounts in order to avoid a damaging gold drain. According to the treaty provisions, the Argentine

25. The Argentine ambassador in Washington reported to his superiors: "It was pleasing for me to confirm that the leading American Banks have understood perfectly the difference between the September movement [Uriburu's coup] and the other revolutions that have occurred in the other South Americans Nations." The suggestion was that Brown Brothers and the other New York banks were aware that the conservative leanings of the new administration would provide security for future loans (ADERA, folder 1980, "Informes de la Embajada en Washington, 1931," letter from Ambassador Manuel Malbrán, January 16, 1931).

26. Much has been written on the effects the Roca-Runciman pact had on the Argentine beef trade. See, e.g., Smith, *Politics and Beef in Argentina*, chaps. 6–8; and Daniel Drosdof, *El gobierno de las vacas, 1933–1956: el tratado Roca-Runciman* (Buenos Aires, 1972). For the broader context of Argentine international trading relations, see Jorge Fodor and Arturo O'Connell, "La Argentina y la economía atlántica en la primera mitad del siglo XIX," *Desarrollo Económico* 13, no. 49 (1973): 3–66.

government would now free these accounts by issuing £13,000,000 (U.S. $65,000,000) in external bonds in England to all private creditors who presented receipts of their blocked accounts in Argentina.

The financial accords of 1933—less-studied by historians than that of the beef quotas—constituted the linchpin of the entire Argentine program for economic recovery. By freeing the sterling accounts, the government was able to restructure both its external and internal debts, to devalue the national currency gradually, and to permit expansion of bank credit, especially for wheat and corn farmers.[27]

The economic success of the Anglo-Argentine alliance was indisputable. By 1937, with a record wheat crop, Argentine exports had climbed back to predepression levels (see Figure 12). Meanwhile, the government was able to continue full service on its external debts and even to liquidate several hundred million dollars worth of foreign bonds in 1937 and 1938. The Argentine economy appeared to prosper in the midst of numberless calamities throughout the world: bread lines and mass unemployment in the industrial nations, the outbreak of the Spanish civil war, the invasion of Austria by Nazi Germany, the conquest of Manchuria by Fascist Japan.

Yet despite the apparent success of the Argentine authorities in negotiating commercial and financial accords with the United Kingdom, relations between the South American republic and the old imperial power were asymmetrical. Argentina depended more on Great Britain than Great Britain depended on Argentina. British investors held the bulk of the Argentine foreign debt, and British-owned companies ran three-quarters of the Argentine railway network, owned half the meat-packing plants in the country, and controlled much of the import-export business. Furthermore, Argentine cattle and wheat producers were entirely dependent on British markets for the sale of their commodities. The external dependency of the wealthiest Latin American nation was clear.

The consequences of dependency were felt in Argentina with increasing force after the onset of World War II. The rivalry between the major powers transformed this South American nation into the pawn of a complex geopolitical and economic conflict. For Great Britain the key issues were maintenance of the meat trade and of the debt service; for the United States the debt question was less important than political and military considerations.

As early as 1940 the British Foreign Office began to take steps to protect its economic position in Argentina, which was considered essential to the overall war effort of the United Kingdom. In October 1940 a commercial mission was sent to Buenos Aires with the specific goal of assuring a con-

27. The best and most succinct analysis of the financial aspects of these accords is Peter Alhadeff, "Dependency, Historiography, and Objections to the Roca Pact," in *Latin America, Economic Imperialism, and the State*, ed. Christopher Abel and Colin Lewis (London, 1984), pp. 367–378.

tinued flow of beef exports to England as well as of obtaining the acquiescence of the Argentine government to the deposit of the proceeds of the meat trade in special "blocked sterling" accounts in the Bank of England.[28] In this way the British government could be sure that its army and navy would have fresh meat supplies without having to pay for them in gold.

The British were not alone in expressing their interest in the role Argentina might play in the war. German agents were also active, playing an important role in the organization of profascist political associations, although German economic interests had been severely curtailed as a result of the British naval blockade of German shipping in the Atlantic.[29] The principal beneficiaries were United States commercial and industrial firms that quickly took over much of the business previously handled by German companies. Yet despite the growing control of the Argentine import business by North American corporations, politicians in Washington were increasingly obsessed with the supposed threat of an alliance between Argentina and Nazi Germany. These fears—as expressed in policy—eventually led to disputes with the British over the question of how to deal with the neutralist stance of the Argentine government.

The British were aware of the increasingly deep ideological splits within the Argentine ruling classes and within the top ranks of the Argentine army. The British ambassador at Buenos Aires, David Kelly, knew that pro-German sentiment had gained considerable strength among nationalist circles. Nonetheless, his reports indicated that he believed that fascist threat in Argentina was much overrated. The ambassador was actually more concerned with the attempts by the United States to establish its politicial hegemony over the Latin American nations, a fact that became clear at the Rio de Janeiro conference of 1942.[30]

At that meeting the United States secretary of state, Cordell Hull, and his assistant Sumner Welles made an effort to oblige all the nations of the hemisphere to sever relations with Germany, Italy, and Japan. The Argentine delegates opposed this proposal and were successful in obtaining ratification of a declaration that merely recommended severance of relations with the fascist powers but did not require it.[31]

---

28. On the Willingdon mission of 1940, see Mario Rapaport, "La política británica en la Argentina a comienzos de la década de 1940," *Desarrollo Económico* 16, no. 62 (1976): 203–228.

29. On the waning influence of Nazi Germany in Argentina, see Ronald C. Newton, "The United States, the German Argentines, and the Myth of the Fourth Reich, 1943–1947," *HAHR* 64, no. 1 (1984): 81–103.

30. Rapaport, "La política británica," pp. 217–218.

31. Gary Frank, *Struggle for Hegemony in South America: Argentina, Brazil, and the United States during the Second World War* (Miami, 1979), pp. 14–15.

The Argentine diplomatic triumph at Rio proved to be a Pyrrhic victory. While the Buenos Aires authorities gained the respect of other Latin American nations for their independent stance, they also won the unyielding hostility of the Roosevelt administration. Henceforward, the United States government refused to consider any Argentine request for economic or military assistance, and after the June 1943 coup, headed by General Pedro Ramírez, tensions intensified. United States intelligence agents considered that the Argentine military government represented a major threat for the other nations of the Southern Cone. As Hull affirmed in strident terms, "Argentina, under the control of the Fascist lawless government, is the refuge and headquarters in this hemisphere of the Fascist movement."[32]

In order to punish and isolate the Ramírez administration, the State Department urged the British government to blockade Argentine trade. But this was too much for Whitehall. In June 1944 Winston Churchill informed President Roosevelt that it would be impossible for him to carry out such reprisals because the United Kingdom depended on Argentina for 40 percent of its meat imports.[33] Moreover, London banking circles were concerned that a break with Argentina would lead to the expropriation of British enterprises in the Río de la Plata and prejudice a favorable solution to the Argentine debt held in England. The bankers were gratified that a large portion of the Argentine blocked sterling accounts was being used to liquidate the old external bonds. They had no intention of castigating a loyal debtor.

After the end of the war, British diplomats continued to promote a conciliatory policy, which allowed them to negotiate a favorable settlement of both the railway and the debt questions with the new president of Argentina, Juan Domingo Perón. In Febuary 1947 an agreement was reached by which the Buenos Aires government ceded the huge sum of £150,000,000 (U.S. $750,000,000) in blocked sterling accounts in London in exchange for the nationalization of the British-owned railway corporations in Argentina. Furthermore, the Perón government used additional export surpluses to pay off all outstanding external bonds still held in Great Britain.[34]

In contrast to the British, the United States insisted on attacking the Perónist administration. However, the motives behind the hard line adopted by such American diplomats as Spruille Braden were essentially political. Braden was incensed about the nationalist positions adopted by the Argen-

32. Ibid., p. 72.
33. Rapaport, "La política británica," p. 225.
34. There is a summary of the essential points of these negotiations in Pedro Skupch, "El deterioro y fin de la hegemonía británica sobre la economía argentina, 1914–1947," in M. Panaia, R. Lesser, and P. Skupch, *Estudios sobre los orígenes del peronismo* (Buenos Aires, 1973), 2:54–70.

tine government, which undermined the attempts by the United States to establish hegemony over Pan-American affairs. On the economic front, by contrast, there were no legitimate motives for criticism of the Argentines. Perón, like his predecessors, paid all off all debts due to the United States punctually and in gold. In 1946 he used $135,000,000 for final repatriation of the dollar-held debt and an additional $85,000,000 to cover the costs of the nationalization of the United River Plate Telephone Company, a subsidiary of the International Telephone & Telegraph Corporation (ITT).[35]

It can be argued that the debt solutions adopted by the various Argentine administrations in power from 1940 to 1947 sacrificed economic advantages for a series of dubious political benefits. Presidents Castillo, Ramírez, Farrel and Perón did not waver in honoring their financial commitments, but they failed to extract significant economic concessions from either the United States or Great Britain. Indeed, the greatest benefactors of the Argentine financial policies of both the 1930s and the 1940s were actually the foreign bondholders who recouped their capital and received full interest payments. In all, between 1929 and 1946 they received payments from Argentina totaling approximately $500,000,000 on capital account and a slightly smaller amount in the way of interest payments.[36]

The enormous economic burden incurred by the Argentine debt strategy can be attributed to two main factors. First, the debt policies adopted from the early 1930s were remarkably rigid, despite substantial political changes inside Argentina. Buenos Aires finance ministers remained committed to payment of interest and sinking fund debits *in full*. Debt renegotiations were not effectively used as instruments of economic diplomacy because the threat of a moratorium or a default was never used by the Argentine authorities to obtain more lenient conditions from foreign creditors.

Second, the Argentine governing elite had difficulty adjusting to the shifting balance of power during World War II, in particular to the new role of the United States as the dominant force in the postwar world. The Perón administration believed that Argentina finally was in a position to establish economic independence from both Great Britain and the United States by paying off its debts and nationalizing the foreign-owned companies that controlled the bulk of the nation's railways, tramways, telephones, and other public services. That this would mean an enormous economic sacrifice was not at first evident, but in the long run it became clear that the price paid to the foreign creditors had been too heavy.

35. For an analysis of United States-Argentine economic relations in this period, see Luis Sommi, *Los capitales yanquis en la Argentina* (Buenos Aires, 1949).
36. These estimates are based on data in the annual *Memoria* of the Ministerio de Hacienda of Argentina for 1940–46, but they require critical analysis.

In contrast to the orthodox financial policies of Argentina, Brazilian officials adopted a more flexible and ultimately more advantageous debt strategy. Following the initial default on the Brazilian external debt in 1931, renegotiations led to several different agreements with foreign creditors in 1934, 1940, and 1943. In each instance the Brazilian government bargained long and hard to extract substantial concessions from the bankers and bondholders. By deftly pitting the British against the Americans over a period of fifteen years, the Vargas administration succeeded in lessening the weight of the debt while at the same time strengthening the Brazilian role in international politics.[37]

The success of the Brazilian financial strategy was surprising. At the time of the Wall Street crash of 1929, Brazil was the largest Latin American debtor. In order to cover payments on more than $1,000,000,000 in loans, the national treasury relied primarily on the income generated by coffee exports. But as these revenues declined, the possibilities of continuing to service external debts evaporated. Therefore, the only way to avoid a full-scale economic collapse was to arrest the fall of coffee prices.

From the onset of the depression, British bankers collaborated closely with the Brazilian financial authorities to stabilize the international coffee markets and to assure an uninterrupted flow of payments on the external debt. The British financiers were committed to helping the Brazilians not only because they were the major creditors of the republic but also because of their large investments in railways, banks, and plantations, as well as because of their considerable stake in the coffee trade. For example, the fact that the Schröder banking firm (of London) owned coffee plantations in Brazil probably influenced its decision to participate in the Coffee Realization Loan of 1930. Thus the loans provided by Schröders, Lazards, and Rothschilds served to protect the large, traditional British role in the Brazilian economy.[38]

The rescue measures implemented from 1930 onward helped defend domestic coffee producers from the adverse consequences of the international economic crisis and helped maintain employment, but from a financial point of view the Brazilian government found itself in an increasingly difficult situation. The outflow of gold caused by the debt service and by the

37. An excellent study of Brazilian financial diplomacy is found in Marcelo de Paiva Abreu, "Anglo-Brazilian Economic Relations and the Consolidation of American Preeminence in Brazil, 1930–1945," in *Latin America*, ed. Abel and Lewis, pp. 379–393.

38. On the British financial position in Brazil in 1930, see Marcelo de Paiva Abreu, "The Niemeyer Mission: An Episode of British Financial Imperialism in Brazil," Centre of Latin American Studies, University of Cambridge, Working Papers no. 10, pp. 1–30.

profit remittances of foreign-owned companies led to the rapid depletion of the hard-currency reserves of the Brazilian banking system.

In order to avoid a possible default, British financial authorities urged the Brazilian finance minister, Osvaldo Aranha, to invite Sir Otto Niemeyer, a well-known British fiscal and monetary expert, to head a mission to investigate the possibility of carrying out a reform of Brazilian public finance.[39] The Niemeyer mission published its recommendations in July 1931. The main proposals were to increase direct taxes, reduce customs duties, reorganize the postal, telegraphic, and railway services, and balance the budget. Furthermore, Niemeyer insisted that Brazil should remain on the gold standard despite the enormous turbulence in international financial circles and urged establishment of a Central Bank to assure convertibility of the Brazilian currency.

The Vargas administration gave lip-service to Niemeyer's proposals but did not take steps to implement them. On the contrary, the Brazilian government rejected the orthodox reforms and abandoned the gold standard. On September 1, 1931, word came from Rio de Janeiro that the government had resolved to suspend sinking-fund payments on all foreign loans except the funding loans handled by Rothschilds. A few days later, interest payments were also frozen.[40]

London and New York banking circles were naturally taken aback by the Brazilian decision. The amount of debt in default was staggering, and they feared that the example of Brazil would be followed by the rest of Latin America. The British bankers reacted most quickly. Abreu notes that it was the firm of Rothschilds, official bankers to Brazil since the time of independence, who made the key proposals for a major debt reform: "At the end of September [1931] Rothschilds recommended that the total debt be divided into three categories: (1) funding loans, (2) secured loans, and (3) unsecured loans. The first category was to receive full service, the second contractual interest only, and the third 25 percent of contractual interest."[41]

The proposal implied that bondholders who had bought securities of the oldest and best-guaranteed loans, such as those of 1898 and 1914, would receive their money's worth, while the remaining creditors would have to accept a reduction in payments. This scheme favored the British and French bondholders over the Americans because the bulk of the funding and secured loans had been placed in Great Britain and in France.[42]

39. At this time Niemeyer was comptroller of the Bank of England, director of the National Bank of Egypt, and director of the Vickers, Armstrong Corporation (Abreu, "The Niemeyer Mission," p. 33).

40. Marcelo de Paiva Abreu, "Brazilian Public Foreign Debt Policy, 1931–1943," *Brazilian Economic Studies* 4 (1978): 112–113.

41. Ibid., p. 113.

42. Most of these loans, which were issued prior to 1914 in London or Paris, had liens on

The Brazilian finance minister accepted the Rothschild blueprint, apparently at the urging of Otto Niemeyer, with whom he maintained close ties. But several months later the Rio de Janeiro authorities announced that they would need additional concessions from the bondholders. Early 1932 saw ratification of a "funding arrangement" by which the interest on most loans would be paid not in cash but in new bonds to be issued in London, New York, and Paris.[43]

Although the accords of 1931 and 1932 brought some financial relief, it was not enough. By 1934 the Brazilian government asked its foreign creditors to discuss a new restructuring of the debt. Once again the ubiquitous Niemeyer appeared as the representative of British interests, and his presence carried additional weight as his services were simultaneously requested by the Argentine government to help set up a Central Bank. Niemeyer submitted an outline of negotiable reforms to the new Brazilian finance minister, Aranha. His suggestions were accepted, and the loans were classified according to a complex hierarchy of seven grades. Grades 1 and 2, which included the Rothschild loans, would receive full interest payments. Grade 3, which included several federal loans plus the bonds issued by the São Paulo Coffee Institute, would receive 30 percent of the interest. The remaining loans, mainly the dollar loans of the 1920s for the federal, provincial, and municipal governments, would receive lesser sums.[44] The representatives of the American bondholders fought unsuccessfully to modify this scheme. The British bankers still had the upper hand.

During 1934–37 the Brazilian treasury complied with this arrangement, paying a total of $150,000,000 in cash to the bondholders. Eventually, however, the Vargas administration reversed its stance and decided to call a halt to further payments. The reasons for the new default, which was announced in November 1937, were complex. On the one hand, the Brazilian economy was suffering the effects of a renewed decline in the international price of coffee. On the other hand, Vargas had adopted a series of measures to reorganize the entire public administration according to a corporatist model called the "Estado Novo." His intentions were to use the new state structure to promote the modernization of the national transport network, to build up heavy industry, and to strengthen the army. To finance these projects, Vargas planned to take advantage of increasingly close commercial ties between Brazil and Nazi Germany. Since 1934, Germany had expanded its acquisition of Brazilian cotton, coffee, and rubber, in exchange for which it sent textiles, chemicals, and armaments to Rio de Ja-

certain tax revenues or state properties, in contrast to many of the American loans of the 1920s that were not so well secured.

43. See Kimber, *Kimber's Record, 1934*, pp. 240–241.

44. Abreu, "Brazilian Public Foreign Debt Policy," pp. 114–115.

neiro and Santos.[45] The new links with Germany led to a weakening of the financial relationship with Great Britain and appeared to justify default.

The reaction of British bankers and government officials to the new Brazilian suspension of payments was bitter. The *Economist* declared: "Brazil needs not make a rigid choice of destroyers or debt service." And Prime Minister Austen Chamberlain announced in menacing terms: "His Majesty's Government view with the gravest concern the loss inflicted on individuals and on the country as the result of default on Foreign Loans."[46]

In contrast to the virulent British response, that of the United States was remarkably mild. This could be ascribed in part to the policy of the Departments of State and of Commerce in support of multilateral trade policies that ran against the British preference for bilateral arrangements. Washington officials did not want to encourage trade with Germany, yet they believed it would be counterproductive to punish Brazil for diversifying its foreign commerce. Above all, however, it was Roosevelt's determination to make Brazil a key actor in the Good Neighbor Policy that shaped relations between the United States and the South American nation. Consequently, no reprisals were taken against the Vargas administration.

In 1939, however, the United States began to press for reimbursement of the foreign loans. By then it had become apparent that the Brazilians were willing to reinitiate some interest payments. Aranha, who had assumed the post as Brazilian ambassador at Washington, met with Treasury Secretary Henry Morgenthau to work out an agreement by which the Export-Import Bank would advance industrial credits to Brazil in exchange for partial renewal of the debt service. The Brazilian government made a token payment of $1,000,000 in New York in July 1939 and invited the various bondholders' associations to send agents to Rio to renegotiate the debt.[47]

Over a period of several months the Brazilian finance minister, Artur Souza Costa, bargained with the bondholders and with a representative of the State Department. In January 1940 Souza Costa made a final proposal based on the old 1934 plan. The American bondholders obtained more favorable terms on their loans, while the British tended to lose ground. This shift reflected the emerging political and military alliance between Brazil and the United States.

---

45. "Vargas and his counselors made a shrewd reading of the international political system during the 1930s. . . . They realized that systemic conditions would allow them to maintain Washington's political support while pursuing a goal seemingly incompatible with that support—the expansion of trade with Nazi Germany. And they pursued that goal relentlessly" (Stanley Hilton, *Brazil and the Great Powers, 1930–1939: The Politics of Trade Rivalry* [Austin, 1975], p. 226).

46. CFBH, *Annual Report, 1938*, p. 8.

47. Abreu, "Brazilian Public Foreign Debt Policy," pp. 122–123.

From the onset of World War II, the United States had been concerned with the degree of Axis penetration of Latin America. Brazil was considered particularly vulnerable because of its large German immigrant population. As a result, the Roosevelt administration began to formulate a policy designed to reduce that threat by establishing close ties with the Brazilian military. Implementation of this policy moved slowly, but after Pearl Harbor (December 7, 1941) the urgency of reaching an agreement with Rio became manifest. In March 1942 four accords between the United States and Brazil were signed, including the supply of anti-tank and anti-aircraft weapons, 300 light and medium tanks, and 50 combat aircraft for the Brazilian forces.[48]

During 1942–45 Brazil became a crucial way-station for the military air-traffic of the United States. As Frank observes, "Some 25,000 combat aircraft were ferried (via Northeast Brazil) to Europe, Africa and even to Asia as well as a good deal of Lend-Lease hardware to the Soviet Union."[49] According to a popular saying, Brazil became the "air funnel to the battle-fields of the world."

The Brazilian government was able to use its now-considerable military and political influence as leverage in its final renegotiation of the foreign debt. Souza Costa began talks with the British bondholders in early 1943, and then in June informed the Americans that the talks were already in progress. Incensed by this news, the State Department immediately dispatched high-level representatives to counter any advantages gained by the British and to obtain equal terms for the American bondholders.[50]

The final Brazilian debt settlement of 1943 guaranteed that the interest payments on the dollar loans would be upgraded, thereby diminishing the discriminatory effect of the 1934 classification scheme. At the same time, major concessions on reduction of part of the interest and capital of the debts were made, allowing the Brazilian government to redeem a portion of the outstanding bonds at low prices. As a result, between 1943 and 1945 the total external debt was reduced by approximately $250,000,000.[51]

By the end of World War II, Brazil still had an external debt of nearly $800,000,000 but it had wrung enough concessions from its creditors to make repayment less burdensome than would have been the case otherwise. This favorable solution was largely the result of strategic cooperation with the United States during the war years. The British government was less flexible. "Whereas the Americans took a rather conciliatory stand, paying

48. Frank, *Struggle for Hegemony*, p. 19.
49. Ibid., pp. 36–37.
50. Abreu, "Brazilian Public Foreign Debt Policy," pp. 127–128.
51. Ibid., table 1, p. 107.

careful attention to their strategic economic and political aims in Brazil, the British tended to worry only about maximization of financial payments."[52]

The success of the Brazilian strategy, nonetheless, was the consequence not only of the war and the military alliance with the United States, but also of the decision by the Brazilian authorities from 1931 onward to use default, or partial default, as an instrument of economic diplomacy. According to one calculation, the financial relief obtained through the various defaults and renegotiations of the 1930s and 1940s allowed Brazil to save a total of approximately $500,000,000 in payments.[53] Despite the constant pressure of foreign creditors, the Brazilians had learned how to play the game of international power politics to economic advantage.

MEXICO: THE BENEFITS OF PROCRASTINATION

In many ways resolution of the Mexican foreign debt quandary was the most complex of all the Latin American financial adjustments of the 1930s and 1940s. Mexico's external debt, valued at approximately $500,000,000 was the third largest in the region, after the debts of Brazil and Argentina.[54] The Mexican debt had been in default since 1914, when as a result of the revolution the treasury had simply run out of money. In succeeding decades, negotiations were carried out with the bankers who represented the foreign bondholders on several occasions, but the amount of payments extracted from the government was insignificant.

The first major renegotiation of the foreign debt of Mexico took place in 1922. The principals involved were the finance minister, Adolfo de la Huerta, and Thomas Lamont, head of the International Committee of Bankers on Mexico. The latter body represented the United States and European investors who had bought the bulk of the government bonds issued before 1914 as well as a large part of the shares of the Mexican National Railway Company.[55] In 1921 the bankers assumed a key role in convincing the State Department to take steps toward formal recognition of the Mexican government. They were opposed by the American oil companies, which demanded political and/or military intervention by the United States government to protect their interests in Veracruz and Tampico. But the views of the bankers ultimately prevailed. The government of President Alvaro Obregón was pleased to receive the financiers in Mexico City, hoping to

52. Ibid., pp. 131–132.
53. Ibid., p. 135.
54. For a precise breakdown of the Mexican debt, see Robert Freeman Smith, *The United States and Revolutionary Nationalism in Mexico, 1916–1932* (Chicago, 1972), figure 1, chap. 8.
55. See ibid., chap. 5, on the formation of the Bankers Committee in 1917–18.

win a reduction of the debt service as well as to obtain funds to help establish a Central Bank.

Despite the preliminary show of goodwill, the negotiations between Lamont and the Mexican finance minister were not cordial. De la Huerta insisted that his government was prepared to recognize the prerevolutionary debts but that it would not sacrifice the welfare of the Mexican people. He affirmed, "Above all, Mexico must survive. . . . If a family finds itself in dire economic straits, the first consideration must be to obtain bread and milk and, after that, to its creditors."[56]

Lamont was adamant, but he eventually convinced De la Huerta to sign a settlement in which the entire original capital of the old debts was recognized, as well as part of the interest in arrears. The Mexican government promised to use oil taxes to establish a fund of $30,000,000 with which to cover the debt service. The agreement was ratified by the National Congress, and during the space of two years the Mexican treasury sent a small stream of silver pesos to New York.

To pay its debts, Mexico relied essentially on the income produced by petroleum taxes, but if there were a marked decline in production of oil the government would find it difficult to pay its creditors. The oil boom had reached its apogee in 1921–22 but waned in years following. The drop in oil income, together with a series of internal conflicts, led President Obregón to announce suspension of the debt service as of June 1924.

The new default stirred the International Committee of Bankers to action again. Lamont now found himself bargaining with another Mexican finance minister, Alberto J. Pani, who proved to be more adroit than his predecessor. Pani argued that export earnings were not sufficient to renew the full debt service immediately, although he promised that his government would do so by 1928. In order to reduce the overall debt burden, however, Pani acceded to the request of the bankers' committee that the National Railway Company be returned to private ownership within one year.[57]

Between 1926 and 1927 the Mexican government deposited $27,000,000 in New York to the account of the Committee of Bankers.[58] Receipt of these funds apparently indicated to the bondholders that Mexico had finally returned to the fold of "creditworthy nations," but they were soon to be disappointed. After 1927 no further payments were forthcoming. To make matters worse, the National Railway Company began running such large deficits that it was impossible to distribute dividends to the foreign shareholders.

56. For details on these talks, see ibid., chap. 8.
57. Secretaría de Hacienda y Crédito Público, *La vieja deuda exterior titulada de México*, (Mexico, 1960), pp. 58–59; and Bazant, *Historia de la deuda exterior*, pp. 195–198.
58. For exact data, see Bazant, *Historia de la deuda exterior*, p. 198.

As before, the cause of the new Mexican default was linked to the fall in value of the nation's exports—silver and oil. From 1926, silver prices had begun to decline, and the mining companies had cut back on their production. Meanwhile, the petroleum fields along the Gulf diminished in productivity, and numerous United States and British firms moved out, shipping much of their drilling equipment to Venezuela, where a great oil boom was in progress.[59]

The world depression aggravated an already grim predicament. In July 1930 the Mexican government signed a new pact with the International Committee of Bankers known as the Montes de Oca–Lamont Agreement. It was short-lived and never ratified by the Mexican Congress. Throughout the decade of the 1930s Mexico remained in complete default on its external obligations.

The turning-point that would lead to the final resolution of the Mexican debt question was the outbreak of World War II. As in the case of Brazil, United States authorities made a concerted effort to establish a political, economic, and military rapprochement with its southern neighbor. In exchange for financial concessions, the leaders of the Roosevelt administration expected that the government of President Manuel Avila Camacho would support the Allied war effort.

The Mexican government was well apprised of the intentions of Washington and determined to strike a hard bargain. In April 1941 the Mexican ambassador at Washington, Francisco Castillo Nájera, wrote to his superiors that during talks with State Department officials Welles and Duggan he had learned that the claims of the United States petroleum companies (which had been nationalized by Mexico in 1938) were to be subordinated to the goal of convincing the Mexican government to sign a series of military and naval treaties. Castillo replied to Welles that the economic and military questions would have to be resolved simultaneously.[60]

The United States strategy of seeking an alliance with Mexico was not predicated solely on military grounds. In fact, as the Mexican ambassador shrewdly observed, Mexico was destined to play a secondary role in the overall military strategy of the United States. On the other hand, Mexico's political contribution to the Allied cause could be decisive, because it would carry great weight throughout Latin America. As Castillo wrote in May 1941: "Our cooperation . . . has, I repeat, political importance because of its impact on the entire hemisphere."[61]

In July 1941 negotiations began on the indemnities claimed by the petro-

---

59. A political and economic history of Mexican oil in this period is Lorenzo Meyer, *México y Estados Unidos en el conflicto petrolero* (Mexico, 1968).

60. ASRE, file III–867–7, detailed report from Castillo Najera, May 3, 1941, p. 23.

61. Ibid., p. 28.

leum companies as well as by American investors who sought monetary compensation for landed estates expropriated during the revolution of 1910–20. At the same time, the Mexican Finance Ministry requested credits from the Export–Import Bank and the Department of the Treasury. It also pressed for a readjustment and reduction of the foreign debt. The economic negotiations were accompanied by military agreements, including the formation of a Mexican-American Defense Commission and the signing of a series of treaties with respect to United States access to Mexican air lanes and seaports.[62]

Mexico made two other contributions of great significance to the United States war effort. It allowed Mexican-born citizens residing in the United States to join the United States Army, and approximately 250,000 did so. And it facilitated the mass migration of Mexican workers across the border to labor in both field and factory, helping to resolve the acute labor shortage of the United States war economy.[63]

The final resolution of the Mexican debt was therefore contingent on a complex set of military, political, and financial factors. The Mexican government's willingness to support the Allied war effort induced the Roosevelt administration to pressure both the oil companies and the International Committee of Bankers to accept a major reduction in their claims. The oil companies were awarded $23,000,000 for the properties that had been nationalized. Mexico agreed to compensate for the surface value and capital equipment, alleging state title to subsoil rights. The oil companies' much greater estimates of their losses included the value of oil in the ground.[64]

The bondholders had to accept a greater sacrifice. According to the final debt agreement signed in 1942 by Lamont and by Finance Minister Eduardo Suárez, holders of Mexican government securities were obliged to accept cancellation of approximately 90 percent of the nominal value of the bonds. Consequently, the Mexican external debt was scaled down from a sum of approximately $500,000,000 to $50,000,000.[65] A similar arrangement was reached with the shareholders of the National Railway Company of Mexico, by which the foreign investors received a net cash payment of $50,000,000 on properties that had been originally valued at ten times that

62. Luis Zorrilla, *Historia de las relaciones entre México y los Estados Unidos de América* (Mexico, 1966), 2:486–495.

63. Ibid.

64. The United States investors who claimed losses on properties during the revolution received another U.S. $40,000,000 in compensation (Bazant, *Historia de la deuda exterior*, pp. 214–215).

65. For the full text of the 1942 agreement, see Secretaría de Hacienda y Crédito Público, *Legislación sobre deuda pública* (Mexico, 1958), pp. 197–578.

sum.[66] In brief, the loans accords allowed the government of Mexico to cancel the bulk of its external debts.

CONCLUSIONS

The Mexican debt settlements of 1942 and 1946 were the most favorable of the Latin American debt renegotiations of the era. Like the Brazilian accords, they were the by-product of the radical change in international relations that had been engendered by the world war. These new circumstances led the United States government to intervene directly in the debt renegotiations, subordinating the private economic interests of the bondholders to the political and military requirements of "hemispheric cooperation."

In contrast to the privileged treatment reserved for Mexico and Brazil, other Latin American nations obtained financial concessions that were not so significant. This may be attributed to the less important role that they played within the geopolitical strategy of the major powers during the war years. But a number of these South and Central American republics did reap some benefits. Bolivia, Chile, Colombia, Costa Rica, El Salvador, Panama, and Peru were able to maintain a moratorium on their respective debts from the early 1930s until the mid- or late 1940s (see Table 8). They later had no other alternative but to resume negotiations with the bondholders. In several instances, however, they were able to obtain a partial reduction of their outstanding debts.

While the Great Depression and World War II severely dislocated the Latin American economies, the defaults helped pave the way for recovery. By unilaterally freezing their external financial commitments, a large number of republics were able to attenuate the impact of the international financial and commercial crisis that had originated with the crash of 1929. The defaults did not lead to economic independence, but they did reduce financial dependency during more than a decade. This was a historical experience that would bear remembering.

66. Secretaría de Hacienda, *La vieja deuda exterior*, pp. 64–70; Bazant, *Historia de la deuda exterior*, pp. 215–227.

A HALF-CENTURY after the crisis of the 1930s, the Latin American nations are once again enmeshed in a vicious debt trap. The financial
disaster of the 1980s is not unprecedented, but its dimensions are much
greater and more complex than preceding crises. Can study of the Latin
American loan cycles of the past provide some lessons for the present? As
always when dealing with highly debatable issues, opinions will differ. It
is certainly possible to single out a number of parallels between the loan
booms and debt crises of the nineteenth and early twentieth centuries and
present-day financial developments. Yet it is perhaps the differences that
are even more significant; they can point to new problems that require
equally new solutions. In other words, a historical perspective can suggest
not only continuities but also significant changes.

The contemporary debt crisis was initially believed to be the result of
short-term liquidity problems, but as it has deepened such a view no longer
seems tenable. Most observers now agree that the causes of the crisis are
deep-rooted and structural, and therefore more difficult to resolve than originally suspected. Among the underlying causes, special attention should be
directed to analysis of the long-term impact of financial, commercial, and
technological dependency and of the unbalanced, deformed pattern of capitalism in Latin America that many writers describe as "underdevelopment." In brief, debt crises, dependency, and underdevelopment go hand
in hand, now as in the past.

The analysis of the successive Latin American loan booms and debt
crises of the past indicates that the debtor nations have had great difficulty
breaking out of this vicious circle. Throughout the present study, we have
emphasized the impact of the cycles of the international economy and their
role in accentuating the boom and bust dynamics of the Latin American
export economies during the nineteenth and early twentieth centuries. Data
on the parallel trends of international trade and loan flows was used to place
Latin American financial history within the theoretical framework presented by the economic and historical literature on economic cycles of that
period.

According to the basic model presented in this study, the loan cycles
reflected the broader swings of the economy on both an international level

229

and a national level. The phases of the loan booms generally corresponded to a period of expansion in the industrial nations that spurred a rise in world trade and the accumulation of surplus capital in international money markets. A substantial portion of these surplus funds were channeled to Latin America in the shape of loans for governments, to be used for a variety of refinancing, military, or public works purposes. The waning of these phases of prosperity was signaled by the outbreak of economic recessions or depression that cut short the flow of funds to Latin America and led to debt crises. That the degree of correspondence between the cycles of the industrial nations and those of the Latin American countries varied over time suggests the increasing complexity of their interaction and indicates the need for additional and detailed case studies on this subject.

The two-phase model of the loan cycles is also characteristic of the contemporary era, but the enormous changes that have taken place in the modern world economy require a new and different analysis. To be more specific, the revolution in international banking, the rise of new capital markets (such as the Euromarkets), and the growing financial power of multinational companies have radically altered global financial flows and added new dimensions to the foreign debt transactions. The remarkable velocity, volume, and variety of contemporary financial transfers stand in striking contrast to the loan operations of the past, which until 1929 consisted essentially of the sale of government bonds on three or four major stock exchanges in Europe and the United States. To these must be added the new role of the governments and central banks of the industrial nations within world finances during the last forty-odd years, as well as the more recent impact of the financial strategies of the oil-exporting nations on the dynamics of international capital flows.

However important these international factors have been, we must focus equally on the evolution of the domestic policies of the Latin American governments taking the loans. For this reason, the present study emphasizes the changing set of objectives of the political elites of the most important Latin American nations during the century following independence. Military and political factors played a dominant role in impelling governments to contract loans during the 1820s and 1860s. By contrast, from the last quarter of the nineteenth century until the crash of 1929, the dominant feature of state loan policies was the desire to attract foreign capital for development of the basic infrastructure required for the growth of the respective national economies.

Once again, however, analysis of past and present experience requires a substantially different perspective and methodology to grasp the implications of the changes in government loan policies. The public works loans of the late nineteenth century, for instance, can be viewed as antecedents to the modern-day "development loans," but their complexity pales in comparison with the loans negotiated for the promotion of petrochemical and steel industries or nuclear power plants in the 1970s by Mexico, Brazil, Argentina, Venezuela, and other nations of the region. This must be attributed to the changes during the last fifty years inside Latin American societies, changes that have been no less dramatic than those of the international financial machinery. The growth of internal markets and the expansion of local industry have modified the economies of the region and led some countries, such as Brazil or Mexico, to enter the ranks of the "semi-industrialized" nations. This process has been closely tied to the crisis of the traditional agrarian economies and to the mass migration of peasants to cities, some of which are now among the largest in the world. At the same time, the growth of Latin American government structures—which are now directly engaged in key spheres of the economy, including heavy industry, transport, electricity, mining and oil, and banking—have forcefully contributed to the transformation of national economic and financial strategies.

In this respect, it is worthwhile to comment briefly in conclusion on some of the basic characteristics of the contemporary debt crisis and on several major contrasts with past experience. To begin with, a first question worth considering is the reason for the delay and uncertainty of politicians, bankers, and economists in grappling with the reality and concept of what would come to be known as the "debt crisis." This delay is probably related to the singular nature of world and Latin American economic cycles during the last forty years.

During the three decades that followed World War II, there were numerous economic crises in different Latin American nations, but there was no major financial upheaval that shook the entire region. Recession, inflation, and balance-of-payments problems were common features of the period, but these were judged to be essentially the result of deteriorating terms of international trade, of unbalanced and technologically dependent industrial structures, and of inadequate economic planning by governments. The gradual expansion of foreign debts did not cause much concern, compared with other problems. It was only as of the mid-1970s, when the loan boom was in full force, that academics and journalists began to call attention to the dangers of this type of financial dependency.[1] But neither borrowers nor lenders recognized the gravity of the situation until the outbreak of the debt crisis.

The modern concept of a "debt crisis" dates from August 1982. It was

1. See, e.g., the pioneering study by Cheryl Payer, *The Debt Trap: The International Monetary Fund and the Third World* (New York, 1974). See also Miguel Wionczek, ed., *Endeudamiento externo de los países en desarrollo* (Mexico, 1979).

then that the Mexican government announced to its foreign creditors that it was on the verge of bankrutpcy. The implications of this news were so ominous that not only the largest international banks, but also the United States government, found themselves obliged to act swiftly to avoid a major panic. The financial rescue package they organized took six months to be ratified by creditors and debtors, but it avoided default on the huge Mexican external debt, then at approximately $80,000,000,000.[2] Some bankers were so relieved they proclaimed the Latin American debt crisis over. However, less than two years later, in June 1984, came news that the Argentine financial authorities were seriously contemplating suspending payments on their foreign obligations. At the same time, reports came from Chicago of the collapse of a major institution, the Continental Illinois Bank. There was much talk in New York of the excess Latin American debt accumulated by the Manufacturers Hanover Bank and by other large financial institutions, and in London rumors were rife that the powerful Midland Bank had overextended itself with Argentine, Brazilian, and Mexican securities. Nonetheless, Argentina did not default, and once again the bankers proudly announced the demise of the crisis.

More recently, in 1986, the specter of Latin American bankruptcies came to the fore again. The precipitous decline of oil prices placed the Mexican treasury in a disastrous situation, and in Peru the administration headed by President Alan García announced it would not pay more than 10 percent of its export earnings to cover the foreign debt service. And from early 1987 the greatest Latin American debtor, Brazil, suspended payments on its foreign loans, threatening to implement a full-scale default if the international bankers did not offer more flexible and reasonable proposals for repayments.

It is now clear that the debt crisis is not over and will not simply go away. Yet one would think that the bankers who were involved in providing the billions of dollars of loans to the Latin American nations would have suspected as much before the event. This shortsightedness may be attributed, largely to the extreme rivalry among the banks for the lucrative Latin American loan business during the 1970s. But it is also manifest that both foreign financiers and Latin American technocrats failed to anticipate the downswing that almost invariably follows the upswing in all foreign loan cycles.

It is here that one can find a first basic parallel between financial developments of the past and those of the present. The two basic stages of the

2. Financial journalists have described the outbreak of the debt crisis in several recent books. See, e.g., Darrell Delamaide, *Debt Shock: The Full Story of the World Credit Crisis* (New York, 1984), pp. 1–29, 96–129.

contemporary "foreign loan cycle" correspond in very general terms to a historical pattern. The first stage, that of the loan boom, took some time to develop. In the 1960s, the number of loans taken by Argentina, Brazil, Mexico, and the other countries of the region began to increase, although not yet spectacularly. Most of these credits were provided by multilateral agencies, such as the World Bank or the Interamerican Development Bank. From 1973 the Latin American loan business picked up speed, and the number of private foreign banks engaged in the transactions multiplied. Finally, during the years from 1978 to 1981 the borrowing governments became so swept up in the financial mania that they took dozens of loans simply to pay back the ones they had previously contracted.

The Latin American loan boom of the 1970s was determined to a large degree by the evolution of the world economy. In the first place, the rise in prices of primary commodities and raw materials increased the revenues of many nations in the Third World, especially of the petroleum exporters. In Latin America the rise in trade income was not as spectacular as it was in the Arab nations, but even so it allowed for a surge in the importation of consumer as well as capital goods. The acceleration of commerce was accompanied by an expansion of international financial flows, impelled by the aggressive strategies of the largest banks of the United States, Western Europe, and Japan.[3] The rapid development of the Euromarkets and of new financial centers around the world testified to the increasing amount of surplus money capital that the banks were handling, a substantial part of it consisting of oil revenues from the Arab countries. The banks not only desired but needed to invest these funds profitably. As a result, when the majority of the Latin American nations began to increase their demands for foreign credits, they were able to obtain the money quickly. In summary, the Latin American loan boom of the 1970s, like previous loan booms, was closely linked to an expanding trade cycle and to acceleration of international capital flows.

The origins of the debt crisis were also similar, in quite general terms, to those of the past. The financial debacle was unleashed by instability in the money markets of the advanced industrial nations. The trigger was the sharp increase of interest rates in the United States during 1980 and 1981, which caused an enormous rise in the debt service that the borrowing na-

3. The internationalization of United States banks had already begun on a large scale during the 1960s, but it was in the 1970s that the globalization of the banking activity of all the major financial powers began to accelerate in unprecedented fashion. On the former developments, an excellent analysis is Harry Magdoff, *The Age of Imperialism: The Economics of U.S. Foreign Policy* (New York, 1966), chap. 3. On more-recent events, see Michael Moffitt, *The World's Money: International Banking from Bretton Woods to the Brink of Insolvency* (New York, 1984), chaps. 2 and 3.

tions now found themselves obliged to pay. This situation was aggravated by economic recession in the United States and Western Europe and by a slowdown of the world economy. As Moffit points out, "In 1981 the value of world trade contracted for the first time since 1958."[4] Soon the international banks cut down on long-term loans to the underdeveloped nations. As a result, most of the Latin American states were forced to seek expensive short-term credits to cover rising trade and balance-of-payments deficits. By mid-1982, however, it became clear that there would be no more short-term loans. There were only two alternatives: rescheduling of debts, or outright default. The rescheduling soon began and has continued ever since. Indeed, it is likely that the renegotiation of external debts will remain the dominant issue governing the relations between Latin American states and foreign bankers for the next decade.

In retrospect, the prolonged nature of the present crisis calls to mind numerous parallels with past debt crises, yet as any economist would be quick to point out, such comparisons are fraught with danger. The changes in the world economy have been so sweeping in the last decades that new theoretical and analytical tools are necessary to explain such complex problems as the evolution of the foreign debts of Latin America. The number of detailed economic studies on this question has multiplied rapidly.[5] But from a strictly historical perspective, it may be useful to single out a few of the major contrasts with previous loan cycles.

One of the most obvious differences from the past is that the present-day foreign debts of the Latin American nations are quantitatively much greater. In 1929 the *public* foreign debt of Latin America, as a whole, barely reached $4,000,000,000 whereas today it surpasses $200,000,000,000.[6] The latter sum bespeaks the enormity of the financial burden that is suffocating the nations and peoples of the region. Nevertheless, the 1929 figure should not be dismissed as insignificant. Any comparison must also take into account such additional factors as the relative value of the dollar and changes in other variables—for example, trade, gross national product,

4. Moffitt, *The World's Money*, p. 202.

5. Three such recent studies are Lawrence G. Franko and Marilyn J. Seiber, eds., *Developing Country Debt* (New York, 1980); John H. Makin, *The Global Debt Crisis* (New York, 1984); and A. Jorge, J. Salazar-Carillo, and F. Diaz, *External Debt and Development Strategy in Latin America* (New York, 1985). In Latin America the number of publications on the current debt problem is extensive. Some of the best studies are in the journal of the Centro de Investigacion y Docencia Economica (CIDE), *Economía de América Latina* (Mexico, 1978–88).

6.Information on Latin American debts in 1929 is in United Nations, Economic Commission on Latin America, *El financiamiento externo de América Latina* (New York, 1964), p. 27. The statistical estimates of the present-day public and private external debts of the Latin American nations change from day to day. The bulletins of the World Bank and of the Morgan Guaranty Bank are among the most frequently cited and reliable sources.

population, and so forth. A per capita debt estimate based on deflated dollars would provide a more reasonable basis for comparison than the gross statistics.

But statistics tell only one part of the story. An equally significant contrast can be found in the new structure of Latin American debts. To be more precise, the types of public entities that have borrowed money abroad are different from the borrowers of the 1920s. At that time, most of the loans went to national, provincial, or municipal governments. In recent years the biggest borrowers have been large, government-owned companies, most of them industrial. Between 1976 and 1981, for example, the most important corporate borrower in the international money markets was the Mexican oil company Pemex.[7] But many other Latin American state-owned firms similarly engaged in the loan frenzy—for instance, Petrobras and Electrobras of Brazil, Corporación Venezolana de Fomento, Ecopetrol of Colombia, Agua y Energía of Argentina, Petroperú.[8] The great debtors of the 1970s were thus typically the most important and technologically advanced industrial enterprises in the fields of oil production, nuclear energy, hydroelectric power, aviation, steel, aluminum, and so forth. In addition, virtually all the state-owned development banks sought funds abroad, using the money for a great variety of industrial and infrastructure projects. In sum, the foreign debt has come to weigh on the most dynamic and complex sectors of the economies of the Latin American countries, binding financial and technological dependency much closer together than ever before in the history of the region.

While a large part of the foreign loans went for productive purposes, it would be erroneous to argue that all of them did so. Indeed, one of the most striking characteristics of the Latin American financial transactions of the 1970s was the huge amount of money used for military objectives. The negotiation of military loans was not unprecedented. There were a considerable number of war loans during the first two-thirds of the nineteenth century, although from 1870 to 1930 this type of loan was relatively infrequent. During the 1970s, on the other hand, the armed forces of several Latin American nations contracted a large but undisclosed number of credits with international bankers to finance arms acquisitions and military industries.[9]

7. The amount of money borrowed by Pemex is a question for speculation. As one journalist observed, Pemex is not noted for publicizing its loans, and at its insistence many have been kept secret ("Latin American Survey," *Euromoney*, April 1981, pp. 55–56).

8. A large amount of data on loans to Latin American state enterprises can be garnered from the financial journals *Euromoney*, *Institutional Investor*, and *Bank of London and South America Review*.

9. There is little published data on the military loans. Some information can be found in the article "Batalla contra las armas," *Visión*, May 20, 1985, pp. 6–22.

The generals of Peru, for example, used a string of loans during the 1970s to acquire hundreds of Soviet tanks and dozens of French Mirage jets, and the dictatorial regime in Brazil used foreign funds to build a powerful and sophisticated military-industrial complex. But the worst offenders were undoubtedly the Argentine and Chilean dictatorships, which in the mid- and late 1970s took billions of dollars in loans in order to foment the war atmosphere that was essential to the maintenance of these repressive regimes. And in all cases international bankers and transnational firms were the most enthusiastic partners in this military madness.

Analysis of singular features of the loan boom of recent years should not obscure equally significant changes in the nature of the contemporary debt crisis with respect to the crises of the past. One important new factor is the preeminence of the largest commercial banks of the world in all spheres of the loan transactions. Prior to 1930 all long-term loans consisted of bond issues that were placed among investors in the stock exchanges. Occasionally some banks took a small percentage for their own portfolio, but the bulk of the securities remained in the hands of a broad circle of individuals, who joined together in bondholder associations to protect their interests. In the 1970s, in contrast, the majority of the Latin American loans were provided directly by the most powerful commercial banks of the United States, Western Europe, and Japan. These banks, rather than the bondholders, are now the principal creditors, and they have determined to manipulate all the instruments at their disposal to recover their loans and maintain the high rates of profits to which they have become accustomed.

The coordination among these financial monoliths is not perfect because they are rivals, but generally they act in concert, using their considerable political influence to get the respective national governments to support their financial strategies. To this must be added the key role of multilateral agencies, such as the International Monetary Fund and the World Bank, which act as guardians for private finance capital at the same time that they design grand strategy to assure the stability of the world economy and to avoid any radical change in the relations between the rich creditor nations and the poor debtor countries.

The combined power of the commercial banks and multilateral agencies is much greater than the power previously wielded by the foreign bankers involved in Latin American loans. Prior to World War II, the investment banks of England, France, Germany, or the United States could usually obtain some diplomatic support from their respective chancelleries to pressure the debtor states to pay instead of declare bankruptcy. But when confronted with a severe international crisis, Latin American governments frequently did default, and in the short run there was little the bankers could do about this. In contrast, in recent years few Latin American states have gone so far as to threaten to default. The governments of Mexico, Brazil, Argentina, and Venezuela have paid an enormous amount in the shape of interest payments—approximately $100,000,000,000 in 1982–85—using most of their export revenues for this purpose.[10] In effect, during the 1980s Latin America has become a net capital exporter (rather than a capital importer, as it was in the 1970s) and has therefore helped the most powerful private banks in the world to survive the debt crisis without suffering a major crackup. This situation would not have occurred had it not been for the enormous pressure brought to bear on the Latin American republics by the financial and political machinery of the advanced industrial nations.

Repayment of the debts has meant enormous sacrifices for the peoples of Latin America. At the urging of the bankers and the officials of the International Monetary Fund, governments have imposed painful austerity programs on their citizens in order to be able to extract sufficient revenue for paying foreign debts. These programs have led to increased taxes, a sharp rise in the costs of essential commodities and basic services, spiraling inflation, expanding unemployment, and decreasing levels of personal income. Apart from hiking up income taxes, all Latin American governments have introduced new sales taxes on basic consumer products. At the same time, all public services—gas, electricity, telephone, and water supplies—have become prohibitively expensive for the majority of the population. The increase in rates has helped governments make interest payments to the bankers, but it has led to a sharp deterioration in basic living standards. Despite these sacrifices, there has been a steady worsening of the economic situation in most countries. Inflation steadily undercuts the already limited buying power of the lower middle classes and workers in the cities and of the peasants in rural towns and villages. And record levels of unemployment intensify the misery and discontent.

There are limits to the suffering that will be borne without protest. Numerous signs of rising indignation in Latin American citizens against the financial blood-letting are heard and seen every day. The number of strikes and demonstrations that link the problem of foreign debts to poverty has increased steadily. The "debt crisis" has become a household word and is constantly on the radio, on television, and in the newspapers. The disillusionment is acute because economic and social progress have come to a halt. During the 1960s and 1970s the increase in the growth rates of most Latin American economies led to some improvements in living standards and to a rise in expectations with respect to better housing, education, medical services, and recreation. These expectations can no longer be fulfilled.

10. See the synopsis of the reports of the debtor's club known as Grupo de Cartagena, published in *Excelsior* (Mexico City), December 26, 1985.

As a result, popular consciousness of the injustice is on the rise. Both the wealthy and the poorest members of Latin American societies are now aware that instead of being able to obtain work and enjoy the fruits of labor, everyone must pay his pound of flesh to the bankers.

The social and political discontent have already spread so widely that many Latin American governments have begun to question the wisdom of continuing to bow to all the demands of the international banks. There have been proposals to create a debtors' cartel, which could oblige foreign creditors to accept the need for concessions that would alleviate the plight of the debtor nations. And in several instances there have been defaults, as in the cases of Bolivia, Costa Rica, and Brazil.

The political implications of the contemporary financial crisis are more widespread than ever before. In the present era the majority of the citizens of the Latin American republics understand the disastrous consequences of the debt debacle because it directly affects everyone. In the past such consciousness was not so extensive. But even so, the history of previous debt crises demonstrates that once the patience of peoples evaporated, revolutions were frequent. In 1890 there was a political and social revolution in Buenos Aires that was the direct result of the misguided financial policies of the government, which had overburdened the society with a huge foreign debt. In the early 1930s one Latin American government after another toppled as a result of strikes and demonstrations by white-collar workers, students, railroad and port laborers, sergeants, and soldiers. They judged the economic depression to be the consequence of political corruption and financial extortion and for these reasons ousted heads of state and pressed for adoption of nationalistic economic policies.

In the 1980s, Latin American citizens are even more acutely aware of the social and economic wrongs engendered by the great loan frenzy of recent years. It is well known that the principal beneficiaries were the technocrats, generals, and businessmen who received secret commissions and contracts on the huge flow of foreign funds. In no period of modern Latin American history has financial corruption reached such heights, and in no period has political repression been so extreme. Indeed, it was largely for this reason that the military regimes in Argentina, Brazil, Peru, and Uruguay were ousted and replaced in recent years by parliamentary governments. The latter have acceded to the demands of the international banking community with respect to repayment of the foreign debts, but their political support will be eroded unless they can obtain significant concessions. If they do not succeed, popular movements will in all likelihood press for adoption of the old and proven practice of unilateral default.

Since independence, debt crises have been a permanent feature of the history of Latin America, being linked to the boom and bust cycles of the economies of the region. They have marked critical junctures in the political, social, and economic evolution of the subcontinent. The contemporary crisis is the most severe to date and that most pregnant with fateful consequences. If historical experience is a reliable guide, we can be sure that its repercussions will be with us for years to come.

APPENDIXES

BIBLIOGRAPHICAL NOTE

INDEX

APPENDIX A

FOREIGN LOANS TO LATIN AMERICAN GOVERNMENTS, 1850–1873

Country and Govt. Entity	Year	Nominal Value (£ thousands)[a]	Interest Rate[b]	Issue Price[c]	Purpose[d]	Bankers[e]
ARGENTINA						
National govt.	1857	1,263	3.0	—	Refinance	Barings (L)
	1865/68	2,500	6.0	72–75	Military	Barings (L)
	1871	6,122	6.0	88	Public works	Murrieta (L)
Buenos Aires Prov.	1870	1,035	6.0	86–88	Public works	Murrieta (L)
	1873	2,041	6.0	90	Public works	Barings (L)
Entre Ríos Prov.	1872	227	7.0	90	Refinance	Barings (L)
Santa Fé Prov.	1874	300	7.0	92	Bank and railways	Murrieta (L)
BOLIVIA						
National govt.	1864	1,000	6.0	Failure	Bank and railways	London County Bank (L)
	1872	1,700	6.0	68	Public works	Lumb, Wanklyn (L)
BRAZIL						
National govt.	1852	1,041	4.5	95	Refinance	Rothschilds (L)
	1858	1,527	4.5	96	Railways	Rothschilds (L)
	1859	503	5.0	—	Refinance	Rothschilds (L)
	1860	1,373	4.5	90	Public works	Rothschilds (L)
	1863	3,300	4.5	88	Refinance	Rothschilds (L)
	1865	6,963	5.0	74	Military	Rothschilds (L)
	1871	3,460	5.0	89	Refinance	Rothschilds (L)
	1875	5,300	5.0	96	Refinance	Rothschilds (L)
CHILE						
National govt.	1858	1,555	4.5	92	Railways	Barings (L)
	1865	450	6.0	92	Military	Thomson, Bonar (L)
	1866	1,121	7.0	92	Military	Morgan (L)
	1867	2,000	6.0	80	Refinance	Morgan (L)
	1870	1,013	5.0	83	Railways	Morgan (L)
	1873	1,227	5.0	89	Railways and military	Oriental Banking Co. (L)
	1875	1,136	5.0	88	Public works	Oriental Banking Co. (L)
COLOMBIA						
National govt.	1863	200	6.0	86	Public works	London County Bank (L)
	1866	7,500	7.0	Failure	—	—
	1873	2,000	4.0	—	Refinance	London County Bank (L)

Country and Govt. Entity	Year	Nominal Value (£ thousands)[a]	Interest Rate[b]	Issue Price[c]	Purpose[d]	Bankers[e]
COSTA RICA						
National govt.	1871	500	6.0	72	Public works	Bischoffsheim (L & P)
	1872	500	6.0	74	Public works	Bischoffsheim (L & P)
	1872	2,400	7.0	82	Railways	Knowles, Foster; Erlangers (L & P)
ECUADOR						
National govt.	1855	1,824	6.0	—	Refinance	Committee of Bondholders
GUATEMALA						
National govt.	1856	150	5.0	—	Refinance	Isaac, Samuel (L)
	1869	500	6.0	70	Public works	Thomson, Bonar (L)
HAITI						
National govt.	1875	1,458	8.0	86	Refinance	Crédit Général Français (P)
HONDURAS						
National govt.	1867	1,000	10.0	80	Railways	Bischoffsheim (L & P)
	1867	90	5.0	—	Refinance	Haslewood & Co. (L)
	1869	2,000	7.0	75	Railways	Dreyfus et Cie. (P)
	1872	15,000	—	Failure	—	—
MEXICO						
National govt.	1864	6,960	6.0	63	Military[f]	Crédit Mobilier (P); Glyn, Mills (L)
	1865	10,000	6.0	68	Military and refinance	Comptoir d'Escompte; Oppenheim (P)
PARAGUAY						
National govt.	1871	1,000	8.0	80	Refinance and railways	Robinson, Fleming (L)
	1872	2,000	8.0	82	Public works	Robinson, Fleming (L)
PERU[g]						
National govt.	1853	2,600	4.5	85	Refinance	Murrieta; Hambro (L)
	1853	400	4.5	—	Railways	Hegan & Co. (L)
	1862	5,500	4.5	93	Refinance	Heywood Kennard (L)
	1865	9,000	5.0	83	Refinance	Thomson, Bonar (L)
	1869	290	5.0	71	Railways	Thomson, Bonar (L)
	1870	11,920	6.0	82	Railways	Schröder (L); Société Générale (P)
	1872	22,130	5.0	77	Refinance and railways	Schröder, Sterns (L); Société Générale (P)
SANTO DOMINGO						
National govt.	1869	785	6.0	70	Public works	Peter Lawson (L)
URUGUAY						
National govt.	1871	3,500	6.0	72	Refinance	Thomson, Bonar (L)
VENEZUELA						
National govt.	1862	1,000	6.0	63	Refinance	Barings (L)
	1864	1,500	6.0	60	Refinance and public works	General Crédit Finance Co. (L)

SOURCES: Corporation of Foreign Bondholders, *Annual Reports* (London, 1873–80); Charles Fenn, *Fenn's on the Funds* (London, 1883); *Investor's Monthly Manual* (London, 1873–76); Irving Stone, "The Composition and Distribution of British Investment in Latin America, 1865–1913" (Ph.D. diss., Columbia University, 1982).

a. The information here is the nominal value of all the bonds offered for sale by the issuing banks. However, because it is difficult to determine exactly how many bonds were actually sold, these figures should be handled with caution.

b. These were the *annual* interest rates payable by the governments issuing the bonds. They do not include amortization.

c. In the different bibliographical sources there are occasional discrepancies in the exact issue price. For several loans—Argentina (1857), Brazil (1859), Ecuador (1855), Guatemala (1856), Peru (1853)—the sources do not provide information on issue price. Because these loans were all conversions of old debts, it can be presumed that the latter were issued at par.

d. Under "purpose" are broad categories that summarize the specific aims of the loans described in the loan prospectuses. However, only a detailed study of the financial archives of each borrowing government can disclose how the proceeds were actually invested.

e. The institutions listed here were the "lead banks" in charge of the overall management of the respective bond issue. They organized broad syndicates of banks, each of which assumed responsibility for the sale of a fixed portion of the securities. The abbreviation(s) following each institution indicates where the banks placed most of the bonds: (L) = London; (P) = Paris.

f. These so-called "Mexican imperial loans" were issued in Paris on behalf of the government of Maximilian, who had been installed as emperor of Mexico by the French government of Napoleon III. The loans were used to pay the expenses of the French occupation army in Mexico (1862–67) and were therefore repudiated by succeeding governments of Mexico.

g. Not included here are two Peruvian loans brought out in Paris in the 1850s, because there is only partial data on them; one was issued by J. Uribarren for approximately £1,800,000, the second was issued by Montané et Cie. for £800,000.

APPENDIX B

FOREIGN LOANS TO LATIN AMERICAN GOVERNMENTS, 1880–1890

Country and Govt. Entity[a]	Year	Nominal Value (£ thousands)	Interest Rate (%)	Issue Price	Purpose[b]	Bankers[c]
ARGENTINA						
National govt.	1881	2,450	6.0	91	Railways[d]	Paris/Bas; Comptoir d' Escompte (P); Murrieta (L)
	1882	817	6.0	90	Military[e]	Paris/Bas; Comptoir d'Escompte (P)
	1882	2,240	5.0	90	Refinance	N.I.
	1884	1,714	5.0	84	National bank	Baring (L); Paris/Bas; Comptoir (P)
	1884	800	5.0	81	Port	Paris/Bas; Comptoir; Cahen (P)
	1886	8,290	5.0	80/85	Ports and railways	Barings; Morgan (L); Paris/Bas; Comptoir; Société Générale (P)
	1887 1889	3,968	5.0	91/97	Railways	Murrieta (L)
	1887	2,017	5.0	90	National bank	Disconto; Norddeutsche; Oppenheim (B,A)
	1887	624	5.0	Par	Refinance	Murrieta (L)
	1887	5,263	4.5	87	Refinance	Barings (L)
	1889	5,290	4.5	90	Refinance	Deutsche; Disconto (B); Murrieta; Baring (L); Heine; Comptoir (P)
	1889	2,750	3.5	Par	Refinance	Stern (L)
	1890	3,000	5.0	NA	Railways	Cahen; Comptoir (P); Disconto (B)
Buenos Aires Prov.	1881	300	6.0	NA	Port[f]	Stern (L)
	1882	2,049	6.0	92	Provincial bank[g]	Barings (L)
	1883	2,065	6.5	NA	Railways	Morton, Rose (L)
	1883	2,254	6.0	94	La Plata City[h]	Morton, Rose (L); Société Générale; Comptoir, Paris/Bas (P)
	1884	2,000	5.0	NA	Railways	Morton, Rose (L); Mendelsohn (B)

247

Country and Govt. Entity[a]	Year	Nominal Value (£ thousands)	Interest Rate (%)	Issue Price	Purpose[b]	Bankers[c]
	1886	2,502	5.0	80	Provincial bank	Deutsche; Disconto; Mendelsohn (B)
	1886	2,040	6.0	92	Provinical bank	Barings (L)
	1887	400	6.0	NA	Railways	Morton, Rose (L)
	1888	1,000	6.0	NA	Railways	Morton, Rose (L)
Catamarca Prov.	1888	600	6.0	95	Provincial bank	Banque Parisienne (P)
Córdoba Prov.	1886	595	6.0	89	Public works	Morton, Rose (L)
	1887	1,190	6.0	91/92	Provincial	Morton, Rose (L)
	1888	2,000	5.0	96	Provincial bank	Comptoir; Société Générale (P); Deutsche (B)
Corrientes Prov.	1889	1,000	6.0	92	Provincial bank	Société Générale (P)
EntreRíos Prov.	1885	1,530	6.0	NA	Railways	Murrieta (L)
	1886	800	6.0	91	Refinance	Murrieta (L)
	1887	1,200	—	97	Provincial bank	Murrieta (L)
	1888	1,745	6.0	NA	Railways	Murrieta (L)
Mendoza Prov.	1888	992	6.0		Provincial bank	Cahen (P)
San Juan Prov.	1888	400	6.0	92	Provincial bank	Cohen (L)
San Luis Prov.	1889	150	6.0	92	Provincal bank	Cahen; Heine (P)
Santa Fé Prov.	1883	1,434	6.0	90	Railways	Murrieta (L)
	1884	1,079	5.0	NA	Railways	Murrieta (L)
	1887	2,190	5.0	84/86	Railways	Murrieta (L)
	1888	390	5.0	90	Provincial bank	Morton, Rose (L)
Tucumán Prov.	1888	600	6.0	92	Provincial bank	Cahen; Heine (P)
Buenos Aires City	1888	1,326	6.0	Par	Public works	Cohen (L)
	1889	1,984	4.5	86	Public works	Barings (L)
Córdoba City	1887	198	6.0	95	Public works	Heinemann (L & P)
	1889	595	6.0	98	Public works	Heinemann (L & P)
Paraná City	1889	212	5.0	92	Waterworks	River Plate Trust (L)
	1889	198	6.0	95	Public works	Morton, Rose (L)
Rosario City	1887	198	6.0	par	NA	Heinemann (L & P)
	1888	992	6.0	103	Public works	Heinemann (L & P)
	1888	297	6.0	NA	Public works	Hambros (L)
Santa Fe City	1889	257	6.0	95	Public works	Heinemann (L & P)
BRAZIL						
National govt.	1883	4,599	4.5	89	Public works	Rothschilds (L)
	1886	6,431	5.0	95	Refinance	Rothschilds (L)
	1888	6,297	4.5	97	Railways	Rothschilds (L)
	1889	19,837	4.0	90	Refinance[i]	Rothschilds (L)
Bahia State	1888	200	5.0	96	Public works	Paris/Bas (P)
São Paulo State	1888	850	5.0	97	Public works	Cohen (L)

Country and Govt. Entity[a]	Year	Nominal Value (£ thousands)	Interest Rate (%)	Issue Price	Purpose[b]	Bankers[c]
Rio de Janeiro City	1889	600	4.0	87	Public works	Morton, Rose (L)
Santos City	1888	100	6.0	100	Public works	Schröder (L)
CHILE						
National govt.	1885	809	4.5	89	Refinance	City Bank (L)
	1886	6,010	4.5	98	Refinance	Rothschilds (L)
	1887	1,160	4.5	97	Nitrate[j] certificates	Rothschilds (L)
	1889	1,546	4.5	102	Railways	Deutsche (B)
MEXICO						
National govt.	1888	10,500	6.0	78	Refinance	Bleichröder (B); Gibbs (L)
	1889	2,700	5.0	77	Railways	Seligman (L)
	1890	6,000	6.0	88	Railways guarantees	Bleichröder (B); Gibbs (L)
S. L. Potosí State	1889	250	6.0	89	NA	Gibbs (L)
Mexico City	1889	2,400	5.0	85	Waterworks	Trustees Corp. (L)
URUGUAY						
National govt.	1883	11,127	5.0	50	Refinance[k]	Barings (L)
	1885	4,255	6.0	82	Public works and refinance	Barings (L)
	1888	2,000	6.0	79	Refinance	Barings (L)
Montevideo City	1889	1,400	6.0	100	Public works	Barings (L)

SOURCES: Corporation of Foreign Bondholders, *Annual Reports* (London, 1880–91); Henry L. Shepherd, *Default and Adjustment of the Argentine Foreign Debt, 1890–1906*, U.S. Department of Commerce Trade Promotion Series, no. 145 (Washington, D.C., 1933); Carlos Marichal, "Los banqueros europeos y los empréstitos argentinos, 1880–1890," *Revista de Historia Económica* (Madrid) 2, no. 1 (1984): 47–82; Jan Bazant, *Historia de la deuda exterior de México* (Mexico, 1968), pp. 125–141; O. Onody, "Les invéstissements étrangers au Bresil," in Centre National de Recherche Scientifique, *Colloque International sur l'Histoire Quantitative du Brésil de 1800 à 1930* (Paris, 1971), pp 302–307.

NA = Information not available.

a. Not included in this listing are several small conversion loans—those of Costa Rica in 1886, £2,000,000; Guatemala in 1888, £887,000; Nicaragua in 1886, £285,000; Paraguay in 1886, £836,000; and Santo Domingo in 1888, £770,000. These did not represent new loans, but simply the exchange of new bonds for the old ones in default since 1873 or 1874. Also not included are the Cuban loans of the 1880s because these depended on the Spanish Crown. For additional references, see footnotes to Table 5.

b. The same categories for "purpose" as noted in Appendix A apply here; the categories of "railways" and "ports" refer to state-owned enterprises in this appendix.

c. The following abbreviations identify where the banks sold most of the bonds: (L) = London; (P) = Paris; (B) = Berlin; (H) = Hamburg; (A) = Amsterdam.

d. All references to "railways" under Argentine national government loans are to the Central Norte and Andino lines.

e. This loan was contracted to pay for expenses incurred in the repression of the revolt of 1880 led by Tejedor, governor of the province of Buenos Aires.

f. Reference here is to the new port built near the city of La Plata.

g. Reference here is to the state-owned Banco de la Provincia de Buenos Aires.

h. La Plata City, the future provincial capital, was built from scratch, financed through this and other loans.

i. In 1889 the Brazilian government also issued a large volume of "internal" gold bonds that actually were placed in Europe.

j. The Chilean nitrate bonds of 1887 were used to liquidate Peruvian debts that had originally been guaranteed by the nitrate fields conquered by the Chilean army in 1880. The Chilean authorities thus succeeded in placating the foreign bankers, who were now disposed to accept Chilean sovereignty over these rich districts.

k. The 1883 Uruguayan loan actually consisted of a conversion of a huge volume of internal debts into external bonds. For this reason the issue price was extremely low.

APPENDIX C

FOREIGN LOANS TO LATIN AMERICAN GOVERNMENTS, 1920–1930[a]

Country and Govt. Entity	Year[b]	Nominal Value (U.S. $ thousands)	Interest Rate (%)	Maturity Years[c]	Issue Price	Purpose[d]	Bankers[e]
ARGENTINA							
National govt.	1923	40,000	6.0	34	96	Refinance	Kuhn, Loeb; Blair
	1924	30,000	6.0	34	95	Refinance	Blair; Chase
	1925	45,000	6.0	34	96	Refinance	Morgan; Nacional City
	1925	29,700	6.0	34	96	Refinance	Morgan; Nacional City
	1926	20,000	6.0	34	98	Refinance and public works	Morgan; Nacional City
	1926	16,900	6.0	34	98	Public works	Morgan; Nacional City
	1927	27,000	6.0	34	98	Refinance	Morgan; Nacional City
	1927	21,200	6.0	34	99	Public works	Morgan; Nacional City
	1927	19,000	6.0	37	97[f]	Military	Hispano Americano (M)
	1927	40,000	6.0	33	99	Refinance	Blair; Chase
Buenos Aires Prov.	1925	14,472	7.5	22	99	Public works	Blair
	1926	10,600	7.0	26	96	Public works	Blair
	1928	41,101	6.0	33	96	Refinance	First National Boston; Hallgarten; Kissel
	1929	11,675	6.5	31	95	Public works	First National Boston; Harris, Forbes
Córdoba Prov.	1925	5,943	7.0	17	95	Public works	Harris, Forbes; First National Boston
Mendoza Prov.	1926	6,500	7.5	25	98	Refinance	P. Chapman; White, Weld
Santa Fé Prov.	1924	10,188	7.0	18	96	Public works	White, Weld; Dillon, Read
Tucumán Prov.	1927	2,122	6.0	23	94	Provincial bank	Paine, Weber
Buenos Aires City	1924	8,490	6.0	31	96	Public works	Dillon, Read; Harris, Forbes; Colony Trust
	1927	3,396	6.0	33	97	Public works	Blyth, Witter; Schröder
	1927	3,396	6.0	33	98	Public works	Blyth, Witter; Schröder
Córdoba City	1927	4,669	7.0	30	98	Public works	White, Weld; Blyth, Witter
	1927	2,547	7.0	10	97	Public works	Ames, Emrich; Strupp & Co.
Santa Fé City	1927	2,122	7.0	18	94	Public works	Blair
Tucumán City	1928	3,396	7.0	23	96	Public works	H. Rollins & Sons

Country and Govt. Entity	Year[b]	Nominal Value (U.S. $ thousands)	Interest Rate (%)	Maturity Years[c]	Issue Price	Purpose[d]	Bankers[e]
BOLIVIA							
National govt.	1922	29,000	8.0	25	101	Public works	Equitable Trust; Spencer, Trask
	1927	14,000	7.0	31	98	Public works	Dillon, Read; Mendelsohn; Pierson & Co. (A)
	1927	23,000	7.0	41	97	Refinance	Dillon, Read
BRAZIL							
National govt.	1921	50,000	8.0	20	98	Public works	Dillon, Read; Blair; White, Weld
	1922	25,000	7.0	30	96	Public works	Dillon, Read; Blair; White, Weld
	1926	60,000	6.5	31	90	Refinance	Dillon, Read (NY); Mendelsohn (A)
	1927	41,500	6.5	30	92	Refinance	Dillon, Read; National City; Blair (NY); Schröder (L)
	1927	42,577	6.5	30	91	Refinance	Rothschilds; Barings (L)
Ceará State	1922	2,000	8.0	25	99	Refinance	Bache
Maranhão State	1928	1,750	7.0	30	94	Refinance	National City; Baker, Kellogg
Minas Gerais State	1928	8,500	6.5	30	97	Public works and refinance	National City; Kissel, Kinnicutt; Schröder
	1928	8,500	6.5	30	97	Public works and refinance	Rothschilds, Barings; Schröder (L)
	1929	8,000	6.5	30	87	Public works	National City; Kissel, Kinnicutt; Schröder
Paraná State	1928	9,720	7.0	30	98	Public works and refinance	Lazards (NY & L)
Pernambuco State	1927	6,000	7.0	20	97	Public works	White, Weld; First National Boston
Rio de Janeiro State	1927	9,374	5.5	22	Par	Refinance	Montagu (L)
	1927	10,218	7.0	37	97	Refinance	Montagu (L)
	1929	6,000	6.5	30	91	Public works and refinance	Rollins; Blyth; Bancamerica-Blair
Rio Grande do Sul State	1921	10,000	8.0	25	99	Public works	Lee, Higginson; Ladenburg, Thalman
	1926	1,000	7.0	40	98	Public works and refinance	Lee, Higginson; Ladenburg, Thalmen
	1927	4,000	7.0	40	97	Public works	Equitable Trust; J. G. White; Otis
	1928	23,000	6.0	40	94	Public works and refinance	White, Weld; National City; Lee, Higginson
Santa Catarina State	1922	4,704	8.0	25	101	Public works and refinance	Halsey, Stuart
São Paulo State	1921	29,190	8.0	15	97	Refinance	Speyer; Blair (NY); Barings; Rothschilds (L)
	1925	15,000	8.0	25	99	Public works	Schröder (L & A)
	1926	48,660	7.5	30	94/97	Coffee Institute[g]	Lazards (L)

Country and Govt. Entity	Year[b]	Nominal Value (U.S. $ thousands)	Interest Rate (%)	Maturity Years[c]	Issue Price	Purpose[d]	Bankers[e]
	1928	32,000	6.0	40	94	Public works	Speyer; Blair (NY); Barings; Rothschilds; Schröder (L)
	1930	35,000	7.0	10	96	Coffee support[h]	Speyer (NY)
	1930	62,323	7.0	10	96 *	Coffee support	Barings; Rothschilds; Schröder (L)
Nitheroy City	1929	3,892	7.0	40	96	Public works	Lazards (L)
Pôrto Alegre City	1921	3,500	8.0	40	99	Public works	Lee, Higginson; Landenburg, Thalman
	1926	4,000	7.0	40	96	Public works	Lee, Higginson; Landenburg, Thalman
	1928	2,250	7.0	40	97	Public works	Lee, Higginson; Landenburg, Thalman
Rio de Janeiro City	1921	12,000	8.0	25	97	Public works	Dillon, Read; Lee, Higginson
	1928	30,000	6.5	25	97	Public works and refinance	White, Weld; Brown Bros.
	1928	1,770	6.0	5	96	Public works	White, Weld; Brown Bros.
Santos City	1927	10,990	7.0	30	97	Public works	Erlangers; Bank of London & Brazil (L)
São Paulo City	1922	4,000	8.0	30	100	Public works	Blair
	1927	5,900	6.5	30	97	Public works	First National Boston; Harris, Forbes; Stone, Webster
CHILE							
National govt.	1922	8,150	7.5	33	95	Refinance	Rothschilds (L)
	1922	18,000	7.0	20	96	Public works and refinance	National City
	1926	13,024	6.0	44	94	Public works	Anglo-South American Bank (L)
	1926	42,500	6.0	34	93	Public works	Hallgarten; Kissel, Kinnicutt
	1927	27,500	6.0	34	93	Public works	Hallgarten; Kissel, Kinnicutt
	1928	44,152	6.0	33	93	Public works and refinance	National City
	1928	25,732	6.0	33	94/95	Public works and refinance	National City (NY)
	1929	19,730	6.0	33	93/94	Public works	Rothschilds (L)
	1929	4,750	6.0	32	88/92	Public works	Swiss Bank Corp.; Credit Suisse (G)
	1930	25,000	6.0	33	91	Public works	National City
National Mortgage Bank of Chile	1925	20,000	6.0	32	97	Bank support[i]	Kuhn, Loeb
	1926	20,000	6.0	35	99	Bank support[i]	Kuhn, Loeb
	1926	10,000	6.0	25	98	Bank support[i]	Kuhn, Loeb
	1928	20,000	6.0	33	95	Bank support[i]	Kuhn, Loeb
	1929	20,000	6.0	33	92	Bank support[i]	Kuhn, Loeb

253

Country and Govt. Entity	Year[b]	Nominal Value (U.S. $ thousands)	Interest Rate (%)	Maturity Years[c]	Issue Price	Purpose[d]	Bankers[e]
Consolidated Municipal loan	1929	15,000	7.0	31	94	Public works	Grace National Bank; Brown Bros.
Santiago City	1928	4,000	7.0	21	100	Public works	Kissel, Kinnicutt; Brown Bros.
	1929	4,750	6.0	33	87/91	Public works	Mendelsohn (A)
COLOMBIA National govt.	1927	25,000	6.0	34	92	Public works	Hallgarten; Kissel; Kinnicutt
	1928	35,000	6.0	33	95	Public works	Hallgarten; Kissel; Kinnicutt
Agricultural Mortgage Bank	1926	3,000	7.0	20	94	Bank support[j]	Dilon, Read
	1927	3,000	7.0	20	97	Bank support[j]	Hallgarten; Kissel; Kinnicutt
	1927	5,000	6.0	20	92	Bank support[j]	Harriman
	1928	5,000	6.0	20	93	Bank support[j]	Harriman
	1929	5,840	6.5	30	95	Bank support[j]	Lazards (L)
Antioquia Dept.	1925/29	20,000	7.0	20	90/93	Public works	Blair; Rollins
	1927	12,350	7.0	30	93/96	Public works	Guaranty Bank
Caldas Dept.	1926	10,000	7.5	20	95/98	Public works	Blyth, Witter; Seligman
Cauca Dept.	1926	4,000	7.5	20	96/98	Public works	Baker, Kellogg
	1928	4,500	7.0	20	96	Public works	Baker, Kellogg
Cundinamarca Dept.	1928	12,000	6.5	31	93	Public works	Rollins; Seligman
Santander Dept.	1928	2,000	7.0	20	94	Public works	Rollins
Tolima Dept.	1927	2,500	7.0	20	93	Public works and refinance	Rollins
Bogotá City	1924	6,000	8.0	21	98	Public works and refinance	Dillon, Read
	1927	2,700	6.5	20	91	Public works	Tucker, Anthony; Baker, Kellogg
Barranquilla City	1925/28	4,000	8.0	20	99/102	Public works	Lazards (NY & L)
Cali City	1927	2,885	7.0	20	93	Public works	Baker, Kellogg; Field, Glore
Medellin City	1926	3,000	7.0	25	93	Public works	Hallgarten
	1928	9,000	6.5	26	93	Public works and refinance	Hallgarten
COSTA RICA National govt.	1926	8,000	7.0	25	95	Public works and refinance	Seligman
	1927	1,800	7.5	22	100	Public works	National City
	1930	1,192	5.0	20	Par	Refinance	Seligman
CUBA National govt.	1923	50,000	5.5	30	99	Refinance	Morgan
	1927	9,000	5.5	10	100	Refinance	Morgan; Kuhn, Loeb; National City
	1928/29	20,000	5.5	4	99	Public works	Chase

Country and Govt. Entity	Year[b]	Nominal Value (U.S. $ thousands)	Interest Rate (%)	Maturity Years[c]	Issue Price	Purpose[d]	Bankers[e]
	1930	40,000	5.5	15	98	Public works	Chase
	1930	36,973	5.5	10	Par	Sugar price support[k]	Chase; National City
DOMINICAN REPUBLIC							
National govt.	1922	10,000	5.5	20	94	Public works and refinance	Lee, Higginson; Dillon, Read; Brown Bros.
	1926	10,000	5.5	14	100	Public works	Lee, Higginson; Dillon, Read; Brown Bros.
EL SALVADOR							
National govt.	1923	6,000	8.0	25	NA	Refinance	Issued in New York[l]
	1924	5,109	8.0	34	NA	Refinance	Issued in New York[l]
	1924	10,500	8.0	34	NA	Refinance	Issued in New York[l]
GUATEMALA							
National govt.	1924/28	4,950	8.0	10	85	Public works	Allgemeine[m]
	1927	2,515	8.0	21	101	Refinance	Schuyler
	1930	2,000	7.0	30	90	Refinance	Swedish Match Co.
HAITI							
National govt.	1922	16,000	6.0	30	96	Refinance	National City
	1922	2,634	6.0	30	75	Refinance	National Railroad of Haiti[n]
	1923	4,349	6.0	30	NA	Refinance	National City
PANAMA							
National govt.	1923	4,500	5.5	30	97	Public works and refinance	Harriman
	1928	12,000	5.0	35	97	Public works and refinance	National City
Banco Nacional de Panama	1926/29	4,000	6.5	20	99/101	National Bank	Otis (NY); Royal Financial Corp. (T)
PERU							
National govt.	1922	6,082	7.5	20	95	Refinance	Barings; Schröder (L)
	1927	15,000	7.0	32	96	Public works	Seligman
	1927	50,000	6.0	33	91	Public works and refinance	Seligman; National City
	1928	25,000	6.0	33	91	Public works and refinance	Seligman; National City
	1928	9,732	6.0	33	91	Public works and refinance	Barings; Schröder (L)
Callao Province	1927	1,500	7.5	17	99	Public works	Seligman
Lima City	1928	3,000	6.0	30	93	Public works and refinance	Grace National Bank; Rollins; Brown Bros.
URUGUAY							
National govt.	1921	7,500	6.0	25	98	Public works	National City
	1926	30,000	6.0	34	96	Public works	Hallgarten
	1930	17,580	6.0	34	98	Public works	Halsey, Stuart
Montevideo City	1922	6,000	7.0	30	97	Public works	Dillon, Read
	1926	9,307	6.0	33	93	Public works	Guaranty Co.

SOURCES: A. Kimber, *Kimber's Record of Government Debts* (London, 1929 and 1934 eds.); Corporation of Foreign Bondholders, *Annual Reports* (London, 1928–35); Foreign Bondholders Protective Council, *Annual Reports* (New York, 1934, 1936). Additional details can found in the country studies listed in the Bibliographical Note at the end of the present work.

NA = No information available.

a. Includes only long-term external bond issues of government entities of the Latin American republics. For some data on short-term loans from United States banks, see Cleona Lewis, *America's Stake in International Investments* (Washington, D.C., 1938), pp. 617–634.

b. Refers to official year of issue; the actual sale of the bonds frequently took place several weeks or months after this year.

c. Maturity refers to the maximum time period for the repayment and cancellation of the bonds. Prior to the final date, however, a certain percentage of the bonds could be retired by using funds from the sinking fund.

d. The terms used here have a meaning similar to those utilized in Appendixes A and B. But given the greater variety of objectives listed in the loan contracts of the 1920s, it is worthwhile to provide additional details. "Refinance" refers here either to conversion of old outstanding external bonds or, alternatively, to liquidation of short-term debts of the government. "Public works" refers to investments in a variety of government-financed development projects, including state railways, urban sanitation and waterworks, pavement of streets, construction of roads, port works, and so on. "Military" refers to expenditures for the acquisition of weapons, gunboats, destroyers, and other war materiel from abroad. It should also be noted that the categories used here refer to the ostensible or "official" purposes of the loans; in numerous instances the loan proceeds were diverted to other uses.

e. "Bankers" refers to the banks leading the issue of the bonds. Unless otherwise indicated, all the banks listed operated out of New York, although they usually placed the bonds among hundreds of brokerage firms throughout the United States. In cases where bonds were also sold outside the United States, the following abbreviations are used for purposes of clarity: (NY) = New York; (T) = Toronto; (L) = London; (P) = Paris; (A) = Amsterdam; (M) = Madrid; (G) = Geneva.

f. Listed on the Madrid Stock Exchange but not on the New York Stock Exchange.

g. The loans for the São Paulo Coffee Institute, established in 1924, were used to regulate Brazilian coffee production through acquisition of sizeable coffee stocks.

h. The proceeds of the loan were used to finance the liquidation of approximately 16,500,000 bags of coffee accumulated at São Paulo. The proceeds were intended to guarantee future interest payments on the São Paulo State external debt.

i. These were gold mortgage bonds to provide support for the sinking fund of the Mortgage Bank of Chile (Caja de Crédito Hipotecario), a government-run financial institution.

j. These were gold mortgage bonds to support the Agricultural Mortgage Bank, an official financial institution.

k. Issued under an agreement between the Republic of Cuba and the National Sugar Exporting Corporation, which pledged as security all the Cuban sugar acquired in exchange for bonds in accordance with the Sugar Stabilization Law.

l. Loan contract signed with Minor Keith, head of the International Railways of Central America (an enterprise closely linked to the United Fruit Company) to pay off outstanding debts of the Republic of El Salvador.

m. Bonds taken by the Allgemeine Elekritäts Gesellschaft, which obtained the contract for construction of the Los Altos Railway and the hydroelectric plant at Santa María, Quetzaltenango.

n. Issued by the National Railways of Haiti in exchange for external bonds of 1911 still outstanding.

A Guide to the Principal Foreign Banking Houses
Engaged in the Issue of Latin American Loans
during the Nineteenth and Early Twentieth Centuries

This guide includes only the principal foreign banking houses engaged in the issue of Latin American loans during the period 1850–1930. A number of small banking firms of England, France, Germany, and the United States have not been included, but information on some of these can be found in Appendixes A, B. and C. There is not enough published information to include data on Belgian, Dutch, and Swiss banking firms that participated in European banking syndicates selling Latin American bonds. For additional information on the banks listed, see "Bibliographical Sources" at the end of this appendix.

BRITISH BANKING HOUSES[1]

Baring Brothers: London merchant bank founded in 1763 by the Baring family to finance trade with the United States and with India. During the Napoleonic Wars it was engaged in large operations for the British treasury. The firm soon became one of the major powers in international finance. Between 1820 and 1870 it was involved in government loans for France, Spain, Portugal, Russia, and Canada, among others. In Latin America it took the 1824 Buenos Aires loan, the 1858 Chilean railway loan, and the 1862 Venezuelan loan. During the 1880s it became the principal banker to the governments of both Argentina and Uruguay, leading syndicates for six Argentine national loans and for three Uruguayan loans. Its excesses led to bankruptcy in 1890. Reorganized in 1892, it reassumed its role as leading banker to Argentina, issuing eight loans for that nation between 1907 and 1914. Subsequently its importance in Latin American finance declined, although it maintained close ties with the Argentine government until 1946 and during the 1920s participated in the issue of two Brazilian loans and one Peruvian loan.

Louis Cohen & Sons: London merchant bank established in 1824. This small but prestigious firm became heavily involved in the issue of Argentine provincial

---

1. Among the British merchant banks we have not included are four firms that were active only between 1822 and 1826, disappearing thereafter: Barclay, Herring & Richardson; B. A. Goldschmidt & Company; Herring, Powles & Graham; and Hullett Brothers. Information on these firms can be found in Chapter 1. We have also not included three British overseas banks that were briefly involved in the issue of several foreign loans during the period 1900–1912 for Argentina, Brazil, and Peru—namely, the Bank of London and River Plate, the Bank of London and Brazil, and the Anglo–South American Bank.

bonds in the 1880s, selling them in conjunction with French and German banking houses.

Erlangers: A cosmopolitan merchant bank with offices at Frankfurt and Paris from the mid-nineteenth century. The sons of the head of the Paris branch, Baron Emile and Baron Fréderic Erlanger, were put in charge of the London branch established in 1870. Its first incursion into Latin American finances came with the issue of the Costa Rica loan of 1872. During the 1880s it became involved in numerous land and railway transactions in the Río de la Plata, leading it to create the great quebracho firm known as La Forestal. It managed the issue of loans for three Argentine provinces in 1909–10 and for several Brazilian states and municipalities in 1909–10 and 1927.

Antony Gibbs & Sons: Merchant bank established in London in 1803 specializing in trade with Spain and Spanish America. In the 1820s it opened branches at Lima and Valparaíso. From 1849 to 1863 Gibbs controlled the finance and distribution of Peruvian guano on a worldwide scale and provided numerous short-term loans to the Peruvian government during the time of its guano contracts. It later became heavily involved in the Chilean nitrate trade. It participated in the issue of the great £10,500,000 Mexican loan of 1888.

Glyn, Mills & Company: London merchant bank established in 1753. During the nineteenth century it acquired a reputation as the "railway bank" because of its active promotion of many railways in England and abroad. From the 1880s it became a major power in the great British-owned railway companies in Argentina and Uruguay. It participated occasionally in Latin American loans, including the 1864 Imperial Mexican bond issue, the Uruguayan conversion loans of 1891–96, 1905, and 1914, and the Argentine railway guarantee bond issue of 1896.

C. J. Hambro & Son: Merchant bank established in London in the early nineteenth century specializing in loans and trade-finance for the Scandanavian countries. It had few direct interests in Latin America, but participated intermittently in the issue of loans for various countries of the subcontinent, including the 1853 Peruvian loan, the 1889 Santa Fé loan, the 1907 Rosario City loan, and the 1911 and 1912 Costa Rica loans.

Lazard Brothers: Originally a firm of cotton merchants established in New Orleans in 1843. It soon became involved in the California gold trade and opened offices in San Francisco circa 1850. Its involvement in international gold markets led to the opening of branches in Paris (1858) and London (1877). It acquired vast business interests in Europe, particularly in France, where it played a dominant role in the gold markets until 1914. From the first decade of the twentieth century, the London branch became involved in the financing of the international coffee trade. This led it to participate in the issue of several loans for the government of Colombia (1906, 1911, 1913, 1916, 1920, 1929) as that nation became a major coffee exporter. During the 1920s it assisted the State of São Paulo with two large loans

(1926) for its coffee stabilization program. At this time, Weetman Pearson, who had made his fortune with Mexican oil companies and public utilities, bought a major stake in Lazards of London. As a result Lazards became heavily engaged in the international petroleum trade.

Lloyds Bank: One of the ''Big Five'' commercial banks of England. It played a minor role in Latin American finances before World War II participating in the issue of two Brazilian loans: the 1911 national loan and the 1913 Bahia State loan. Since the 1950s Lloyds Bank has become a major force in Latin American finance through its control of the Bank of London and South America (BOLSA) and all its subsidiaries.

Midland Bank: Also one of the ''Big Five'' English commercial banks. It had no branches in Latin America, but it developed interests in Chile, participating in the issue of the Chilean national loan of 1893 and the Valparaíso City loan of 1912.

J. S. Morgan & Company (later known as Morgan, Grenfell & Company):   Merchant bank established at London in 1838 by the United States traders George Peabody and Junius Spence Morgan. The firm specialized initially in the importation of tobacco and cotton from the United States to Great Britain and the export of British railway equipment to North America. It soon was selling large amounts of shares of American railway companies on the London Stock Exchange, working in intimate connection with its sister branch at New York, the famous J. P. Morgan & Company. J.S. Morgan soon broadened its international financial activities, issuing loans for France, Spain, China, and various Latin American nations. It managed the issue of three of the earliest Chilean loans (1866, 1867, 1870) and two later Chilean railway loans (1922, 1923). It participated in two large public works loans of Argentina in the 1880s, as well as in the great Argentine Funding Loan of 1891 and the loans of 1907, 1909, and 1910. In Mexico it played a part in the issue of the conversion loans of 1899, 1910, and 1913.

Morton, Rose & Company: Merchant bank established at London in 1864. It maintained close ties with both Canada and the United States. Among its partners was John Rose, former Canadian finance minister, who joined the firm in 1869. This bank specialized in the issue of Canadian government loans and in the financing of Canadian railway companies. It had a sister branch at New York, Morton, Bliss & Company. During the 1880s it became heavily involved in the issue of Argentine government bonds to finance construction of state railways; it issued five loans for the province of Buenos Aires and loans for the provinces of Córdoba, Entre Ríos, and Santa Fé.

Cristobal de Murrieta & Company: Merchant bank established at London in the mid-nineteenth century by Spanish-Basque capitalists. The Murrietas were merchants from Bilbao; they played a major role in the financing of trade between the Basque country and Great Britain. In Latin America they participated in the issue of the 1853 Peruvian loan. They later acquired interests in Mexican rails and mines.

Their largest Latin American interests, however, were in Argentine railways, land companies, and loans. They participated in one Argentine national loan and three provincial loans between 1870 and 1874. During the 1880s they managed the issue of three Argentine national loans and six provincial loans. Their large Argentine commitments led the firm to bankruptcy following the Baring Panic of 1890.

N. M. Rothschild & Sons: One of the most famous and powerful of the London merchant banks. Established in 1815, it maintained close links to the banking houses of the Rothschilds at Frankfurt, Paris, Milan, and Vienna. Each branch of the Rothschild banking empire played an important role in nineteenth-century finances, but the wealthiest and most influential houses were those of London and Paris. The London Rothschilds participated actively in the international trade in silver, diamonds, copper, and coffee and were engaged in the promotion of important companies like the Rio Tinto Mining Corporation. In Latin America they were official bankers to Brazil from the first half of the nineteenth century; they issued a grand total of twenty-one Brazilian national loans between 1825 and 1914. From the 1880s they became official bankers to the Chilean government, issuing ten national loans between 1886 and 1911. During the 1920s they continued to play an important role in Brazilian and Chilean finance, co-managing the issue of four Brazilian loans and three Chilean loans.

J. H. Schröder & Company: The Schröders, originally from Hamburg, opened their merchant banking house in London in 1815. By mid-century they were actively engaged in the international loan business, participating in loans for the Confederacy (1863), the 1864 Swedish loan, the Russian railway loan of 1868, and a loan for Japan in 1870. In Latin America their first major financial involvement came as a result of their co-management of the great Peruvian railway loans of 1870 and 1872. During the first decade of the twentieth century, they participated in the issue of two Chilean loans and of the Cuban gold bonds of 1904 and 1909, jointly with Speyer Brothers. In the 1920s they became heavily engaged in Brazilian loans, probably as a result of their interest in the coffee trade, dating back to 1850, and their ownership of coffee plantations in São Paulo. They co-managed the issue of three national Brazilian loans (1927, 1928, 1929) and of three São Paulo State loans (1926, 1928, 1930).

Stern Brothers: Merchant bank established at London in 1833, in close association with the firms of J. S. Stern of Frankfurt and A. J. Stern of Paris. The London house specialized in the financing of telegraphs and railways in Spain, the tobacco monopoly in Italy, and Portuguese government loans. Its first major incursion in Latin American finances was in connection with the 1872 Peruvian railway loan. Subsequently it specialized in Argentine loans, including two short-term loans in the 1870s and two long-term loans in the 1880s for the national government, as well as loans for the provinces of Buenos Aires (1881) and San Juan (1888).

Thomson, Bonar & Company: Merchant bank established at London in the early nineteenth century. By the 1860s they were prominent international bankers, participating in loans for the Russian government, but they apparently made a specialty of Latin American business. Between 1863 and 1869 they held the Peruvian guano contracts and issued two large Peruvian foreign loans (1865, 1869). They also participated in the issue of the Chilean loan of 1865, the Guatemalan loan of 1869, and the first Uruguayan foreign loan (1871). In later years, however, their name was no longer linked to Latin American finances.

FRENCH BANKING HOUSES[2]

Banque de Paris et des Pays Bas: One of the first and greatest French investment banks. Established at Paris in 1872, it financed metallurgical, electrical, gas, and transport firms. From its inception it held a large block of shares in the great and allied commercial bank of the Société Générale. From the end of the nineteenth century, Paris/Bas was the French bank most active in the placement of international loans, specializing above all in loans for Russia, the Balkan countries, and the Latin American nations. It helped finance a variety of private French enterprises in Latin America, including railway and port firms in Brazil and Argentina, but it stood out particularly in the field of government finance. It participated in the issue of six loans for the Argentine national government between 1881 and 1889 and three additional Argentine loans in 1909–10. It participated in various Brazilian loans, including the Bahia State loans of 1889, 1904, and 1910, the national railway loan of 1908, and the 1905 and 1907 São Paulo State loans. It co-managed the Mexican national government loans of 1910 and 1913 and had a major role in the placement of the Uruguayan conversion loan of 1905 and public works loan of 1909.

Banque de l'Union Parisienne (BUP):   Paris investment bank founded in 1904 by French and Belgian bankers; among the former were several of the best-known firms of the "haute banque," Heine, Hottinguer, Neuflize, Mallet, and Vernes; among the latter was the powerful Société Générale de Belgique. These banks worked together with the BUP in the issue of shares for industrial companies or bonds for governments. The BUP specialized in the financing of electrical and metallurgical enterprises in France and abroad. In Latin America it had interests in Brazil, Chile, and Mexico, but above all in Argentina, where it promoted railways, land companies, and local banks, including the Banque Hypothecaire Franco-Argentine and the Banco Francés del Río de la Plata. It was less active in the loan field than in the sphere of direct investments, but it participated in the issue of the 1911 national loan of Argentina as well as in several Argentine provincial loans, the 1905 Bahia City (Brazil) loan, the 1910 Haitian loan, and the 1913 Mexican conversion loan.

Bischoffsheim and Goldschmidt: Cosmopolitan merchant banking firm—with branches in Frankfurt, Brussels, Paris, London, Amsterdam, and Antwerp—that for several decades was among the most important European financial houses. It

---

2. The French banks listed were responsible for the management of numerous Latin American loans. Many other French financial institutions collaborated with them in the sale of the securities but did not have equal responsibility in the organization of the loan transactions.

played a key role in the establishment of the Banque de Paris et des Pays Bas and had interests in the Société Générale and the Crédit Foncier Colonial. The Bischoffsheims also established the Banque Franco/Egyptienne, which later served as the vehicle for the creation of the Banco Nacional de México (1884), the most important bank in Mexico until 1910. Although principally engaged in large financial transactions in Europe and the Near East, they also found it profitable to take shares in the sale of Honduras and Costa Rica bonds in the early 1870s.

L. Cahen d'Anvers: Merchant bank established at Paris in 1849 by L. Cahen, a Belgian Protestant financier. Associated with the "Haute Banque" of Paris, this firm built up close links to the Crédit Mobilier and the Société Générale. In Latin America its role was limited basically to participation in Argentine loans during the 1880s, including the national loans of 1881, 1882, 1884, and 1889, as well as bond issues for the provinces of Corrientes, Mendoza, and Tucumán in 1888.

Comptoir National d'Escompte: One of the great French deposit banks, established in 1848 by Parisian merchants, the city of Paris, and the French government. In the 1860s it began opening branches throughout France and several in the Near East. It participated in a great many international loan operations. In Latin America it was involved first in the issue of the Mexican Imperial loan of 1865 to finance the French occupation of Mexico (1863–67). Later in the 1880s it participated in the issue of no less than seven Argentine national government loans. During the first decade of the twentieth century it participated in the sale of a Brazilian railway loan (1908), two Mexican conversion loans (1910, 1913), and the Uruguayan public works loan of 1909.

Crédit Lyonnais: Established at Lyons in 1863, this firm soon became one of the largest French commercial banks. In the international field it devoted most attention to loans for the Ottoman Empire and Russia. It apparently had few interests in Latin America, but it did participate in the 1909 Argentine national government loan and the 1910 Mexican conversion loan.

Crédit Mobilier: Investment bank established at Paris in 1902. It specialized in investments in the metallurgical industry, in promoting of French companies abroad, and in the sale of foreign government bonds. Its principal spheres of activity abroad were in Russia, Algeria, Turkey, and Latin America. It participated in the issue of the Imperial Mexican loan of 1864, in the 1911 Argentine national loan, in two loans for the province of Buenos Aires (1909, 1913), and in two Brazilian national loans (1909, 1910). It also had a direct interest in several Argentine enterprises, including the Rosario Port Company and several electrical and financial firms in the Río de la Plata.

Louis Dreyfus et Cie.:   Merchant firm founded in 1851 by Leopold Dreyfus, a grain merchant from Basel. In 1875 the firm established its main headquarters at Paris, and from there it managed its growing business in the international grain trade, importing cereals from Russia, India, and Argentina. It soon moved into merchant banking. Its activities in the South American trades led it to participate in the 1911 Argentine national loan, in bond issues for the provinces of Mendoza (1909) and Tucumán (1909), and in Brazil in the 1910 Ceará State loan.

Heine et Cie.:   One of the most prestigious of the Paris private investment banks. During the 1880s it participated in two spheres of Latin American finances. The first was in the notorious Panama Canal Company, in which all the Paris banks speculated until its spectacular collapse in 1889. In the same decade Heine participated in the issue of two Argentine national loans (1885, 1889) and four provincial loans (all in the year 1888).

Société Générale pour favorier l'Industrie et le Commerce: The Société Générale was founded in 1863 with the support of the Bischoffsheim financial firm, among others. This powerful commercial bank soon established a network of branches in France, Italy, Spain, and elsewhere in Europe. In Latin America it participated in many loans, including the 1865 Imperial Mexican transaction, the two great Peruvian loans of 1870 and 1872, four Argentine loans in 1888–89, two Brazilian loans (1907, 1908), two Mexican loans (1910, 1913), and the Uruguayan public works loan of 1909.

German Banking Houses[3]

S. Bleichröder & Company: Private Berlin bank established in 1803. It played a major role in German finances during the nineteenth century. Gerson Bleichröder, son of the founder, became Bismarck's financial adviser. The bank participated in the issue of two Argentine loans (1885, 1886), but its main interests in Latin America were linked to Mexican finance. On behalf of the Mexican government, it co-managed the great 1888 conversion loan, the 1890 railway loan, the 1893 national loan, and the conversion loans of 1899, 1910, and 1913.

Darmstadter Bank: Established in 1853 at Darmstadt, this firm grew rapidly, becoming one of the great German commercial and investment banks. It specialized mainly in industrial promotion but did not eschew the foreign bond business. Its first incursion into Latin American finances was apparently a short-term credit for the Peruvian government in 1868 in exchange for guano. In the late 1880s it participated in two loans for the national government of Argentina as well as in one provincial loan and two municipal loans. It also participated in the issue of the 1888 Mexican conversion loan and the 1890 Mexican railway loan.

Deutsche Bank: Established in Berlin in 1870 by Georg von Siemens, this bank soon became the most powerful German commercial and investment bank. It played

---

3. A large number of German financial firms collaborated with the major commercial and investment banks in the distribution of Latin American bonds in capital markets through Germany, but we have included only the principal banks involved.

a major role in many of the largest German industrial firms, but also participated in numerous foreign loans. It soon established an international network of branches, including the Banco Alemán Transatlántico in Buenos Aires (1886). It participated in various Argentine loans, including national bond issues in 1887 and 1889, and in a 1885 loan for the province of Buenos Aires, the national loans of 1907 and 1909, and the Buenos Aires City loan of 1913. In Chile it participated in the 1889 loan. In Mexico it participated in the conversion loans of 1899, 1910, and 1913.

Disconto Gesellschaft: Berlin banking firm established in 1851. It soon became one of the most important in Germany, rivaling the Deutsche, Darmstadter, and Dresdner banks (the four "D" banks). It became engaged in Latin American trade finance from an early date, establishing a small bank in Buenos Aires in 1872: the Deutsche-Belgische La Plata Bank. Later, in conjunction with the Norddeutsche Bank, it founded the Brasilianische Bank (1885) and the Bank für Chile (1895). In Argentina it had close links to the Buenos Aires financial firm of Tornquist y Cia., through which it took a stake in four national loans and one municipal loan in the 1880s, the 1907 and 1909 national loans, and the 1913 Buenos Aires City loan. It also provided a controversial loan to Venezuela in 1898 that was subsequently the cause of a violent military-diplomatic conflict between Germany, Great Britain, and the Venezuelan government.

Dresdner Bank: Established in 1872, it became a powerful commercial and industrial bank. By 1886 it was the third largest bank in Germany. It promoted German industrial exports to Latin America and for this purpose established the Deutsch-Sudamerikanische Bank in 1905. It participated in the 1905 São Paulo loan, the 1907 Argentine national loan, the 1910 Buenos Aires loan, and the Mexican loans of 1893, 1899, 1910, and 1913.

Norddeutsche Bank of Hamburg: Important commercial bank of Hamburg that became engaged in South American trade finance starting in the 1870s. During the 1880s it participated in four Argentine loans.

Mendelsohn & Company: Berlin private bank established in 1795. It proved important in making Berlin an important financial center. In the mid-nineteenth century the Mendelsohns were leading bankers to the Russian government. During the late 1880s the bank participated in the issue of two national loans for Argentina and one provincial Argentine loan.

S. Oppenheim, Son & Company: Private bank established in 1798 at Cologne. Among the leading banking firms of the Rhineland during the nineteenth century, had extensive international contacts through sister branches at Paris and London and was heavily engaged in Egyptian finances. In Latin America its loan activities were apparently limited to participation in four Argentine loans in the late 1880s.

Blair & Company: A private investment bank of New York, established in the nineteenth century. By the 1920s its partners sat on the boards of more than one hundred American and foreign corporations. In 1929 Blair was acquired by A. Giannini's Transamerica banking consortium, but intense struggles inside Wall Street subsequently led to the sale of most of the former Blair interests to the National City Bank. Blair had few direct interests in Latin America, but in the early 1920s it participated in the issue of three loans for the national government of Argentina, five loans for the province of Buenos Aires, three Brazilian national loans, and two large Chilean loans in 1928 and 1930.

Brown Brothers: Established in 1833 in Baltimore, it later opened branches in Philadelphia, New York, and Liverpool, devoting most of its attention before 1860 to the financing of the cotton trade. Subsequently it became involved in investment banking, raising money for many important American railways. In Latin America it acquired interests in Nicaraguan railroads and in Cuban and Dominican sugar companies in the early twentieth century. It participated in the issue of the 1909 Nicaraguan loan, several Dominican loans in the 1920s, three loans for Argentina (1922, 1927, 1928), the 1928 Rio de Janeiro City loan, and the 1928 Santiago de Chile City loan.

Chase Securities Corporation: The investment branch of the Chase National Bank, a large New York commercial bank established in the nineteenth century. In Latin America the Chase group acquired large holdings in Cuban sugar companies and participated in many loans during the 1920s, working jointly with Equitable Trust and Harris, Forbes & Company. Together they managed the sale of more than $100,000,000 in Latin American securities between 1917 and 1931. Chase sold the bonds of thirteen Argentine loans, two Cuban loans, two Brazilian loans, two Chilean loans, and several Colombian issues.

Dillon, Read & Company: A large New York investment banking firm specializing in the sale of foreign bonds and securities. Between 1917 and 1930 it managed the sale of $500,000,000 in Canadian bonds, $500,000,000 in European securities, and $200,000,000 in Latin American bonds. It played a major role in the issue of Brazilian loans (1921, 1922, 1926, 1927) in conjunction with Rothschilds of London. It also participated in Bolivian and Colombian bond issues.

4. As in the case of the larger German and French banks, the big United States banks distributed Latin American bonds through widespread syndicates of investment and brokerage firms. Among the more-active firms selling Latin American bonds during the 1920s *not* included in our listing were the following: Paine, Weber & Company; White, Weld & Company; E. H. Rollins & Sons; Lee, Higginson & Company; J. S. Bache & Company; Baker, Kellogg & Company; Landenburg, Thallman & Company; Halsey, Stuart & Company ; and W. A. Harriman & Company

Hallgarten & Company: Established in 1850, this banking and brokerage house made a reputation in the 1920s as New York's most active middle-sized financial firm engaged in the sale of South American bonds. Between 1920 and 1930 it was responsible for the issue of $240,000,000 in foreign bonds, of which 92 percent were for Latin American governments. In this decade it managed seven Colombian bond issues, three loans for the province of Buenos Aires, three Chilean loans, and two Uruguayan loans.

Kuhn, Loeb & Company: Financial firm established in New York in 1867. It specialized in the financing of North American railways, attracting much European capital for this purpose. In Latin America they had few direct interests—except in Mexico, where they helped finance railways and were major stockholders in the Mexican National Railways (1904). They participated in the issue of the Cuban loan of 1914 and in the Argentine national loan of 1923.

J. P. Morgan & Company: Banking firm established at New York in 1860 by J. P. Morgan, son of the leading partner of J. S. Morgan & Company of London. By the 1880s it had become the most powerful investment bank in the United States, playing a dominant role in railway finance. It later promoted several of the largest industrial corporations, such as General Electric and United States Steel, and took virtual control of two important commercial banks, Bankers Trust and Guaranty Trust. In Latin America its main interests were in Mexico (in railways) and in Cuba (in sugar companies). It participated in the Mexican conversion loans of 1899, 1910, and 1913. In Cuba it managed the issue of the loans of 1914, 1923, and 1927. It also played a role in the finances of Argentina, co-managing six loans of that nation during the 1920s.

National City Bank: Established at New York in the nineteenth century by an important group of financiers, merchants, and industrialists. By 1910 such powerful capitalists as Stillman, Schiff, Harriman, McCormick, Grace, and Armour were on the board of directors. It specialized in commercial banking and the financing of international trade. From 1914 it was the New York bank that devoted the most energy to the conquest of Latin American markets and resources. It opened branches throughout the region. It also directly promoted major investments in Chilean and Peruvian copper mines and in Cuban sugar plantations and refineries. During the 1920s it participated in the issue of five Argentine national loans, one Brazilian loan, five Chilean national loans, one Costa Rica loan, one Haitian loan, three Peruvian loans, and one Uruguayan loan.

Seligman Brothers: Established in the early 1850s in San Francisco, this banking firm prospered with the gold boom and subsequently opened branches in New York, London, Paris, and Frankfurt. It helped finance the Union during the Civil War by raising funds through Jewish-German bankers in Europe. It also financed many railway firms. In Latin America the Seligmans were involved in financing the first stages of the construction of the Panama Canal in the 1880s, participating in banking syndicates led by French bankers. Later in 1900–1914 their firm sold five loans for Brazilian provinces in Europe, three for Pará State, and two for Rio de Janeiro. It was also involved in the notorious Nicaraguan loan of 1909. During the 1920s it took a major stake in Cuban sugar firms and promoted the 1927 Cuban government loan. It also played a major role in Peruvian finance, providing three loans (1927 and 1928) for the dictator, Leguía.

Speyer & Company: The Speyers were originally an old Frankfurt family of merchant bankers. Like many Frankfurt Jews, various Speyers emigrated to the United States, opening a New York office in 1837 and later a London office in 1861. They maintained close ties with their fellow bankers—for example, the Lazards, Erlangers, Sterns, and Seligmans. They channeled much European capital into North American railways, playing a major role in the investment of German capital in California railroads. Their interests in Latin America centered in railways, particularly in the Mexican National Railways. They managed the issue of three Mexican loans (1904, 1908, 1912) and two Cuban loans (1904, 1909), and participated in two São Paulo loans in 1928 and 1930.

BIBLIOGRAPHICAL SOURCES

This appendix is based on a variety of sources, including those cited in Appendixes A, B, and C, various banking almanacs and guides, and numerous bank histories. On the British merchant banks and commercial banks, the following were most useful: A. S. Baster, *The International Banks* (London, 1935); Paul Emden, *Money Powers of Europe in the 19th and 20th Centuries* (New York, 1938); Paul Emden, *Jews of Britain* (London, n.d.); Roger Fulford, *Glyn's, 1753–1953: Six Generations in Lombard Street* (London, 1953); Ralph W. Hidy, *The House of Baring in American Trade and Finance: English Merchant Bankers at Work, 1763–1861* (Cambridge, Mass., 1949); Leland Jenks, *The Migration of British Capital to 1875* (New York, 1927); David Joslin, *A Century of Banking in Latin America* (Oxford, 1963); and D.C.M. Platt, *Foreign Finance in Continental Europe and the USA* (London, 1984).

On the role of the French banks, important sources are Edmond Baldy, *Les Banques d'affaires en France* (Paris, 1922); Jean Bouvier, *Un Siècle de banque française* (Paris, 1973); Jean Bouvier, *Le Crédit Lyonnais de 1863 à 1882*, 2 vols. (Paris, 1961); Henry Coston, *L'Europe des banquiers* (Paris, 1963); Bertrand Gille, *La Banque en France au XIXe siècle* (Paris, 1970); David Landes, *Bankers and Pashas: International Finance and Economic Imperialism in Egypt* (Cambridge, Mass., 1979); Jacques Thobie, *La France imperiale, 1880–1914* (Paris, 1982).

On the history of the foreign activities of the German banks, the following are informative: Georges Diouritch, *L'Expansion des banques allemandes a l'étranger* (Paris, 1909); Willis Parker, ed., *Foreign Banking Systems* (New York, 1929), chap. 8; Jacob Riesser, *The Great German Banks and Their Concentration* (Washington, D.C., 1911); Fritz Stern, *Gold and Iron: Bismarck, Bleichröder, and the Building of the German Empire* (London, 1977).

On the history of United States investment banks and bankers, useful sources are Vincent Carosso, *Investment Banking in America: A History* (Cambridge, Mass.,

1970); Lewis Corey, *The House of Morgan* (New York, 1930); Edwin J. Perkins, *Financing Anglo-American Trade: The House of Brown, 1800–1880* (Cambridge, Mass., 1975); Stephen Birmingham, *Our Crowd* (New York, 1970); Fritz Redlich, *The Molding of American Banking, 1781–1910*, 2 vols. (New York, 1947, 1951). On the banks' Latin American loans in the 1920s, see U.S. Congress, Senate Committee on Finance, *Sale of Foreign Bonds or Securities in the United States* (Washington, D.C., 1932).

BIBLIOGRAPHICAL NOTE

THIS bibliographical note is highly selective. It provides the reader with a general orientation to the principal publications on the history of Latin American foreign debts. Additional references are in the footnotes.

BIBLIOGRAPHIES

The literature on Latin American public finances and in particular on foreign debts is varied and scattered. Given the lack of specialized bibliographical guides on the subject, researchers must rely on more-general reference tools. Perhaps the most comprehensive bibliography on the economic history of Latin America is Roberto Cortés Conde and Stanley Stein, eds., *Latin America: A Guide to Economic History, 1830–1930* (Berkeley, 1977). A useful complementary source is Harvard University Bureau of Economic Research on Latin America, *The Economic Literature of Latin America: A Tentative Bibliography*, 2 vols. (Cambridge, Mass., 1935). Both these works have special sections on public finance by countries. Additional references are in R. A. Humphreys, *Latin America: A Guide to the Literature in English* (Oxford, 1960). Other basic research tools are *Handbook of Latin American Studies* (Cambridge, Mass., 1936–51; and Gainesville, Fla., 1951–); and Xerox University Microfilms, *Latin America and the Caribbean: A Dissertation Bibliography*, 2 vols. (Ann Arbor, Mich. 1977, 1981). An extensive listing of works on the history of foreign investments and loans in Latin America is in Marvin Bernstein, ed., *Foreign Investments in Latin America* (New York, 1966), pp. 283–305; an updated version of this work would be useful for both students and researchers.

ARCHIVAL SOURCES

Although the present study is based mainly on published materials, it is essential to comment briefly on the manuscript sources available in Latin America, the United States, and Europe on the history of Latin American foreign debts. The relevant archives in Mexico and Argentina that I was able to explore are illustrative of the wealth of materials on foreign debts in the archives of many other nations of Latin America.

In Mexico, important manuscript sources are in the historical archive of the Secretaría de Relaciones Exteriores, which contains many documents and letters from Mexican legations abroad that provide information on foreign debts dating from 1823. Another major repository is the Archivo General de la Nación, which houses the papers of the Secretaría de Hacienda y Crédito Público. The historical archive of the Banco Nacional de México contains manuscripts related to the foreign loan contracts between 1884 and 1914. And the Banco de México has a large group of documents in its "Archivo de la Vieja Deuda Exterior Titulada" that relate to the loans of 1888–1914.

In the case of Argentina, a great fund of unpublished documents on public foreign debts can be found in the "Archivo de la Deuda Exterior" in the Ministerio de Economía. When I consulted this repository in 1976, it was located in the ministry's Department of Parliamentary Information. The loan contracts and correspondence for each of the national, provincial, and municipal loans from 1880 to 1930 were in individual folders. The other main source on Argentine finances is the collection of papers of the Ministerio de Hacienda, housed in the Archivo de la Nación; here also are the personal papers of high-ranking politicians engaged in the loan negotiations. Additional documents (which I was not able to consult) are in the archives of the Ministerio de Relaciones Exteriores, the Banco de la Provincia de Buenos Aires, and the Banco de la Nación, as well as in the private archive of the Tornquist family.

While there are similarly rich materials on the history of national debts in many other Latin American countries, important manuscript sources are also held in archives in Europe and in the United States. The wealth of information on financial negotiations that is contained in the diplomatic correspondence of the creditor nations is best illustrated by Heraclio Bonilla, *Guano y burguesía en el Perú* (Lima, 1974), which uses British and French documents to analyze Peruvian nineteenth-century finances. Of equal interest are the historical archives of banks, such as that of Baring Brothers, on deposit at the Guildenhall Library in London, which has been explored by D.C.M. Platt, *Foreign Finance in Continental Europe and the USA, 1815–1870* (London, 1984); that of the Bank of London and South America, held at the University of London and studied by David Joslin, *A Century of Banking in Latin America* (Oxford, 1963); and that of the French branch of the Rothschilds, in the Archives Nationaux at Paris, which has been studied by Bertrand Gille, *Histoire de la Maison Rothschild*, 2 vols. (Geneva, 1965). In the United States there is a large amount of material on Latin American finances in the historical files of the State Department in the National Archives at Washington, D.C. Complementary sources are the private papers of important bankers and politicians involved in the loan transactions with Latin American states; a partial list of these is in the bibliographical sections of the studies by Robert Freeman Smith, *The United States and Revolutionary Nationalism in Mexico, 1916–1932* (Chicago, 1972) and *The United States and Cuba, 1917–1960* (New York, 1960), and in Frank Mackaman, "United States Loan Policy, 1920–1930" (Ph.D. diss., University of Missouri, 1977), 2:823–824.

Printed Sources

Serials and Journals. The most important serials that provide information on the external debts of the different Latin American nations are the annual reports of the respective ministries of finance. In most cases these include a special report by the corresponding Department of Public Credit of the ministry. To determine how the loan monies were invested, however, it is essential to analyze the financial accounts (cuentas de inversión) that were normally published in a second volume, accompanying the annual report. Additional data can be gleaned from the publications of other economic ministries, such as those of public works, as well as from the transcripts of the congressional debates of each country.

A fundamental complement to the government documents is the financial press of the nineteenth and early twentieth centuries. The number of journals (published in the Latin American nations) that dealt with financial and economic questions is legion. A listing of the principal Mexican journals and newspapers, for example, can be found in Enrique Florescano et al., *Bibliografía general del desarrollo económico de México, 1500–1976* (Mexico, 1980), 2:523–566. Of similar importance are the financial journals published in Europe and in the United States that carried information on Latin American economic affairs. The best guide to these journals is T. Jones, E. Warburton, and A. Kingsley, *A Bibliography on South American Economic Affairs: Articles in Nineteenth-Century Periodicals* (Minneapolis, 1955).

Other serials that provide information on Latin American foreign bonds are Corporation of Foreign Bondholders, *Annual Reports* (London, 1873–); Foreign Bondholders Protective Council, *Annual Reports* (New York, 1935–); and a variety of annual guides to stock exchange securities, such as the informative Albert Kimber, *Kimber's Record of Government Debts* (New York, 1918–36).

Secondary Literature. Most of the secondary literature on the history of Latin American finances focuses on individual nations, but there are a few works that offer a comparative perspective. Three important studies that provide statistics on foreign investments on a regionwide basis are James F. Rippy, *British Investments in Latin America, 1822–1949* (Minneapolis, 1959); Irving Stone, ''The Composition and Distribution of British Investments in Latin America, 1865 to 1913'' (Ph.D. diss., Columbia University, 1962); and United Nations, Economic Commission for Latin America, *El financiamiento externo de América Latina* (New York, 1964), pp. 1–35. An equally wide-ranging but more analytical interpretation is D.C.M. Platt, ed., *Business Imperialism, 1840–1930: An Inquiry Based on British Experience in Latin America* (Oxford, 1977), which is based on the company archives of British firms engaged in Latin American trade and finance. A classic study of the legal aspects of Latin American international finances is William Wynne, *State Insolvency and Foreign Bondholders*, 2 vols. (New Haven, 1951). Finally, an excellent collection of essays that deal with the financial problems of the 1920s and 1930s is Rosemary Thorp, ed., *Latin America in the 1930s: The Role of the Periphery in World Crisis* (New York, 1984).

There are many published works on the history of the foreign debts of the individual Latin American republics, but they are usually difficult to locate. What follows is a brief listing of studies that refer to the larger Latin American nations.

On the history of Argentine foreign debts, there are two overviews: the ponderous work by Jose Garcia Vizcaíno, *La deuda pública nacional* (Buenos Aires, 1972); and the more illuminating monograph by Harold E. Peters, *The Foreign Debt of the*

Argentine Republic (Baltimore, 1934). A number of specialized studies have analyzed the first foreign loan of Argentina negotiated in 1824. See, among others, Samuel Amaral, "El empréstito de Londres de 1824," *Desarrollo Económico* 23, no. 92 (1984): 559–588; Armando Chiapella, *El destino del empréstito Baring* (Buenos Aires, 1975); and Juan Carlos Vedoya, *La verdad sobre el empréstito Baring* (Buenos Aires, 1972). A mine of information on Anglo-Argentine financial relations during the nineteenth century is H. Ferns, *Britain and Argentina in the Nineteenth Century* (Oxford, 1966). On the loans of the 1880s there are several studies; among the more useful are John H. Williams, *Argentine International Trade under Inconvertible Currency, 1880–1900* (Cambridge, Mass., 1920); Horacio Cuccorese, "La version histórica sobre la crisis de Baring Brothers," *Investigaciones y Ensayos*, vol. 20 (Buenos Aires, 1976), pp. 265–321; and A. G. Ford, "Argentina and the Baring Crisis of 1890," *Oxford Economic Papers*, n.s. 8, no. 2 (1956): 127–150.

On the history of Bolivian foreign debts, two excellent sources are Margaret Marsh, *The Bankers in Bolivia* (New York, 1927); and Charles McQueen, *Bolivian Public Finance* (Washington, D.C., 1925). A more-recent overview that ties historical problems to contemporary finances is J. M. de la Cueva, *Imperialismo y oligarquía* (La Paz, 1983).

On Brazilian nineteenth-century finances, the classic work is Liberato de Castro Carreira, *História financeira e orçamentária do Império* (Rio de Janeiro, 1889; reprint ed. 1980). Other general studies are Gustavo Barroso, *Brasil colonia de banqueiros: história dos empréstimos de 1824 a 1934* (Rio de Janeiro, 1937); two studies by Valentin F. Bouças: *História da dívida externa* (Rio de Janeiro, 1950), and *Finanças do Brasil: história da dívida externa estadual e municipal* (Rio de Janeiro, 1942); and José de Nascimento Brito, *Economia e finanças do Brasil, 1822–1940* (Rio de Janeiro, 1945). More recently, research on the history of Brazilian finances has been carried out by several scholars; see, e.g., Steven Topik, "The Evolution of the Economic Role of the Brazilian State, 1889–1930," *Journal of Latin American Studies*, no. 11 (November 1979): 325–342. On the debt renegotiations of the 1930s, see Marcelo de Paiva Abreu, "Brazilian Public Foreign Debt Policy, 1931–1943," *Brazilian Economic Studies*, no. 4 (1978): 37–88, as well as other essays by the same author cited in the footnotes to Chapter 8.

Statistical data on the Chilean foreign debts of the nineteenth century can be located in Republic of Chile, Dirección de Contabilidad, *Resumen de la hacienda pública de Chile desde 1833 hasta 1900* (Santiago, 1900). A historical monograph on the subject is Alfonso Ferrada Urzúa, *História comentada de la deuda externa de Chile, 1810–1945* (Santiago, 1945). A useful source on Anglo-Chilean financial relations is Hernan Ramírez Necochea, *História del imperialismo en Chile* (Santiago, 1960).

On the foreign debts of the Colombian government in the early nineteenth century, two key sources are David Bushnell, *The Santander Regime in Gran Colombia* (Newark, Del., 1954); and Vicente Olarte Camacho, *Resumen histórico sobre la deuda exterior de Colombia* (Bogotá, 1914). On the loans of the 1920s, see J. F. Rippy, *The Capitalists and Colombia* (New York, 1931); and J. Echavarria, "La deuda externa colombiana durante los 20s y los 30s,'' *Coyuntura Económica* 12, no. 2 (1982): 24–42.

During the nineteenth century the financial relations of Cuba were subject to the Spanish Crown. The island's foreign debt was in practice part of the Spanish public debt. References to nineteenth-century loans are in Julio Le Riverend, *História económica de Cuba* (La Habana, 1974). Three useful studies on the loans the Cuban government took after 1898 are Leland Jenks, *Our Cuban Colony* (New York, 1927); Robert Freeman Smith, *The United States and Cuba*, cited above; and Oscar Pino Santos, *La oligarquía yanqui en Cuba* (Mexico, 1975).

The number of works on the history of the finances of Ecuador is small. This has been largely remedied by the recent publication of Linda Alexander Rodríguez, *The Search for Public Policy: Regional Politics and Government Finances in Ecuador, 1830–1940* (Berkeley, 1985).

There is an abundance of publications on the Mexican foreign debts of the nineteenth and early twentieth centuries. Two particularly incisive and informative analyses of the early foreign debt of the republic are Lucas Alamán, *Liquidación general de la deuda esterior de la Republica Mexicana hasta fin de diciembre de 1841* (Mexico, 1845); and Joaquín Casasús, *História de la deuda contraída en Londres* (Mexico, 1885). The most detailed overviews are Thomas Lill, *The National Debt of Mexico: History and Present Status* (New York, 1919); Walter McCaleb, *The Public Finances of Mexico* (New York, 1921); and Jan Bazant, *História de la deuda exterior de México* (Mexico, 1968).

An old but still useful history of Peruvian debts is Charles McQueen, *Peruvian Public Finance*, Department of Commerce Trade Promotion Series, no. 30 (Washington, D.C., 1926). The fundamental sources on the Peruvian foreign debts of the nineteenth century are the study by Heraclio Bonilla, *Guano y burguesía en el Perú* (Lima, 1974), and the informative monograph by Carlos Palacios Moreyra, *La deuda anglo/peruana, 1822–1890* (Lima, 1983).

On the history of Uruguayan finances, there are several studies. A detailed overview is found in Juan Ferrando, *Reseña del crédito público del Uruguay*, 2 vols. (Montevideo, 1969). A more analytical study is that of Carlos Zubillaga, *El reto financiero: deuda externa y desarrollo en Uruguay, 1903–1933* (Montevideo, 1982).

On the Venezuelan foreign debt of the early nineteenth century, a basic source is Francisco Pimentel y Roth, *História del crédito público en Venezuela* (Caracas, 1974). On the Venezuelan debts of the last decades of the nineteenth century, see Miriam Hood, *Gunboat Diplomacy, 1895–1905: Great Power Pressure in Venezuela* (London, 1971).

Additional references to works on the foreign debts of the Latin American republics are in the footnotes of this study as well as in the general bibliographies previously cited. Information on Latin American loans is also contained in the published histories of numerous banking firms cited at the end of Appendix D.

INDEX

The index provides references to the first, and complete, citation of all works cited more than once in the footnotes.

Abel, C., and C. Lewis, 215n.27
Abreu, Marcelo de Paiva, "Brazilian Debt," 220n.40
Agarragaray, Eduardo, 143
Alamán, Lucas, 23, 62, 64
Alberdi, Juan Bautista, 68, 81n.28
Alvear, Torcuato, 135
American Atlantic and Pacific Ship Canal Co., 73
American Foreign Banking Corp., 192
American International Corp., 181
American Locomotive Sales Corp., 181
Amin, Samir, 9
Andrews, Joseph, 25
Anglo-Paraguay Land and Cattle Co., 124
Anglo-South American Bank, 259n.1
Argentina: banks and bank crises, 105, 137–42, 155–59; bond quotations, 54n.33, 58, 109, 205; debt renegotiations, 58–59, 159–70, 211–18; debt service, 177, 178n.16; foreign loans, 34–35, 80, 92–94, 127–48, 185, 243, 247–49, 251–52; foreign trade, 50–51, 90–91, 214–15; railways, 93–94, 133–35; silver mines, 23–26, 52; stock markets, 152–53; trade crises, 49–50, 105; war with Brazil, 50; war with Paraguay, 92–93, 118
Armstrong, Thomas, 19
Avellaneda, Nicolás, 105, 168
Avila Camacho, Manuel, 226

Baldwin Locomotives Co., 134
Balfour, Williamson & Co., 83
Banco Belgo/Alemán (Buenos Aires), 105
Banco Comercial (Montevideo), 143
Banco de Buenos Aires, 34

Banco de Italia y Rio de la Plata, 157n.22
Banco de la Nación (Argentina), 158
Banco de la Providencia (Lima), 88n.52
Banco de la Provincia de Buenos Aires, 91, 93, 137–40
Banco de la Provincia de Santa Fé, 105
Banco del Perú, 88n.52
Banco del Pobre (Santiago), 106
Banco de Valparaíso, 83
Banco Español (Havana), 192
Banco Francés del Rio de la Plata, 127n.4
Banco Hipotecario de la Provincia de Buenos Aires, 130
Banco Hipotecario Nacional (Argentina), 130, 139–40
Banco Mercantil (Buenos Aires), 105
Banco Nacional (Buenos Aires), 105, 130, 137–39, 151, 153–60, 167
Banco Nacional (Montevideo), 143–44
Banco Nacional de Chile, 83, 106
Banco Nacional de Cuba, 192
Banco Nacional del Perú, 108
Banco Nacional de México, 127n.4
Banco Thomas (Santiago), 106
Banco Transatlático (Montevideo), 144
Bank of Antwerp, 156n.16
Bank of England, 44–45, 122, 149, 156, 160, 220n.39
Bank of France, 149
Bank of London and Brazil, 259n.1
Bank of London and River Plate, 121n.54, 143, 156–57, 160n.29, 162, 259n.1
banks. See foreign banks; names of individual banks and names of individual countries
Banque de l'Union Parisienne, 263
Banque de Paris et des Pays Bas, 171, 263

Banque Nationale d'Haiti, 180
Baran, Paul, 9
Barclay, Herring, Richardson & Co., 26, 28, 39–41, 49n.19, 53–55, 259n.1
Baring, Alexander, 13, 43, 61
Baring Brothers: early loans to Latin American nations, 28, 34, 37, 41–42, 46n.10, 54, 63; history of firm, 259; loans in 1920s, 196; loans to Argentina and Uruguay in the 1880s, 129, 133, 135, 143, 146–47; public works and military loans to Chile and Argentina at mid-century, 73n.15, 77, 84, 92–93, 96, 105, 113; role in panic of 1890, 149–51, 159–63, 171
Barron, Eustaquio, 64
Barroso, Gustavo, 35n.53
Baxter, Dudley, 102n.12
Bazant, Jan, 34n.50
Beer, Julius, 118n.49
Bello Andrés, 38
Benecke & Co., 46
Bernardes, Artur, 197n.57
Bernstein, Marvin, 127n.4
Bethmann, G., 46
Bischoffsheim and Goldschmidt, 96, 115–18, 263–64
Blair & Co., 199, 267
Bleichröder, S., & Co., 265
Bolívar, Simón, 4, 12, 15–18, 29–33, 38, 41, 53
Bolivia: debt renegotiations, 122–23; default, 107, 120, 203, 212; foreign loans, 80, 205, 208, 243, 252; foreign trade, 201, 207; political crisis, 202
bondholders: renegotiations with Latin American governments, 56–61, 119–25, 205–6. See also Corporation of Foreign Bondholders; debt renegotiations under names of individual countries
bonds, Latin American. See bond quotations under names of individual countries
Bonilla, Heraclio: Gran Bretaña y el Perú, 48n.15; Guano y burguesia, 79n.27
Borja Mignoni, F., 38
Bouças, Valentim: Finanças do Brasil, 198n.59; Historia da dívida externa, 92n.61
Boyer, Jean-Pierre, 35
Braden, Spruille, 217
Brazil: bond quotations, 94, 109, 205; debt renegotiations, 219–24; default, 203, 212; financial crisis, 106; foreign loans, 14, 28, 35, 80, 92–94, 128, 185, 194–99, 244, 249, 252–54; foreign trade, 48–49, 75, 91, 195–97; government loan policy, 174, 177–78, 194–99; railways, 93; war with Argentina, 50; war with Paraguay, 92–93, 118
British banks, engaged in Latin American loans, 259–63. See also foreign banks; names of individual firms
Brittain, James, 19
Brown, Shipley & Co., 149
Brown Brothers, 180, 192, 267
Brunlees, James, 117n.46
Buell, Raymond, 190n.36
Buenos Aires (city): banking crisis, 155–58; debt renegotiation, 167; port loans, 34, 135–36; real estate boom, 152–53; revolution in, 154; stock exchange, 139–40, 152–54
Buenos Aires (province): debt renegotiation, 164; foreign loans, 28, 34, 136
Buenos Aires Water Supply & Drainage Co., 147, 166–67
Bukharin, N., 8
Bunge, Emilio, 143
Buschental, José de, 142
Bushnell, David, 26n.36
Byron, John, 12

Cahen D'Anvers, L., et Cie., 156n.16, 264
Cairncross, Alec, 6, 114n.38
California gold rush: impact on Latin American trade, 71–73, 81–82
Calvo, Carlos, 161
Canning, George, 16
Casares, Vicente, 157
Casasús, Joaquin, 62n.46
Casey, Edward, 143
Castillo Najera, Francisco, 226
Castlereagh, Robert S., 15, 32
Castro, Felix, 34
Castro Carreira, Liberato de, 92n.63
Central America (Federation of): debt renegotiation, 60; foreign loans, 14, 28
Central Peruvian Railway, 89
Central Railroad (Brazil), 197
Central Uruguay Railway, 143
Chamberlain, Austen, 222

Chase National Bank, 190n.36, 192–94, 208

Chase Securities Corp., 267

Chile: bond quotations, 64, 205; debt renegotiations, 57–59, 212; default, 55, 203, 212; foreign loans, 14, 28, 33, 80, 84–85, 128–29, 185, 244, 249, 254–55; foreign trade, 72, 81–82, 178, 201, 207; railways, 83–85; silver mines, 23–26, 51–52; stock markets, 78, 83; war with Peru (War of the Pacific), 107; war with Peruvian-Bolivian Confederation, 56

Chilean and Talcahuano Railway, 85n.42

Chilean Mining Association, 26

Chilean Nitrate Co. (COSACH), 207

Chincha Islands, 86

Churchill, Winston, 217

City Bank Ltd., 85n.42

Clapham, John, 149n.1

Clarke, Hyde, 102n.12

Clarke, William, 89n.54

Cockerill & Co., 134

Cohen, Louis, & Sons, 115n.41, 146–47, 259

Colombia: bond quotations, 205; debt renegotiations, 58–59, 212; default, 55, 203, 212; fiscal system, 30–31; foreign loans, 14, 28, 32–33, 53n.32, 80, 182, 185, 244, 255. See also Gran Colombia

Colombian Mining Association, 23n.27, 26

Comptoir National d'Escompte, 96, 150, 264

Connally, Tom, 206

Continental Illinois Bank, 232

Cooke, Jay, & Co., 99n.5, 100n.7

Corporation of Foreign Bondholders, 121n.53, 124

Cortinez, Santiago, 133

Costa, Braulio, 34

Costa Rica: bond quotations, 111; debt renegotiations, 60, 123–24, 212; default, 107, 120, 204, 212; foreign loans, 80, 114–15, 185, 244, 255; railways, 114–15

Credit-Anstalt Bank, 209

Crédit Lyonnais, 264

Crédit Mobilier, 96, 171, 264

Crowder, Enoch, 191

Cuba: banks in, 192–94; default, 211–12; foreign loans, 29, 94, 128–29, 186, 191–94, 255–56; foreign trade, 191; political crisis, 202–3; railways, 94; U.S. policy toward, 179–80, 191

Cuban Sugar Cane Corporation, 192

Cuccorese, Horacio, 148n.49

Cumberland, William, 189n.35

D'Amico, Carlos, 134–36

Danatbank, 209

Darmstadter Bank, 265

Davis, Norman, 193

debt crisis: concept of, 5–8; in contemporary era, 229–39. See also Latin America, defaults; references to defaults and debt renegotiations under names of individual countries

defaults. See Latin America, debt crises and defaults; references to defaults under names of individual countries

De la Huerta, Adolfo, 224–25

Deutsche Bank, 171, 265–66

Dillon, Clarence, 206

Dillon, Read & Co., 182, 195–96, 206, 267

Disconto Bank, 161, 171, 266

Disraeli, Benjamin, 24, 54n.34

Dominican Republic: bond quotations, 111; debt renegotiations, 123; default, 107, 120, 204, 212; foreign loans, 80, 118, 186, 245, 256; political crisis, 202

Drabble, George, 143, 160n.29

Dresdner Bank, 266

Dreyfus, Louis, et Cie., 264–65

Dreyfus Frères et Cie., 90, 96, 110, 125

Duggan, Thomas, 143

economic crisis. See international financial crises; Latin America, debt crises and defaults; references to bank and trade crises under names of individual countries

Ecuador: debt renegotiations, 59, 123; default, 107, 212; foreign loans, 80, 244

Egaña, Mariano, 23, 39

El Salvador: debt renegotiations, 60, 212; default, 212; foreign loans, 186, 256

Entre Rios (province): foreign loans, 94

Erlangers, 115n.41, 260

Escandón, Manuel, 62

Everett, Walker & Co., 28

Export-Import Bank, 222, 227

export of capital. See Germany, loans and investments in Latin America; Great Brit-

export of capital (*cont.*)
ain, investments in Latin America;
France, loans and investments in Latin
America; United States, investments in
Latin America

Famatina Silver Mining Co., 25, 52
Federal Reserve Bank of New York, 188
Federation of Central America. *See* Central
America (Federation of)
Fenn, Charles, 57n.39
Feis, Herbert, 6
Ferdinand VII (of Spain), 16
Fernández, Manuel A., 83n.35
Ferns, H., 19n.20
Ferrando, J., 143n.38
Ferrocarril Andino (Argentina), 94n.67,
133, 154
Ferrocarril Central Norte (Argentina),
94n.67, 133–34, 154
Ferrocarril Oeste de la Provincia de Buenos
Aires, 130, 134, 154, 156
Ferrocarril Santiago, 85n.42
First Boston Corp., 199
Flahaut de la Billarderie, Count, 65
Fleming, George, 118n.50
Fletcher, Alexander & Co., 28
Folkman, David, 72n.13
Forbes, William, 64
Ford, A. G.: "Argentina," 152n.10; *Gold
Standard*, 142n.35
foreign banks: engaged in Latin American
loans, 259–69. *See also names of individual firms*
foreign loans. *See* debt crisis and defaults;
*references to foreign loans under names
of individual countries*
Foundation Co., 190
France, relations with Latin America:
French banks in Latin America, 77, 95–
96, 171–72, 263–65; intervention in
Mexico, 65–66; loans and investments in
Latin America, 127n.4, 133, 146; policy
toward Peru, 125; trade with Latin America, 47–49, 74
Frank, Gary, 216n.31
Freeman Smith, Robert: *U.S. and Cuba*,
191n.40; *U.S. and Mexico*, 224n.54
French banks, engaged in Latin American

loans, 263–65. *See also* foreign banks;
France; *names of individual firms*
Fries and Co., 46
Frys & Chapman, 28, 37
Furtado, Celso, 9

Galarza, Ernesto, 203n.7
Galmarini, Raúl, 26n.33
Garcia, Alan, 232
Garcia del Rio, Juan, 37
Gayer, A., and W. Rostow and
A. Schwartz, 13n.3
German banks. *See* foreign banks; Ger-
many; *names of individual firms*
Germany, relations with Latin America:
German banks in Latin America, 46, 146,
171, 265–66; loans and investments in
Latin America, 146; trade with Brazil,
221–22; trade with Latin America, 47–49
Gibbs, Antony, & Sons, 20, 50, 77, 83,
86–87, 149, 160n.29, 260
Giffen, Robert, 101
Gille, Bertrand, 26n.36
Glyn, Mills & Co., 146–47, 149, 160, 260
Goldschmidt, B. A., & Co., 26, 39–41, 46,
49–50, 53, 259n.1
Gómez Farias, Valentin, 64
González Casanova, P., 180n.23
Goschen, Viscount, 149
Gowland, Thomas, 19
Graham, Richard, 68n.1
Graham, Rowe & Co., 83
Gran Colombia (Federation of), 28–34; de-
fault, 43, 55; foreign loans, 30–33; for-
eign trade, 48; loan renegotiations, 59
Grant, Albert, 96
Grant, Ulysses S., 118
Great Britain, relations with Latin America:
British banks engaged in loans to nations
in Latin America, 259–63; diplomatic re-
lations with Latin America, 15–17, 38,
56, 104; investments in Latin America,
78, 127, 138; merchants in Latin Amer-
ica, 18–22, 77–83; parliamentary investigation of Central American loans, 111–
19; political/financial negotiations with
Argentina, 214–18; political/financial negotiations with Brazil, 219–24; trade with
Latin America, 47–49, 74–76, 104–5

Great Southern Railway of Buenos Aires, 134
Greenhil, Robert: "Merchants," 20n.23; "Shipping," 82n.30
Guadalajara (state): foreign loans, 29
Guardia, Tomás, 112n.34, 115, 122
Guatemala: debt renegotiations, 60, 123; default, 107, 120, 212; foreign loans, 80, 186, 208, 244, 256
Guatemala Mining Co., 23n.27
Gunder Frank, André, 9
Gutiérrez, Carlos, 117n.47

Hackshaw, John, 135
Haiti, 204; foreign banks in, 180; foreign loans, 29, 35, 80, 186, 212, 244, 256
Hale, S. y Cia., 139n.27, 143
Hallgarten & Co., 182, 268
Halperin Donghi, Tulio, 57; Guerra y finanzas, 17n.3; Historia contemporánea, 69n.2
Hambro, C. J., & Son, 149, 160n.29, 260
Hambro, Everard, 149
Hartmont, Edward, 96, 118n.49
Haussmann, Baron, 135
Head, Francis, 25
Heine et Cie., 265
Herrera, César A., 97n.73
Herring, Charles, 26n.35
Herring, Powles & Graham, 20, 26, 28, 32, 39–41, 49n.19, 53, 259n.1
Heureaux, Ulysse, 123
Holguin, J., 32n.46
Holland, Lord, 15
Honduras: bond quotations, 111; debt renegotiations, 60, 123; default, 107, 120; foreign loans, 80, 115–17, 212, 244; railways, 115–17
Honduras Inter-Oceanic Railway Co., 115
Hood, Miriam, 121n.54
Hoover, Herbert, 195
Hope & Co., 46n.10
Huergo, Luis, 134–35
Hull, Cordell, 216
Hullett Brothers, 23, 25, 28, 33, 37, 41, 54, 259n.1
Humphreys, Robin A.: British Consular Reports, 16n.12; Liberation, 23n.27; Tradition and Revolt, 19n.19
Hurtado, José Maria, 23, 38, 53

Hylsop, Maxwell, 20
Hylsop & Co., 20, 26, 50

Ibañez, Carlos, 183, 202, 207
Interamerican Development Bank, 233
international financial crises: 1820s, 43–47; 1870s, 99–104; 1890s, 149–52; 1920–21, 179, 182, 186–88; 1930s, 201–11. See also debt crises; money market
International Financial Society, 115n.41
International Monetary Fund, 237
International Telephone and Telegraph Corp., 218
Irigoyen, Hipólito, 211
Irisarri, Antonio de, 23, 37
Istúriz, 65
Iturbide, 17, 34

Jecker, Juan B., 65
Jenks, Leland, 6, 192; Migration of Capital, 13n.4; Our Cuban Colony, 174n.9
Johnson, Hiram Warren, 210
Joslin, David, 143n.37
Juárez, Benito, 65–66, 80
Juárez Celman, Miguel, 137, 140, 147, 152–54, 156, 168
Juglar, Clement, 46, 47n.12

Kahn, Otto, 206
Kapp, Bernard, 49n.17
Keith, Minor, 99, 115, 124
Kelly, David, 216
Kemmerer, Edwin, 188–89
Kinder, Thomas, 21, 25, 28, 33, 37, 40–41
Kindleberger, Charles, 6
Kissel, Kinnicutt & Co., 182
Knowles & Foster, 96, 115n.41
Kondratiev, Nicolai, 101n.9
Kuhn, Loeb & Co., 180, 182, 206, 268

Lacroze, Julio, 134
Laing, Samuel, 97
Lake Nicaragua, 73
Lambert, Charles, 25
Lambert, Eric, 15n.10
Lamont, Thomas, 206, 224–27
Landes, David, 77n.23
La Plata (city): foreign loans, 136
Larrea, José de, 33
La Serna, Viceroy, 20

Latin America (region): banks engaged in loans to nations in, 77–78, 259–69; debt crises and defaults in, 43–44, 53–61, 104–19, 201–13; foreign loans to nations in, 80, 94–97, 127–29, 184–91; international trade of, 68–69, 81, 98, 104–6, 126, 175–79, 201–2, 209; railways, 79–80, 98–99, 127. *See also references under names of individual countries*
Lawson, Peter, & Son, 96, 118n.49
Lazard Brothers, 196, 219, 260
Lefevre, Charles, 116–17
Leguía, Agustin, 183, 189–90, 202
Lenin, V. I., 6, 8
Lewis, Charles, 113
Lewis, Cleona, 173n.8
Lidderdale, William, 149
Liehr, Reinhard, 34n.50
Lill, Thomas R., 189
Lindmark, Knut, 134
Lizardi, Manuel, 62–64
Lloyds Bank, 261
loans. *See* foreign loans
London Stock Exchange. *See* money market, Europe
López, Vicente, 154–61
López Mendez, F., 31
Love, Joseph, 196n.53
Luis, Washington, 197n.57
Luxemburg, Rosa, 6, 8, 46n.12

MacGregor, Gregor, 38
Machado, Gerardo, 190, 193–94, 202
Macintosh, Ewen, 64
Mackaman, Frank, 189n.35
Mackau, Admiral, 35
Madero, Eduardo, 135
Magdalena River, 72
Magnasco, Osvaldo, 168
Malbrán, Manuel, 214n.25
Manufacturers Hanover Bank, 232
Marichal, Carlos: "Los banqueros," 134n.18; "The State," 94n.67
Martel, Julián, 152n.10
Martinez del Rio, Gregorio, 62
Mathew, W. M.: "Anglo-Peruvian Debt," 33n.48; *House of Gibbs*, 77n.22
Mauá, Barón de, 106, 142
Maximilian, Archduke, 66, 80, 95
Maxwell, W. and A., & Co., 20

Medina, Rafael, 116
Meiggs, Henry, 84–85, 89, 112, 115
Mendelsohn & Co., 266
Mendieta, Carlos, 204
Mercantile Bank of the Americas, 192
merchant banks. *See names of individual firms*
Mexican National Railway Co., 224–27
Mexico: bond quotations, 54n.33, 64, 205; debt renegotiations, 59, 123, 213, 224–28; default, 55, 107, 178, 224–26; foreign loans, 14, 28, 34, 80, 128–29, 244, 250; foreign trade, 49; silver mines, 23–26, 52; war with France, 65–66; war with Texas, 63; war with United States, 56, 64, 71
Mexico City, foreign loans, 130
Michelena, José, 39
Midland Bank, 232, 261
Miers, John, 25n.32
Miller, John, 12n.1
Miller, William, 18
Minas Geraes (state): foreign loans, 198
Mitchell, Charles, 206
Moneta, Pompeyo, 134
money market, Europe: early loans and investments in Latin America, 13–14, 21–23, 27–29, 38–41; effects of crash of 1825 on, 44–46; impact of banking crisis of 1931 on, 209–10; impact of economic crisis of 1870s on, 99–104, 110–14; investments in Latin America in prewar era, 171–73; role in Latin American loan boom at mid-century, 69–70, 95–97; speculation in Latin American bonds in 1880s, 145–48
money market, United States: impact of crash of 1873 on, 99–100; impact of Great Depression on, 201, 204–6; investments in Latin America during war and 1920s, 179–84; investments in Latin America in prewar era, 173–74
Morgan, J. P., 161
Morgan, J. P., & Co., 100n.7: history of firm, 268; loans to Argentina, 161; loans to Latin America in 1920s, 172, 181–82, 192–93, 206
Morgan, J. S., & Co.: history of firm, 261; loans to Argentina, 146–47, 149, 160n.29, 161, 169n.51; loans to Central

American republics, 115n.41, 118; loans to Chile, 85, 96
Morgenthau, Henry, 222
Morrison, Charles, 118n.49
Morrow, Dwight, 193
Morton, Rose & Co., 118, 134, 146, 160, 261
Muchnic, Charles, 181
Mulhall, Michael, 91n.59, 145
Murrieta, Cristobal de, & Co.: history of firm, 261; loans to Argentina, 94–96, 105n.21, 115n.41, 133, 146–47, 160

Napoleon III, 66, 135
National City Bank, 180–82, 190–93, 268
New Brazilian Mining Co., 24
New York Stock Exchange. *See* money market, United States
Nicaragua, 38; civil war in, 202; debt renegotiations, 60; foreign loans, 213; impact of California gold rush on, 72–73
Niemeyer, Otto, 220–21
Norddeutsche Bank of Hamburg, 266
Norton, Henry K., 171

Obregón, Alvaro, 224
O'Higgins, Bernardo, 4, 17, 29, 33, 37
Olmedo, José Joaquin de, 53
Oppenheim, S., & Co., 266
Oppenheimer, Robert, 78n.25
Orellana, José Maria, 183
Oriental Bank Corporation, 85n.42
Ottoman Empire: debt crisis in 1870s, 102–3
Overend, Gurney & Co., 26, 93

Pacific Steam Navigation Co., 84
Palacios Moreyra, Carlos, 87n.50
Panama: default, 204, 213; foreign loans, 186, 256; railway, 72, 115
Panama Canal Co., 127n.4
Pani, Alberto J., 225
Paraguay: bond quotations, 111; debt renegotiations, 124; default, 107, 120, 213; foreign loans, 80, 118, 245; war with Brazil and Argentina, 92–93, 118
Pardo, Manuel, 88
Paris Stock Exchange. *See* money market, Europe
Parish, David, 46

Parish Robertson, John and William, 19, 25, 34, 37, 40–41, 50
Paroissien, James, 25, 37
Pasco-Peruvian Mining Co., 25
Payno, Manuel, 64
Paz, Máximo, 140
Pellegrini, Carlos, 135–36, 154–62
Peña, José, 160n.32
Perón, Juan Domingo, 217–18
Peru: banks, 88, 108; bond quotations, 109; debt renegotiations, 59, 124–25, 213; default, 43, 53, 108–10, 120, 208, 213; foreign loans, 14, 28, 33–34, 80, 87–90, 186, 245, 256–57; foreign trade, 47–48, 85–87, 108, 201, 207; railways, 88–90; war with Chile (War of the Pacific), 107; war with Spain, 71n.8, 88, 95
Peruvian Corporation, The, 124–25
Pessoa, Epitacio, 197
Platt, D.C.M.: *Business Imperialism*, 20n.23; *Foreign Finance*, 99n.4; *Latin America*, 18n.16
Plaza, Victorino de la, 159–62
Pole, Peter, Thornton & Co., 44
Porter, D., 18n.15
Potosi, La Paz and Peruvian Mining Association, 23n.27
Powles, John, 54
Poyais: loans to, 29, 38

Ramirez, Pedro, 217
Randall, Robert, 23n.27
Rapaport, Mario, 216n.28
Real de Catorce Mining Co., 52
Real del Monte Co., 25, 52
Regla, Count of, 25
Reichenbach and Co., 46
Reus, Emilio, 143–44, 147
Revelstoke, Lord, 147, 149
Richardson, T., 26n.34
Ricketts, Charles, 21, 50
Rippy, J. Fred: *British Investments*, 14n.6; *Capitalists and Colombia*, 174n.9
Rivadavia, Bernardino de, 4, 16, 23, 29, 34
Rio de Janeiro (city): foreign loans, 198–99
Rio de la Plata Mining Association, 25, 52
Rio Grande do Sul (state): foreign loans, 198
Rivero, Manuel del, 43
Robinson, Fleming & Co., 96, 118n.50

Roca, Julio, 126, 132, 154–55, 168
Rocafuerte, Vicente, 36n.55, 39, 53
Roddy, William, 189
Rodriguez O., Jaime, 26n.35
Romero, Juan José, 162–63
Roosevelt, Franklin Delano, 217
Rosas, Juan Manuel, 56, 58
Rostow, Walt W., 101
Rothschild, Lord, 156, 160
Rothschild, Nathaniel de, 114
Rothschild, N. M., & Sons: bankers to Chile and Brazil in early twentieth century, 171, 175, 196, 208, 219–21; early loans to Latin America, 28, 35n.53, 41–42, 53–54; history of the firm, 262; loans to Brazil at mid-century, 77, 92, 94, 96, 106; role in panic of 1890, 149
Rothschild Committee, 160, 167
Rubio Cayetano, 62, 64
Russell, John, 65

Saenz Peña, Luis, 162
Salisbury, Lord, 162
Sánchez Albornoz, Nicolás, 17n.13
Sandino, Augusto, 202
San Luis Potosí (state): foreign loans, 130n.9
San Martín, José de, 4, 15, 18, 29, 40–41
San Martín, Ramón Grau, 202
Santa Anna, Antonio, 63
Santa Fé (province), foreign loans, 94
Santander, Francisco, 29, 31
Santo Domingo. See Dominican Republic
São Paulo (city): foreign loans, 198–99
São Paulo (state): coffee export policies, 195–96; debt renegotiations, 221; foreign loans, 195–96
São Paulo Coffee Institute, 195–96, 208, 221
Sarmiento, Domingo, 81n.28, 132, 168
Sater, William, 83n.34
Saul, S. B., 100n.7
Sayers, R. S., 44n.3
Scalabrini Ortiz, Raúl, 137n.23
Schneider, John, & Co., 63
Schröder, J. H., & Co., 90, 96, 196, 219, 262
Schumpeter, Joseph, 101
Seidel, Robert, 188n.33

Seligman, J. and W., & Co., 180, 182, 184, 187, 190, 192, 268
Shepherd, H. L., 160n.30
Siles, Hernando, 202
Simon, Mathew, 76
Sismondi, J.C.L., 46
Smart, William, 13n.4
Smith, Payne & Smith, 149
Smith, Peter, 179n.17
Snare & Co., 190
Sociedad de Crédito Argentino, 144
Société Générale (Paris), 90, 96, 265
Sommi, Luis, 137n.24
Souza Costa, Artur, 222–23
Spain, 12, 15; loan claims on Mexico, 65; naval war with Peru, 71n.8, 88, 95; policy toward Latin American independence, 14–16
Spanish American War, 179
Speyer, James, 206
Speyer & Co., 195–96, 206, 269
Staples, Robert, & Co., 20, 25, 37, 50
Stein, Stanley, 91n.60
Stephenson, Robert, 25–26
Stern Brothers, 96, 146–47, 160, 262
Stewart, Watt: *Henry Meiggs*, 84n.39; *Minor Keith*, 99n.3
stock exchange. See money market
Stone, Irving, 29
Suárez, Eduardo, 227
Sucre, Antonio, 12, 29, 32
Suez Canal, 103
Swedish Match Corp., 208

Tajes, Máximo, 143
Tehuantepec (isthmus), 72
Tenenbaum, Barbara: "Merchants and Mischief," 64n.52; *Politics of Penury*, 17n.13
Thomson, Bonar, J., & Co., 88n.51, 96, 262–63
Thorp, R. and C. Londoño, 203n.9
Thorp, Rosemary, 173n.6
Tooke, Thomas, 7, 44n.12, 46
Tornquist, E. y Cia., 139n.27
Trujillo, Rafael L., 204
Trust Co. of Cuba, 192–93

Ubico, Jorge, 202

Ulen & Co., 190
United Fruit Co., 124
United Mexican Mining Association, 23, 52
United River Plate Telephone Co., 218
United States, 12, 18, 33, 38; banks in
    Latin America, 172, 179–84; investments
    in Latin America, 173, 179–84; loan poli-
    cies, 189, 206, 210–11; role in renegotia-
    tion of Latin American debts, 216–18,
    222–24, 226–28; trade with Latin Amer-
    ica, 75, 183
United States banks, engaged in Latin
    American loans, 267–69. *See also* foreign
    banks; United States, banks; *names of in-*
    dividual firms
Uriburu, José Evaristo, 156, 169
Uriburu, José F., 202, 211
Uruguay: banks, 142–43; default, 107, 120,
    203, 213; foreign loans, 127–28, 142–44,
    186, 245, 250, 257

Vanderbilt, Cornelius, 73
Vanderlip, Frank, 181
Varela, Rufino, 153
Vargas, Getúlio, 220–23
Veliz, Claudio: "Egaña, Lambert," 23n.27;
    Historia marina, 72n.11
Venezuela: default, 107; foreign loans, 80,
    245; loan renegotiations, 59, 123
Vetch, James, 25
Victoria, Guadalupe, 61

Villanueva, Guillermo, 134

Walker, William, 73
Ward, George, 23n.26
Waring, Charles, 99, 112, 113n.35, 115,
    121n.54
Warren Brothers, 190, 193
Welles, 118n.49, 216, 226
Wentworth, Chalmer & Co., 44
Westendorp Corp., 123
Wheelwright, William, 84
White, George Henry, 113
Wilde, Eduardo, 147
Williams, John, 136n.21
Wilson, Joan H., 182n.28
Wilson, Robert, 65
Wilson, Thomas, & Co., 28
Winkler, Max, 173n.8
Wirth, Max, 146n.45
Woods, Edward, 117n.46
World Bank, 233
World War I: impact on Latin American
    economies, 7–8, 172–81
World War II: impact on Latin American fi-
    nances, 215–28
Wright & Co., 29
Wynne, William, 65n.56

Zalduendo, Eduardo, 93n.66
Zayas, Alfredo, 192–93
Zea, Francisco, 32, 36